THE CAMEROONS

from Mandate to Independence

THE CAMEROONS
from Mandate
to Independence

by Victor T. LeVine

UNIVERSITY OF CALIFORNIA PRESS
BERKELEY AND LOS ANGELES
1964

UNIVERSITY OF CALIFORNIA PRESS
BERKELEY AND LOS ANGELES, CALIFORNIA

CAMBRIDGE UNIVERSITY PRESS
LONDON, ENGLAND

To
NATHALIE

Preface

On January 1, 1960, the former Cameroun under French trusteeship became an independent state, the Cameroun Republic. Eighteen months later the present Cameroun Federal Republic was born of a union of the Cameroun Republic and the former Southern Cameroons under British trusteeship. The political entity that, in the eyes of the United Nations, had achieved the titular maturity of "statehood" in 1960 was shaped during the relatively short span of seventy-five years. For the first thirty years—after Gustav Nachtigal raised the German imperial flag at Douala on July 14, 1884—the territory was a German protectorate; then, in 1916, the Germans were driven from the "Kamerun" and the protectorate was partitioned by France and Britain. It is the political development of the French Cameroun during the period between the end of the German protectorate and the establishment of the Cameroun Republic that forms the basis and the primary focus of this study.

There are at least five compelling reasons to undertake such a study: (1) the Cameroun underwent a dual colonial experience—first German, then French rule; (2) it experienced two forms of international tutelage, being both a mandate of the League of Nations and a United Nations trust territory; (3) it is a "developing area"—its economy is essentially preindustrial, and its remarkably diverse social patterns have only partly emerged from traditional or tribal forms; (4) the growth of political groups in the Cameroun followed a pattern unique in French-speaking Africa; and (5), the Cameroun Republic came into being during a period in which many other areas of the African continent were also in the process of political self-assertion. It rode, as it were, the African "tide of independence."

This work focuses mainly on the nature and concatenation of the many forces, factors, and processes that went into defining the political community of the Cameroun Republic and, to this end, it is organized on two levels. The first is a general study of the Cameroun's premandate history, of its geographical and human environment, and of the most important sociopolitical factors that have influenced its political growth. The second level is an analysis of the territory's political development during the mandate and trusteeship periods.

There is much that can be criticized in this study of "nation-building" in Africa south of the Sahara,[1] and not the least of such criticism can be directed at the choice of emphases within the study, or to its organization. It may be argued, and with considerable justice, that greater attention should have been given to such matters as economic development, the impact of the French cultural presence in the Cameroun, the personalities of the more important Camerounian leaders, and the growth and influence of trade unionism. These are areas that, admittedly, have either not been treated at all or have been discussed all too cursorily. There is no defense against such criticism except, perhaps, that which lies in the need to establish priorities of relevance so that the end product will neither founder in too much detail nor be so brief as to be meaningless. To the end, then, of resolving—at least partially—some of these difficulties, several central propositions were used to give focus to the study as a whole and they in turn suggested the choice of material for emphasis:

1) With almost no exceptions, nation-building in sub-Saharan Africa is at an early stage.[2] This being so, then the discussion must have a temporal dimension that only historical perspective can give it. Accordingly, the factors, forces, people, and groups that give shape to the Camerounian polity are examined not only in their contemporary contexts, but also in terms of their growth, their transmutations over time, and the effect that events in the Cameroun's political past has had upon them.

2) Nation-building, in the African context particularly, involves overcoming ethnic particularisms.[3] (The term "tribalism" is often used in this connection, but it has become suspect as an analytical concept because of the heavy normative overlay it has acquired.) Consequently, the facts of Cameroun ethnic particularism and its effects on political and social life are stressed throughout this study. Parts of Chapters III, VI, VII, VIII, and IX take up this vital aspect of Cameroun political life in various contexts.

3) Nation-building, whether Africans wish it or not, involves the creation of an entity whose models are implicitly Western and whose construction therefore involves the use of ideas, institutions, and methods explicitly borrowed or adapted from the West.[4] Consequently, it becomes necessary to examine in detail some aspects of the so-called Westernization process as it affects or affected the Cameroun. The growth of an exchange economy, as the basis of the present economy; urbanization, as the process that accelerated contact with Western economic and social patterns; and education, as one of the primary vehicles for the Westernization, and, later, for the political socialization of youth, are all stressed in Chapter III. Some of the institutional and political adaptations developed in the process are seen in depth in Chapters VI through IX.

4) Crucial to nation-building is the growth of groups that give voice to nationalist aims and organize the varying interests that come to have a stake in the economic, social, and political growth of the country. In the African context, the old labels "political party" and "political movements," even though utilized by the participants themselves, cannot always be used to characterize the many groups that begin to make their claims upon the emerging polity. Consequently, this study examines a fairly wide range of such groups, from "politicized" tribal or economically functional groups to political parties self-consciously modeled in organization, method, and even language upon Western models. They are seen, in Chapters VI, VII, and VIII, against the backdrop of the constitutional and general political advance that they helped direct, and, in Chapters VIII and IX, in the perspective of present-day political trends and events.

5) It is a truism that the policies and institutions of a former colonial power have often indelibly marked the institutions and the character of political life in states just freed from colonial control. This would have been true of the Cameroun even if it had not also experienced the international tutelage of the League of Nations and the United Nations. The fact of international tutelage adds a dimension that makes it necessary to examine (*a*) colonial policy and institutions, (*b*) colonial policy and institutions under the impact of the mandate and trusteeship systems, and (*c*) the combined effect of both the international tutelary systems and the colonial systems on the shaping of indigenous political demands, groups, and ideas. These considerations provide another important emphasis found almost throughout the study, in varying degrees.

Although the primary emphasis of this work is on the French Cameroun, the rise of nationalism in the British Cameroons is an integral part of the Camerounian story; events in the British trust territory will therefore be treated at some length insofar as they illuminate developments in the French area. Further, inasmuch as the British Cameroons was an undifferentiated part of the German protectorate, and so much of the pre-World War I story involves that area, it is included in the discussions in the first two chapters dealing with the geographic, ethnic, and historical aspects of Cameroun development.

To the Ford Foundation, I am indebted for the generous fellowship that enabled me to undertake a year's research tour in the Cameroons during 1960 and 1961. I am similarly indebted to the African Studies Center and the Graduate Council of the University of California, Los Angeles, for a three months' preliminary study tour in the Cameroons during the latter part of 1959. My research in the Cameroun Republic could not have been conducted without the kind assistance and permission of the Cameroun Government; in particular, M. Jean-Faustin Betayené, former Foreign Minister of the Federal Republic, M. Didier Nzogang, Secretary-General of the Cameroun National Assembly, and M. Jean Audat, Technical Counselor to the Cameroun National Assembly were unfailing in their courtesy and their willingness to permit me access to crucial political materials. Mention must also be made of the Cameroun Service des Archives, which permitted me free use of its materials, and of the Institut des Recherches Camerounaises, which opened its library and facilities to me. A special note of gratitude is owed to the United State Embassy in Yaoundé for taking me and my wife under its protective wing and helping in every way to make our stay in the Cameroun both profitable and enjoyable. In the British Cameroons, Shirley and Edwin Ardener, of the Nigerian Institute of Social and Economic research, and Mr. P. E. N. Malafa, principal information officer to the Southern Cameroons government, were especially amiable and helpful. In Paris, M. Paul-Marc Henry, of the French Ministry of Foreign Affairs, kindly provided several letters of introduction which helped to open a number of important official doors in the Cameroun. The cordiality of Africans and Frenchmen alike throughout the Cameroun was so generous and spontaneous that it would be difficult to name all those to whom I am indebted for both information and hospitality.

A number of people read all or parts of this manuscript; I am particularly grateful to Dr. Paul Gebauer, who read Chapter I, to Mr. Claude Welsh, who read the entire study, and to Professor Reuben Frodin, who read several sections during the early stages of the manuscript's preparation. Their insights and critical comments proved immensely valuable, and are deeply appreciated. Mrs. Mary Virginia Kahl, of the University of California Press, provided invaluable assistance, both by wielding a keen and skillful editorial scalpel and by shepherding the manuscript through the Press.

Further, I gratefully acknowledge a debt that, by its very nature, can be neither repaid nor measured. It is the intellectual and moral debt I owe to Professors James S. Coleman, Robert G. Neumann, and J. A. C. Grant of the University of California, Los Angeles. Without their guidance and encouragement this study would not have been realized.

Finally, it must be added that however large my debts to others, the defects of this study and any errors of fact or analysis are my responsibility, and mine alone.

V. L. V.

Note to Reader

To avoid confusion from the outset, a few words about the terminology used in this study are essential. There appears to be, first of all, no *official* single orthography for "Cameroons," a difficulty stemming from the fact that the present federation is bilingual; in one part (the former British Southern Cameroons) English is the common language, and in the other (the former Cameroun Republic) French is the dominant tongue. Thus, both "Cameroun Federal Republic" and "République Fédérale du Cameroun" are acceptable designations. To compound the difficulty, renderings in other languages have been and are still used: "Kamerun" (German), "Camarones" (Spanish), and "Camaroes" (Portuguese, and the original version of the name, which means "prawns").

One way out of this thicket is to recognize that the terrirory (or parts of it) was consistently referred to in only one way by the administering powers, and to follow their usage:

1) the German spelling, "Kamerun," can be used for the period of the German protectorate;

2) the French spelling, "Cameroun," can be used in references to the French mandate, the French trusteeship, and the Cameroun Republic;

3) the English spelling, "Cameroons," can be used in reference to both the British mandate and the trusteeship, the latter divided administratively into the Northern and Southern Cameroons.

Another way out is to be entirely arbitrary in the interests of consistency.

This study will use some aspects of each method. Inasmuch as it deals principally with the period when there were in fact *two* Cameroons, the spelling "Cameroons" will be used in general references to both territories as well as to the British mandate and trusteeship; "Kamerun" will be used for the German protectorate, and "Cameroun" will be used in designations to the Federal Republic and its component parts, the East and West Cameroun. It might be added that there is at least some sanction for the latter usage; the place plaque at the United Nations General Assembly reads "Cameroun."

Contents

MAPS

TABLES

THE CAMEROONS
from Mandate to Independence

MAP 1. Africa, showing location of Cameroons (Cameroun Federal Republic)

CHAPTER

I The Geographic and Ethnic Context

GEOGRAPHY OF THE CAMEROONS

The political frontiers of the Cameroons before 1961—taking both the Republic and the British trust territory together as a unit—had one thing in common with those of most other African territories: they followed neither geographic nor human boundaries. The colonial scramble which delineated political frontiers in West Africa, usually marking them on north-south axes from the sea, cut blindly across the natural regions along which human settlement and migration had moved before the coming of the West. The position of the Cameroons at what has been called "the hinge of Africa" (see map 1), where the coast takes a sudden right-angled turn southward near the equator, makes it privy not only to the north-south boundary illogic of the Guinea coast, but also to a similar east-west border irrationality of the central-southwestern coast of the continent. The nineteenth-century scramble for colonies in Africa produced what is roughly a triangle (see map 2), the base of which extends 450 miles eastward from the sea, roughly along the parallel two degrees north to the juncture of the Ngoko and Sangha rivers. Its apex rests in Lake Chad, and its western (left) side runs south by southwest to the Atlantic, skirting west of Mount Cameroon (13,350 feet) at the edge of the sea. Oddly enough, the Cameroons' jagged eastern frontier is the most logical of the three; it follows for much of its length the course of six rivers, tributaries of the great river basins of the Congo, the Niger-Benué, and the Chad-Logone. The Cameroons is not only a transitional zone between two kinds of African boundary-making (that delineated north-south axes and that made along east-west axes), but it is also the joint between what are usually called West and Central Africa. A fault zone and a chain of volcanic and semivolcanic mountains and hills can be followed northeast from the offshore volcanic islands of Fernando Po to Mount Cameroon on the mainland to the Mandara Hills just south of Lake Chad. The axis of this chain of mountains, broken only in the north

1

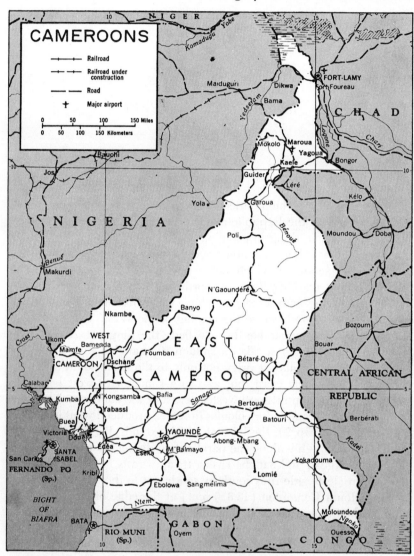

MAP 2. The Cameroons

by the valley of the Benué and the plain around Lake Chad, formed a natural border between the Cameroun Republic and the British trust territory.

The Cameroons triangle is roughly 770 miles long, and before 1961 contained some 195,881 square miles, of which about 80 per cent lay within the Cameroun Republic and 20 per cent in the trust territory. The Federal Republic now has an area of only 178,381 square miles, as the Northern British Cameroons (17,500 square miles) became a part of Northern Nigeria on July 1, 1961.

According to topography, climate, and vegetation, it is possible to divide the Cameroons into five natural regions (see map 3):

The first is the coastal forest plain bordering on the Atlantic; it is from 50 to 90 miles wide, largely covered with dense forests, with characteristic West African marshes and mangrove forests on the coastal strip. The climate is hot (averaging 80° F,) and humid, and rainfall is high—about 150 inches a year. One village, Debuncha, in the West Cameroun near Mount Cameroon receives an average of 400 inches a year.

Immediately bordering the littoral plain, often with an abrupt change of altitude, is the southern region, extending from the Sanaga River to the edge of the Middle Congo basin. It is a region of plateaus (average altitude 2,100 feet) and dense equatorial forests, with a hot and humid climate and an annual rainfall of between 60 and 80 inches. Most of the region lies within the area drained by the Sangha and three of its tributaries, the Dja, the Boubé, and the Ngoko; it forms the outer edge of the immense Congo basin and is generally covered with dense tropical vegetation. It is also the area in which the remaining pygmoid peoples live in isolated clusters, many still untouched by Westernizing influences.

North of the Sanaga River, which traces approximately the northernmost limits of the southern forest east of its junction with the Mbam, begins the central plateau region, also called the Adamawa Plateau region. This is an area of transition between the forested south and the northern savannahs. Altitudes here range between 2,600 and 5,000 feet, and rainfall averages about 20 inches a year.

The plateau region merges gradually into the northern savanna region, comprising the Benué and Chad plains, which are mainly savanna and steppe. November through May is the dry season; during the other five months the rains come, causing a vast area around Lake Chad to become inundated or swampy, and forcing the Benué and its tributaries out of their banks and onto the neighboring lowlands. Both

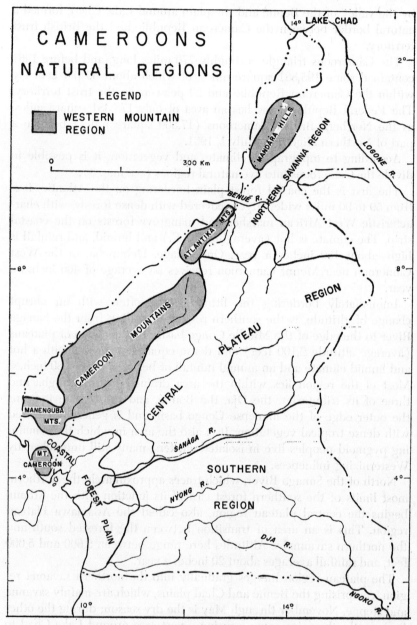

MAP 3. The Cameroons—natural regions

floodings, however, provide the basis for the limited agriculture that exists in the north.

The fifth region is the western mountain region, extending along the western side of the Cameroons triangle. Mount Cameroon, which last erupted in January, 1959, is the only remaining active peak in a volcanic belt that extends from the islands of Annobon, Principe, and Fernando Po north-northeast through Mounts Cameroon, Kupé, Manenguba, and Bambouta, almost to the edge of Lake Chad. The region lies largely in the former British trust territory; in fact, the division of the British trust territory into two parts conformed to a break in the mountain chain where the valley of the Benué passes between the Atlantika Mountains and the Mandara Hills. The mountain chain, followed northward, becomes progressively lower; the 13,350 foot height of Mount Cameroon gradually gives way to the Mandara Hills, whose highest peaks do not exceed 3,700 feet. In between is some of the most beautiful scenery in the world including peaks up to 8,000 feet, the incomparable Mambila Plateau, and the ranges of the grassy highlands of Bamenda. The invigorating climates of the region also make it ideal for human habitation; it contains some of the most densely populated areas south of the Sahara—and, of course, some of the most vexing political problems as well.[1]

PEOPLE OF THE CAMEROONS—*Ethnic Grouping and Distribution*

There is no dearth of examples to demonstrate that political institutions and often entire political systems are shaped by ethnic divisions. For instance, the federal basis of the Nigerian Republic stems from a recognized division between the Yoruba, the Ibo and the Hausa-Fulani, each group occupying a fairly well-defined geographical area and, most important, decisively influencing political institutions in their respective areas. The basis of Ceylonese political institutions before 1960 rested on explicit and implicit recognition of the multiracial character of the country; representation both in legislature and on executive levels was dominated by the Sinhala majority yet invariably included members of the Tamil minority. Canada is an excellent example of a comparable Western country in which political institutions reflect ethnic division, as one of the bases of Canadian federalism is in the constitutional balance between the English-speaking majority and the French-speaking minority. A similar balance was embodied in the constitution of Cyprus. The complexity of ethnic divisions in the Cameroons constitutes yet another example of the influence of ethnic factors on the political system. It is certainly an area in which these influences can be seen in sharp relief; their very nakedness is testimony to the degree to which they color the contemporary Cameroonian picture.

The Cameroons is not only the meeting place of northern, western, and central geographic regions, it is also the confluence of three of Herskovits' great African culture-areas: Guinea coast, Western Sudanic, and Congo.[2] Herskovits' cultural classification represents a useful framework within which to begin description of the ethnocultural complexities of the Cameroons. Represented in the Cameroons are branches of the Nigritic peoples of the Guinea coast, the Fulani and Arab peoples of the Western Sudan, and the Bantu-speaking peoples of the Congo basin. This taxonomy generally follows the more usual classification by language groups; the "culture areas" roughly correspond to what Greenberg[3] designates as the West Atlantic and Central branches of Nigritic linguistic stock, and the Chad subfamily of the Hamitic stock. Murdock,[4] who follows Greenberg's system with some modification, calls the three groups the Atlantic (Nigritic or Greenberg's West Atlantic), the Bantoid (Greenberg's Central branch), and the Chadic (Greenberg's Chad). Without entering into the controversy over whether the Bantu and so-called semi-Bantu languages are or are not completely distinct from the Nigritic,[5] Murdock's classification, which seems the most usable for this work, will be followed. (Map 4 shows the main ethnic groups, mostly identified according to Murdock's scheme.)

Recent tabulations listed some 136 identifiable ethnic groups in the Cameroun Republic[6] and about 65 such groups in the British Cameroons.[7] Available ethnic maps (of which map 5 is a composite) confirm the picture of an unusually complicated ethnic configuration. The figures mentioned above need, however, to be taken with the proverbial grain of salt; they are by no means accurate, since tabulations are at most provisional and depend on the system of classification used. What does stand out, and what the authorities are agreed upon, is that there is an unusually large number of tribal and ethnic groups in the Cameroons, and that classifying them presents extraordinary difficulties because of their number, their origins, and their current dispersion.

The largest of these ethnic groups, and, at the time of this writing, still the most troubled, is the Bamiléké, numbering some 550,000 persons who are found largely in the Cameroon highland area (see maps 4 and 5). Most of them currently live in the East Cameroun, within the five *départements* (administrative divisions) that, before 1961, comprised the Bamiléké *Département*.[8] Another 100,000 have left the Bamiléké region to take up residence elsewhere in the Cameroun. Directly related to these people are the various tribes of the Bamenda Province of the West Cameroun, most of them of Tikar origin, and numbering

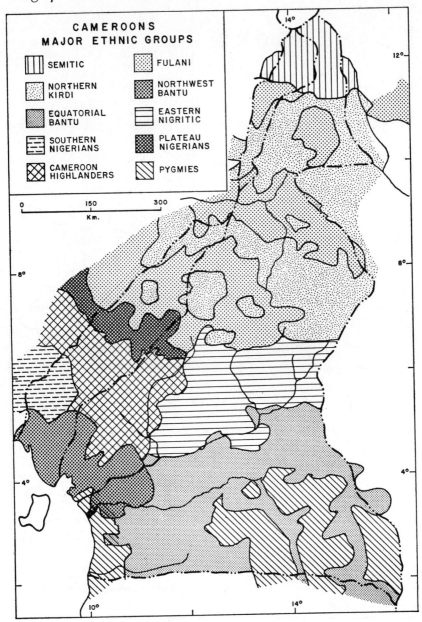

MAP 4. The Cameroons—major ethnic groups

MAP 5. The Cameroons—ethnic map

close to 300,000 persons.[9] The densely populated area around Dschang (see map 6) is the one inhabited by the Bamiléké, and that around Bamenda is the center of Tikar population. To the south, in the area where the equatorial Bantu are dominant, the main ethnic group is a widely distributed linguistic agglomerate, the Beti-Pahouin, which includes the tribes inhabiting the Yaoundé area. This Beti area comprises the second most densely populated area in the Cameroun. (See maps 4 and 6.) The group is principally made up of the Ewondo-speaking tribes (459,000), the Bulu-speaking [Boulou] Bantu (129,000) and the Fang-speaking tribes (48,000). The Beti-Pahouin have a total of about 655,000 speakers, of which the Ewondo are the most important.[10] The most numerous of the northwestern Bantu are the Bassa-Bakoko, who number about 195,000 and generally occupy the southern area of the Sanaga River valley. This latter group is important not only because of its numerical strength, but also because it was the first southern tribal group to participate in the political violence that began in 1955. Another northwestern Bantu group, the Douala, the first to make contact with Europeans coming to the Cameroons and to experience Westernization, is also of great political and economic importance. The Douala now number about 45,000 and live mainly in the area in and around Douala and the estuary of the Wouri.[11]

Pygmies, the original inhabitants of the southern forest area, now number only about 6,500 and are widely dispersed in small villages or families in the equatorial forest.[12] Some Pygmies live in the southeastern towns, where they are often respected and protected for magical qualities attributed to them.

Within the loose system of classification shown in map 4 the strongest ethnic and cultural group, numerically speaking, is that of the peoples called "Kirdi" (pagans) by the Fulani. The term Kirdi is, admittedly, unacceptable to anthropological classification, as it includes peoples of eastern Nigritic, plateau Nigerian, Sudano-Nigritic, and Chadic stock, but it does have a value recognized by a number of French authorities in that it provides an inclusive designation for the non-Muslim, predominantly negroid peoples of the general area north of the central plateau region.[13] These people are concentrated in the northern section of the western mountain region (especially the Atlantika Mountains and the Mandara Hills), even more heavily in areas between the Mandara Hills and the Logone River (in the so-called duckbill and along the Mayo Kebbi River), and in fairly isolated clusters in hilly and mesa areas south of the Benué. About 725,000 Kirdi are found in the East Cameroun[14] and about 367,000[15] in the former British Northern Cameroons. In the northern regions of the East Cam-

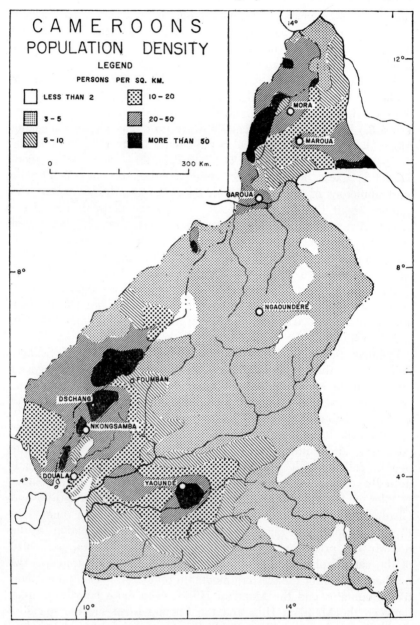

Map 6. The Cameroons—population density

eroun they comprise around 57 per cent of the total population; in the former British Northern Cameroons they are a similar percentage of the total. In both the British trust territory and the Cameroun they outnumbered the Islamized Fulani peoples, their traditional overlords, but they showed no signs of asserting themselves politically until very recently.

The Fulani, whom Murdock suggests stem from the Tukolor people of the Senegal Valley and savanna regions of Fouta Toro immediately southward,[16] extended their sway over the Negro peoples of the Chad area during the eighteenth and nineteenth centuries. Some of the native plateau Nigerians and eastern Nigritic peoples were converted to Islam, but a larger group—the Kirdi of the north—remained both unconverted and politically uncontrolled. The Fulani now include about 395,000 individuals in the East Cameroun, some 73,000 in the former Northern Cameroons trust territory,[17] and the 1953 Nigerian census listed about 10,000 in the Southern (now West) Cameroons. The Fulani cluster loosely, for the most part, around the towns that formed the principal outposts of the Adamawa emirate in the nineteenth century: Garoua, Maroua, and as far south as Ngaoundéré, with the main concentrations found along the valleys of the Benué and its southern tributaries. Two other northern groups complete the tally; the Islamized Negroes (mostly Kotoko and Mandara), and the Choa (Shuwa) Arabs and Kanuri around Lake Chad itself.

In 1961, an official estimate put the total population of the East Cameroun at approximately 3,300,000 inhabitants, with the greatest concentrations clustering around the towns of Douala, Garoua, Maroua, Yaoundé, and Dschang. About 1,230,000 live in the six northern *départements*.[18] The most recent estimate of the population of the British trust territory put the total at about 1,632,000, with 841,000 in the Southern (now West) Cameroons, and 791,000 in the Northern Cameroons.[19] The total population of the Cameroun Federal Republic was estimated in the December, 1961, *U.N. Monthly Bulletin of Statistics* to be about 4,907,000. Considering the lack of accurate data, this figure must be regarded with caution. Table 1 provides a summary of the numerical strength of the various ethnic components of the territory and an indication of their distribution between the two Cameroons.

TABLE 1

PRINCIPAL ETHNIC GROUPS IN THE CAMEROONS: THEIR DISTRIBUTION AND ESTIMATED STRENGTH

(Latest available figures)

Group	East Cameroun	British trust territory[a]	Notes
I. *Southern Nigerians*		155,000	Ibo (25,800), Ekoi-Anyang-Boki, etc. Mainly now in W. Cam.
II. *Northwestern and Coastal Bantu*			Group with first European contacts. *Ca.* 70,000 now in W. Cam.
Douala	45,000	2,000	
Bakwiri-Mboko		18,600	
Mbo (Bakundu)	25,000	44,410	
Bassa-Bakoko	195,000		
Other	2,000	4,000	
	267,000	69,010	
III. *Equatorial Bantu*			Beti-Pahouin includes:
Beti-Pahouin	655,000		Ewondo 459,000
Maka	64,000		Bulu 128,000
Djem	41,000		Fang 48,000
Other	13,000		
	773,000		
IV. *Pygmy*	6,500		Mostly dispersed in isolated clusters.
V. *Cameroon Highlanders*			Bamiléké in E. Cam. living in *départements* of
Bamiléké[b]	549,000	51,800	
Emigré Bamiléké	100,000		
Tikar and affiliates	12,500	260,000	

(*Full citations of works mentioned briefly below will be found in the bibliography.*)

  [a] The figures given here are for the Northern *and* Southern Cameroons. Inasmuch as the last census for the Southern Cameroons is the 1953 Nigerian census, the population of the West Cameroons must be estimated for 1962 at close to 900,000. *Report on the Cameroons* (1959), p. 120, estimates the population of the Southern Cameroons at mid-1959 to be *ca.* 841,000. It is interesting to note that Art. 60 of the constitution of the Cameroun Federal Republic fixes the population of the West Cameroon at 800,000, apparently for representational purposes. See the 1959 *Report*, p. 127, for a rough ethnic breakdown of the Southern Cameroons population, based on the 1953 Nigerian census.

  [b] Tardits, *Les Bamiléké* . . . , estimated the Bamiléké population in 1961 to be between 492,000 and 606,000; 549,000 is his medial figure.

Table 1—*Continued*

Group	East Cameroun	British trust territory[a]	Notes
Widekum and other Bamenda		114,000	Dschang, Bafoussam, Mbouda, Bafang, and Bangante. Emigrés live outside these five *départements; ca.* 427,800 of this group now in W. Cam.
Bamoun	80,000	2,000	
Banen	28,000		
Yambasa	26,721		
	796,221	427,800	
VI. *Plateau Nigerians*			
Mambilla	12,500	36,000	In trust territory, mainly hill pagans in Benué and south Adamawa provinces. *Ca.* 30,000 of this group now in W. Cam.
Tigon		15,000	
Jukun		10,000	
Ndoro and Jibu		10,000	
		71,000	
VII. *Eastern Nigritic*			
(G)Baya	84,000		Mostly pagans. Those in the E. Cam. often included as Kirdi. *Ca.* 20,000 of this group now in W. Cam. Chamba includes Bali.
Mbum	74,000		
Duru-Verre	43,000		
Vute (Bute)	17,000		
Namchi	16,000		
(T)Chamba	10,000	30,000	
Other	4,000	20,000	
	248,000	50,000	
VIII. *Kirdi* (*northern pagans*) Approx. total	450,000	367,000	
Prin. groups:		Prin. groups:	Mostly pagan groups north of Benué River. See map 4 for broader definition. In Brit. trust territory, mainly in N. Cam.
Masa	80,000	Fali	
Tupuri	62,000	Koma	
Matakam	60,000	Bata	
Musgum	35,000	Highi	
Mofu	35,000	Marghi	
Gisiga	25,000	Njai	
Fali	25,000	Sukur	
Kapsiki	20,000	Bude	
Daba	18,000		
Mundang	15,000		

Table 1—*Continued*

Group	East Cameroun	British trust territory	Notes
IX. *Islamized pagans*			
Mandara	40,000	50,000	
Kotoko	25,000		
	65,000		
X. *Chadic*			
Shuwa (Choa)			
Arabs	45,000	52,300	Islamized Negroes of
Kanuri	5,000	131,000	the Saharan fringe.
Hausa	5,000	12,800	Approx. 15,000 of
	55,000	196,100	this group now in W. Cam.
XI. *Fulani (Peul, Fulbe, Foulah, etc.)*			
	395,000	72,400	Approx. 15,000 Fulanis now in W. Cam.
XII. *Other*			
Non-Cameroons Africans	80,000	101,000	Mainly in South.
Nonindigenous	16,400	1,142	Mostly Europeans and Americans, but includes Levantines, etc.
Composite grand totals	3,164,121	1,560,452	
Latest official estimates of total populations	3,223,517 (1959)[c]	1,632,000 (1959)[e]	The 1963 *U.N. Demographic Yearbook*
	3,300,000 (1961)[d]	1,586,000 (1958)[f]	estimates total population of Cameroun Federal Republic at midyear 1962 at 4,326,000.

[c] *Guide Economique du Cameroun, 1959*, Chambre de Commerce and d'Industrie du Cameroun (Yaoundé, 1959), p. 5.

[d] Service de la Statistique Générale (Yaoundé), 1961. No complete census of the East Cameroun has ever been undertaken.

[e] *Report on the Cameroons* (1959), p. 120.

[f] See notes 17 and 18 to Chapter I.

OTHER SOURCES: *Rapport du Cameroun* (1957), pp. 16–26; Ardener, *Coastal Bantu of the Cameroons*, pp. 14, 15; McCullough *et al., Peoples* . . . , pp. 14–16, 54, 88–91, 135, 155, 165; Lembezat, *Cameroun;* Dugast, *Inventaire* . . . ; *The Northern Cameroons; Supplément au Bulletin de la Statistique Générale, 1958*, p. 47; *Population Census of the Eastern Region of Nigeria*, 1953, Bulletins 1, 2, 5, Census Superintendent (Lagos: 1954).

CHAPTER

II *The Historical Context*

INTRODUCTION

There is no simple, satisfying explanation for the impetus that drove the nations of Europe to establish colonies all over the world. There is only a complex of motives and pressures as various as the situations in which they operated: the colonization of South America differs as much in its underlying motivations as the conquest of India by Britain differs from the European penetration and colonization of sub-Saharan Africa. Each case presents its own pattern of cause and effect; each instance its own unique characteristics. In Africa, many important factors seem to have been operative: the curiosity of the first European seafarers to venture south of the Pillars of Hercules; the competition of the great trader nations for the slaves, palm oil, and gold of a continent; the need for raw materials to feed the burgeoning European industrialization of the eighteenth and nineteenth centuries; the simple factor of rivalry for colonies and the need to keep others from getting there first; and even the less tangible factors of prestige and military security. This list is by no means all-inclusive; these are just some of the more important motives.[1]

All these factors operated in the making of the Cameroons. The first visitors were curious Carthaginians, awed by the volcanic sights along the Bight of Biafra. Later the Portuguese came to exploit the wealth of the Guinea coast and, after the colonies in the New World had been launched, toward the beginning of the sixteenth century, they were joined by other nations in search of the most precious commodity the continent had to offer—slaves. With the passing of the agricultural tradition that gave slavery its raison d'etre and the beginnings of industrialization in Europe and America, the quest for slaves turned into a search for raw materials, both agricultural and natural. It had been possible to "cultivate" the slave-producing Guinea and Cameroons coasts from a distance by using coastal tribes as middlemen; the new era demanded permanent settlements from which the newer exploitation could be conducted. Quite naturally, the rapidly industrializing nations of Europe entered into vigorous competition for unclaimed slices of the continent.

15

Britain, France, and Germany all sought footholds on the Cameroons coast: the winner was Germany. As the Cameroons became important to Germany for economic reasons, so did it also assume a military importance in the light of the diplomatic and military fencing that preceded World War I. By the time the war broke out in 1914, the Cameroons was an economic, military, strategic, and political prize. So it remained during the years between the wars, and to its possession was added the element of enhanced prestige. Germany, shorn of her colonies by her defeat in 1918, continuously complained that her empire had been stolen from her and demanded the return of the Cameroons as a measure of the Third Reich's power and prestige. But German aspirations were doomed to disappointment, and the Cameroons remained with the Allies.

There is then no discernible "grand design" or "Kamerunsgeist" operating to shape the Cameroons over the course of its history. A number of circumstances, accidents, forces, and events can be seen as keys to an analysis of that history. Nothing more is claimed for their selection than that they were chosen to illuminate the historical background to today's Cameroonian political life.

PRE-COLONIAL CAMEROONS

THE COMING OF THE WEST

According to some texts left us by Greek and Latin historians, in the fifth century B.C. the Carthaginian, Hannon, claimed to have sailed the coast of the "Lybic lands beyond the Pillars of Hercules." Hannon wrote of seeing a large volcano, which he named "The Chariot of the Gods," and which later commentators sought to identify as Mount Cameroon.[2]

More exactly, the Cameroons—at least the coastal region—enter history with the great Portuguese discoveries near the end of the fifteenth century. During the reign of King Alphonso V (1438-1481), seafarers in the pay of a rich Lisbon merchant, Fernando Gomez, arrived, possibly in 1472, in the Bight of Biafra and visited the island of Fernando Po. As the Portuguese sailed into the estuary of what is now the Wouri River, they were struck by the presence of innumerable prawns, easily taken and delicious to eat. They named the river Rio dos Camaroes, or River of Prawns, and it was by that name that it appeared on the first Portuguese maps of the region.[3] They also named the mountain Mount Ambozes, after the early natives of the region, a name by which Mount Cameroon was known for nearly two centuries. The Portuguese failed, however, to establish any fixed stations on the Cameroons coast. Their base of operations was at São Tomé island, from which they sent ships to visit their *resgates*, or trade points at the mouths of various coastal rivers. Content with their lucrative ivory and gold trade along the Gold Coast, the Portuguese did not undertake any extensive exploration of the Cameroons hinterland. The dense coastal mangrove forest, the humidity, the insect-borne diseases, and the hostility of the coastal tribes all discouraged penetration into the interior, and, moreover, Benin, a few hundred miles west, offered far more promising prospects for slave trade.

By 1493, however, the Portuguese had begun to colonize both São Tomé and Fernando Po, and by the 1520's their settlers had developed first-class sugar plantations worked by slaves bought along the coast.

THE SLAVE TRADE AND THE CAMEROONS COAST

Columbus' discoveries in the West Indies and the growth of the Caribbean plantation system marked an important change in the complexion of European trade along the West African coast. After 1530, slaves became the most important export commodity of the region. Until the end of the sixteenth century the Portuguese were the most important suppliers of slaves for the burgeoning plantations of the New World. In the process, Fernando Po and São Tomé were converted into collection depots from which slaves could be conveniently shipped west. Though slave trade lured other major European states to West Africa, it was the Dutch, toward the beginning of the seventeenth century, who finally broke the Portuguese monopoly on this trade. By 1642, the Dutch had managed to capture São Tomé and threatened the Portuguese hold on Fernando Po by establishing a trading post at the mouth of the Rio dos Camaroes. With the extension of the trade in slaves during the seventeenth and eighteenth centuries, not only Dutch and Portuguese, but also French, English, Swedish, Danish, and Brandenburger slavers visited the Cameroons coast in search of human booty. Calabar, about eighty miles west of Mount Cameroon, Bimbia and Douala on the Rio dos Camaroes, and Rio del Rey had become famous by the beginning of the nineteenth century as centers where slaves were sold and from where they were shipped abroad.[4] Despite the frequency of their visits, the Europeans made no effort to establish permanent footholds; most of them remained aboard ship, dealing with the coastal tribes that served as middlemen. These coastal tribes, of which the Douala, Bakweri, and Bulu were among the most prominent, both obtained slaves and aided in the distribution of goods brought by the Europeans.

In 1807 the British declared their own slave trade illegal and, inasmuch as they had by then become the dominant power along the Nigerian and Cameroons coast, began to take active steps to suppress slaving in the Gulf of Guinea. In 1827 they obtained permission from the Spanish to occupy Fernando Po, which had fallen to the latter in 1777, and to base a squadron there to control the shipping of slaves from the Bights of Biafra and Benin.[5] The British took advantage of their settlement on the island to encourage several Bristol and Liverpool enterprises to set up floating hulks as trading posts in the Cameroons River. It is interesting to note that the use of pidgin English, still spoken as a lingua franca along the West African coast, began to spread during this period.

By 1830 traders along the Cameroons coast had established trading posts and factors' stations, and had made contacts and agreements with native chiefs from Calabar to Campo.[6]

THE FIRST SETTLEMENTS

When the British, with Spanish permission, settled Fernando Po in 1827, they brought with them a number of manumitted slaves from Freetown, center of their antislavery activities in West Africa. The presence of these freed slaves and the suppression of the slave trade spurred English missionary societies into establishing missions on the Cameroons coast, long known as the most active slave-trading region in West Africa. In 1844 the Jamaican branch of the English Baptist Missionary Society landed forty-two volunteers at Clarence (Santa Isabel on Fernando Po), where the Reverends Clark and Prince had established a small church two years before. Some months later, in 1844, the society established a church and school at the Bimbia trading post, but these were forced to close by 1849. Clarence's position was also becoming increasingly uncomfortable, inasmuch as the Spanish Jesuits on the island, outraged by the presence of Protestants on Spanish soil, were pressuring the governor for their expulsion. Alfred Saker, who had taken over at Clarence, left the island under protest and purchased from the native king of Bimbia, "King William," a strip of land ten miles long and five miles deep beside Ambas Bay at the foot of Mount Cameroon and along the coast opposite Fernando Po. There in 1858, Saker established Victoria, the first permanent settlement on the Cameroons coast,[7] and became *de facto* governor of the new colony in the absence of an officially appointed administrator.

Even though the mainland had already been explored by Englishmen (Lander, Oldfield, Baird) in the 1830's and 1840's and the King of Bimbia had offered to cede to the British government part of his territory from Bimbia to Rio del Rey, official British interest continued to be directed toward the suppression of the slave trade rather than toward the acquisition of new territory. British interests were deemed sufficiently well served by the periodic visits of the British consul for Fernando Po and the Oil Rivers (the Delta of the Niger), who had at his disposition several small gunboats that patrolled the nearby coastal waters.

In 1842 the British consul signed a treaty with two native kings in the Cameroons River district to encourage the legitimate trade in palm oil and ivory, on the condition that slave trade cease. Nevertheless, slaving continued on a clandestine basis for several years after the treaty, and it was finally eliminated only when the riverain Douala, long middlemen in the slave trade, found the trade in palm oil and ivory more profitable. By virtue of this latter commerce, the town of Douala became the principal trading center along the Cameroons coast. Thomas Lewis, the missionary in charge at Victoria in 1884, reported that at that time, on the rivers near Douala there were six floating hulks belonging to English traders, and two shore establishments at Akwa and Bell towns belonging to the German Woermann firm.[8]

Relations between the traders and the natives at Douala were not always harmonious. When they became so strained that all compromise seemed impossible, the British and German traders and the chiefs agreed on the formation of a "Court of Equity" to settle all outstanding and future disagreements between them. The court was also to maintain the peace:

. . . a purpose not easily achieved because of the almost continuous civil war that prevailed among the rival chieftains. The court reported to the British Consul and referred serious matters to him on the occasion of his infrequent visits. It had the power by fines and other penalties to enforce decrees necessary for the peace that prosperous trade needs. In extreme cases, when peaceful methods failed, British gunboats could be called upon to lend a helping hand in the enforcement of law and order. On occasion the bombardment of native villages had been necessary to keep the peace and end interference with trade. So accustomed had the natives become by 1880 to the authority of the British Consul that the latter's recognition was felt necessary to establish the position of a native king.[9]

THE BRITISH PRESENCE

At Douala the British and German traders coöperated fruitfully. The latter participated in the Court of Equity without complaining, and, up to 1880, had shown little sign of wanting to challenge British supremacy in the Gulf of Guinea. The British saw as their principal threat the French, who were active along the coast from

Oil Rivers to Campo. Already, by the 1870's the French had established trading centers at Malimba, Big Batanga, and Campo. Both British traders and native chiefs were anxious to secure an official British protectorate over the Cameroons coast, the former for obvious reasons, the latter because they had become accustomed to the British and found it easier to deal with them than with the French. Between 1877 and 1884 the various native kings along the coast directed numerous requests for protection and annexation to the British government, either directly to London or to Consul Hewett in the Gulf of Guinea.[10]

King Akwa's letter to Queen Victoria, dated August 7, 1879, suggests both the nature of these requests and some of the reasons for them:

Dearest Madam—We your servants have join together and thoughts its better to write you a nice loving letter which will tell you about all our wishes. We wish to have your laws in our towns. We want to have every fashioned altered, also we will do according to your Consul's word. Plenty wars here in our country. Plenty murder and idol worshippers. Perhaps these lines of our writing will look to you as an idle tale.

We have spoken to the English Consul plenty times about an English government here. We never have answer from you, so we wish to write you ourselves.

When we heard about Calabar River, how they have all English laws in their towns, and how they have put away all their superstitions, oh, we shall be very glad to be like Calabar now.[11]

The native kings were not alone in their anxiety to secure the establishment of a British protectorate of the Cameroons coast; the missionary settlement at Victoria, and the Liverpool, Manchester, and London traders in the region had since 1880 repeatedly made their wishes on this subject known to the government.

THE BRITISH AND ANNEXATION

The British government procrastinated until 1882, when it finally instructed Consul Edward Hyde Hewett to make a lengthy stay on the coast, visit the Cameroons River, and report on the kings, the people, and the trade of the territory so that the government could give the question of annexation full consideration.

Hewett's report gave a minute description of the Cameroons River area. As far as a hitherto indifferent home government was concerned, however, the most significant parts of Hewett's report were those dealing with the increasing French trade along the coast, especially in the Oil Rivers district and the Niger Delta. Hewett had been apprised by a letter from Kings Akwa and Bell in April, 1883, that the French were signing a treaty with King "Pass-All" (Mukoko) of Malimba. Frequent correspondence from British traders along the coast, letters from Victoria, and messages from various missionaries seemed to confirm Hewett's reports about the threat posed by the French. Alarmed, the Gladstone cabinet approved Hewett's suggestions that the entire area along the Nigerian and Cameroons coast be supervised by a "floating consulate" and four vice-consuls. In addition, Hewett recommended that treaties be concluded with native chiefs, binding them to cede no territory to foreign powers without the consent of Her Majesty's government.[12] The cabinet approved the general scheme late in November, 1883, and, after some delay, voted to send Hewett out with treaty forms for the native chiefs to sign, and to keep the entire affair completely secret until the last of the treaties had been concluded.

By July 6, 1884, Hewett had met at Bonny with the senior officer of the West African Fleet, Captain Brooke of HMS *Opal,* and worked out with him the details for putting the scheme into operation. According to the plan, Hewett was to proceed along the Nigeria coast with his treaty forms, and Brooke was to proceed to Big Batanga to have the pro-English king there sign one of the treaties. While Brooke was at Big Batanga he learned that a German gunboat, the *Möwe,* was going to the Cameroons River, and immediately he dispatched Lieutenant Moore on the *Goshawk* to Douala to reassure the native kings and ask them to make any treaties until Hewett showed up. Moore arrived in Douala on July 10, and on July 11 sent Brooke a report in which he indicated that the local German traders were holding nightly meetings with the natives and telling them that the Germans wanted to annex their country. Moore had also called on King Bell, who, though threatening to turn his land over to the Germans because of the repeated rebuff from the British, nonetheless agreed not to make treaties with anyone before Hewett arrived. King Bell, according to Moore, wanted the English consul to come "soon, within one week," because he (Bell) might have made a conditional promise to the Germans.

Hewett, treaty-making on the coast near Bonny, did not learn about the coming of the *Möwe* until July 14:

He suddenly changed his plans and sailed aboard the *Flirt* for the Cameroon River. Engagements of various kinds made it impossible for him to get there before Saturday, July 19; and then only to discover that he had come too late, for Kings Bell and Akwa had already made their treaty with Dr. Nachtigal [on the 12th] who had come with the *Möwe* under instructions from Bismarck to establish German rule. It was a bitter day for Hewett. Everything had been kept secret by the English in order to anticipate possible French moves, with nobody dreaming that Germany had even the slightest colonial ambitions.[13]

Hewett's trip had not, however, been entirely in vain. Two days before arriving in the Cameroons River he had stopped at Victoria and officially declared it a British possession. The big prize, though, had eluded him.

The German Coup

Nachtigal's presence in Douala, astonishing as it was to the British, was certainly no accident. Since April, 1883, the German government had been quietly taking steps to effect the occupation of the Camerouns. The various German traders with interests in the Cameroons, of which the most vocal and important was Adolf Woermann of Hamburg, had long asked Bismarck to extend imperial protection over the region. The British-Portuguese agreement of February, 1884, to neutralize the Congo Basin, the increase of French and British diplomatic and trading activity along the West African coast, served to convince the Chancellor that it would be necessary to act to annex African territories before either Britain or France did so. On April 19, 1884, Bismarck sent up a smoke screen in the form of a communication to Lord Granville, British foreign secretary, informing him that Nachtigal was being sent to West Africa "in order to complete the information now in possession of the German Foreign Office at Berlin on the state of German commerce on that coast," and that he was "authorized to conduct on behalf of the Imperial Government negotiations connected with certain questions."[14] Granville took the bait. So convinced was he by Bismarck's repeated avowals of opposition to colonization that he assured him that British authorities on the coast would be instructed to aid Nachtigal. Despite the fact that several German newspapers tipped Bismarck's hand in the month preceding Nachtigal's departure, the British remained unsuspecting.[15]

Bismarck's man for this venture was already known as an intrepid explorer and was at the time of his appointment the German consul-general in Tunis. He sailed as soon as he received his final instructions; by July 2 he arrived in Togoland, and by July 6 he had signed several treaties by which Togo became a German protectorate. Nachtigal then set sail immediately for the Cameroons, arriving on July 11, and by the next day Kings Akwa and Bell had signed the treaty establishing their protectorate. Lieutenant Moore had reported correctly: the German traders, be it by cajolery, bribes, alcohol, or alluring promises, had succeeded in convincing the local kings that the British were not to be trusted in word or deed and that their future lay with Germany.

On July 14, 1884, Nachtigal had the imperial flag hoisted near the

German factors' station on the right bank of the river, and salutes were fired in nearby towns.[16] He stayed long enough to install his assistant, Dr. Buchner, as temporary imperial representative on July 19, to greet Hewett when he arrived that same day, to assure British traders that their interests would be safeguarded, and to attempt (but fail) to alter the Court of Equity. Nachtigal sailed on July 20, and between July 21 and 26 had raised the German flag at five other trading posts along the Cameroons coast.[17] Hewett remained behind for several days to remonstrate unavailingly with King Bell and to convoke a meeting of the Court of Equity, during which he appointed a British trader, Buchan, as vice-consul. Buchan was instructed to keep in touch with the natives who had not signed the treaty, especially with the disaffected inhabitants in Hickory Town, across the river, and before long:

. . . German authority suffered a good deal from the fact that the numbers of Englishmen, the frequent re-appearance of English gunboats, and the English-controlled Court of Equity tended to reduce the outward appearance of [German authority] . . . with the passage of time and with British intrigue, the situation in the river became increasingly serious.[18]

THE GERMAN PROTECTORATE
CONSOLIDATION

After Nachtigal had raised the German flag at Douala, he left his colleague, Dr. Buchner, as the temporary official German representative in the region until a permanent government could be inaugurated. Buchner found himself in immediate conflict with the British merchants and missionaries, most of whom refused to accept German rule. Many of them felt that prior British claims had been unjustly neglected, and accused the Germans of treachery in seizing the area. Their domination of the Court of Equity, their numerical superiority over the German traders in Douala itself, the frequent visits of the British consul to Douala, all contributed to the uneasiness of the German position. In addition, Buchan, left behind by Hewett as British vice-consul, became active in openly advocating resistance to the Germans among the disaffected natives on both the east and west banks of the Cameroons River. Even the Germans were forced to admit that their treaties were not popular with many natives, who expressed their disapproval by openly shouting insults.

Meanwhile, the British and Germans were engaged in a race for written agreements with the native rulers in the area west and northwest of Victoria. A Polish adventurer of doubtful reputation, Rogozinski, and his aides, all in British pay, led the English treaty-makers by concluding thirty-five "temporary" treaties during 1885. Needless to say, Bismarck was not pleased by this further evidence of what he considered British obstructionism.

In December, 1884, disaffection at Douala came to a head with the rebellion of King Lock Priso of Hickory Town, who had not accepted German rule, against King Bell, who had. Dr. Buchner at once called in the German Admiral Knorr, who proceeded to put down the rebellion with naval gunfire and the help of marines. The English mission at Hickory Town was leveled and several persons (including four Germans) were wounded or killed. Knorr took over from Buchner and began issuing decrees which firmly established German rule. The Court of Equity, long a thorn in Buchner's side, was summarily dissolved, despite British protest. By February of 1885 the British government, in a series of notes to Bismarck, was taking a more conciliatory tone than it had since December; it agreed to ship Buchan home and to surrender a number of claims based on the "temporary" treaties concluded by Rogozinski and his cohorts. The English merchants were asked to cease their agitation among the natives and to coöperate with the new government. By the end of that year matters were once again on an even keel, and a "business as usual" atmosphere prevailed among both German and English traders. (The last remaining obstacle to complete German control of the Cameroons, the British missionary colony at Victoria, was eliminated in 1887 when the English Baptist Missionary Society sold its holdings to the Basler Mission after two years of negotiations.)

One of the causes for the weakness of German authority in the protectorate in the period leading up to the uprising in December, 1884, was the tug-of-war between Bismarck and the German traders in the area. Bismarck had long sought to have the traders accept administrative responsibility for the protectorate which, as he pointed out repeatedly to them, had been created at their request and on their behalf. The Hamburg merchant king, Adolf Woermann, who represented the traders and whose firm had the greatest holdings in the colony, was a good friend of Bismarck and sought to convince him of the necessity for strong, central imperial control over the colonies. Woermann pointed out, with some justification, that German traders refused to administer a government, to collect taxes, to enforce the law, to care for schools, and to become, for all practical purposes, the government in a region where they were the commercial rivals of resident English firms.[19]

Bismarck's reluctance to establish a full-scale colonial government was not a position he maintained out of simple personal conviction. Strong and continued opposition to colonial schemes came from the Reichstag, especially from the Centrist and Freisinnige parties, which balked whenever money was to be allocated for colonial ventures. Bismarck had been able to convince the Reichstag of the necessity for the Togo and Kamerun protectorates only by claiming that they were to exist to protect the German traders from the menace of English and French competition. Moreover, and most important, he had promised that the new colonies would cost little to run and hinted that the main administrative costs would be borne by the traders themselves. By the time Knorr had put down the rebellion, Bismarck and the traders were still at an impasse over the issues outstanding between them. The rebellion, together with Knorr's strongly worded recommendations, forced Bismarck into the humiliation of asking the Reichstag in 1885 for appropriations to set up a government in the Kamerun. Not only had he to acknowledge publicly that the traders were unwilling to assume governmental responsibility, but also that the death of Nachtigal, and Buchner's return home owing to illness, had left the Kamerun devoid of any imperial representatives.

Von Soden

On July 3, 1885, the Kamerun's first governor, Julius von Soden, took charge to rule until 1891. He at once set up a three-man advisory council to assist him, appointed a legal counselor (chancellor), and created the forerunner of the Mixed Courts (Schiedsgerichte) to supplant the abolished Court of Equity. Von Soden was an advocate of a gradual rather than the rapid and forceful opening of the hinterland that the traders favored—although they were not, however, prepared to support any such exploration with money. In December, 1885, the governor sent his financial deputy, Puttkamer, and the explorer Krabbe to study Mount Cameroon and establish German authority over the Bakweri living on its slopes. On this trip Puttkamer managed to convince the natives that their treaty with Rogozinski had been superseded, and he also raised the German flag at Buea, which later became the capital of the protectorate. The excellent climate at Buea and the fertility of the volcanic soil around the mountain convinced the Germans of the desirability of establishing extensive plantations in the area. As a matter of fact, almost immediately after the transfer of Victoria to Germany, the firms of Woermann and Jantzen und Thoermahlen started plantations on the lower slopes of Mount Cameroon. By 1913 the plantations owned about 100,000 hectares (close to 40,470 acres) in the Victoria area, of which less than one-third was under cultivation in 1885.

During von Soden's tenure, the Germans consolidated their hold on the coastal region. The German commercial establishments built up their trade and set up an ever widening circle of contacts with the hinterland natives. The Basler Mission, which had taken over the English Baptists' mission at Victoria, set up a mission and catechistic seminary at Douala.[20] Von Soden was also instrumental in setting up the botanical gardens at Victoria, where experimental agricultural work was carried on by the government in an attempt to improve cash-crop strains and to discover new areas of agricultural exploitation.

Von Zimmerer, von Puttkamer, and Expansion

Under von Zimmerer, von Soden's successor, beginnings were made—by such men as German explorers Zintgraff and Kurt Morgen—in opening the interior of the Kamerun to trade and administrative control. It was also during von Zimmerer's term of office that the most serious scandal in the Kamerun's history took place. Acting for him during a period of absence in Germany was his chancellor, Kleist, whose immorality and cruelty led to a violent uprising among the Dahomean soldiers whom the explorer Gravenreuth had purchased from a native king who was about to kill them as sacrifices. Not only did Kleist underpay and mistreat the troops, but he had their women publicly whipped, an act which shocked both the troops and the general public. Kleist was subsequently (in 1894) tried and convicted for his misconduct by the special Disciplinary Court of Potsdam.[21]

Von Zimmerer was succeeded by Jesko von Puttkamer, whose tenure lasted from 1895 to 1907. Under him the Kamerun developed greatly. He encouraged penetration into the northern areas, and played a prominent part in getting plantations established on a large scale. Von Puttkamer was instrumental in the creation of a private trading corporation, the *Gesellschaft Süd-Kamerun* (1898), specifically organized to exploit the rich southeast forest region. The new concessionaire took over the management and administration of the concession area, and succeeded in establishing a German monopoly in the rubber and ivory with which the region abounded. Furthermore, the move effectively foreclosed the activities of the French, Belgian, and Dutch traders operating in the area. A similar society, the *Gesellschaft Nordwest-Kamerun*, was created in 1899 to exploit the Bamoun and Bamiléké regions (see map 7).

Von Puttkamer considered himself a "realist" in administrative matters, and there is little question that some of his support of the commercial enterprises was given at the expense of the natives. His harsh attitude toward them came to be much discussed in the Reichstag; he favored corporal junishment, was unwilling to improve the working

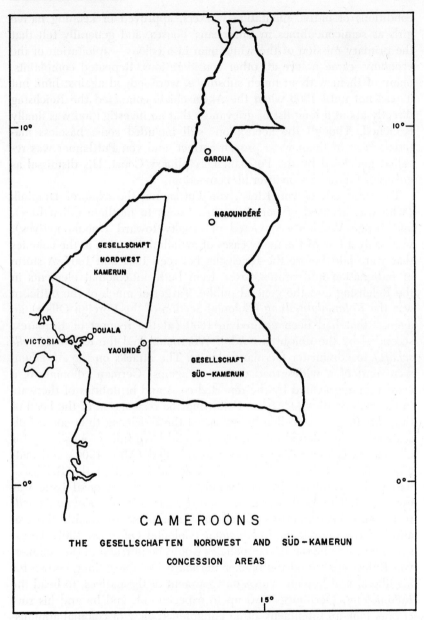

MAP 7. The Cameroons—German concession areas

conditions of native plantation workers, approved of keeping native girls as semiconcubines in Europeans' houses, and generally felt that the primary mission of the white man in a colony—exploitation of the economy—came before all other considerations. Repeated complaints, many of them without much substance, were lodged against him, but it was not until 1906 when the Akwa chiefs contacted the Reichstag directly about a long list of grievances that an investigation was finally launched. Though the accusations still included some baseless material, most of them were proven correct, and von Puttkamer was recalled and tried by the Potsdam Disciplinary Court. His dismissal as governor followed soon after his conviction.

The misdeeds of von Kleist, von Puttkamer, the explorer Dominik (who was accused of permitting his troops to mutilate fallen foes), and Judge Wehlan (convicted of cruelty toward Douala natives), were only a few of the many cases of maladministration in the colonies that were laid before the Reichstag between 1901 and 1907. A storm of indignation and protest arose from both anticolonial elements in the Reichstag and the general public. Target of much of the criticism was the *Kolonialabteilung* (Colonial Section of the Foreign Office), an agency that had been created in 1890 (at the request of Bismarck, seconded by the ubiquitous Adolf Woermann and the *Kolonialgesellschaft*) to administer German colonies. The attacks on the *Abteilung* were part of a widespread campaign against German colonialism, a campaign aggravated by the reported costs and brutalities of the wars in German Southwest Africa. Following the resignation of the head of the *Abteilung*, Chancellor Bülow asked the Reichstag to create a full-scale separate colonial ministry that would have full responsibility for all matters colonial. Von Bülow was rebuffed (May, 1906) and matters came to such a head over the colonial issue that the Reichstag had to be dissolved. In the ensuing election the colonial issue was uppermost. The result was a resounding success for the *Kolonialgesellschaft* and the supporters of colonialism, and made possible the creation of the permanent *Kolonialamt* (Colonial Office) in 1907. To assure that more humanitarian policies would be pursued in the colonies, von Bülow appointed the banker Bernhard Dernburg, long known for his liberal and humane views on treatment of the natives, to head the *Kolonialamt*. Dernburg lived up to expectations, and he and his successors took an intelligent, often enlightened view of colonial administration. The excesses of the pre-1906 era were largely eliminated, and a series of able administrators was appointed to fill key colonial posts.

Seitz, Gleim, and Ebermaier: the Prewar Years—1907-1913

Puttkamer's successor, Theodor Seitz (1907-1910), was an appointee in the Dernburg spirit, who brought with him to the Kamerun a determination to remedy the wrongs of previous administrations. He was concerned with native welfare as no other governor before him; he championed increased native representation on local councils, the elimination of control of certain kinds of domestic slavery, and restrictions on the sale of alcoholic beverages; he sought elimination of forced labor, flogging, and the other abuses commonly practiced on plantations, and he turned a sympathetic ear to complaints about the misuse of the head-tax system.

A noteworthy event during Seitz's term was the negotiation of the addition to the Kamerun of a large part of the French Congo in 1911. The cession came about as a result of the Anglo-French Convention of November 4, 1911, when, as compensation for the surrender of German rights in Morocco, the imperial government received from France about 107,000 square miles of the French Congo. Originally, the Germans had demanded some 16,000,000 hectares (61,776 square miles), which, however, would have cut the French Congo in two and deprived the French of some of the most extensively developed areas of their territory. The final agreement gave the Germans an outlet to the Congo River and drew the southern boundary so that it enclosed Spanish Rio Muni (see map 7). The Germans gave up part of the so-called duckbill lying between the Logone and Shari Rivers. The area acquired by the Germans, known as "New Kamerun," was alleged to contain some one million in population, and virtually doubled the size of the protectorate.[22]

Seitz was followed by Dr. Otto Gleim, who held the governorship until 1912, when he was replaced by Karl Ebermaier, who was governor until the Allied occupation in 1916. Until the outbreak of the war in 1914, both Gleim and Ebermaier were faced with the increasingly serious resistance of the Douala people—resulting from a highly unpopular attempt on the government's part to move the Douala out of the city and expropriate some of their lands. The government sought, according to its spokesman, to improve health conditions and prevent speculation on the land that a few of the Douala had been selling in ever larger amounts. It was contended, with some justification, that it was impossible to get the natives to follow the most elementary sanitary practices, and as a result malarial mosquitoes, which also carried filariasis and which bred in the native areas, were a constant menace to the white community as well. Furthermore, the Douala, whose monopoly as "middlemen" in the Douala-town trade had been whittled down by the white traders, had been forced into other ways of earning their living. One method was the sale of land, which European traders sought to buy for later speculation. A notable instance involved some 280 hectares (722 acres) fronting on the river, property which, the Douala people alleged, was not to be taken away from them under the terms of the 1884 treaty. The Douala people objected most strenuously—objections which were shared by Governor Gleim and some of the missionaries and traders—and their king, Rudolph Douala Manga Bell, repeatedly petitioned the Reichstag for redress. One petition was sent in November, 1911, and another in March, 1912. The actual work of moving the natives from the land was begun in 1912, despite Manga Bell's protests to Governor Ebermaier and local officials. On February 20, 1913, Manga Bell submitted a formal note of protest against the expropriation, and asked a German lawyer to represent Douala interests in Berlin. The government, through Colonial Secretary von Solf, refused to change its program and defended its policy against numerous critics in the Reichstag. Manga Bell thereupon sent letters to various Kamerun chiefs asking for their support, claiming a breach of the 1884 treaty. He also later admitted that he had tried to get in touch with foreign powers for support in his efforts to keep his people from losing their lands. The coming of the war in 1914 made it appear that Manga Bell had been plotting with Germany's enemies, and he was arrested, tried, and hanged for high treason.[23]

The expropriation of the Douala's property and the execution of their chief left them bitter and rebellious. Probably one of the reasons the Germans abandoned Douala soon after a British force sailed into its harbor was that they were unwilling to face both the British and the hostile natives, one on the sea and the other in the town. The German expropriation left a legal tangle that was not finally unsnarled until 1952. In the interim, the French administration was forced to face a perennially discontented Douala population, highly vocal, and capable of embarrassing the government with telling effect.

Whatever the Douala case, however, it became unimportant to the Germans once war had broken out, and when it had, they tried to keep the Doualas quiet by harsh and repressive measures. Very soon, however, the Germans' military position became untenable and they vacated the town, retreating toward Mount Cameroon.

THE WAR AND THE PARTITION
OF THE CAMEROONS

World War I was declared in Europe in August, 1914, and it was not long until a three-pronged attack was launched upon the Kamerun by forces based in neighboring territories. General Aymerich attacked from the French Congo; General Dobell led a seaborne expedition against Douala, using Nigerian, British, and French troops; and a third column entered the protectorate from the north.

The Germans were kept on the defensive throughout the campaign; Allied superiority in men and matériel did not, however, prevent the Germans from inflicting severe checks upon the Allies and from putting up a spirited defense. They hoped that German arms on the Continent would decide the issue for them, and consequently sought to extend the conflict as long as possible.

The campaign lasted eighteen months, and ended with the internment of the German force, including Governor Ebermaier, in Rio Muni by the Spanish. About 6,000 troops and 14,000 friendly civilians reached the safety of neutral internment. The figure for interned soldiers is significant; if it is to be believed, then by comparison the Allied losses were tremendous. It would appear that the Germans ended the war in the Kamerun with almost as many men as they started with, yet the Allies lost about 3,500 killed and wounded, or about 35 per cent of their strength.[24]

There is ample evidence that the Kamerun campaign, from the Allied side, was badly handled. It must, however, be admitted that tactically the advantage lay with the Germans, who had a superior knowledge of the terrain, prepared positions, and available local levies. They were able to check both the northern and eastern advances; their northern strong point, Mora, fell more than a year after the Nigerian-Chad columns had unsuccessfully assaulted it. Even Allied commanders praised the Germans' defense.[25]

The Condominium, the Partition of the Territory, and the Creation of the Mandate

The departure of the Germans from Douala after its fall to the Allies on September 26, 1914, presented the occupying forces with the problems of administering and caring for the welfare of the newly conquered areas. Initially, and with characteristic thoroughness, the British had brought with them personnel ready to take up administrative roles: the expeditionary corps landed a finance officer and a treasury staff, a branch of the Bank of West Africa, a transport and requisitions agent, a military quartermaster's service, an engineering service staff, a naval roads-and-ports service staff, a customs service staff, an information service, and a staff for administering property and commerce.[26] Not to be outdone by the well-prepared British, the French subsequently brought their own personnel to assure a joint administration of the newly won territory.

The condominium that existed in principle was established in fact following the exchange of a series of notes between M. Delcassé, Sir Francis Bertie, and Sir Edward Grey (September 21 and 24, 1915). It was decided that until the enemy had been completely defeated in the territory, the Allies would provide joint ad hoc or provisional administration. With the collapse of German resistance, Britain and France decided to divide the Cameroons and permit the interested nations to administer their respective areas according to their own methods and without interference from others. The agreement of March 4, 1916, ended the condominium and delineated the zones of influence of France and Britain:

1) Territories ceded to Germany in 1911 would be returned at once to the administrative aegis of French Equatorial Africa, and would initially be treated as occupied territory.

2) The British and French zones were defined so that the French obtained four-fifths of the total remaining area (to be administered under the Department of the Colonies in Paris, separately from AEF), and the British obtained two disconnected pieces bordering Nigeria. The provisional frontiers thus established have, with only minor variations, remained unchanged until today.

The British and French generals were charged with effecting the transfer. A decree issued April 7, 1916, named General Aymerich as commissioner of the French Republic and instructed him to install military government in the areas delimited by the March 4 agreement.[27] A similar Order in Council was issued to General Dobell, who took charge of the new British Cameroons possessions. Raoul Nicolas, a French judge who witnessed the transition, commented on conditions in the territory when hostilities had ceased:

The beginnings were extremely difficult, the territory having been disorganized by the state of war; the indigenous [population] abandoned its villages and hid in the bush or the forest; the [administrative] posts were burned down. Finally, a considerable number of natives (about 14,000) had been dragged along by the Germans in their retreat to the Spanish Muni [sic]. Left without control, the natives went back to their old ways: exactions by the chiefs, rebellions against them, wars between villages, and private vengeance. Pillage prevailed in the [inhabited] centers. Finally, the Germans, counting always on the success of their arms, had carried away or hidden many vital documents.[28]

It may be added that slavery reappeared and instances of ritual cannibalism became more frequent. Probably the most vexing problem facing both British and French in the early days of the condominium was the continued presence of the German military and civilian personnel interned by the Spanish. Following the termination of hostilities, most French and British troops used in the campaign were sent elsewhere on the continent to assist in the conquest of the other German colonies, so that the Germans and their native auxiliaries, although interned by the Spanish, were numerically superior to the combined Anglo-French forces left in the area. The Spanish, under the resulting pressure from Aymerich and the British, first transported 845 Germans to Cadiz, among them Ebermaier and Colonel Zimmermann. In April, the Spanish began moving the remaining Germans, the native troops, and most of the native civilians to Fernando Po. Aymerich estimated that 55 European officers and noncoms, about 6,000 native levies, and about 10,000 native civilians were involved in the transfer.[29] The soldiers were interned in camps, and most of the civilians were sent to the interior of the island where they were put to work on the labor-hungry plantations. The French and British continued to protest the presence of the internees at Fernando Po for two reasons: one, that they were spreading unrest among the civilian population of the island, and two, that their numbers constituted a potential military threat to the Douala-Victoria-Buea area. When Aymerich left for home in October, 1916, the problem had still not been resolved. In 1919, however, about 6,000 native troops and 7,000 civilians were repatriated to the Cameroons.

The wholesale departure of the Germans meant that the initial task of the occupying forces was to provide the territory with a completely new administration to replace the one that had disappeared. Not only had the Germans created a highly organized and relatively well-functioning colonial bureaucracy, but they had succeeded in creating habits of acceptance of their rule among the natives with which the French and English would have to reckon when setting up their own systems. It is interesting to note that the occupants of some traditional chieftaincies still legitimize their authority by reference to German symbols of office.[30]

Characteristically, the French, in their section of the Cameroons, set up administrative structures closely resembling those in force at the time in French Equatorial and West Africa (AEF and AOF). At first, military personnel manned and directed the vital services. When the military regime was converted into a civilian one and a government was appointed, on September 5, 1916, the public works, maritime controls, railway management, finances, and customs were either transferred to civilian personnel, or the military personnel occupying the positions were placed under the administrative control of the civil governor. The country was divided into the traditional *circonscriptions,* and these in turn into *subdivisions.* A political bureau and an economic bureau were created, and a number of official decrees and ordinances (*arrêtés* and *ordonnances*) were issued to provide some direction in social and economic matters. Of considerable importance was the reorganization of the court system to correspond closely to the system in the AEF. Native courts, presided over by a European administrator and assisted by native assessors, were to dispense justice according to custom if the latter were not in conflict with what Nicolas called "the principles of our civilization."[31] Along with these courts, it was deemed wise to continue, but on a narrower scale, the Mixed Tribunals or *Schiedsgerichte* that had been set up before the Germans came and continued during their occupation. These courts, it will be recalled, were originally established to settle disputes between European traders and native rulers, and were usually presided over by a representative of the dominant power. Their forerunner was the Court of Equity of Douala. The French found that, by the time they came to establish their own judicial system, these courts enjoyed a vigorous existence in a large number of towns. Therefore, under a provision of the Hague Convention of 1907 and until the French Cameroons had officially become mandates, the French continued to enforce most of the German legislation in effect at the end of the war.

On May 7, 1919, the Supreme Allied Council allocated the various German colonies in Africa to their respective conquerors. The Council declared that, although other territories would definitely become mandates, the status of Togo and the Cameroons should be settled by negotiations of the French and British governments. The two nations were invited to make a joint recommendation on the two territories in question.[32]

The French were not prepared, however, to agree to a conversion of Togoland and the Cameroons into mandates. Expansionist sentiment ran high in France toward the end of the war, and M. Simon, the French colonial minister, argued for "annexation pure and simple." He contended that, since France had won both Togo and the Cameroons by force of arms, she was not obliged to place these territories under League of Nations control. In a speech before the Chamber of Deputies on September 7, 1919, he referred to the New Cameroons as a colonial Alsace-Lorraine, and indicated that it would return to the "full sovereignty" of France. As for the other territories, Simon admitted that France was bound by the general obligations of Article 22 of the Treaty of Versailles. The extent of these obligations, however, was only to give the members of the League of Nations the benefits of the "open door" to the two colonies; France would take measures to abolish the slave trade and forced labor, and to limit the commerce in arms and alcohol. She would also publish an annual "yellow book" (report) on the administration of the territory, but would reserve the right to recruit natives to serve in Europe, to establish a customs and administrative union with adjoining territories, and to maintain entire liberty with regard to public works. Subject to these qualifications, the French government would agree to "administer without a mandate but in the spirit of a mandate." The chief difference between this arrangement and a mandate under the League would be that France would not be responsible to the Council of the League for the fulfillment of these obligations.[33] By accepting a mandate under the League, France would also have had to submit to international controls, a situation to which she was unwilling to agree.

During negotiations with the British Foreign Office, however, the French government finally gave up this point of view and agreed that both Cameroons and Togo should be held under League mandates,[34] although it was not until July 20, 1922, that the two mandates were finally confirmed by the Council.

The mandate ushered in a new phase of the Cameroons' development. Arbitrarily sundered into three parts, the territory lost whatever unity it had achieved during the protectorate. The two Cameroons under separate administrations moved off in different directions, propelled by the force of colonial policies often diametrically opposed to one another. The artificial bisection of the territory created the reality of two distinctly different Cameroons, with different social, economic, and political traditions. It would be thirty-five years, almost two generations, before the possibility of reunifying the two Cameroons could be raised as a meaningful issue.

THE LEGACY OF THE GERMAN PROPRIETORSHIP

Although the end of the German protectorate over the Cameroons in 1916 was marked by the wholesale departure of all German nationals in the territory, from Governor Puttkammer to the fathers of the Pallotine Order, it did not mean that the German presence would soon be forgotten. The Cameroons' experience under Germany remained very much a live issue during the interwar period. The physical return of German planters to the British Cameroons after

1924, the tangible and intangible remains from the German period, and the increased volume of German propaganda for the return of her former colonies, all served to keep alive the memory of the Germans. Even after World War II, when the question of returning Germany's former colonies to her had finally been totally settled, the semimythical unity of the two Cameroons under the Germans continued to serve as a nationalist symbol and a political weapon for those desiring such reunification.

Tangible evidence of the German period was not hard to find; indeed, it served to remind both Cameroonians and Europeans of the economic and physical development of the country under the Germans and, inevitably, came to be used as a yardstick for comparing the old order with the new.

Mention has already been made of the extent of the physical plant left behind by the Germans: harbor facilities at Douala, Kribi, Campo, and Tiko-Victoria; the Nordbahn and Mittelbahn rail lines, as well as the Victoria plantation narrow-gauge railway; a large number of bridges, roads, and paths; and well-constructed government and private buildings, many of which are still in use today. The value of the many plantations and development projects started during the protectorate can hardly be underestimated; the French and British inherited an established basis for economic development—that is, a basic infrastructure and a productive agricultural economy, both with considerable potential.

The intangible legacy of the German period is, obviously, harder to measure. In its aggregate, however, it also represents something lasting and influential. The Germans initiated the Cameroonian Africans into the novelties of the exchange economy by drawing them into the cash-wage nexus, and by introducing notions of ownership foreign to the native societies. The Germans inculcated habits of obedience and deference to authority without which the successors to its regime would have been unable to function. Also, some of the Germans' repressive policies, especially the attempt to change the face of Douala by moving the Douala out in wholesale lots, fostered protest movements containing the seeds of future political action. By their actions, the Germans encouraged the growth of an African social stratum capable of mediating between the Europeans and the African Cameroonians of the hinterland; in this the administration consciously used education and Christian missionary activity as instruments of penetration and modernization. It was no accident that the Douala early became the most Westernized Cameroonians in the territory. Despite their rebelliousness, they served the German administration well, providing it with indigenous teachers, traders, government officials, and missionaries. In all, it must be said that the Germans effectively paved the way for their British and French successors.

Yet the mandatory powers in the Cameroons soon discovered the difficulties of building upon a foundation laid by others. Whatever else could be said of their motives, the Germans (according to objective scholars) maintained a colonial administration that could be compared favorably with any other in Africa at the time.[35] Rudin reports that during his travels in the Cameroons in the 1930's he heard frequent praise of the Germans, usually unsolicited, and often reflecting genuine affection for German officials. Informed commentary seems to agree that, on the whole, German rule in the Kamerun was strict, often harsh, but usually just. The Germans did not try to conceal the fact that their primary purpose in the colony was to exploit it; yet in the process they brought intelligent, often enlightened, administration. Consequently, there were many Cameroonians who genuinely regretted the end of the protectorate, not the least of whom were the traditional chiefs, with whom the Germans had been content to deal on what were virtually "indirect rule" principles. The Sultans of Bamun and Ngaoundéré had special reason to regret the passing of the Germans; they were both later deposed by the French. Many other chiefs lost their prerogatives under French rule; the seeds of anti-French rebelliousness often lay in resentful comparisons between the two regimes.

It can be argued with some justice that, for many Cameroonians, the Germans shone in the distorted light of retrospection; their administration seemed that much the better for being past, and hence that much more available for disparaging comparisons with the current regime. The Germans undoubtedly were guilty of many harsh acts toward the African Cameroonians; yet they were also concerned with their welfare. It must be recalled that the Reichstag forced many a humanitarian program on the imperial administration. All in all, objective evaluation of the protectorate period leads to the conclusion that the German colonial administration was not as black as it was often painted. In a larger sense, however, the quality of the German administration becomes irrelevant in the light of the political context in which the question was often raised. For the Cameroonians desiring to attack the French or British administrations for alleged wrongs of commission or omission, the brighter the German experience could be painted, the handier it became as a weapon. During the interwar period, many travelers came away from the Cameroons with the impression that, compared to the current French or British administration, a substantial number of Africans thought the former German regime to have been a paragon of mildness and fairness. Raymond Buell, who chronicled the defects of the French mandate during the 1920's, was struck by this,[36] as was Harry Rudin later on.

The question of the use of the Kamerun era as a symbol for political ends will be discussed in greater detail in Chapter VI, but it is interesting to note here that even during the interwar period the alleged unity of the Cameroons under the Germans was cited by some Douala who claimed sovereignty over the whole of the territory.[37]

In all, it can be maintained that the German impact on the Cameroons was important not only for the obvious reasons, that is, the physical development left behind, but also for the less tangible ones of sentiment and political action. The German experience remains, for many Cameroonians, at once a political touchstone and a potent symbol of a half-mythical golden age when the Cameroons were one.[38]

THE CAMEROONS NORTH

Until the turn of the century, the Cameroons' history was largely the history of the coastal regions. The vast areas above the tropical rain forest and the plateaus did not become important as parts of the territory until the Germans had established their hegemony from the sea to Lake Chad. Thereafter, the northern areas of the Cameroons began to be increasingly significant in the political evolution of the territory. In fact, much of the political history of the Cameroons, and indeed many of the country's contemporary problems, cannot be understood without reference to the unique traditions and ethnic patterns of the north, such as the Fulani emirates, the Muslim traditions, and the Fulani-Kirdi dichotomies. All of these contributed their part to French and British policy during the 1920's and 1930's.

The Cameroons north, above the great equatorial forest and the plateaus which effectively barred contact between peoples of the coast and the savanna, does not become a historical entity until the great explorations of the eighteenth and nineteenth centuries mapped and described it. In an even stricter sense, there is no Cameroons "north" until 1901 when the Germans succeeded in taking Ngaoundéré and Garoua, thus eliminating what were virtually the only blocks to full control of their Kamerun. Though delineated by treaty in 1890, 1894, and 1911, the frontiers of the German protectorate were not finally settled until 1913.

In the broad sense, it is the mid-Sudanic plain, the area around Lake Chad, that we find mentioned first in the oral and written traditions that have come down to us. It is known that by the eighth century A.D. the Chad plain was already inhabited by diverse animist peoples, and that in that century pastoral Berbers and semi-Arabs appeared from the west and north and began conquering the animist negroid peoples around Lake Chad.[39] Some of these latter peoples, who fled into inaccessible regions of the Logone and into the mountains, have succeeded in remaining free until today, despite later Fulani pressures.[40] Others, who at first managed to avoid Berber domination, later succumbed to the Islamizing pressures of the Fulani.[41] Around the western and southern perimeter of Lake Chad, then, in an area where Berbers and natives merged with one another, arose the great Muslim state of Bornu in the tenth century. West of Bornu, at the same time, emerged the seven senior Hausa states, the *Hausa Bokwoi*—Daura, Kano, Zaria, Gobir, Katsina, Kano, and Biram—whose influence spread widely to the south and southwest. Islam reached the Hausa states in the fourteenth century and, though never wholly accepted as a religion by their people, greatly influenced their systems of law and education. Bornu also became progressively more Islamized as it developed closer ties with North and East Africa.

THE FULANI

As early as the thirteenth century the Fulani (Fulbé) began to make their appearance in Hausaland. A pastoral people, probably originating in Tekrur in the ninth century, they arrived among the Hausa from the west, driving their herds before them.[42] Some settled in the cities and became Islamized, and others continued their primitive life and remained pagan. By the eighteenth century the Fulani had become well assimilated, mostly by peaceful integration, within the Hausa states.

To the east, several groups of pagans who had successfully avoided incorporation into Bornu had set up a small but powerful empire, Mandara, in the rugged Mandara Mountains, some 130 miles south of Lake Chad. During the sixteenth century this empire was attacked by the Bornuans, who managed to Islamize and subdue all but a few of its tribes, which have remained pagan to this day. Bornu set up a vassal Mandara sultanate which existed until the Fulani attack in the beginning of the nineteenth century.

By the end of the eighteenth century the Fulani immigrants had established themselves not only in the Hausa states but had infiltrated east as far as the edge of the Bornu and Mandara empires, and southwest into the valley of the Benué itself. East of Hausaland, the Fulani

mostly accommodated themselves to local existing authority where-
ever they settled. They intermarried extensively with the Bata along
the Benué, with the Kilba, and submitted (at first) to the pagan rulers
in the areas southwest of Bornu.[43]

DAN FODIO AND ADAMA

Toward the end of the eighteenth century an urban Fulani and a devout
Muslim, Usuman [Osman] dan Fodio (1754-1810), began to preach . . .
against the debased Islamic faith of the Hausa States, and achieved a considerable following among the *Fulani Gidda* [urban Fulani]. The Hausa
rulers in Gobir and elsewhere became alarmed at this criticism of their way
of life and tried to repress the sect. Usuman dan Fodio then declared a
jihad, in which, between 1804 and 1810, the Fulani conquered all the Hausa
States and for a time even occupied much of Bornu.[44]

Dan Fodio's *jihad* marked the transition of the Fulani from peaceful
dwellers among the Hausa and the Kirdi to the dominant ethnic group
in the northern Nigeria–Lake Chad area. The success of the Fulani
came about not only because they fought with fanatic, missionary zeal,
but also because they were mounted and possessed firearms. Only those
pagan peoples who were able to flee to hilly country where the Fulani
horsemen could not operate were able to save themselves. In 1806 a
Fulani noble, Adama, returned east from Sokoto to his people in the
region southwest of Bornu, bringing the news of Dan Fodio's *jihad*
against the unbelievers. "Many of the local Fulani had already em-
braced Islam, and Adama persuaded the various clans to combine and
follow the crusading example of Sokoto."[45] Usuman dan Fodio gave
Adama a flag, and

. . . in his letter of appointment he conferred on Adama the title of *Lamido
Fumbina,* with a *firman* to propagate the faith from the Nile to the Bight of
Biafra, and allowed him to recruit Fulani volunteers (*Toronkawa*) in Sokoto.
Their ranks were swelled by Hausa mercenaries fired by the prospect of
slaving, and Adama thus acquired a nucleus for the Adamawa Army which
he was to raise on his return.[46]

Adama made Yola, on the Benué, his headquarters, and it still remains the traditional capital of the Adamawa emirate carved out by
Adama and his successors. In the campaigns conducted by Adama
until his death in 1848, he extended the emirate south as far as the
Bamun sultanate of Fumbam (including the towns of Banyo and
Tibati); southeast to Ngaoundéré; east to Rei, on a tributary of the
Benué; northeast to Maroua, Mindij, and Bogo; and north up to parts
of Bornu and including much of the Mandara kingdom, whose combined forces he defeated in 1823.

ADAMA'S SUCCESSORS

Two of Adama's sons, Lawal and Zubeiru, extended and consolidated the empire carved out by their father. In the process, the Bornuan empire fell under Fulani domination. By the time Zubeiru succeeded to the throne, in 1890, the Germans had established their protectorate and were pushing up from the coast. The British had begun pressuring Adamawa from the west, and the French, in control of the areas north and east of Lake Chad, were challenging Zubeiru as well. It was Zubeiru's melancholy fate to watch and succumb to the reduction of the emirate by the hated infidel Europeans. At best, he was able to fight only a hopeless, though spirited, rearguard action. His successors have all, until recently, held their titles under the protection (and by permission) of the European powers who came to dominate the Chad plain. (See table 2.)

TABLE 2

GENEALOGICAL TABLE OF THE LAMIDOS OF ADAMAWA[a]

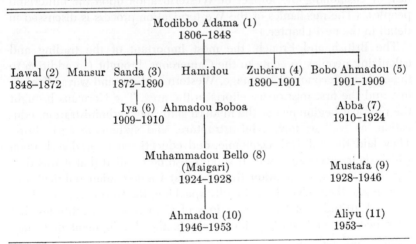

Modibbo Adama (1)
1806–1848

Lawal (2)   Mansur   Sanda (3)   Hamidou   Zubeiru (4)   Bobo Ahmadou (5)
1848–1872   1872–1890   1890–1901   1901–1909

Iya (6) Ahmadou Boboa   Abba (7)
1909–1910   1910–1924

Muhammadou Bello (8)
(Maigari)   Mustafa (9)
1924–1928   1928–1946

Ahmadou (10)   Aliyu (11)
1946–1953   1953–

[a] The table traces both the descent of the lamidos of Adamawa (designated by the numbers in parentheses) and the genealogical successors of the first lamido, Modibbo Adama. Note that four of Adama's six sons themselves became lamidos; of the four, Zubeiru (1890–1901) was the last to exercise independent sovereignty.

SOURCE: A. H. M. Kirk-Greene, *Adamawa, Past and Present* (New York: Oxford University Press, 1958), p. 147.

CONCLUSION

This discussion of the course of Cameroonian history to the beginning of the League of Nations mandate has, of necessity, been cursory, and only the highlights have been touched upon. What emerges most forcefully from the facts is the impression of the remarkable number and diversity of influences that have contributed to the making of the territory. Slavers, traders, missionaries; British, French, Germans, Fulani; all brought significant ingredients destined to become part of the Cameroonian tradition and important in shaping its future political life.

The early slavers and traders brought the first Western contacts, which proved destructive and negative in most instances. However, most important for future political development, they created a semi-Westernized African coastal society that was both willing and able to cultivate the exchange economy and to act as the carrier of Western culture into the hinterland. This society also performed the important task of cushioning the impact of Westernization upon the hinterland peoples. (The mechanics of the Westernization process is discussed in detail in the next chapter.)

The British and French, the most important of the trading and colonizing peoples to come to the Cameroons, brought (in addition to the exchange economy) language, Western customs and ways of thinking, and the first missionary efforts in the area. The Germans brought the physical beginnings of the modern state: law, administration, education, as well as towns, infrastructure, and systematic agriculture. They laid the political, economic, and educational groundwork upon which their successors built. It should also be recalled that it was during the German occupation that the first Cameroonian political stirrings made themselves felt. Broadly speaking, the Germans shaped the political attitudes of two generations of Cameroonians, attitudes that later became an important ingredient in the development of Cameroonian nationalism.

Finally, the impact of the Muslim Fulani on the Cameroons north should not be underestimated. The Fulani established a pattern of authority and administration, plus a way of life, that retarded the Westernization of the north—with important consequences for education and general social development—and that eventually produced political forces destined to counterbalance those that arose in the south.

The influence of the Christian missions, only lightly covered in this chapter, was most important in relation to their contributions to formal education. (Education is one of the Westernizing influences to be discussed in the next chapter.) It may be added that, just as the Muslim Fulani formed the political forces in the Cameroons north, so did the missions have a key role in providing educational orientation to significant political forces in the south.

Essential as these elements are to an understanding of the subsequent political history of the Cameroons, before the narrative can be taken up again it is important to examine the Westernizing forces brought into the Cameroons and the manner in which they affected the territory. Such an analysis should add depth and substance to the broader historical perspective attempted here.

CHAPTER

III *The Westernization**
of the Cameroons

In the centuries before the advent of the European colonial powers, most traditional societies in the great West African rain-forest regions were relatively closed worlds. The external limits of these groups were most often defined by the geographical extension of the clan, and usually comprised, at best, no more than a loose agglomerate of neighboring villages. Contacts with groups outside the clan tended to be hostile, frequently taking the form of raids for women, slaves, or food. The occasional appearance of major kingdoms or ethnic aggregations, such as the kingdom of Dahomey, the Ashanti Confederation, the Yoruba, and the Mossi, did little to disturb the basic isolation of the peoples of the Guinea coast. Even the great empires of the western Sudan were as a rule unable to penetrate to the coastal regions; they too played themselves out against the hostility of their neighbors and the southern tribes. The insularity of the indigenous societies of West Africa stayed more or less unbroken until the eighteenth and nineteenth centuries. Even though coastal tribes had been in contact with European traders since the sixteenth century, the lack of good harbors, the proximity of the plateaus to the coast (which made it impossible to sail inland for any great distance before encountering rapids), and the harshness of the climate, all militated against permanent European settlement. It was not until European traders began to create permanent or semipermanent installations on African soil that the impact of the West began to be felt in other than purely negative ways.

Slave trading was not conducive to the establishment of permanent trading posts; usually, regular visits to supply stations and to those points where the trade was most brisk or needed protection, and to small collection and gathering facilities and quasi forts, were sufficient to keep

---

* The term "Westernization," as used in this chapter, refers to the variety of cultural, political, and technological changes that occurred in the Cameroons as a result of European penetration, occupation, and administration.

44

the trade going. The coastal tribes were themselves hostile to permanent installations as potential threats to their own collection efforts or, more often, to their position as middlemen with respect to tribes in the interior who did the work of collecting for them. The suppression of the slave trade in the early part of the nineteenth century and the increase in demand for the mineral and agricultural products of the continent contributed not only to the rise of a number of important trading towns but to the scramble for territorial possessions. During this period the trading posts on the Cameroons coast, such as Bimbia, Douala, Big Batanga, Kribi, and Campo, were converted and expanded into communities based on European models. The acculturative processes by which Western influences began to change, and eventually to transform or to destroy, traditional societies in the Cameroons began with the creation of the trading communities on the coast; consequently, the coastal tribes were first and most profoundly affected.

Once permanent or semipermanent trading facilities had been erected, it became necessary to ensure a peaceful environment. Where the indigenous population had not come to terms with the traders or had actively tried to prevent them from carrying out their work, pacification became a necessity. When the trading areas became the bases for political domination and territorial expansion, pacification, often against stubborn resistance, became one of the major activities of the new colonial regimes. After 1884, when the Germans established their protectorate over the Cameroons, they had to subdue Bakweri, Douala, Bassa, and Bulu tribesmen before they could even begin to move into the hinterland. It was not until 1911 that the Germans were able to subjugate all the indigenous groups as far north as Lake Chad. The immediate effect of the establishment of a *pax Europea* was the substitution of one set of authority figures for another. In a deeper sense, it involved a displacement of traditional authority symbols by a European administrator, the creation of a "king" or chief from a senior notable or councilor (Ardener suggests the spate of Bakweri and Douala "kings" stems from just such arrangements),[1] or by the removal of one chief and the substitution of another more amenable to his conquerors.[2] Once the authority systems of traditional societies had been breached, other forces began to accelerate the process of disintegration.

GROWTH OF AN EXCHANGE ECONOMY

A consequence of the trading system introduced by the West, and a process that went hand in hand with pacification and the growth of trade, was the growth of an exchange economy.

Coleman calls it the "commercialization of land and labor," and defines it as ". . . the . . . shift from an almost wholly subsistence economy, based upon the coöperative bonds of lineage and a variable, but comparatively stabilized system of stratification, to a dynamic money economy based upon the cash nexus, individual profit, and wage employment."[3]

The introduction of an exchange economy, however, need not necessarily exert "Westernizing" influence in the sense that it brings with it a set of distinctly "Western" values. Such an economy is an essentially valueless nexus involving certain manipulative relations and it is a misconception to append a value system (ethnocentrically, the "Western" one) to it.[4]

Before the coming of the European traders the coastal Bantu tribes of the Cameroons were, for the most part, self-sustaining societies. The Douala, their coastal affiliates, and the Bassa had all engaged in subsistence agriculture, supplemented by ocean and river fishing. Patrilineal descent was the normal practice, and clan lines were seldom extended beyond neighboring villages. Chiefs among the Bakweri and Douala usually functioned more as lineage symbols than as decision-makers; the most important decisions were made by local assemblies and/or councils, with village elders supplying informal leadership.[5] The development of slavery, and later the establishment of trading posts, radically altered their way of life. The Douala shifted from their subsistence economy to the more lucrative slave trade and the exchange economy. They became the principal suppliers of slaves in the Wouri River—Mount Cameroon area, and developed a near-monopoly in slaving that was not broken until the trade itself was abolished during the early years of the nineteenth century.[6]

When the slave trade was at its height, not only the Douala, but other littoral tribes as well acted as middlemen and collectors for the European traders who came to the coast. As the trade disappeared during the nineteenth century (in the Kamerun, slavery was not officially forbidden until 1902), the Douala turned from being middlemen in slaving operations to being middlemen in the trade for oils, ivory, and other products. The Bassa and Bulu similarly turned to middleman activities of a like nature, but, unlike the Douala, found it impossible to maintain their positions against the ever deeper penetrations into the hinterland by German traders and explorers. A result of the eventual tension that built up over the understandable reluctance of the coastal tribes to give up their lucrative position was a series of armed rebellions in which the Bakweri, the Bassa, and the Bulu sought to prevent further penetration into the interior. The Germans overcame all three, with considerable loss of African lives. In their treaty with the Douala "kings" in 1884, the Germans had promised to respect the Douala middleman monopoly; the promise proved impossible to keep and the Douala avoided the fate of neighboring tribes only by giving in with a minimum of protest. In the process of becoming "contact agents" for Western traders, the Douala lost their cultural solidarity, accepting progressively weaker "kings" as rulers, usually abandoning their traditional agricultural and fishing activities and giving primary attention to the acquisition of money, goods, and Western habits and skills. They became, as a result, the first and most Westernized indigenous group in the Cameroons, and eventually the first politically active group. The intransigence of the Bassa and the Bulu militated very strongly against their becoming Westernized at the same rate as the Douala; as a consequence, the former groups adopted the exchange economy only in a limited way and hence managed to retain considerable ethnic solidarity. Both interior and coastal tribes were, however, finally drawn into the exchange economy by three other important factors: the need for labor (to work the new plantations and to move goods to coastal ports), the rise of the plantation system itself, and the acquisition of land by Europeans through purchase or outright occupation.

The increase in the coastal trade during the latter part of the nineteenth century made it imperative that an ever increasing flow of goods reach the coastal trading centers and ports. The almost total lack of roads and draft animals of any sort—it must be recalled that the Cameroons coast and much of the equatorial forest was malarial-mosquito and tsetse-fly country—put the work of transport squarely on the backs and heads of African porters. One estimate, for example, puts the number of porters operating on the 120-mile Yaoundé-Kribi road in 1913 at 80,000.[7] At the same time there were some 18,000 laborers on the plantations.[8] The important point here is that these laborers were wage earners, usually paid either on an ad hoc contract basis or for a specified length of time. Drawn into the cash nexus, these laborers inevitably used their wages to purchase Western goods available at company stores and in the towns. Later on, significantly, money began to be used as a substitute for animals or goods in setting and paying bride-wealth.[9] The contract relationship introduced a highly disintegrative element into communal life. It provided an alternative, and often a most seductive alternative, to the traditional relationships within the community which allowed the individual little possibility of escaping the communal obligations of village, clan, or family.

The plantations, which will be discussed in greater detail later, stimulated the growth of the exchange economy by concentrating individuals from diverse tribal backgrounds, having little in common except their employment, together in plantation villages. Most of the workers were paid by the month, and had shelter, food, and other amenities provided them. All had access to company stores, and the plantation owners much preferred to pay wages partly in goods that could be purchased in them. Therefore, the concentration of workers in the plantation provided for them, as it were, an enforced course in the mechanics of the exchange economy.

Western concepts of property and contract, on which the exchange economy is largely based, when applied to land, constituted another important factor of change in the Cameroons context. Basically, three kinds of tenure existed (and still exist) among the Cameroons tribes. The first, and most prevalent, vests all land in the community as a whole, with the chief of the clan community acting as trustee. A second type, prevalent among the Islamized northerners, vests all land in the traditional ruler, and occupancy and use are entirely at his discretion. A third type, common among the Cameroons highlanders, vests the land in the community, with the fon (Bamenda) or chief possessing rights of administration and allocation without corresponding rights to any of the fruits of the land.[10] The permanent alienation of land was unknown; one might acquire tenancy or usufructuary rights to a plot or area, but never outright ownership of the land itself in the Western sense.

The sale of littoral lands to the European planters, merchants, and traders did not at first create many difficulties, because the land sold was largely unused forest land between indigenous settlements. "King William's" sale of land to the English Baptists in 1858 was apparently made with this consideration in mind, as were some of the other sales to German plantation societies in the 1880's. Most of these purchases did not include settled lands.[11] The difficulties came later, when it became possible for colonists to assert possessory rights in the face of customary rights, which never recognized alienation in the first place. More serious were the difficulties resulting from the sale of land in or near the growing coastal towns. As it became obvious that more land would be needed by these towns, both natives and Europeans began to indulge in wholesale speculation. Despite the official policy of opposition to speculation and the various safeguards set up to preserve sufficient land for native use, the Africans themselves began to traffic in worthless land. A somewhat jaundiced French view describes the process:

Very quickly also, in the proximity of towns such as Douala he [the

African] discovered that the needs of urbanism gave considerable value to some marshes which he had always neglected; each parcel, formerly without value, found itself a "customary" proprietor, and with the aid of politics, several hectares of swampy sand became worth millions in exchange. The psychological shock was so great that entire groups lost their heads over the prospect of millions so easy to obtain; the example of certain lands, where ten millions had been paid for 246 uncultivated hectares, of which half was marshy and which, furthermore, had already been classed as German Crown land, swept away what remained of the desire to work, honesty, and loyalty in the neighboring inhabitants. The Administration which had sought to restrain this folly became "the enemy." "Why discuss it?" publicly stated a ranking chief. "Give us our ten millions so that we can go have a drink."[12]

Although these transactions might not have robbed Africans of "the desire for work" (a Western projection), "honesty," and "loyalty," there is no question that it encouraged the growth of the exchange economy and most certainly of the mercantile spirit among the Douala people.

URBANIZATION

Hand in hand with the growth in trade and the development of the exchange economy came increased urbanization.[13] The burgeoning coastal towns, centers of the exchange economy, created an elite based on nontraditional values, such as industrial skill, education, money, and so forth, and thereby hastened the breakdown of traditional social structures. The new elite could assert its economic independence from the traditional groups, and in so doing escape as well from the ancient hierarchies of status and birth.[14] This dual dissociation completed the breakdown of the traditional Douala political system, and is well on the way to destroying that of the Yaoundé (Ewondo-Beti) group. At the time of the German annexation in 1884, the Douala had institutionalized their chiefs as "kings" (probably in response to Western needs) and had shifted the balance of their traditional political system from one loosely organized to one based on hierarchical principles. Today, the descendants of Kings Akwa and Bell, who signed the treaties with the Germans, live in Douala and are accorded traditional honors as "princes." They are, however, devoid of any but symbolic powers. Whatever influence is wielded by "Prince" Alexandre Douala Manga Bell, present titular holder of the "kingship," is owing to the force of his personality rather than to his position. If the Douala have any voice as a group, it is through the Ngondo, of which mention has already been made. This voice, however, is somewhat feeble, and not often heeded.

TABLE 3

PRINCIPAL URBAN CENTERS IN THE (EAST) CAMEROUN

Urban centers	Population (1962, approx.)	Location (approx.)	Primary activities (See key, end of table)
		Coastal region:	
Douala	130,000	Wouri estuary	P, Tr, Adm, Rh
Edéa	12,000	Sanaga River	Power, Hvy Ind
Kribi	7,000	Kienke River estuary	P, Tr, Adm
		W. mountain region:	
Nkongsamba	31,991	Nkam Dept.	Tr, Adm, Rh
Dschang	15,000	Dschang Dept.	Tr, Adm
Bafoussam	8,600	Bafoussam Dept.	Tr, Agr, Adm
Foumban	18,000	Bamoun Dept.	Tr, Agr, Adm, Ls
		Southern region:	
Yaoundé	60,000	Nyong-et-Sanaga Dept.	Tr, Adm, Rh, Lt. Ind (national capital)
Mbalmayo	5,500	Nyong-et-Sanaga Dept.	Tr, Rh, Agr, Pl
Ebolowa	15,000	Ntem Region Dept.	Tr, Adm, Pl, Agr
Eséka	6,593	Sanaga-Maritime Dept.	Tr, Agr, Pl
Sangmélima	7,500	Dja et Lobo Dept.	Agr, Pl, Tr, Adm
		Central plateau region:	
Ngaounderé	15,000	Adamaoua Dept.	Ls, Adm, Tr
Batouri		Lom et Kadei Dept.	Agr, Pl
		Northern region:	
Garoua	15,400	Benoué Dept.	P, Tr, Ls, Adm
Maroua	18,000	Diamaré Dept.	Tr, Ls, Adm

KEY TO ABBREVIATIONS: Agr = Agriculture; Adm = Administration; Ls = Livestock (cattle); Lt Ind = Light Industry; Hvy Ind = Heavy Industry; Tr = Trade, Commerce; P = Port; Rh = Railhead; Pl = Plantations Center.

SOURCES: *Guid-Cameroun, 1959* (Paris: Diloutremer, 1959); *Supplément au Bulletin de la Statistique Générale*, Etat du Cameroun, Service de la Statistique Générale, no. 3 (September, 1958), p. 9.

In point of time, Douala was the first urban agglomerate in the Cameroons to receive the full impact of the Westernization process. In 1884, when the Germans signed their treaties with Kings Akwa and Bell, the coastal Douala probably comprised no more than five thousand people inhabiting a cluster of eight adjoining villages, and not more than fifty European traders and missionaries. Another ten thousand

Doula probably lived within a perimeter of from twenty to fifty miles from the site of Douala town. The Victoria missionary settlement, historically the first *permanent* settlement, was founded in 1858. Yaoundé did not become a European settlement until the Germans opened a station there in 1890. Other trading stations (the most important being Edea, Batanga, Kribi, Campo, Lolodorf, and Nkongsamba) grew into towns only after the Germans turned them into ports or centers of commerce. But it was Douala that became, and has remained, the largest city in the Cameroons. It provides a striking example of the West African urbanization pattern and of some of the accompanying ethnic difficulties. (For recent figures on the populations of major towns in the Federal Republic, see table 3.)

Prior to 1900, one of the sources of recurrent complaints voiced by German entrepreneurs in the Kamerun was what apeared be an almost endemic shortage of labor. When the Germans established their protectorate, the coastal region was sparsely settled because of the generally unhealthy climatic conditions in which malaria and other tropical diseases spread rapidly once they got started. Planters and traders vied for whatever labor could be persuaded to leave the cooler highlands or to come from other countries. In the early days, the change in climate, with its accompanying lowering of resistance to infection, was responsible for very high death rates both in plantations and on the portage trails.[15] After 1900, the Germans paid more attention to health and sanitation; compulsory innoculations, dispensaries, and frequent official checks on working conditions did much to reduce the death rate among workers who had come into the coastal belt. This, plus the construction of the rail lines east and north from Douala, brought a surge of migration toward that city. German figures, which show total population for the Douala district (*bezirk*) only, nonetheless indicate a gradual increase between 1907 and 1913:[16]

1897	20,000
1907-1908	52,420
1908-1909	75,160
1909-1910	63,615
1910-1911	63,615
1911-1912	76,954
1912-1913	91,808

During the military campaigns in the Cameroons between 1914 and 1916, the Germans abandoned or destroyed their medical facilities as they retreated. Their campaigns against malaria and sleeping sickness

TABLE 4

POPULATION GROWTH IN DOUALA, 1926–1957

Year	Population	No. of non-Africans included	
1926	19,590		
1931	26,987	862	
1933	27,853	728	
1936	39,080	730	
1937	36,572	730	
1938	42,542	730	
1941	42,780	780	
1945	38,918	1,362	
1947	51,077	1,406	Total conurbation for 1947: 59,899[a]
1950	102,250		
1952	110,000		
1954	110,398	5,080	
1957	124,703	5,846	

[a] This figure represents the first attempt to estimate the total population for the so-called metropolitan Douala conurbation, that is, Douala, Bonaberi (across the Wouri River), and other suburban towns and villages. Subsequent figures for Douala are for the city only.

(Full citations of works mentioned briefly below will be found in the bibliography.)
SOURCES: *Résultats du Recensement . . . de Douala, 1955–56*, p. 4; Guilbot, *Petite Etude . . .* , p. 8; *Rapport du Cameroun* (1954, 1957); Guernier, *Cameroun, Togo*, p. 65.

came to a halt, and endemic diseases of various kinds spread rapidly after 1914. Exact figures are not available on the numbers of Africans who died or fled the coast to return to their traditional tribal areas, but their numbers must have been considerable because the first census under French auspices, in 1926, gave the total number of inhabitants for the old *bezirk* (district) Douala (Douala plus M'banga administrative subdivisions) as 53,879.[17]

With the reëstablishment of peace, the renewal of health and hygienic campaigns, and the entrance of new capital into the newly mandated territory, Douala began to grow once again. Table 4 gives some indication of that growth. The figures are cited with considerable reservation; their accuracy is certainly doubtful before 1939. The Service de la Statistique Générale du Cameroun, for example, cites figures up to 1939 as representing the population of the *city* of Douala;[18] Kuczynski, seventeen years earlier, gave the same figures for the whole Douala *Région*.[19] With these reservations, however, the general picture shows a rather slow increase in Douala's population up to the outbreak of World War II. After the war, the figures show a startling increase—from 51,077 in 1947 to 125,000 in 1957. This change did not reflect an increase in the local population, but rather mostly immigration channeled into the city along the axes of the Douala-Nkongsamba and Douala-Yaoundé rail lines, drawing into Douala those peoples through whose areas the railroads pass.

Table 5 shows the radical changes in the ethnic composition of the city by comparing 1947 and 1955-1956. Of special importance is the absolute and relative increase in the Bamiléké population as compared to the static situation of the Douala, the indigenous group. In 1943, 1,432 Bamiléké lived in Douala, but by 1945 this figure had risen to 4,167. In 1947 there were about 8,120 Bamiléké, or 16.3 per cent of the total city count; in 1955-1956 this figure had risen to 29,650, or about 26.2 per cent (29.8 per cent if neighboring Highlanders are included) of the total city count. In contrast, the Douala numbered 22,927 (46

TABLE 5

CHANGES IN THE ETHNIC COMPOSITION[a] OF DOUALA, 1947 AND 1955–1956

Group	Of 1947 total of 51,077		Of 1955–1956 total of 125,000	
	Number	% of total	Number	% of total
Douala	22,927	46.0	23,075	20.4
Bassa	7,408	14.9	7,696	7.0
Bakoko			12,445	11.0
Bamiléké	8,120	16.3	29,650	26.2[d]
Beti (Ewondo)	8,118	16.3	12,258	10.8
Central Bantu	incl. in Beti[c]		7,453	6.6
Bakundu	incl. in Douala[c]		3,432	3.0
Non-Cameroonians[b]	4,504	6.2	6,608	5.8

(Full citations of works mentioned briefly below will be found in the bibliography.)

[a] Principal ethnic groups only; for town proper.
[b] Including Europeans and other non-Africans.
[c] Number small enough to be unimportant to totals.
[d] Tardits, *Les Bamiléké* . . . , gives 23,370 as the 1956 Bamiléké figure.
SOURCES: *Résultats du Recensement . . . de Douala*, p. 10; Guilbot, *Petite Etude . . .*, p. 8; Dugast, *Inventaire . . .*, p. 121.

per cent of the total) in 1947; in 1955-1956 they had only increased to 23,075 (or about 20.4 per cent of the total). As a matter of fact, all ethnic groups except the Douala increased in absolute numbers over the eight-year period, if not in relative standing.

Guilbot's study,[20] from which the 1947 figures are taken, cites statistics to show that even though the Douala had a considerably larger potential labor force to draw from than did the Bamiléké or the Beti, only 29.4 per cent of that potential was actually employed. Without going into the social reasons for the low Douala employment (health seems not to have been a factor), the contrast suggests that the immigrant peoples were on their way to dominating the town's labor market. The urbanized Douala, long the leading trading and commercial element in the indigenous population, were unable to keep up with the immigrants from the northern and eastern plateaus. By 1947, the Douala had already ceded their numerical primacy in the manual-labor market; only 9.8 per cent of Douala town's labor force was engaged in such work that year. Yet their hold on the so-called intellectual trades—as secretaries, clerks, health workers—was not, according to Guilbot's sample, challenged by any other ethnic group. About 30 per cent of the Douala labor force was engaged in these pursuits, as opposed to 7.3 per cent of the Bassa, the next-closest group. By 1956,[21] even though the Douala had raised their employment quotient to 55 per cent of their total force, they were beginning to be pushed out of the intellectual trades by the numerically stronger Bamiléké and the equally vigorous Bakoko and Beti. Table 6 graphically indicates the situation. Note, for example, that the Bamiléké had, in 1956, taken strong numerical positions in every occupational category except the arts, and fishing and livestock farming. In contrast, the Douala retained strong showings only in those occupations in which special skill, or experience, or a natural monopoly had prevented inroads from being made by immigrant groups. They could claim relatively high percentages in missionary work, the arts, public utilities, banking and insurance, and fishing and livestock farming. An interesting contrast is to be found in the figures for those employed in government and in administration. In 1947, most indigenous personnel employed in administration were Douala; in 1956, the Douala could claim only 15.3 per cent of the total so engaged; the Bamiléké had 25.3 per cent; the Beti, 18.2 per cent; and the Bassa-Bakoko, 17.8 per cent. The rest was spread among other, smaller groups.

As a result of the foregoing changes in the ethnic composition of the city of Douala, the indigenous Douala people were overwhelmed by

TABLE 6

THE ETHNIC COMPOSITION OF THE LABOR FORCE IN THREE CAMEROUN TOWNS: DOUALA, YAOUNDÉ, AND EBOLOWA

Ethnic groups		Total nos. each group	% of total population	Administration and govt.	Missions	Fishing and animal husb.	Forestry, lumbering	Public utilities	Extractive industries	Secondary industry	Construction and pub. wks.	Commerce and retailing	Transport and hauling	Banks and insurance	Liberal professions	Domestics	Unemployed	Undeclared, doubtful
Douala (Douala)[a]	D	23,075	20.4	15.3	20.9	63.0	9.4	18.3	17.3	12.3	7.8	11.2	11.7	30.8	15.1	0.5	15.1	29.3
(Yaoundé)[b]	Y	1,276	2.34	i.s.	i.s.	i.s.	i.s.	i.s.	i.s.	i.s.	i.s.	i.s.	i.s.	i.s.	i.s.	i.s.	i.s.	i.s.
(Ebolowa)[c]	E	256	1.75	i.s.	i.s.	i.s.	i.s.	i.s.	i.s.	i.s.	i.s.	i.s.	i.s.	i.s.	i.s.	i.s.	i.s.	i.s.
Bassa-Bakoko	D	20,141	18.0	17.8	23.5	14.6	15.4	26.0	11.6	17.4	26.1	9.0	8.3	14.3	9.0	12.9	22.4	13.1
	Y	2,816	5.18	7.3	5.8	i.s.	12.5	7.2	6.4	2.5	8.1	4.8	6.2	12.0	7.0	2.8	5.1	3.6
	E	922	6.46	8.4	6.7	i.s.	3.6	i.s.	i.s.	9.6	13.1	6.5	1.4	14.0	4.6	4.7	6.1	3.3
Equatorial Bantu	D	7,453	6.66	6.8	4.8	6.7	7.4	9.2	7.2	8.6	7.0	3.9	6.8	1.0	3.8	8.7	5.9	42.2
	Y	3,253	5.98	7.0	4.9	i.s.	12.5	3.1	6.4	4.6	4.8	4.1	5.0	8.0	7.3	10.7	5.2	5.9
	E	1,074	7.52	8.2	6.4	i.s.	12.0	i.s.	i.s.	7.2	9.3	7.4	4.8	i.s.	3.7	19.0	6.9	16.6
Beti-Pahouin	D	12,258	10.8	18.2	11.6	1.9	28.9	15.3	19.5	16.2	17.6	7.1	8.5	5.9	3.8	8.1	9.7	7.5
	Y	29,655	54.6	61.9	79.2	13.3	37.5	61.4	32.2	55.5	64.5	32.3	43.3	50.0	51.0	39.0	59.1	47.1
	E	8,996	63.0	62.3	75.1	25.0	65.0	66.6	66.6	28.8	40.7	36.3	54.1	42.5	72.5	38.1	65.5	35.0
Bamiléké	D	29,650	26.2	25.3	21.8	1.9	21.4	19.0	19.8	28.7	21.6	47.0	45.3	22.8	26.4	41.3	29.4	28.2
	Y	7,835	14.4	7.1	3.3	6.6	12.5	11.4	12.9	18.1	6.1	35.9	25.7	6.0	9.7	8.5	12.7	17.6
	E	1,492	10.45	4.4	2.6	i.s.	8.4	i.s.	i.s.	29.3	6.5	25.3	25.3	i.s.	0.9	5.9	8.8	18.0
Fulani-Hausa, etc.	D	910	0.8	i.s.	i.s.	i.s.	i.s.	i.s.	i.s.	n.d.	n.d.	n.d.	n.d.	i.s.	i.s.	i.s.	n.d.	n.d.
	Y	4,391	8.08	0.5	i.s.	46.6	i.s.	i.s.	i.s.	4.0	n.d.	8.3	5.0	i.s.	9.7	i.s.	4.2	5.0
	E	358	2.3	i.s.	i.s.	n.d.	i.s.	i.s.	i.s.	n.d.	n.d.	n.d.	n.d.	i.s.	i.s.	i.s.	n.d.	n.d.
Non-Cameroun Africans	D	6,608	5.8	4.5	6.3	2.9	5.9	5.7	7.6	6.4	6.4	10.5	6.5	7.9	30.0	7.2	5.6	6.2
	Y	604	1.1[d]															
	E	358	2.5[d]															

Percentage of Labor Force (Males 14 & Older) by Occupation

KEY: i.s. = insignificant; n.d. = no data.

[a] Figures are for 1956
[b] Figures are for 1957
[c] Figures are for 1958
[d] % in every category insignificant

SOURCES: Ministère des Affaires Economiques, Etat du Cameroun, Service de la Statistique Générale, *Résultats du Recensement ... de Douala; Résultats du Recensement ... de Yaoundé; Résultats du Recensement ... d'Ebolowa.*

aggressive immigrant groups that challenged their social preëminence by invading the "learned professions" and virtually monopolizing the most lucrative occupations. The immigrant's assiduity, his willingness to begin at a menial job and save his money, his eagerness to be educated, won for him the deference given to the possessor of money, skill, and property. It is particularly significant that the Bamiléké have turned to commerce and transportation in such large numbers; in an expanding urban context it is the shopkeeper, the small capitalist, the expediter, and the transporter, who stand to gain most from growth. The urban social order, previously dominated by the well-educated and experienced Douala, has been progressively restructured.

The tensions resulting from the rapidity of this social and ethnic restructuring are present not only in Douala, but in such centers as Yaoundé, Mbalmayo, Ebolowa, and Nkongsamba. They are also present to some degree in the northern centers of Ngaoundéré, Garoua, and Maroua. Basically, the problem lies not so much in the process of adaptation to Western ways in the cities, but in the competition for the symbols and emoluments of Westernized living: money, material goods, education, and political participation.

In many African territories an important factor in the political life of communities undergoing urbanization has been the special position held by, or disproportionate influence exerted by, a dominant indigenous group.[22] In most urban centers in the Cameroons the opposite tendency has prevailed: traditionally dominant ethnic groups have been or are being displaced, socially, economically, and politically, by an extralocal group or groups. The example of Douala has been noted. Equally striking, if to a lesser degree, are the examples of Yaoundé and Ebolowa. Table 6 presents the statistical picture and demonstrates that the Douala pattern is repeated to a remarkable degree in the latter towns. A talented young East Camerounian writer, Alexander Biyidi, known by his nom de plume of Mongo Beti, describes the social contrasts in Mbalmayo, another town near Yaoundé, much more vividly than do the statistics:

But it is above all a town of *margoulins,* of merchants of shoddy wares whose expansion, in the colonial context, has only a limited perspective. It is this almost exclusively mercantile character which explains the heterogeneity of its population. Besides the Europeans, and insofar as they are inhabitants, in the city itself only individuals from other African countries or other regions of the Cameroun can be seen. The Bamiléké, for instance, have a monopoly in transportation and practically one in retail trade, a sector from which they rapidly ousted the Levantines and Balkan Slavs, still numerous on the eve of the second world war. . . . Thus, the town of M'balmayo seems, for the most part, a stranger in a land which is the vast domain of a Bantu tribe, the Bané, whose forested territories hem in the tiny city. Under a Christian veneer . . . the Bané, faced with colonization in all its forms, stand aloof and on the defensive. They willingly send their children to school, but they fear educated men. Their great weakness, other than an excessive taste for strong drink, is a prodigious political indifference.

The Bané and the strangers to the town quarrel continually, though it is not something so desperate that the colonial police need interfere (alas! they stick their noses into these affairs too often!). The outsiders dread the Bané, who is always quick to take offense [*prendre la mouche*], or to do some mischief; they consider the Bané incorrigibly lazy, and like all lazy people, to be a nihilist, ready to put to the torch the riches others have accumulated with great difficulty, and precisely because he has no idea of their value.

The Bané considers all strangers to be thieves; people who, fleeing their own lands where they were dying of hunger, have come to enrich themselves at his expense. And perhaps he is right in this (perhaps I'm being partial, since this concerns my own tribe). The Bané is, admittedly, not a great worker, but he is certainly not a sluggard, considering that he places immediately after the Bulu in the production of cocoa. How, then, to explain the rapid prosperity of these strangers, white or black, who arrive pale and penniless, and several months later, drive around in a car? In this trading economy, how is it that these intermediaries manage to earn their living, almost as if the work of the Bané were truly nonexistent?

It is simply that the Bané has a horror of working as a day-laborer in the city; when he is not in his village, cultivating cocoa or peanuts with good humor, what he adores is working in an office. Ah! an office, a necktie. . . .[23]

Despite the tone of this passage, it reveals many of the underlying tensions in the urban centers in the Cameroons. Significantly, the author notes the unwillingness of the indigenous population to soil its hands in manual labor. A longer exposure to Western ways has made it value the prestigious symbols of officialdom more than those of private enterprise.[24]

Finally, a special southern urban problem, one with serious political repercussions, is the presence in the towns of masses of unemployed. Official censuses of the unemployed in Douala put their number at 5,000 in 1954, 12,000 in 1957, 17,000 in 1958, and close to 25,000 in 1960.[25] Georges Chaffard points out that if one includes the idle who have never held a job and consequently have never been counted as "unemployed" by the *Inspection du Travail,* approximately one-fourth of the population of Douala (including New Bell) is composed of men without visible means of support and "living on the fringe of society."[26]

Similar estimates give Yaundé about 16,000 unemployed, and Nkong-samba about 8,000. Whatever the reasons that draw increasingly large numbers of people into the towns, the fact remains that they swell the ranks of the unemployed, increase urban tensions, and give rise to un-healthy physical and social conditions.[27] It is hardly surprising that the growing urban slums in the East Cameroun south, erupting periodically with violence, should have become the favorite haunts of political agitators.

ETHNIC TENSIONS

Since 1955, with the eruption of civil violence in the Bassa and Bamiléké *Régions,* the so-called Bamiléké problem has been the most vexing ethnic problem confronting the Cameroons. It is a problem with repercussions widely felt in the political, social, and economic spheres of Cameroun life. We have already discussed the problem, if only peripherally, in its urban character. The immigration of the Bamiléké from their traditional villages into the cities and larger towns and the resultant pressures on the local populations is only one aspect, albeit one of the most significant, of what is a veritable social revolution. That social revolution has had so profound an impact on the life of the country because it involves the Bamiléké, one of the most energetic and dynamic peoples in west Africa. The Bamiléké crisis is a cultural crisis of the first order, with serious political ramifications. Within the Bamiléké community itself traditional authority structures are under sharp attack. Externally, the numerical expansion of the dynamic Bamiléké has brought them into conflict with other ethnic groups. The tensions generated in both these internal and external spheres are sufficient to evoke what is often violence of the most sanguinary sort. Without going into a full-scale analysis of *le problème Bamiléké,* something beyond the scope of this work, it is possible to examine the essentials of the various situations whose concatenation has produced the explosive social crisis of the Bamiléké.*

The Cameroons highlands are extremely well suited for human habitation: a combination of relatively fertile soil, favorable climate, and excellent natural defenses made the Cameroons plateau desirable for settlement. The highlands were not occupied by their present inhabi-

---

* The term "Bamiléké" is collective: it refers to a loose agglomeration of tribal groups organized as chiefdoms. The bond between the various Bamiléké is based on common cultural characteristics and traditions of common origin rather than on any existing political arrangements between individual tribes. The latter unions do not tend to be long lasting.

tants until the seventeenth century, during which successive waves of Fulani invaders drove large numbers of Sudanic and sub-Sudanic Negroes south, most of them into the Cameroon highlands (into what is now the Bamenda area of the West Cameroun and the Bamiléké *départements* of the East Cameroun), and the rest into the semiplateau, semi-savanna country of the Bamoun region. The original inhabitants of the highlands were either pushed out or assimilated. The Bamiléké highlanders managed to avoid conquest and conversion by the Islamized Fulani, but the Bamoun came to be dominated by the Fulani and themselves began a series of wars on their Bamiléké neighbors, hostilities which they abandoned only in 1931. Paradoxically, also during the period of conflict the Bamoun-Bamiléké boundary became blurred owing to the intermarriage of a number of members of the contacting groups.[28]

Among the Bamiléké proper, social organization revolves around the chieftancy. The chief is not only the head of the extended tribal family, but the titular owner of all land, dispenser of justice, hereditary trustee of the tribal totems, intermediary between the tribe and the tribal deities, and the guarantor of the earth's fertility through his contact with both the tribal ancestors and the gods of the earth. In addition, he exercises well-defined plenary and administrative power over the chiefdom in collaboration (often unwilling) with the local representatives of the central government. In the five Bamiléké *départements* (Mbouda, Dschang, Bangangté, Bafoussam, and Bafang) there are at present over one hundred chiefdoms, ranging in population from 50 (Bossinga) to over 30,000 (Bandjoun), often organized into different combinations of alliances (usually based on common kinship), associations, or, more often, independent chiefdoms.[29] A large number of age-grade associations, secret societies of socio-religio-political purpose, and intertribal associations, exist among the Bamiléké. Admission into the associations and secret societies, and consequently into the positions of deference and honor that such membership confers upon the individual, is controlled by the local chiefs, themselves heads of the societies.

There are three main factors that precipitated the Bamiléké crisis: (1) overpopulation and its consequent pressures on the available land, (2) nonadaptive factors in the Bamiléké social system, and (3) the return of immigrants from the cities. The Bamiléké region has experienced a steady population growth since it was first settled. Between 1931 and 1958 the population increased by about 136,000, a figure that does not include the more than 100,000 Bamiléké who have migrated south and east. The 1931 figure (see table 7) comprises almost all

TABLE 7

POPULATION OF THE BAMILÉKÉ REGION: INCREMENT SINCE 1931

Year	Population	Notes
1931	345,001	
1933	364,977	
1934	369,596	
1936	383,589	
1937	394,136	Includes Bamoun
1938	415,988	
1941	430,690	
1943	460,079	
1945	468,454	
1949	417,070	
1951	455,281	
1953	454,080	
1955	460,096	Does not include Bamoun
1957	476,911	
1958	480,850	
1961	492,000–606,000	for all five Bamiléké *départements;* does not include Bamoun.

(*Full citations of works mentioned briefly here will be found in the bibliography.*)

SOURCES: *Rapport du Cameroun* (1947–1957 incl.); Kuczynski, *Cameroons . . . ,* p. 95; McCullough *et al., Peoples . . . ,* pp. 89, 90; *Supplément au Bulletin de la Statistique Générale,* 1958, no. 2, p. 47. The 1961 figures are from Tardits, *Les Bamiléké . . . ,* p. 63, who suggests them as the range of estimates possible varying according to rates of increase from 1.5 per cent to 2.5 per cent, using an official 1956 figure of 459,000 as his base.

Bamiléké in the East Cameroun; the large emigration was just beginning at that time. The total increment over the twenty-seven year period is something on the order of 65 per cent from the 1931 base. By 1946-1947, as Delarozière's figures indicate, the density of population in some chiefdoms had reached astonishing proportions. Three chiefdoms in the Bafoussam *Subdivision* (see table 8) had attained density figures of over 800 persons per square mile, with pressures on the available land becoming increasingly greater. The Bamiléké are agriculturists, once mainly engaged in semisubsistence farming, now increasingly driven to subsistence farming in most districts. The women and girls are responsible for planting, sowing, and reaping, although the men may help with the initial work of clearing the ground; the men also erect fences, build and repair huts, and engage in trade.[30]

The diminishing returns from agriculture, a result of the intensification of cultivation owing to overpopulation where subsistence or semi-subsistence farming is the rule, was coupled with an increasingly greater fragmentation of agricultural holdings. For the most part, the population is dispersed in habitation patterns that utilize virtually all arable land and define individual occupancies in an extremely rigorous manner. There are very few true villages; the only exceptions are the semiurban agglomerations that have grown up around the various administrative posts. Each family lives on the land it cultivates, each plot separated from the next by hedgerows or bushes, with a single narrow

TABLE 8

DENSITY OF POPULATION, BAFOUSSAM SUBDIVISION, 1946–1947

Chiefdom	Popu-lation	Approximate area		Approximate population density	
		In sq. kilo-meters	In sq. miles	Per sq. kilo-meter	Per sq. mile
Bandjoun	27,257	80	31.2	340.7	872.0
Baham	13,144	70	27.3	187.7	480.5
Bangou	8,404	45	17.5	186.7	477.9
Baya(n)gam	8,255	25	9.8	330.2	845.3
Bamougoum	13,838	40	15.6	345.9	885.5
Bamendjou	11,252	70	27.3	160.7	411.3
Bafoussam	7,681	150	58.5	51.2	131.1
Baleng	9,480	300	117.0	31.6	80.9
Batoufam	4,359	30	11.6	145.3	371.9
Bameka	6,480	20	7.8	324.0	829.4
Batie	7,602	80	31.2	95.0	243.2
Bahouan	3,468	20	7.8	173.4	443.9
Bangam	2,159	18	7.0	119.9	306.9
Badenkop	3,163	20	7.8	158.1	404.7
Badrefam	1,270	15	5.8	84.6	216.6
Bapi	1,092	10	3.9	109.2	279.5
Bandeng	440	15	5.8	29.3	75.0
Settlement on left bank of Nun River	2,358	180	70.3	13.1	33.5
Total	131,702	1,188	463.2	110.8	264.3

(Full citations of works mentioned briefly here will be found in the bibliography.)

SOURCES: Delarozière, *Les Institutions* . . . , p. 13; McCullough *et al.*, *Peoples* . . . , p. 90. The chart was constructed by the latter author, but was based mainly on the work of the former.

entrance to the parcels. The amount of land cultivated by each family varies, of course, according to the density of population and the amount of available arable land in the chiefdom. Marginal and unused land remains under the domain of the chief and is often between 25 and 40 per cent of the total available land, without counting marshes or unusable areas. In Bangangté, for example, where the average population density is about 250 persons per square kilometer, an average family (a man, one or two wives, and from three to seven children) occupies from two to four hectares. Under the circumstances, it becomes difficult, if not impossible, to fragment existing holdings, or find new ones for new claimants.[31] The size of cultivable parcels must be reduced to accommodate the larger numbers of claimants on the land. At first, inasmuch as the available land that could be allocated in each chiefdom was strictly limited by the size of the chiefdom, marginal land was turned over to cultivation, and, after that had been exhausted, the individual holdings were themselves fragmented. Part of the pressure on the land was alleviated by emigration; such relief, in most instances, was only transitory. The chiefs, ultimately responsible for allocating the land, were caught in a series of politically dangerous dilemmas. First, they had to decide whose land had to be split, a decision bound to create friction among those affected. As a rule, the chiefs had rarely interfered in inheritance or with allocation itself, as this was usually performed by their lower-echelon agents. With changing conditions, however, they were forced to interfere more and more often. Second, the chiefs more often than not refused to fragment their own holdings, under cultivation by their own wives, or their hereditary grazing areas, or those grounds on which stand their residences and the buildings and places set aside for the use of the men's societies meeting under their aegis. As a result, it often appeared as if everyone's holdings except the chief's were getting smaller and less productive. Third, the chiefs were forced to reallocate lands that had been under cultivation by the families of individuals who had emigrated, and often without the latter's knowledge. In some cases, it is alleged, land still under cultivation by the wives of a temporary emigré was reallocated without the emigré's or his wives' consent. In most of these situations, the ultimate right of the chiefs to allocate the land did not come into question, as the members of the tribe usually had only usufructuary rights stemming from a present or former grant by the chieftancy. Largely, it was that the traditional rules governing land tenure were becoming inapplicable or, worse, irrelevant in the new situations, and the chiefs became, rightly or wrongly, the targets for the frustration and resentment created by the changes. The situation was, and still is, aggravated by the fact that, under Bamiléké customary law, property passed from father to son is indivisible. Most often, land passed in this manner is too small to support several households. As only one son may inherit, the others must of necessity leave at the age of twelve or thirteen and seek employment elsewhere in manual labor, apprenticeship, commerce, or domestic service so as to be at most a minimal burden on the family. At sixteen or eighteen, many emigrate to other parts of the country.[32] Another custom, the bride-wealth system, causes a substantial number of young men to leave for the urban centers in the hope of earning the often-exorbitant sums involved.[33]

In addition to all this, the return of many of the younger men from the urban centers precipitated a series of new crises. Many young Bamiléké had left their tribal areas with the understanding that their social and economic positions in the home community would remain safe for them, pending their return. Returning home, often after having accumulated some savings and impressed with the opportunities and conveniences of town life, they were obliged to submit themselves to the traditional authority of their elders and chiefs, often were unable to find land to cultivate, and, not infrequently, were unable to find marriageable women. Again, their discontent focused on the authority system, notably on the chiefs. At once, two groups of potential and actual opposition to the authority system grew in strength in the Bamiléké region, the domestic dispossessed and the returnees. Both groups were ready to turn to political action as the internal situation became worse; the political group known as the UPC, which will be discussed in greater detail later, provided that solution, while disorder grew apace, often into unmanageable proportions.

Another source of resistance to traditional authority, and an even greater source of striving for modernization, grew among the emigré Bamiléké. Littlewood[34] writes of the migrations south into the adjoining Mungo region:

Early in the Century, Bamiléké loaned their services to the indigenous agriculturists of this region, working mostly on the prosperous cocoa farms. As a result of the economic crisis of 1928-32 the owners of the farms were forced to make payments to their Bamiléké labourers in the form of portions of the plantations; this handing over of the plantations became the current practice so that many of the Bamiléké are now in charge of their own farms. . . .

During . . . 1933-45 there was an added impetus to move into the region since the rapid expansion of agricultural enterprises created a strong demand for labourers. The majority of the immigrants were men who left their wives and children behind, being joined by them later when they had become well established in the area.

Littlewood cites Dugast's 1947 figures to show that in the administrative subdivision of Nkongsamba there were 10,727 Bamiléké out of a total population of 21,876. We have already noted the pattern of Bamiléké immigration into Douala, in another connection, and the presence of the Bamiléké in M'balmayo. Significant Bamiléké movement has also been recorded to the east and southeast. A 1957 census in Yaoundé records 7,835 Bamiléké in a total population of 58,099 (or 14.42 per cent of a total indigenous population of 54,343). Not unexpectedly, they have a larger number of individuals engaged in commerce than any other group (1001 as against 939 for the Beti and less than 300 for all the rest); they already have large numbers in administration, industry, and transport. In Ebolowa, about eighty miles south of Yaoundé, the Bamiléké, mostly male, constituted 10.45 per cent of the total indigenous population. As in Yaoundé and Douala, they have concentrated their activities in commerce (236 out of a total of 846), industry (67 of a total of 266), and transport (37 of a total of 146).[35]

The immigrants rarely break the bonds linking them to their territory of origin, and in the urban centers they tend to group themselves either according to the chiefdoms from which they came, or, where this is impracticable, more generally in local Bamiléké societies. In many instances, such local societies are themselves under the nominal tutelage of an emigré chief or elder. Groupings according to tribe or region of origin are found in both Douala and Yaoundé; in Douala, for example, the *Quartier* Babouté has a Bamiléké chief, as has the *Quartier* Bafoussam (the name of one of the Bamiléké *Départements*) in Bonaberi-Douala. The emigré chiefs often serve to crystallize sentiment for reform directed at the home area, as do the Bamiléké intellectuals whose numbers are increasing every year. Delarozière gives some interesting examples of the extent of Bamiléké emigré solidarity:[36]

Along the trade route of Kola nuts originating in the Chiefdom of Batoufam (Subdivision of Bafoussam), the *emigré* Bamiléké form a sort of relay. [The nuts] pass through the hands of Bafoussam men all the way to markets at Garoua or Maroua. This organization is one of the reasons for the commercial strength and dynamism of the Bamiléké.

These *emigrés* remain in close contact with their groups of origin, and as proof I cite a recent example: in 1947, on hearing the news that a sacred forest in Batoufam was about to be reclassified [apparently preparatory to being cut down], the *emigrés* of Batoufam living in many distant parts of the Cameroun protested and demanded that the project be abandoned.

There is more. It often happens, upon the initiative of energetic *notables,* that the Bamiléké area, groups of *emigrés* spontaneously organize them-selves on the model of their former chiefdoms, and with three fundamental elements: chief, hierarchy, and associations. This is the case, for example, in Nkongsamba. What is lacking, apparently, is the religious substratum which gave such structures additional power when organized at home. At least, there is an instinctive recognition, and generally by youthful elements, al-ready *evolué,* and very often converted, of the social value of traditional institutions, especially for those who live in unfamiliar lands and who are fre-quently on the defensive.

This creation of an artificial chiefdom in no way implies a rupture with the group of its origin.

Delarozière continues by pointing out that the new chiefs, whatever their nominal rank in the local administrative structure, remain never-theless loyal to the titular chief of their home tribe. Delarozière made this point in 1947; since then a number of emigré chiefs have become highly critical of affairs in the home area, and some have even become the organizers of reform groups. In addition, educated and highly vocal Bamiléké have become quite numerous and take every oppor-tunity to press their criticisms by all available means. This latter group most often records its discontent in the local newspapers; the *Presse du Cameroun,* published in Douala and the largest daily in the Came-roun, carries frequent articles by emigré Bamiléké on *le problème du tribalisme, le problème Bamiléké,* and the like. Their tone is almost invariably hostile to the traditional authority system. One such article, representative of most of the others, states:[37]

We are far from believing that the strife [*guerre*] in the Bamiléké Region is political in origin. Rather, it is a *guerre de régime* because the peasants are excessively harassed by their chiefs. Peace is born of justice; this is the rule, pure and simple, that the traditional chiefs must henceforth keep in the pockets of their *gandouras* [a native garb; the phrase is the equivalent of our English "Let them put that in their pipes and smoke it!"]. In 1959, it is no longer possible to count on monarchical power to keep docile a people who have already grasped the sense of liberty. . . . [The writer then inveighs against what he considers unjust levies of chiefly tithes. He goes on:] One knows very well that Camerounians, who for forty years have been trained to live *à l'occidentale,* that is, in a liberal fashion, can no longer live according to the opposite of democracy. They can no longer admit of Pharaonic methods, the principles of trickery and fraud. They no longer wish to live in a world where the master's will becomes the only rule in men's lives, where the mass has no voice but the intentions of the chiefs; in short, they want democracy, from the chiefs and for the people, from the chiefs who merit honor, but who must also possess certain qualities:

honesty, truthfulness, and justice, [qualities] which will automatically lead to a *détente*, to a land in which the people exercise total sovereignty. . . .

The writer then blunts his attack with a plea for the retention of the symbols of chieftaincy:

Nevertheless, we cannot permit the suppression of the chiefdoms. To wipe out summarily the faults that are degrading our chiefs does not in the least mean that their presence will be unnecessary in the emerging situation, because they remain valuable intermediaries between the peasants and the administration, [and because] they are also the true trustees [*gérants*] of Camerounian tradition, the repositories of customary powers.

The social and economic revolution of the Bamiléké has been translated by the new generation into political demands whose urgency is hard to ignore. I have suggested that entrenched custom, the resistance to change on the part of much of the traditional elite, and the internal and external social and economic pressures on the chiefdoms have all contributed to the creation of a political climate in which frustrated demands for reform easily channel into destructive outlets. Another factor, undoubtedly, is the slowness and hesitancy of administrative reform in the Bamiléké region. For the moment, it is sufficient to note that the key to this latter aspect of the problem lies in an inability to reconcile the prefectural system of administration with the political expediencies of maintaining traditional authority intact. In all, the situation remains volatile in the extreme, and will plague the East Cameroun government for some time to come.

Le problème Bamiléké provides an instructive example of what can and does happen when a fairly large, homogeneous ethnic group undergoes rapid changes and begins to move out of its traditional geographic area. An illuminating parallel can be found in the example of the Ibo peoples of Eastern Nigeria.[38] A similar pattern appears to be unfolding in the northern areas of both the East Cameroun and the former Northern British Cameroons with the so-called Kirdi (pagan) peoples of Adamawa, Bornu, and the northern East Cameroun *départements*. It will be recalled that the Kirdi do not have the linguistic and social community of the Bamiléké, despite the fact that both terms refer to *groups* of tribes. Kirdi is simply a convenient designation used in studies of these peoples; they do not behave as a group, or indeed have any feeling of being anything more than a part of the limited tribal configuration. They do, however, have certain similarities that make it useful to speak of them as a whole. The most important of these are:

1) Their "paganism"; that is, the fact that they are neither Muslim nor Christian, but usually practice forms of animism coupled with ancestor worship and divination.[39]

2) Their opposition to the Fulani, whose conquest of the Chad plain in the nineteenth century was marked by attempts to Islamize or at least subjugate them. The Mandara and the Kotoko are examples of tribes that were both conquered and Islamized. Most of the other pagan tribes were either driven into the hills of Mandara or the mesas of the Benué plain where they took up quasi-independent existences, harassed by the Fulani until the turn of the twentieth century, remaining largely hostile to and aloof from the surrounding cultures.

3) Their primitive ways, in contrast to the more advanced cultures of the Fulani, Arabs, Kanuri, and Hausa. Characteristically they are wary of outsiders, aggressive, and suspicious of the Muslim culture of their traditional overlords, the Fulani. Many of them have adopted some aspects of Fulani, Arab, and Kanuri culture, such as dress, but most still cling to seminudity, the simplest agricultural methods, and the barter economy.

The stirrings among the Kirdi have not yet been formally recorded or studied, except perhaps in scattered anthropological works. However, more and more of the pagan tribes have come to accept, even to demand, education.[40] A case in point are the Fali, whose tribal area is just north of Garoua. In 1959 and 1960, for the first time, primary schools were opened in their areas. Also, an increasing number of Kirdi are beginning to appear in northern towns such as Garoua, Maroua, and Yagoua. Some have taken jobs in the towns and assumed the dress and customs of urban life. Like the Bamiléké, most of the Kirdi tribes have a high birth rate, and, again like the Bamiléké, they are beginning to move out of fairly circumscribed traditional tribal areas. The 1953 *Rapport du Cameroun* noted that "in the North, the mountain-dwelling Kirdi . . . are avoiding coming down into the plains so as not to have contact with the Fulani."[41] At that time the Kirdi were estimated to comprise about 725,000 persons. In 1960, unofficial estimates gave them approximately 750,000, with increasing numbers settling near traditionally Fulani-controlled towns. The political significance of the large Kirdi population in the north of the Cameroons (they are a majority in both the former Northern British Cameroons and in the northern *départements* of the East Cameroun) is just becoming a matter of concern to politicians; it is generally conceded that, if the Kirdi begin to use the franchise available to them, Fulani domination of elective offices may be seriously challenged. The possibility that this may come to pass in the near future was driven home by the November, 1959, plebiscite in the Northern British Cameroons, where the results—rejection of association with Northern Nigeria after Nigerian independence in October, 1960—can be explained only by reference to the Kirdi voters who participated. Apparently sufficient numbers of Kirdi voted against association—reasoning, perhaps, that continued association with Northern Nigeria meant a prolongation of Fulani domination —to reject the proposed incorporation. It is significant to observe that the 1959 Northern Cameroons plebiscite marked the first time the Kirdi had voted in anything like large numbers. Between the November, 1959, and February, 1961, plebiscites in the Northern Cameroons, the government of Northern Nigeria conducted an extensive political campaign in the Northern Cameroons, aiming its heaviest propaganda guns at the Kirdi. The strategy apparently paid off because, in the February, 1961, plebiscite, it was the Kirdi who once again tipped the voting balance, this time in favor of integration with Northern Nigeria. This political potential of the Kirdi makes their awakening a matter of tremendous concern to the government of Northern Nigeria.[42]

The connection between the areas of ethnic tension discussed above and the political life of the two Cameroons is unquestionably a crucial one. Some of the political reflections of these tensions have been mentioned in passing. In anticipation of the arguments of subsequent sections, and to give the foregoing sharper focus, it may be useful to suggest some other general consequences of these tensions:

1) The creation of tribal or ethnic organizations whose political purpose is to reflect the group's solidarity on social, economic, or political issues. These groups, on the whole, function more like pressure groups than political parties seeking office. About a third of the registered political parties and associations in the Cameroun Republic was of this nature.[43]

2) Group programs, statements, manifestos, and so on, aimed negatively at "strangers," "non-Cameroonians," and the like. The manifestos of both the Kamerun National Congress and the Kamerun National Democratic Party, the West Cameroun's two major parties, have reflected anti-"non-Cameroonian" sentiment. The East Cameroun government party, the *Parti d'Union Camerounaise*, has used the fear of southern domination in its appeals in the north of the East Cameroun.

3) The results of elections in urban centers such as Douala or in areas where tensions are highest, such as in the Bamiléké, Mungo, Sanaga-Maritime, and Nkam *départements*. The issues tend to be defined in ethnic terms by the principal parties involved, and an elec-

toral decision frequently reflects the success or failure of a call to tribal or ethnic solidarity, rather than a choice for a party, a policy, or a personality.

4) Demands for ethnic representation in governmental agencies, and/or in the administrative structure. Witness, for example, the distribution of posts in M. Ahidjo's 1958 cabinet when he balanced "northern" and "southern" seats.

The systems of education in the Cameroons have mediated and considerably softened the impact of ethnic tensions in the two territories. Both as a Westernizing influence and as the main instrument shaping the new Cameroonian elite, the systems of education have had crucial roles.

Until 1961, the British Cameroons' educational system was tied to that of Nigeria, which was itself based on the British model. After the creation of the Federal Republic, important questions about the accommodation of the West Cameroun's system to that of its new partner began to be raised. Some of these problems will be noted in Chapter VIII. However, since the focus of this study is the East Cameroun, an examination of that state's educational system and its problems is immediately in point.

EDUCATION

Professor James S. Coleman has stressed the role of formal education in the creation of new elites:

> Western education has been at once the most revolutionary of all influences operative in Sub-Saharan Africa since the imposition of European rule. It has been the instrument for the creation of a class indispensable for imperial rule, but one which invariably has taken the leadership in displacing that rule. Western education has created the new African elite. . . .[44]

In the Cameroun as elsewhere in Africa it is necessary to distinguish between mission education, long the only operative educational system, and the public system which developed later. That the secular system began to take on the characteristics of its religious predecessor is no surprise; the mission schools led the way in the creation of the "new African elite," and when this elite later began to assume the reins of responsibility, the education system it created bore the marks of the orientation of its founders.

The missionary societies came not only to effect conversions, but to provide the "civilized" context within which the varied values of Christianity (as interpreted by each sect) could best be propagated.

The missionary effort was and is devoted not simply to encouraging people to *act* like Christians, but to *live* like Christians, an orientation that involves a whole new set of behavior patterns that might include a range of activities from wearing clothes to attending religious services.

A useful model is that of Victoria, the missionary settlement founded by Alfred Saker in 1858 on Ambas Bay, facing Fernando Po. Saker's Victoria sought to provide a Christian *community,* both as an example of how such a community lived, and as a magnet with which to draw the natives. Indeed, most of the missions in the Cameroons tried to create microcosmic Christian communities according to whatever vision their particular sectarian allegiance dictated. It might also be pointed out that the message of "Christian living" had other overtones as well; to a German Protestant it amounted to living like a German Protestant; to the English and French missionaries it was coupled with English and French modes of life. In this context, the Christian school represented what was probably the most useful and lasting vehicle of the religio-secular message of the missions. The reasons are simple:

1) The educative process took a number of years, which kept both children and parents close to the mission for a long period.

2) The pupil-teacher relationship was ideal for the long-range inculcation of values and proved most useful for the missions, since both children and adults are reached, either one through the other, or simultaneously.

3) The complexity of the demands of the "Christian life" is best taught in an atmosphere where receptivity is usually high, that is, in the controlled atmosphere of a school.

4) Education became coupled with conferred status, and, more often, with the economic advantage that being "mission taught" brought to those who participated in it.

It cannot be stressed too often that the mission schools flourished in the Cameroons and elsewhere in West Africa because they were at first means to the ends sought by the missions themselves, and later to the ends sought by many Cameroonians. Until the secular authorities began providing acceptable substitutes for mission education, the mission schools continued to be highly sought after as places where the African might learn the white man's skills, and, with them, find work that would provide economic rewards and a measure of deference from both Africans and Europeans. Thus, in many instances, the mission schools produced Africans with literacy and manual skills, but with only a thin veneer of Christianity. Instances abound of Cameroonians in responsible positions who married a first wife according to Christian rites, had themselves and the first wife baptized, and later contracted other polygamous unions according to traditional ritual. This attempt to "get the best of both worlds" has, as could be expected, been severely criticized by the missions, but it continues (as do other similar practices) despite the moral indignation heaped upon it.[45]

Another important agency for education has been the commercial company. Margaret Read points out that

European thought in the seventeenth and eighteenth centuries saw no incompatibility between establishing "forts" to regulate the slave trade and educating a very limited number of Africans to assist them in their enterprises. The education implied as a rule conversion to Christianity, and in this respect the early trading companies anticipated the work of the missions.[46]

In the Kamerun, the first school was opened in Douala in 1888 by one Christaller, who had been appointed to the post upon the recommendation of the Basler Mission and who taught according to a program whose principles Adolf Woermann, head of the most important firm operating in the Kamerun, had worked out. In a memorandum to Bismarck, Woermann had suggested that the curriculum of the new schools include the teaching of arithmetic, reading and writing German, and some religious instruction; he also suggested an agricultural school to give the natives some idea of the principles involved in tilling the soil. In 1889 a second school was opened at Deido (Douala), and a few years later a third school was founded in Victoria, chiefly at the request of Pastor Joseph Wilson, a native Baptist for whom the Germans had a liking because of his efforts to win support for Germany among the pro-English natives of that community.[47]

Christaller's first school, and the early schools of Douala and Victoria, had an unusual semiofficial, semimissionary-trader flavor. Some of the Douala schools were temporarily taken over by the Basler mission in 1897, which had also assumed control over the school in Victoria. Following its efforts to introduce schools in the southern part of the protectorate, the government sought to extend its school system in the north. In 1906 the government opened a school in Muslim Garoua, manned by a locally born African teacher, named Steane, from Victoria. To allay the fears of the Muslim population that the school might become a center for Christian proselytizing, it offered Arabic as well as German, and compelled students' attendance at the local mosque every Friday for religious services.

In 1907 Governor Seitz called a conference on education at Douala and invited not only government officials but representatives of the missions as well. The conference sought to develop a standard curriculum for all schools, placing primary emphasis on the German language, with arithmetic next, and special attention given to geography, history, and general science. The government favored compulsory attendance, but, since this appeared impossible to enforce, settled on a general tightening of the attendance requirements. In 1910 all mission schools were obliged to follow the program laid down by the government in order to obtain financial assistance, which set a precedent for the formula still observed today. Also in 1910 two trade schools were established in Victoria and Buea, respectively, one to teach agricultural methods, and the other to provide instruction in cabinet-making and upholstery work. The agricultural school in Victoria operated in conjunction with the Government Botanical Gardens there, accepted only graduates of a mission or government school, and then only on the signing of a bond obligating the students to serve the government for five years after the completion of the course. By 1913 two additional trade schools had been opened, one in Douala, and another in Victoria.

The government, however, limited its own work very much to the number of schools or classes it thought necessary to train staff to work in administration, and preferred to rely mostly on the missions to carry out the general education of the people. By 1913, throughout the colony there were only four government schools, with 833 pupils, but there were 631 mission schools, with 49,000 pupils. Under the German system, in both government and mission schools great stress was laid on practical matters. Instruction was given in shoemaking, tailoring, carpentry, brick-making, sewing, washing, and numerous other crafts that could enable the pupils to earn a living. Such teaching won the warm approval of the traders and planters, who felt that most other missionary activity was of a sentimental or impractical nature.[48]

In the Kamerun at the outbreak of the war three of the four Protestant missions were German; the Basel (Basler), the German Baptist, and the Gossner Societies. The American Presbyterians, working in the south of the territory, ranked as neutrals until 1917. Their educational effort included some 97 schools with 6,545 pupils. The Basel Mission, whose original inheritance was the work transferred to it by the Baptist Missionary Society at the time of the German occupation, had developed a network of stations extending into the hinterland with a considerable educational agency: in 1914, 384 schools were reported with an enrollment of 22,818. The German Baptist mission, serving the

Baptist churches that had refused to come under the rigid discipline of the Basler Society, in 1913 had 57 schools and 3,151 pupils. The third German Protestant mission, the Gossner Society, had just begun operations in the Kamerun in 1914 by opening a mission and a school when the war destroyed their efforts. The Catholic effort was represented by the Pallotine Fathers, who had been at work in the Kamerun since 1890. In 1913 they operated 151 schools with a total of 12,532 pupils. In 1917 the Fathers of the Holy Ghost (*Congrégation du Saint-Esprit*) took over the work of the Pallotine Fathers, who had remained the principal Catholic mission in the territory, except in the British Cameroons where the Mill Hill Fathers took over the Catholic missions.[49]

From August, 1914, to March, 1916, both official and mission schools were closed. In many instances the Anglo-French expeditionary forces used the school buildings as billets. The European teachers and their native assistants were mostly incorporated into the German forces, and the missionaries, mobilized by the government, ceased all instruction. In 1916, the occupation authorities decreed the reopening of all public and mission schools, and by 1917 some official primary schools had reopened, staffed by several European teachers and forty-seven native assistants. The mission schools were slower to recover, as reopening the schools often involved transfer of the school and mission property to an English or French mission society, in addition to finding operating funds. The second problem was especially difficult to overcome as most of the mission schools had to seek new sources of private funds, and attempt to regain some measure of the public assistance previously provided by the German government. By 1918 the American Presbyterian, French Protestant (Baptist), and Catholic missions had reopened, subsidized according to the number of pupils undergoing instruction in French (in the area under French jurisdiction) and the number of teachers and assistants following the official course of study.[50]

During the period from 1921 (when the schools were officially set up again and courses of study prescribed on all levels) to 1928, the administering authority in the French mandate sought to develop an educational system along the lines of the system in French West Africa. Three types of public instruction were recognized: elementary-primary (*primaire-élémentaire*), secondary and professional (*supérieur et professionel*), and technical. This pattern has been followed, without major modifications, until the present day. Currently, the East Cameroun's educational system still follows traditional French lines, utilizing the bifurcated seven-year primary course, followed by the seven-year secondary course leading to the *baccalauréat.* In addition, technical and teacher-training courses on the secondary level are available separately from the standard academic secondary courses. The details of the entire system are not immediately relevant here, but in order to understand some of the Cameroun's educational problems, a brief summary of the system is useful at this point:[51]

1) Primary: Primary education consists of two stages. The first lasts four or five years, depending on whether one or two years are spent in preparatory (kindergarten) classes before entering the first academic class; a competitive examination then screens entrants into the two-year second stage. In all, there are five years of standard formal education, not including the preparatory or infants' classes lasting one or two years. Emphasis was—and still is—on French, arithmetic, hygiene, simple science, agricultural principles, and, for the girls, domestic skills. In addition, rural and urban two-year primary sections offer adults training in literacy skills, homemaking, and agricultural methods. Children usually enter the first class at age seven; they usually complete the second primary cycle at twelve.

2) Secondary: Those who want to continue their education take competitive examinations that screen them and guide them into one of several alternative secondary courses. The full six-years-plus-special-terminal classes leading to the second *baccalauréat* examinations are offered in fifteen East Cameroun institutions (ten private and five public *lycées* and *collèges*). These are the so-called long courses; they emphasize either academic or technical subjects. The end of the "third" year of the secondary course (actually the fourth *chronological* year of the secondary course, as the French system enumerates secondary years in reverse order, starting with the "sixth" year) marks the standard midpoint screening of the long courses (first baccalaureate examination). This is the terminal point for most of the East Cameroun's secondary schools, and is usually designated as the short course. The short courses tend to attract students taking technical training or training to become *moniteurs* (probationary teachers) in rural areas, as well as those with limited educational aspirations. "Assistant teachers" are trained in a five-year secondary cycle; regular primary or secondary teachers take the full seven-year secondary normal-school course.

3) Higher: Until 1960, when the college-level École Camerounaise d'Administration was opened, and 1962, when the Université Fédérale du Cameroun in Yaoundé was opened, Camerounian students seeking higher education were almost invariably sent to universities or governmental training institutions in France. The new university, which

started with an initial enrollment of 588, now permits graduates of the long secondary course to continue their studies without going abroad. Since 1963, the university has had three faculties (law, letters, sciences) and two attached schools (the Ecole Normale Supérieure and the Ecole Normale Camerounaise d'Agriculture), which produce teachers for the first secondary cycle, inspectors of primary education, and instructors for teacher-training institutions.

The growth of this present system, whether by accident or design, seems to have followed fairly rational lines. Further, a functional balance—corresponding to shortages in finance, staff, and operating equipment—between private and public education has been struck. Whether the system is adequate to meet the needs of the country for trained, literate citizens, is another question. Some possible answers may lie in a summary examination of a few of the more vexing problems that have arisen in the process of the system's evolution. Among them and of primary importance, are the educational disparity between the northern and southern areas, the lag in the education of women, the vast gap between the number of school entrants and graduates, the relations between the private and public systems, the technical and educational inadequacies of most teachers, the low priority given to educational financing, and the development of higher education.

It is noteworthy that educational advance has generally been more rapid in the southern areas of the East Cameroun than in the north, where progress has been retarded by the poverty of communications and by the hesitancy of members of the Muslim community to send their children to what popular prejudice condemned as "Christian," "heathen," or "unfriendly" schools. This writer heard all three terms used by members of the Fulani (Muslim) community in the north. Recently, however, considerable educational progress has also been made in the northern areas. Enrollments have increased at the government schools in the main urban centers, a move often led by local Fulani chiefs who set persuasive examples by sending their sons to the schools. In Garoua, I saw the heir to the lamidate of Garoua enrolled at the Collège du Nord, and was informed that other local chiefs, in increasingly greater numbers, had been sending their sons to the elementary schools. Whatever educational facilities, public or private, existed in the northern areas of the Cameroun prior to World War II were principally among the Muslim Fulani. The northern Kirdi began attending mission and public schools in the north in appreciable numbers only after 1947. Their increased participation in schooling has already been noted elsewhere; it must be added here that they usually attend government rather than mission schools.

Despite the increase in school attendance in the northern areas, the latter are still far behind the south. Of the approximately 427,129 children attending both public and mission primary schools in the Cameroun in 1962, only 56,693 (about 11 per cent) were enrolled in schools in the five northern *départements* and Adamaoua. Even more marked is the northern resistance to the education of women. In the southern *départements,* of the 370,436 children attending both public and mission primary schools in 1962, 30 per cent were girls. In the north, only 18 per cent of the 56,693 enrollees were girls. In the Bami-léké areas, the proportion of girls to the total school enrollees is seldom more than 8 per cent. Taking the country as a whole, however, there has been considerable progress. In 1936 there were only 1,536 girls enrolled in the schools, but by 1958 this had risen to 103,713. Seen another way, this means that in 1936 only about 1.5 per cent of all schoolchildren were girls; in 1958, 30 per cent were girls.[52]

This statistical leap has important political and social consequences. It represents the creation of a segment of an informed public likely to affect the outcome of future elections, and indeed, to make itself felt in political programs and in the creation of political groups. For example, both major parties in the British Cameroons instituted local women's wings, and at least two important women's political organizations (one of which is an affiliate of the UPC) made their appearance in the East Cameroun.[53] Woman's role in the politics of Federal Republic will undoubtedly become increasingly important.

However imposing the growth in school attendance in general and of girl students in particular during the past several years, the unhappy fact remains that by the end of the six-year primary course, barely one-fifth of those who began receive their diplomas or school-leaving certificates. About half of those who begin primary schooling (first class) drop out at the end of the first year; by the end of the third year, three-fourths of the original number have left. Even more distressing is a comparison between input at the beginning of the primary course and output at the end of the (long) secondary course (second *bachot*): often only 0.1 per cent of those who start primary school finish their secondary education. The 1962 UNESCO Camerounian Educational Planning Group's preliminary report traced the classes of 1946, 1947, and 1948 through both their primary and secondary years:[54]

Class (yrs. of study)	Number enrolled in 1st cl. prim.	Number obtaining prim.-school leav'g cert.	Number winning places in 6th cl. (lycée)	Number obaining *brevet* elem.	Number obtaining *bachot*
1946–1959	40,626	1,317 (3.2%)	639	421 (1.01%)	81 (+0.1%)
1947–1960	60,231	2,157 (3.2%)	874	261 (1.8%)	82 (+0.1%)
1948–1961	77,838	3,266 (4.1%)	1,370	690 (0.8%)	92 (+0.1%)

The report noted that the situation tends to be aggravated by excessive repetitions in the primary grades, and by the general lack of qualifications of over three-quarters of the teachers. It is not too much to suggest that unless more students can be brought through the primary and secondary cycles, the nation will continue to be abysmally poor in the skilled manpower it now needs and will need in the future.

One of the most difficult problems for the East Camerounian administration has been the sharp difference between the rates of growth and enrollments of the voluntary agency schools and official schools. The crux of the problem is that as late as January, 1958, approximately 70 per cent of all individuals registered in all primary and secondary schools in the territory were attending schools run by the voluntary agencies. Enrollments in the government schools did not rise appreciably after 1919, when the first official attempts to rebuild the educational structure were begun. In 1938, immediately before the outbreak of World War II, there were only 10,637 enrolled in the official schools. In contrast, the private schools reported 92,491 enrollees for that same year. In 1919 the mission schools had an approximate enrollment of 3,000 pupils, while 1,690 were reported for the official schools. Between 1919 and 1938, the growth rate of the private schools was approximately five times that of the official schools (see table 9). In other words, during the nineteen-year period in question, private-school enrollment went up about thirty-one times but official-school enrollment only about six and a half times.

Both public and private primary schools follow the same official curriculum, are subject to the same rules regarding methods of instruction, qualifications of teachers, and the condition of physical equipment. The crucial differences between them (and probably the two main reasons that the private schools continue to command the financial support of the government) are that the private schools have extensive,

TABLE 9

SCHOOLS AND SCHOOL ATTENDANCE IN (EAST) CAMEROUN BY TYPE
OF SCHOOL OR AGENCY: SELECTED YEARS, 1919–1962

(n.d. = no data)

Type of school and year	Total enrolled	Public		Voluntary agency	
		Students enrolled	No. of schools	Students enrolled	No. of schools
Primary:					
1919	4,190	1,690	27	2,500	25
1921	6,122	3,122	38	3,000	25
1925	57,322	6,785	78	50,537	n.d.
1930	72,206	5,880	74	66,326	n.d.
1935	81,679	8,550	68	73,129	n.d.
1938	102,600	10,109	76	92,491	n.d.
1947	113,678	18,600	157	95,078	1,188
1953	172,758	48,258	364	126,508	1,500
1957	294,000	89,309	649	204,691	1,814
1958[a]	330,893	103,072	649	227,911	1,814
1962	427,129	151,635	977	275,494	1,453
Secondary:					
1919	—	—	—	—	—
1921	—	—	—	—	—
1925	72	72	1	—	—
1930	147	147	1	—	—
1935	85	85	1	—	—
1938	136	136	3	—	—
1947	925	723	5	203	2
1953	2,911	1,722	6	1,189[b]	11[b]
1957	3,597	1,618	5	1,979	16
1958[a,b]	7,570	3,785	n.d.	3,785	n.d.
1962	18,387	5,975	22	12,412	62
Teacher-train-ing:					
1919–1931	—	—	—	—	—
1935–1938[c]	—	—	—	—	—
1947	203	—	—	203	3
1953	n.d.	438	4	—[d]	—[d]
1957	2,136	499	5	1,637	15
1958	1,808	570	5	1,238	7
1962	n.d.	n.d.	n.d.	n.d.	n.d.

[a] Figures for the Cameroun are dated February, 1959, and probably are those for the fall semester, 1958. Secondary-school figures include normal schools.

[b] Includes normal schools.

[c] Secondary schools provide teacher-training.

[d] Included with secondary schools.

Table 9—*Continued*

Type of school and year	Total enrolled	Public		Voluntary agency	
		Students enrolled	No. of schools	Students enrolled	No. of schools
Vocational:					
1919–1921	—	—	—	—	—
1925[e]	n.d.	376	8	n.d.	n.d.
1930[e]	n.d.	n.d.	n.d.	n.d.	n.d.
1935[e]	n.d.	n.d.	n.d.	n.d.	n.d.
1938[e]	n.d.	65	n.d.	n.d.	n.d.
1947	280	180	2	100	2
1953	1,310	222	6	1,088	22
1957	4,376	1,778	35	2,598	28
1958	5,127	1,652	37	4,775	28
1962	5,740	2,691	51	3,049	20
Higher and post-secondary students abroad:					
1935	n.d.				
1938	—				
1947	45[f]				
1953	148[f]				
1957	1,166[g]				
1958[g]	1,050				
1962	1,084 (444 on scholar- ships)				
Higher, in Cam. 1962:	703				
Cam. Fed. Univ.:	588				
Cam. Nat'l School of Administra- tion:	115				

[e] Vocational training included at both primary and secondary levels as part of the ordinary course.

[f] Scholarship students only.

[g] Including nonscholarship students.

Table 9—*Continued*

Type of school and year	Total enrolled	Public		Voluntary agency	
		Students enrolled	No. of schools	Students enrolled	No. of schools
Totals, all categories:[h]					
1919	4,190	1,690	27	2,500	25
1921	6,122	3,122	38	3,000	25
1925	57,394	7,233	47	50,537	n.d.
1930	72,352	6,027	75	66,326	n.d.
1935	81,764	8,635	69	73,129	n.d.
1938	102,736	10,310	79	92,491	n.d.
1947	115,131	19,503	144	95,584	1,195
1953	177,088	50,640	380	128,785	1,533
1957	305,275	93,204	694	210,904	1,873
1958[a]	346,538	109,079	n.d.	237,709	n.d.
1962[i]	454,851	161,574	1,057	292,193	1,542

[h] Totals are of figures given above; they will not, in many instances, agree with the sources' totals as they include or omit figures cited or omitted by the sources. The figures given above are, therefore, only suggestive.

[i] Figures are approximate; accurate figures on teacher-training were not available.

(*Full citations of works mentioned briefly here will be found in the bibliography.*)

Sources: *Rapport du Cameroun* (1923, 1925, 1930, 1935, 1947, 1953, 1957), (Paris); *Supplément au Bulletin de la Statistique Générale*, Etat du Cameroun, Ministère des Affaires Economiques, Service de la Statistique Générale, February, 1958, no. 2, p. 48; Hailey, Lord, *An African Survey, Revised 1956* (New York: Oxford University Press, 1957), pp. 1204–1206; *Bulletin*, Direction de l'Enseignement et de la Jeunesse du Ministère de la France d'Outre Mer, no. 10 (Jan., 1958); Nicolas, Raoul, *Le Cameroun depuis le Traité de Versailles* (St. Armand/Cherbourg: Imp. A. Leclerc, 1922), p. 53; Costeodat, René, *Le Mandat français et la réorganisation des territoires du Cameroun* (Besançon: Imp. Jacques et Demontrand, 1930), pp. 118–126, *passim*; *Info-Cameroun*, no. 2 (Feb., 1959); United Nations Educational, Social, and Cultural Organization, *World Survey of Education, Vol. III, Secondary Education* (New York: International Documents Service, 1961), pp. 316, 317, 1267; Federal Republic of Cameroon, Ministère de l'Education Nationale, *Statistiques Concernant les enseignments Secondaire, Technique et Supérieur, 1962/1963* (Yaoundé: 1963); UNESCO, Camerounian Educational Planning Group, *Report Drawn Upon Return of the First Mission, 10 March–20 May, 1962* (Paris: 1962), mimeo.

widely dispersed facilities and that they have maintained a self-perpetuating system for the training and maintenance of large numbers of teachers. Initially, it will be recalled, the missions brought their own teachers, often missionaries, to their new schools, or trained native converts to teach in them, all with the aid and approval of the budget-minded German administration. At the end of the war the French administration found it easier to rely on the already well-established system than to go about the difficult task of creating a new system from scratch. The mission schools had the advantage of being there, and, most important, of being able to provide their own teachers and much of the money needed to run the schools. Content to concentrate on other matters, such as health, the administering authorities apparently felt the cause of primary education was sufficiently well served by the private agencies. What effort was devoted to education was concentrated on technical education and on the establishment of regional, second-level primary schools in various communities.

In the meantime, the private agencies trained large numbers of their primary-school graduates to be *moniteurs,* or student teachers, in addition to establishing many trade and technical schools. In 1938, just before the beginning of World War II, the official schools reported a teaching staff of 192 persons, including 172 native student teachers. The private schools, divided into "recognized" schools (teaching the official curriculum in French) and "unrecognized" schools (following other curricula or teaching in a native language), had a teaching staff which together probably exceeded 1,250, of which about 1,100 were native student teachers.[55] After the war, the French authorities began to give more serious thought to the creation of a larger teaching cadre; by 1957 three normal schools had been opened for men and one for women, together graduating between 120 and 150 Camerounian teachers a year. In addition, new courses for *moniteurs* were instituted in the north, summer courses were begun so that teachers could improve their skills, and each year eight selected instructors were, and are, sent to France for a four-months' study tour at government expense.[56] The 1960 figures show the results of the postwar teacher-training program: the public schools are reported to have a teaching and administrative staff of 2,250, of which about 2,100 are native Camerounians. The private schools, in contrast, show a staff of 5,250, of which about 4,500 are Camerounians.[57]

Whatever optimism can be generated over the increasing Camerounization of the teaching staff and the augmented teacher-training facilities, the outlook, insofar as the quality of teaching is concerned, is far from encouraging. Not only do the teacher-training institutions turn out too few teachers to meet the growing enrollment—teacher output per year for the primary grades amounts to less than one-third of those needed—but over 70 per cent of all teachers on the public

elementary level have substandard qualifications, that is, they are un-
certificated *moniteurs* or assistant teachers. In private elementary institutions, 82 per cent of the teachers are *moniteurs*. In 1962, in the
East Cameroun's public schools, for every teacher with a *baccalauréat* there were eight assistant teachers and twenty-seven *moniteurs*.[58]

If the educational system is to provide the necessary trained and
literate manpower without which it cannot hope to grow, it follows
that expenditures must be adequate to meet the need for more and
better teachers, more classrooms, and better teaching facilities. By any
standard, according to the 1962 UNESCO Study Group, the East
Cameroun's projected financing for educational development is plainly
inadequate.[59] The First Five Year Plan, designed to cover all phases
of national development, and put into effect in December, 1960, distributed projected funding as follows:[60]

	Million francs CFA	*Approximate %*
Studies	2,399	4.5
Productions	16,224	30.4
Infrastructure	25,460	47.8
Social equipment	9,099	17.1
Total	53,182	100

"Social Equipment," which included education, was broken down
thus:

	Million francs CFA
Public health	3,564
Education	1,460
Adult education, youth, and sport	2,000
Housing and town planning	2,075

The figure for education, the smallest of those in the "Social Equipment" rubric, amounts to only 2.7 per cent of the total investment
projected for the five years 1961-1965. Only slightly more optimistic
is the Cameroun's Twenty Year Plan, promulgated in 1960, of which
the Five Year Plan is the first installment. The Twenty Year Plan estimated its total cost to be approximately 44,420 million francs CFA
(since 1963, CFA has stood for Communauté Financière Africaine) (or
about $180 million), and allocated 3,050 million francs CFA (about
$12.4 million) to education; here the percentage for education, of the
whole, was 6.8 per cent.[61]

TABLE 10

I. Scholarship students in France
  A. Higher education (*supérieure*), by specialization:

1. Law	43	
2. Letters	23	
3. Sciences	24	
4. Medicine	59	
5. Pharmacy	19	
6. Veterinary medicine	2	
7. Dentistry	3	
8. "Grandes Ecoles"[a]	9	
9. Prep. for "Grandes Ecoles"	13	
10. Engineering	1	
11. Beaux-arts	4	
12. Miscellaneous	95	
Total, higher education		295

  B. Other schools, by type:

1. Secondary schools, "long course"	25	
2. Technical schools	171	
3. "Perfectionnement"[b]	20	
4. Miscellaneous	20	
Total, other schools		236
Total, scholarship students in France		531
II. Nonscholarship students in French higher education		585
III. Students in Dakar, all types of schools and specializations		39
Total, all students abroad		1155[c]
Per cent on scholarships		45.6

[a] St. Cyr, the Ecole d'Administration d'Outre Mer, the Conservatoire National des Arts et Métiers, and similar institutions.

[b] Includes various types of in-service training in administration, government, and business.

[c] Does not include students attending denominational schools.

Note: The figures cited above do not include Cameroun students in France or elsewhere receiving higher or other education in denominational schools.

(*Full citations of works mentioned briefly here will be found in the bibliography.*)

Sources: *Rapport du Cameroun* (1957), p.297; *Bulletin*, Direction de l'Enseignement de la Jeunesse du Ministere de la France d'Outre-Mer, no. 10 (Jan., 1958).

With independence, the Cameroun, no less than other African states, began to realize the crucial role of postsecondary and university-trained manpower in the development of the country. Such manpower would be needed not only to handle the administrative apparatus left by France, but the skills and knowledge acquired in higher education would become critical to the political management of a country in which literacy and political sophistication had become and would become increasingly widespread.

After 1947, it became obvious that the local secondary schools were insufficient to train the cadre necessary to the expanding administrative structure and for the growing needs in professional groups of various kinds. The war had interrupted plans to send eight students on scholarships to metropolitan France to study at higher institutions there, but in 1947 twenty-four students were given scholarships to attend courses in medicine or law in the *métropole,* another group of twenty-one was sent to Dakar, fifteen to the Ecole de Médecine et Pharmacie Africaine, and five to the Ecole des Sages-femmes (school for midwives). By 1958 the number of students studying abroad had increased to 1166, of which thirty-nine attended schools in Dakar—notably the Institut des Hauts Etudes—and the rest in France. The government also provided Cameroun students in the Paris area with a Foyer des étudiants Camerounais à Paris (Cameroun students' center), toward whose maintenance, in 1959, it allocated about $4,100.[62] Table 10 indicates main areas of study and sources of students' funds for a representative year, 1957. It highlights the large number of students studying law or medicine, fields that are unmistakable status professions in a country where little more than 10 per cent of the population is literate. It also illuminates the large number of students studying under nongovernmental auspices; I was told that some received funds from private organizations, some from business firms, some worked to sustain themselves, but that most were supported by their families.

The cost of the overseas scholarships has been underwritten by the Cameroun government, with the assistance of funds from various official French sources. The 1959 budget allocated 133,000,000 francs CFA (approximately $554,166) toward scholarship awards for students studying abroad. Included in this figure was 3,000,000 francs CFA toward scholarships in Arab-speaking countries, a new development in the scholarship program. The 1960-1961 budget allocated 183,500,000 francs CFA (approximately $749,000) for the same purposes.

In 1960 the Ecole Nationale d'Administration was opened in Yaoundé, followed in 1961 by the creation of the National Center for Advanced Study which, in 1962, became the Cameroun Federal University.

UNESCO assisted in the formation of the new university, and France made available most of the staff now teaching there. Although over a thousand East Camerounians were still studying at foreign (principally French) universities in 1962 and 1963, the creation of the two local institutions of higher learning has many obvious advantages for the Cameroun government, not the least of which is supervision of the curricula—and consequently of the students' training itself—and, probably even more important, of the students' postgraduate disposition. Not a few young Camerounians studying in France delayed their return home, or even refused to be repatriated after their training was completed. In France, many became culturally Frenchmen, imbued with French values and mores, if not with a love of France itself. In France, also, many young Camerounians had their first contacts with the extreme radicalism of many French university students and the leftist organizations catering to African students. A significant number of African students became, if not communists, certainly captivated by the glitter of socialist promises. The organization of Cameroun students in France, *l'Union des Etudiants Kamerunais* (UNEK), made no pretense of concealing its hostility to the Ahidjo government and of its sympathies with the aims of the UPC.[63] The return of these students to the Cameroun, often to assume important government posts, has been a source of much misgiving on the part of both French and Cameroun authorities. Some of the students, however, quickly lose their radicalism when confronted with the realities of administrative responsibility. Others do not change, and become nuclei for dissension or disaffection within the governmental apparatus or at large in the country. Whatever the experiences of the government with students studying outside the Camerouns—and there is little indication that the government wishes to discontinue sending students abroad—the new institutions in Yaoundé do provide a higher measure of political control over the students than was previously possible. In addition, leaving academic considerations aside, the government has without question added considerably to national pride by the very fact of having a university; given the high status values associated with higher education, the possession of a university is a matter of no small political prestige both at home and abroad.

Several noteworthy points emerge from this hurried survey of Camerounian education. One is the variety and scope of the influences on the present-day system; another is the variety of the human product of that system. Together, the two suggest that, rather than being hurt by an "educational pluralism," the Cameroun has, in fact, considerably benefited from it.

To recapitulate, among the most important of the educational influences that need to be taken into account are: the several missions'
schools, the German system, a changing educational orientation over
the years of the mandate and the trusteeship by the French administration, the education of Camerounians abroad, commercial interests
in the Cameroun, and the policies of Cameroun governments after
1956.

The mission schools brought the Christian vision of the good life
according to the dictates of each sect. They also, significantly, inculcated various attitudes to authority, from the deference to hierarchy
found in Catholicism, to the voluntarism of the American Presbyterian
mission. (One suspects that one of the main reasons for the Catholic
mission's relative impotence in the Muslim north is a clash between
two different hierarchically based authority systems.)

The Germans brought a rigidly defined, strictly enforced system
whose cornerstones were deference to authority and the creation of a
technical proletariat.

The French initially emphasized simple literacy and technical skills
as their main aims, later broadened them to provide for the creation
of a Gallicized native elite.

Some of the largest of the various commercial interests operating in
the Cameroun not only supported the expansion of the missions, and
thereby mission education, but eventually either opened schools of
their own or provided technical or commercial and technical education for their employees.[64]

The African Camerounian governments after 1956 were given full
charge of the educational program within the country. One of the first
and principal tasks assigned to the schools, whether public or private,
was to develop a sense of "Camerounism," that is, an appreciation of
the territory's history, traditions, and political future. In short, in addition to teaching literacy and technical skills, the schools became
agents for the politicization of the younger generation.[65]

By and large, one suspects that these varied educational influences
have had a salutary effect on the East Cameroun. The percentage of
Camerounians with any education is growing, though literacy is still
low, so that the territory's "educational pluralism" can only be bene-
ficial. The East Cameroun has been assured—and to its good fortune—
of the diversity of ideas, orientations, and skills that make for political
vitality. It remains to be seen, however, if, in the face of the considerable problems still facing Cameroun education, that vitality can be
maintained.

OFFICIAL SCHOOL PROGRAM SET UP BY [GERMAN] IMPERIAL ORDINANCES
OF 25 APRIL 1910 AND 23 APRIL 1913
FOR THE FIVE-YEAR PRIMARY SCHOOLS

[Hours per week]

First year
    Reading and writing (German)   2 hrs.
    Moral principles and behavior   2 hrs.
    Simple arithmetic   2 hrs.

                                                    6 hrs.

Second year
    Reading and writing (German)   3 hrs.
    Moral principles and behavior   2 hrs.
    Simple arithmetic   3 hrs.

                                                    8 hrs.

Third year
    Elements of grammar, orthography (German)   4 hrs.
    Natural history   2 hrs.
    Arithmetic   3 hrs.
    Geography   1 hr.

                                                10 hrs.

Fourth year
    Reading, writing, explanation of selected pieces (German)   4 hrs.
    Arithmetic   3 hrs.
    History of the territory   1 hr.
    Natural history   1 hr.
    Domestic skills   1 hr.

                                                10 hrs.

Fifth year
    Exercises in grammar (German)   4 hrs.
    Metric system   3 hrs.
    History of the German Empire   1 hr.
    Natural history   1 hr.
    Domestic skills   1 hr.

                                                10 hrs.

SOURCE: René Costeodat, *Le Mandat français et la réorganization des terri-toires du Cameroun* (Besançon: Jacques et Demontrond, 1930), pp. 118-119.

IV *The Growth of Political Life and Institutions in the Interwar Period*

An analysis of the pattern of political development in the French Cameroun between World Wars I and II reveals
that three main factors influenced that development. First was the
complex of institutions and policies the French administration formu-
lated, both to govern its territory and to solve the various problems
that arose during the course of the nearly forty years of French
rule. By and large, these types of institutions and policies also
existed elsewhere in French Africa; typically most of them had, in
fact, been conceived in Paris for broadcast application in the French
overseas dependencies. The second factor was the Camerounian response, or series of responses, to these policies and institutions. It is
true that such local reaction was seldom, if ever, effective in forcing a
change during this period, but it is still important to assess the inter-
play as it gave rise to attitudes important in their turn as the source of
future political demands. The third factor, not to be underestimated,
was the influence of the German presence in the two Cameroons—
especially in the British mandate. The activities of German planters, and
Germany's international campaign for the return of its former colonial
possessions, increasingly influenced the course of official action in the
French mandate up to the outbreak of World War II. In a very real
sense, the German presence in the Cameroons, which Britain and France
tried to supplant—with varying degrees of success—returned to plague
them with a vengeance. It becomes important, therefore, to examine
the nature and force of this influence.

A. FRENCH POLICIES AND INSTITUTIONS

FRENCH COLONIAL POLICY

Until the startling course of events after 1944
forced recognition of the increasing political ferment in its colonial
empire, France never doubted that the *métropole* and the colonies

would develop into a single, integrated political and economic unit. Unlike Great Britain, France never conceived of self-government for most of its colonial possessions. Even though specific institutions and policies have often reflected the practical realities that have led elsewhere to policies of "differentiation," the French have clung, at least theoretically, to the ideas of identity inherent in their universalist thinking.[1] In practice, this led to a political schizophrenia whose illogicality and painful consequences did not become apparent until after 1944. On the one hand, it was possible for French policy to champion "assimilation" and tender what appeared to be political and economic equality to her colonies. Article 109 of the French constitution of 1848, which embodied this principle, stated that colonies are French territory in the same way as the *métropole* and enjoy the same position in private and public law. Thus, it was no surprise when in 1848 the inhabitants of Senegalese coastal towns were granted both French citizenship and the franchise.[2] On the other hand, the realities of anti-French Muslim feeling in North Africa, and the great cultural gap between the inhabitants of most of French Black Africa and those of metropolitan France turned many French administrators into proponents of a doctrine that was in substance antiassimilationist. Lyautey, Gallieni, and de Lanessan advocated a *politique de protectorat* in terms not unlike Lugard's formulations on "indirect rule." Jules Harmand, who brought the doctrine to its fullest expression, distinguished between situations in which Europeans simply *dominated* a large indigenous population and those in which "the true *colon* was the Native and the great colonizer the State."[3] Harmand argued that the social standards of the indigenous inhabitants were too far removed from those of Frenchmen for assimilation to be practical, and that there should accordingly be instituted a policy of "association" which would involve some measure of indirect administration and a general respect for indigenous institutions.

Albert Sarraut, who became Colonial Minister in 1922, put the "policy of association" into operation throughout the French colonial empire. The policy, as he defined it,[4] had several significant aspects:

1) It assumed that in most situations the coördination of economic and political policies of the colonies with France proper that was implied in the "policy of assimilation" would be unworkable. Local differences would be taken under consideration and coördination of policies would not be stressed so long as the aim of a total development of the colonial empire was kept in mind.

2) Instead of all-out political assimilation, there would be a kind of functional collaboration between the French rulers and the native elite

who had accepted French civilization. Education would gradually raise the social standard of the masses to the point where, eventually, assimilation might become feasible.

3) Great stress was placed upon a planned *mise en valeur* (economic development) by which the economic potential of each colony would be developed along lines most profitable in each situation. In this way, Sarraut argued, both France's needs and the colonies' development could work to each other's benefit. French destinies, wrote Sarraut, depended on increased production. Colonial and metropolitan action had to dovetail, and the colonies were to become reservoirs of raw materials and emporia for home manufacturers.[5] Instead of the "improvised empiricism" of prewar years, there would be what he called "colonial incorporation," a term that expressed the mutualism and necessity of coöperation between *métropole* and colonies.

Wieschhoff noted another aspect of this stress on economic development. He noted[6] that it was an emphasis

. . . quite characteristic of French colonial policy in general. It is thought that economic penetration along French lines will bring about a progressive association with French social institutions, just as French methods of administration will result in the ultimate introduction of French political institutions. Traditional African institutions have value only insofar as they can be utilized for purposes of administration, or as they may serve the general policy of association. There is no tendency to uphold native political organizations or to modernize such existing political institutions; on the contrary, attempts have been made to abolish them wherever feasible.

The *politique de protectorat* also gave rise to a French version of a policy of "differentiation." This was expressed in an administrative separatism that applied different policies and standards to inhabitants of the colonies depending on the degree to which they had "evolved" toward the French social ideal. In nonofficial terminology and usage, individuals came to be identified as *français* or *européen* (covering any white Frenchman or non-African), *assimilé* ("assimilated," or as close as an African could come to being *européen*), and *évolué* ("evolved," or Africans educated and considerably Gallicized). The terms continue to find currency today, and are often used by Africans themselves, usually without the original connotations of condescension or paternalism. Throughout French Africa, separate legal systems existed to distinguish those Africans assimilated to European law (*citoyens*) from those subject to native custom (*sujets*). *Citoyens* had the civil and political rights of persons of French origin. *Sujets* might become *citoyens* by showing evidence of having become Europeanized through education or employment of a "European character." *Citoyens* were exempt from the obligation of compulsory labor and also from the *régime de l'indigénat* (or disciplinary penalties) which could be summarily administered by an administrative officer.[7]

FRENCH POLITICAL AND ADMINISTRATION INSTITUTIONS

The most significant indices of the nature and strength of the French mandate in the Cameroun were the political and administrative institutions France brought into the territory. These reflected, often unconsciously, the failings of French colonial policy, as well as its successes. They also reflected the distorted image of the mythical "African," in whose name and on whose behalf France claimed to have undertaken her "civilizing mission" in Africa. The image persisted in the Cameroun until the eve of World War II; it was the image held by those who saw the African in the paternalistic light of an earlier epoch, and one that blinded French officialdom to the extent that any rapid advance in the political education of the Camerounians was virtually precluded. This is not to say, however, that French policy and institutions did not undergo considerable change in the period of the mandate. On the contrary, the institutions were constantly being retooled to fit new situations, even if the basic policies underlying them changed much more slowly. In the next several sections we shall observe this differential rate of change operating in several institutional sectors of the Cameroun administration, and including some of the most important institutions: the *Conseils de Notables* (Councils of Notables), the indigenous chieftaincies, and the system of justice and the *indigénat*.

1) *Territorial institutions.* The institutional arrangements that the French brought to the Cameroons differed only slightly from those already in operation in their Equatorial African territories.[8] The chief administrative functions were vested in a civil Commissioner of the Republic, responsible to the Minister of Colonies. The Commissioner, in addition to possessing the administrative and military powers of other French colonial governors, appointed regional administrators, district officers (*chefs de circonscription*), as well as an advisory body, the *Conseil d'Administration* (Administrative Council). This body, composed of important administrative personnel and European *notables*, was consulted by the Commissioner on most important ques-

tions, and especially on those involving budgetary matters, land, taxes, expenditures, and public works. The Commissioner was not, however, required to accept its advice, although he usually did so as a matter of policy. The Council's membership was periodically expanded, but it was not until 1927 that two indigenous *notables* were given seats. By 1945 there were four African Cameroonians on the Council, which also included heads of the various administrative services and two representatives of the chamber of commerce.

In addition to the *Conseil d'Administration,* the administration created Agricultural Commissions concerned with the dissemination of information and advice, and Commissions of Hygiene, charged with duties of inspection in matters of public sanitation and of supervising campaigns against endemic diseases. The Agricultural Commissions, created in 1923, included in each district chiefs and *notables* through whom the Commission worked.

2) *Conseils de Notables.* It has been previously noted that the French administration saw collaboration between itself and the indigenous elite in terms suggesting that political institutions to include native participants would be organized and would function solely to further policies conceived at the highest administrative echelons. The creation and operation of the *Conseils de Notables* is an instructive example of this policy in operation.

In 1923 it was thought advisable to curb the powers of a new ruler in the Moslem town of Ngaoundéré. The sultan of the town was a young man apparently unwilling to coöperate fully with the French. The administration claimed the sultan had misused funds in his trust, was "badly counselled," and hence had to be deposed. It replaced him with a local notable who was to wield his powers in conjunction with a so-called Council of Notables.[9] The administration was not prepared, however, to permit this new Council of Notables to represent anything more than the official French *politique.* Passages from Commissioner Marchand's letter to the Ngaoundéré *chef de circonscription* suggesting the creation of the Council of Notables, are highly revealing in this respect:

I leave you the task, according to these directives, of conceiving and of proposing to me the creation of an organ destined, under your presidency, to examine problems having to do with farming, animal-husbandry, and the improvement of human capital.

It goes without saying that considering the inorganic state of indigenous society, there would be no question of any form, however vague and distant it might appear, of a representative *régime.* You will inform the *notables* chosen as members of this council of the primary principles of the evolution of peoples, such as have been derived from the colonial experience of France. You will generate expressions of opinion based on a knowledge of the *milieu* where the *notables* exercise their influence; you will seek such opinion as will give your directives and your suggestions the force necessary for their success. And you must seek to instill in each [participant], by the consideration with which you listen to the views expressed, a feeling of pride in his share of this modest form of participation in the conduct of public affairs. I rely on your tact, on your care to see that in these matters you will display high regard for human dignity, [as well as] the measured liberalism, appropriately nuanced, that has always characterized our overseas actions, according to the situation and the degree of evolution of the [indigenous] races.[10]

Marchand's strictures are especially interesting as he was dealing with a sophisticated, complex political system dating back to the beginning of the nineteenth century, one in which institutionalized means for resolving the very problems posed by the actions of the young sultan had already existed for more than a hundred years before the French arrived. As a matter of fact, the French did recognize this, but only obliquely. In the language of the annual report to the League of Nations:

Still, it is necessary to say that we find in Ngaoundéré a special situation, in the fact that the dignitaries of the lamidate, already formed into an embryo of Muslim civilization and accustomed to participate in the internal affairs of their group, are better prepared to fulfill the role we wish to assign them than the minor chiefs and notables of the forest region.[11]

By 1925, the administration had apparently overcome its doubts on this matter, and it gave its sanction to the creation of similar Councils of Notables in each district.[12] The new Councils followed the pattern set in Ngaoundéré, though they were to some extent more representative than their prototype. They were composed of between ten and twenty members, including superior, cantonal, and regional chiefs, as well as representatives of each major ethnic group in the district chosen on the basis of one representative per five thousand inhabitants. Appointments were made by the *chef de circonscription* from lists of nominees submitted to him each fall. The lists contained twice as many names as there were to be councilors. According to the rules, members of the councils had to be over thirty years old, possess land and dwellings in the *circonscription,* have visible, acceptable sources of income (*disposant de ressources d'origine bien établie*), and never have been convicted of any criminal act nor have been subject to any correctional punishment imposed either by an official native court (*tribunal des races*) or by a European court. In addition, penalties were assessed for nonattendance of meetings, and any councilor convicted of any criminal offense by a native or European court, or of any offense under the *indigénat*, was subject to dismissal from the Council. The Councils had to be consulted on certain specified matters such as labor levies for public works and head taxation; the agenda was set by the *chef de circonscription*, who presided over meetings of the Council.

In French legal terminology, a duty to consult (i.e., Art. 12 of the *Arrêté* of Oct. 9, "*Le conseil de notables est obligatoirement consulté . . .*") does not also imply an obligation to follow advice given upon such consultation. The Councils, therefore, were in effect completely powerless, having no greater function than criticism and no funds whatever at their disposal. Apart from the chieftaincies and the various functional official commissions, the *Conseils des Notables* long remained the only local political organs in which Africans participated.

It was not until 1949 that any substantial revision of the *Conseils* was made. The *arrêté* of January 28, 1949, enlarged the *Conseils* from thirty to forty members and included representatives of traditional associations, economic societies, local coöperatives, and trade unions. Members of the newly created Territorial Assembly were guaranteed a seat on the *Conseils* of larger administrative units, the *régions*.[13] With the growth of other local administrative structures such as the urban and rural *communes*, the *Conseils de Notables* fell into disuse and remain today only in the northern *départements* where rural *communes* have not yet been instituted. Their unrepresentative character has also changed considerably: they have become more truly consultative organs and considerably more heedful of the local populations and their wishes. This latter change, however, occurred only after World War II, and in the wake of the greater political awareness and the reforms of the *loi-cadre* and similar measures.

3) *The chiefs.* The shift of administrative power away from indigenous authorities, implied by the institution of the *Conseils de Notables*, went hand in hand with a reduction in the power of the indigenous chief, a shift which, in many instances, preceded the creation of the *Conseils*. The slow revision of the chieftaincy system is another excellent example of the French policy which sought, by means of a gradual erosion of the power of indigenous political authority, to introduce a French-created system of local control.

Initially, in 1917, in accordance with the provisions of the 1907 Hague Conventions, the French saw the expediency of continuing the so-called Mixed Courts (*Schiedsgerichte*) that the Germans had instituted in Douala, Edea, and Yaoundé, and hence also recognizing the judicial power of the chiefs. This recognition lasted only until 1922, when a full-scale reorganization of the chieftaincies was undertaken. In 1921 the native courts were suppressed on the grounds of confusion.[14] The judicial powers of the southern chiefs were vested in the official district heads or in official native courts. In the north, in a number of places where the traditional judicial powers of lamidos, sultans, and the like were maintained, the French courts were set up as alternatives in the firm belief that once the natives recognized that they would get better treatment in the official courts, the judicial powers of the traditional chiefs would wither away. Also, certain types of cases were reserved for the courts of the district head; in all, it was expected that the new system would,

. . . by the administering of a more human justice, create in the minds of the natives of these regions a confidence in the European judge, which will make it possible progressively not to destroy the local law, but to lead the natives in search of a jurisdiction which will insure them more guarantees in fact. . . .[15]

The suppression of the judicial powers of the chiefs led to a wholesale reorganization of the chieftaincies themselves. A number of districts were created in which several chiefdoms were grouped under a single appointed *chef de région*.[16] These regional chiefs were chosen by the *chefs de circonscription* "because of their intelligence" and because of their eagerness to serve French authority. The French had few illusions about the realities of the new chieftaincies. The 1922 *Rapport*[17] states quite frankly: "The regional chiefs, a creation of the French administration, have only the authority which is delegated to them; they have no power of their own; they are above all administrative organs."

The chiefs chosen for the new positions were either one of the chiefs of the villages included in the *région*, or, often, simply someone the French felt they could trust. Probably the most notable example of such an artificial chief was Charles Atangana. He was an interpreter who had first served in the German administration as an instructor of Beti at government schools in Hamburg and Berlin; later, during the war, he was a second lieutenant in the German army. In 1912, in recognition of his services, the Germans made him chief of the

Yaoundé (Ewondo) people. At the conclusion of the Cameroons campaign, Atangana was interned in Rio Muni along with the remaining German forces. He then asked the French to be allowed to return, a request that was granted. The French thereupon not only reinstated him in his former position in Yaoundé, but also extended his authority to include the Bané tribe, which is related to the Beti-Yaoundé.[18] Atangana died in 1943, at sixty, still chief of the Ewondo and Bané. A statue was erected in his honor in Yaoundé in May, 1959, and he was eulogized by both the mayor of Yaoundé and the prime minister, M. Ahidjo.[19]

A *cause célèbre*, involving the use of artificial chiefs, was the deposition of Sultan Njoya of Bamun, in 1931. Njoya, through a combination of ruthlessness, cunning, intelligence, and political savoir faire, had managed to maintain his throne through German, British, and then French administrations. A man of remarkable intellectual abilities,[20] he had retained his traditional prerogatives by making himself indispensable to successive colonial regimes. Even the French were reluctant at first to disturb his position. It was not long, however, until Njoya's near-sovereignty came into conflict with the role the French administration wished to assign to traditional chiefs. In 1924, the government created a number of local chieftaincies in Bamoun whose incumbents were to be responsible directly to the administration rather than to Njoya. Njoya sought to avert further incursions on his powers by trying to provoke a rebellion against the new regime. The administration retaliated by cutting him off from his traditional tribute moneys and putting him on an annual official *allocation*. Njoya and the administration feuded for six years; the unequal struggle ended with Njoya's deposition by Commissioner Marchand himself in 1931. The sultan was exiled to Yaoundé, but, like the Sultan of Ngaoundéré, continued to draw an annual pension (24,000 francs). Njoya died in exile in 1933 and his son, more amenable than his father, succeeded to the throne.[21]

What is instructive about *l'affaire Njoya* is the means employed by the government in its attempt to make the sultan into what Marchand termed a "nominal sovereign." In the Atangana case, a chief was created where only the most tenuous legitimacy could be offered for his presence. In Bamoun, the administration brushed aside considerations of legitimacy; it simply created alternate chieftaincies, withdrew financial support from the sultan, and waited for him to topple. When he did not do so, it removed him and replaced him with a "first degree" chief of its own choosing. It appeared almost coincidental that the new sultan could also claim traditional legitimacy.

The French recognized early that chiefs appointed under the new regime would not be respected unless they were accepted by the people over whom they were to rule; official credentials were not enough. The principle that local opinion should be consulted before appointments were made was formally recognized in the Cameroons in 1928,[22] and in 1932 a model *arrêté* laid down that *chefs de village* (the lowest echelon of chiefs) should be chosen by heads of families by majority vote.[23]

Subsequent modifications of the 1922 statute created several types of chiefs and arranged them hierarchically according to importance. By the end of the mandate period three "degrees" of chiefs had been recognized:[24]

"First degree" chiefs: *lamibé* (plural of lamido), sultans, and *chefs supérieurs,* all presumed successors (under French direction) of feudal chiefs of the former days.

"Second degree" chiefs: chiefs of so-called *groupements* and *cantons* (both designations artificially made for administrative convenience, sometimes disregarding traditional lines of demarcation), and *laouanes.* These latter were a sort of assistant chief to a lamido; the institution had died out during the German occupation, but was revived by the French to insure greater administrative control. *Laouanes* were appointed by the *lamibé,* with the concurrence of the *chefs de circonscription.*

"Third degree" chiefs: village chiefs and *chefs de quartier* (chiefs-designate, usually with popular approval, of the separate ethnic "quarters" in the larger towns and cities).

The method of paying indigenous chiefs also demonstrated the function they were expected to play in the administrative scheme of things. Initially, chiefs on most levels were not paid salaries, but received a percentage rebate or *remise* on collected taxes. Lower-echelon chiefs did the collecting themselves; higher-level ones had emissaries or the lower-level chiefs to do it for them. All received their percentage: for example, in 1938, in northern areas, *laouanes* kept 5 per cent of taxes they collected, and the lamidos kept 3 per cent of the gross taken by their several *laouanes.* The rebates amounted to large sums. In 1938, the Lamido of Maroua (one of the best paid in the country, who had the distinct advantage of drawing taxes from the densely populated Kirdi settlements in the so-called duckbill area) earned 25,252 francs by these means.[25] Buell reports[26] that in 1926 there were four exceptions to this system, who were paid regular indemnities, or *allocations:* Charles Atangana, the Sultan of Bamoun (Idrissou Njoya), a "deported lamido" (probably the Lamido of Ngaoundéré, of whom mention has been made), and a number of Kirdi chiefs (including Bamiléké and northern chiefs).[27]

As the institution of the chieftaincy evolved, other local administrative institutions made their appearance. A new stage in municipal administration was begun in 1941 with the creation of two so-called *communes mixtes urbaines.* Douala and Yaoundé were the pilot cities chosen for the new system; a municipal administration was created, to be headed by an Administrator-Mayor, assisted by a *commission municipale.* Both mayors and councils, however, were to be appointed by the High Commissioner. By the end of the mandate period plans were already being made to convert the appointed municipal councils into freely elected ones.[28]

In sum, then, by 1947 local administration had evolved into a quasi-direct system of institutions and practices. On the one hand, key appointive and veto powers were still in the hands of the French administration, at whose apex sat the High Commissioner of the Cameroun, responsible to the *Ministère des Colonies.* The seventeen *régions* were administered by *chefs de région* (almost wholly professional French colonial administrators), with the assistance of the *Conseils de Notables* appointed by them. Some forty-six *subdivisions* were administered either by French colonial administrators or by French-trained Camerounians. In many localities, the traditional chiefs acted as administrators, responsible only to the *chefs de région* and the High Commissioner. Usually village and *quartier* chiefs were responsible for the management of affairs in their jurisdictions but they were nonetheless answerable to the *subdivision* or *région* administrators. However, many of them, especially those in the north and west, continued to wield considerable, and frequently powerful, influence over affairs at the local level. The Bamiléké chiefs are one example of traditional chiefs who retained much of their former powers, despite French attempts to curtail them. The selection of the *Conseils de Notables* was liberalized to cater to a wider spectrum of local interests, and a recognition of local sentiment went into the selection of both councils and traditional rulers. African representation was guaranteed on the Agricultural and Public Health Councils as well as on the newly created (1942) Advisory Councils for Economic and Social Affairs.

THE COURTS, THE INDIGÉNAT, AND THE LEGAL
SYSTEM

Until the enactment of the constitution of 1946,
throughout French Africa a distinction was made between persons
subject to native custom (*sujets*) and those assimilated to European
law (*citoyens*). The latter had civil and political rights identical with
persons of French origin. As noted, the differentiation was made on
the basis of varying standards of achievement toward the French cultural ideal. At the very least, it involved knowledge of the French
language, acceptance of French law (which involved a rejection of
such practices as polygamy plus a willingness to serve in the French
army), and the practice of some "civilized" profession. It is, however,
in the *indigénat*, the system of summary disciplinary punishment from
which *citoyens* were exempt, that the practical distinctions between
the two types of status become most apparent.

When it was introduced into the Cameroons, the *indigénat* was already in effect in French West and Equatorial Africa. The official
reasoning behind the move to extend the system to the new mandate
can be found in an interesting cover letter to the decree establishing
the *indigénat* in the Cameroun.[29] The Minister of Colonies Daladier
thus wrote to President of the Republic Doumergue:

Paris, the 8th August 1924

Monsieur le President,

The Order of the Chancellor of the Empire, dated April 1896, regulated
(in the Cameroons under German domination) the application of disciplinary
punishment to the natives: the stipulated penalties were imprisonment in
irons for a period of fourteen days and the cudgel or whip up to the limit
of twenty or twenty-five blows, respectively.

Since 14 May 1916, the Commissioner of the Government in the occupied
territories of the Cameroun has substituted for the penalties imposed by the
German laws penalties more in conformity with our principles of civilization: simple imprisonment or a fine. . . .

Despite certain similarities, the indigenous races which populate the
Cameroun present certain apparent differences from those of French
Equatorial Africa: their social and moral level seems, on the whole, to be
higher.

It appears, under these conditions, that it is of interest to regulate (by a
special decree) this important question and suggest [for adoption] the text
already proposed for the Territory of Togo. . . .

The decree itself[30] (to which reference will hereafter be made by

Article) exempted not only *citoyens* from its application, but also the following types of *indigènes:*

(Art. 4) 1. *Indigènes* who served in the [French] colonial forces, including their wives and children.

2. *Chefs de région.*

3. Indigenous agents of the administration receiving fixed salaries.

4. Indigenous members of deliberative or consultative assemblies.

5. Assessors serving on Native Tribunals.

6. *Indigènes* who have been decorated either with the Legion of Honor or the Medaille Militaire.

The exemptions did not put those involved on the same level with *citoyens;* the former might still be subject to the penalties if the Commissioner thought it proper (Art. 5). They might also be subject to the extraordinary penalties ("internment" for ten years or more, sequestration of property, collective fines) that the Commissioner might impose in instances where public security was menaced by insurrection or "grave political troubles" (Arts. 21, 22, 23). It is of further interest to note some of those besides *citoyens* who were not included in the list of exemptions: village chiefs, *chefs de quartier,* a wide variety of northern Kirdi and Muslim chiefs who were not *chefs de région* nor receiving salaries from the administration, or members of the *Conseils de Notables.* The French view (at least initially) of what constituted the elite seems to have been somewhat narrow.

The penalties prescribed by the decree, imprisonment up to fifteen days or fines up to 100 francs, or both (Art. 18), were not in themselves excessive. What was extraordinary was the variety and nature of the acts that constituted violations under the decree.[31] A full list will be found in Appendix C; a few of the violations were:

Acts of disorder.

Organizing a game of chance.

Circulating rumors of a nature to disturb the public peace.

Giving aid to malefactors, agitators, vagabonds, natives who have fled their village, and to all persons wanted by the administration.

Hindering traffic on public highways, routes.

Vagabondage.

Practice of sorcery when consequences do not lead to a court appearance.

Reluctance in paying taxes.

Attempts to simulate or aggravate natural ills or wounds in order to be dismissed from a public work project.

Allowing dangerous animals or animal nuisances to stray, or allowing domestic animals to stray onto another's property.

Administration of the *indigénat* fell directly upon the *chefs de circonscription* and *chefs de subdivision* (Art. 2). Appeal was possible from decisions under the *indigénat* up to the Commissioner himself; he might change a sentence imposed by a *chef de circonscription* or *subdivision,* and *chefs de circonsription* were given powers of review over the decisions of the *chefs de subdivision* within their jurisdiction (Arts. 10, 20).

The *indigénat* was roundly condemned by the French administrators attending the Brazzaville conference in 1944. As a consequence of this and attacks on it made elsewhere in French Africa, it was abolished in 1945 and 1946 in the various French territories.[32] The obvious defect of the system lay in its arbitrariness; any colonial administrator might inflict summary, extrajudicial punishment for a list of offenses vaguely defined and poorly differentiated. It placed what was often unnecessarily broad discretionary powers in the hands of minor officials, who were often too far from their superiors to heed the guarantees of review. The *indigénat* was used in the Cameroons to punish natives who failed to cultivate their gardens or work on the railway, who failed to pay their taxes within three months of its levy,[33] who failed to take off their caps in the presence of the local administrator, who spat on the floor of a government office, who had not kept an appointment with the local *chef de subdivision,* who had come late to work on a works project, and so on.[34] Of the Camerounians who recalled prewar days, and with whom I spoke, there were few who did not speak of the *indigénat* with some bitterness.

The system of dual legal status that made the *indigénat* possible found further expression in the courts and the legal system in general. Until the reforms following the Brazzaville conference eliminated the *indigénat* and clarified the legal status of the various peoples under French control, *citoyens* and *sujets* were subject to two entirely different systems of courts and laws. The system of *justice de droit français* was applied through a system of courts resembling as closely as possible those in metropolitan France.[35] For *citoyens* in the Cameroun (as in French Equatorial Africa) the full set of metropolitan codes (civil, commercial, penal, and *instruction criminelle*) were applicable. A *Parquet du Procureur de la République* performed the usual prosecutory functions, as well as handling official representation before the French courts in the territory. An Appeals Council heard appeals from the Court of First Instance (a civil court) and from the civil side of the various Justice of the Peace courts. The Criminal Court heard most criminal matters arising in Douala or Yaoundé, and criminal appeals from the Justice courts.

The system of *justice indigène,* created in the Cameroun by the decree of April 23, 1921, was administered by a *tribunal de races,* one or more of which was usually found in each administrative district and was presided over by the European administrator.[36] The administrator was assisted by native assessors chosen from a list of *notables* or chiefs designated annually by the Commissioner of the Republic. The assessors had a "deliberative" vote on civil matters, but merely an advisory vote in criminal matters. The assessors' opinions were entered in the record, and their judgment could not be challenged (save, presumably, by the administrator in charge). These tribunals, which had jurisdiction over all Camerounian *sujets,* followed procedure prescribed by local custom and "applied customary laws so long as they do not conflict with the principle of French civilization."[37]

In instances where native custom decreed excessive or cruel punishment, the administrator could impose whatever penalty he felt the crime merited.[38] The difficulty with this situation was that there existed no statutory limitations on the imposition of such ad hoc punishment. The sole check on the judicial powers of the administrators lay with the Court of Homologation in Douala, which could only pass on the record, and then only in cases in which the penalty imposed was for more than three years' imprisonment. The *Procureur Général* might ask the Court to set aside or decrease a sentence given below. In fact, an examination of the reports to the League of Nations shows that the Court of Homologation set aside or modified a considerable number of criminal judgments between 1923 and 1938. There is evidence that the authorities kept some check on abuses of the administrators' judicial discretion. In balance, the most serious defect in the system lay, of course, in the *indigénat* and the broad disciplinary powers it conferred on French and French-trained native administrators.

The system engendered considerable antagonism in the territory, and made the judicial work of the regular native courts that much more difficult to perform. In addition to the *indigénat*, Buell points out that the procedure of extrajudicial conciliation in civil matters (by a European official or native assessor), which was recommended by the regulations on native justice, broke down because of the overload of judicial business before the courts and administrators, and because of the tendency of indigenous assessors to abuse their powers. Furthermore, the almost total reliance of European administrators upon native interpreters created situations in which the interpreters often willfully used the courts for their own purposes. Sometimes they even prevented cases from appearing before the administrators. Buell claims that, in the Yaoundé district, most of the interpreters were in the secret employ of the chief, Charles Atangana, and were consequently in a position to prevent anyone from complaining to the administrator against Atangana's exactions.[39] The story does not appear exaggerated in view of the record and of Atangana's general reputation.[40]

The judicial reforms introduced by the decree of July 31, 1927,[41] modified the form of the system, but not much of the spirit. It did, however, provide for increased participation by chiefs and notables on all levels. Local chiefs were given the power of "conciliation" in civil matters, and were encouraged to persuade litigants to settle their disputes before taking them to court. Buell notes that under the old system of conciliation as administered by native assessors these officials settled most of the innumerable civil disputes that arose.[42] It is probable that, by giving the power of conciliation to the chiefs, the French tacitly recognized that they were exercising judicial power anyway and that little could be done to prevent it. If conciliation failed, civil matters were heard by the *Tribunaux du Premier Degré* (local courts), which also exercised original jurisdiction in minor criminal matters. As many of these courts might be created in a *subdivision* as there were separate ethnic groups or as the need indicated; they were presided over by *chefs de subdivision* and two native assessors with "deliberative" votes.

Appeals in both civil and criminal matters might be taken from these courts to the *Tribunaux du Second Degré* (regional courts). These courts were established in the principal town of each *subdivision* and *circonscription* (later *région*). They were presided over by the *chef de subdivision* or *circonscription* in which they were located, and operated with the assistance of two native assessors with "consultative" (advisory) votes. The regional courts had original jurisdiction over a list of criminal acts that included most matters considered *crimes* under French law (the approximate equivalent of the Anglo-Saxon felony), such as murder, rape, robbery, arson, and maiming, as well as cannibalism, slavery, group pillage, and crimes committed by native officials or agents of the administration.

The structure was capped by the old *Chambre d'Homologation* presided over by a professional French judge (president of the highest French law court) and two assessors chosen by the Commissioner of the Republic upon recommendation of the *Procureur Général*. One assessor was a European, the other an African. The court reviewed the record only, and could recommend revision or annulment after so doing. With very few minor changes this system remained in force until World War II.

It is clear that the three institutions discussed above were functional to the basic *politique de protectorat,* only thinly veiled as a *politique d'association.* In each case, the administration tried to utilize existing traditional institutions, but only insofar as basic policy objectives in each situation might be attained. The *Conseils de Notables* used one of the oldest traditional institutions in Africa, the village or clan council, and transformed it into a ratificatory body which could be used to give the added weight of tradition to policies made not in the council, but by the administration. If the institution proved educational as well, and taught local *notables* some degree of responsibility in administrative matters, so much the better; basically, however, it was created and used as an instrument of the European administration. This was even truer with the chieftaincies, whose titular holders very often ruled under a legitimacy conferred by the administration rather than by tradition. So also with the legal system, which used customary law as an administrative weapon and created distinctions that permitted and encouraged differential treatment of Africans according to a cultural rather than a legal yardstick.

FORCED LABOR AND THE MANDATE

If French policies and administrative institutions created anti-French bias in many parts of the Cameroons, the widespread use of forced labor to effect certain aspects of the *mise-en-valeur* generated a similar ill-will among the rural populations in particular. The French used *corvée,* or forced labor, most extensively in the Cameroun during the early years of their administration when major railway and road projects were undertaken, such as the extension of the Douala-Yaoundé rail line (the old German Mittelbahn), the construction of a number of main trunk roads linking principal urban centers in the south, and the building of the main roads linking the south with the towns of the north. The animus created among a number of southern tribes toward the French administration persisted long after forced labor had been abolished and tended to make suspect the introduction of the rural commune system. Even after that, a general suspicion of French motives usually accompanied the initiation of public works projects and hampered the recruitment of labor for them.

The Germans had little hesitation in using forced labor to construct roads, railways, and other public projects. Under their administration, taxation had been limited to the imposition of a labor tax which was restricted to thirty days in the year and commutable into cash.[43] In only two localities did the Germans waive the labor tax and substitute a form of income tax.[44]

Under the French mandate, Camerounian Africans became subject to obligations similar to those of the inhabitants of other French territories in Africa. The French abolished the German labor tax, contending that it was "scarcely humane" and in "fundamental conflict" with French institutions.[45] In its place, they instituted a head tax system, whose rate might vary according to district, but which was the same for all taxable individuals within it. The tax was imposed on all men and women and, in two northern districts, on children over twelve.[46] The tax on women, unknown during the German administration, was met with open hostility by the women in some parts of the territory.[47]

In addition to the capitation tax, the French administration imposed upon Camerounians of *sujet* status the so-called *prestation,* a form of compulsory labor obligation which the French denied was in any way a continuation of the German system. Raymond Buell, who visited the Cameroun during the late 1920's concluded that the prestation system was, however, "practically the same as the German labor tax."[48] When one considers the details of the system, it is not difficult to agree with Buell.[49] All males were obligated to furnish the government with ten days of free labor a year. After ten days, if they remained on the job, they were paid a minimal fixed rate set at so much per kilometer of road or track finished. Commutation of the prestation was possible at the rate of two francs per day of labor, although the administration admitted that such was rarely allowed, and then only as a "special favour" as it "preferred the natives to carry out their forced labour in person."[50] Initially, recruitment was done through the local chiefs, but when these began to use their powers to recruit free labor for their own or private purposes, the administration (in 1930) gave the task to government administrators.

Criticism of the French system of forced labor in general and the situation in the Cameroons in particular took two main forms, one legal and the other humanitarian. At first, critics of forced labor found nothing to attack in the system itself; indeed, it was a common feature of colonial administration and existed to some degree in all the African mandates.[51] Some critics pointed out that the original terms of the French mandate for the Cameroons stipulated that "the mandatory power . . . shall prohibit all forms of forced labor or compulsory labor except for essential public works and services, and then only for adequate remuneration."[52] The French system, they noted, provided no pay for the first ten days of the period of servitude, and consequently violated the terms of the mandate agreement. The French complained that a literal compliance with the provision in the agreement was not possible, as they were forced to undertake large-scale projects with only the limited funds provided by the territorial budget.[53] However, in 1925, by instituting a commutation of two francs for each day worked, the administration attempted to satisfy its critics on this point.[54] The move satisfied few critics because (as was noted) the commutation was permitted only rarely, and then as a special privilege.

In the meantime, many instances of maladministration in the system and of wholesale abuse of the workers themselves had begun to attract attention, The French representative to the Permanent Mandates Commission stated in 1924 what was virtually to become a model for subsequent French defenses of the system:

It was very unpleasant for the government authorities to have to say that they have recourse to forced labor, but the labor was needed for public works, the non-execution of which would have been detrimental to the prosperity of the country. It was only in the case of such works that recourse was had to compulsory labor. Wages were not paid the first ten days, but at the end of this period the workmen were paid at the same rate as free workmen. The natives worked very little for other people, even if paid. As soon as they had acquired the taste for work and for remuneration, compulsory labor would disappear even for public works.[55]

According to this position, it was necessary to force the Camerounians to work for their own good. It would, consequently, be necessary to overcome an understandable reluctance by efficient methods of recruitment. Initially, traditional chiefs were given the task of local recruitment, and were in fact, in the case of compulsory road work, paid a lump sum for the work done. As late as 1931, in a report to the German newspaper *Kölnische Volkszeitung*, Catholic missionaries claimed that forced labor had assumed revolting proportions in the Cameroons, recruiting sometimes taking the form of manhunting. Natives would be captured in their cabins during the night, and, when brought to the workshops, would be badly fed, housed, and generally mistreated. Questioned on these and other charges, the French administration, significantly, avoided the issue, contending that the statements were "either pointless or made far too late." The administration admitted that some native chiefs had indulged in bad practices, but added that when they had been caught they had been punished.[56]

Buell charged that, in addition to permitting abuses in the conscription of *prestation* and compulsory labor, many chiefs used their power to conscript labor for their own plantations, which the French had encouraged them to develop, and of which a sizable number had been started, especially around Yaoundé. One chief, reported Buell, had a cocoa plantation of eighteen thousand trees; another had a rubber plantation of twenty-six thousand trees. Charles Atangana planted over four hundred hectares (988 acres) of land. Buell, who visited Yaoundé in 1925, claimed that Atangana had

. . . about two hundred police, each wearing a badge with his initials, who roam the country, and according to dozens of complaints, forcefully oblige natives in the villages to come and work on Atangana's plantations. In some cases these police tell them they are being taken for the government. Natives thus captured are obliged to work without pay until they can escape; and in some cases, they are obliged to have their food brought to them from their homes.[57]

Buell noted that, in a case before Yaoundé court, the Bané people complained that Atangana's men, through the subordinate chiefs, demanded twice the number of men from the villages as the government had requisitioned. They claimed the excess were used on Atangana's plantations.[58] According to Buell, and to testimony before the Permanent Mandates Commission, these practices were widespread in the southern part of the territory, except in the Douala area. Buell thought that, because the government was so dependent on the food and labor furnished by the important chiefs, it was "difficult for it to inquire too closely into abuses which the big fellows commit."[59]

Buell's revelations and the large number of complaints received by the Permanent Mandates Commission prompted that body to undertake an investigation into some of the charges made by Buell. It agreed substantially with him and suggested the French administration do something about the abuses by the chiefs.[60] The French, through Commissioner Marchand, contended that Buell's work was full of errors and mistatements but they did not attempt to refute them. "That Chiefs should employ natives for their own profit," admitted Marchand, "was sometimes so habitual that the Administration could only note the fact with a view to taking energetic sanctions."[61] Some of the most flagrant instances of such abuse were later remedied, but the frequency of complaints, even after 1930, indicated that the government either found such practices difficult to abate or failed to stop other violations of a like nature.

Working conditions on the various government projects came in for even greater criticism. The most widely publicized project, and the one at which most criticism was directed, was that involving the extension of the Midlands Railway (the old German Mittelbahn) from Njock (the farthest point of German construction) to Makak and Yaoundé, a distance of 133 kilometers. The line was to pass through an extremely unhealthy forest region that was humid, insect infested, and practi-

cally devoid of population. Buell pointed out that, as the administration had paid "inadequate attention" to the problem of maintaining
proper health conditions on the project, and that, as a result of the
lack of proper medical attendance, "the death and mortality rates
[*sic*] became excessive. . . . Even today the word 'Njock'—the center of
railway construction during this period—connotes to the natives a form
of servitude from which death is the most probable form of escape."[62]
The French reports between 1922 and 1926 gave the impression that
the death rate on the project was quite low. An analysis of the figures
and the percentages given led both Buell and members of the Permanent Mandates Commission to estimate mortality rates at a scale
considerably above that given or implied by the French administration.
In 1925, for example, Buell noted that the report stated that the death
rate was 0.51 per cent or 5.1 per thousand, although his investigations
showed the actual rate to have been 61.7 per thousand.[63] Commissioner
Marchand revised the 1925 estimate to 0.71 per cent, but Mr. Grimshaw
of the Permanent Mandates Commission estimated the figure to be
between 50 and 60 per thousand.[64] Similar differences occur for each
of the other years.

It was not surprising that the death rate was so high. Some six
thousand workers, of which only 25 per cent (at best) were voluntary,
put in a fifty-hour week under the most extreme climatic conditions,
were given little opportunity for diversion, and, in an area infested
with malarial mosquitoes and tse tse flies, were provided with only a
single doctor for all their medical needs. African overseers often mistreated the men under them, and flogging was not rare.

Evidence of the ill-repute in which the rail projects were held was
given by the widespread attempts to emigrate to other countries during
the period of the main construction. Buell reported migrations of large
numbers of Africans from the French Cameroun into the British
Cameroons, while still others went into the French Gabon, to Spanish
Rio Muni, or to Fernando Po.[65] To counteract this, the administration
put a number of curbs on movement out of and within the territory.
The Decree of July 9, 1925, forbade Africans to leave the country except upon personal authorization from the Commissioner of the Republic or the authorized district head, and upon payment of a bond
of 500 francs which was to be reimbursed upon return. In addition, a
special passport was required, for which the recipients paid twenty-
five francs.[66]

Questioned on the large-scale exodus of Africans from tribes usually
tapped for conscript labor, the French denied that the migrations were
in any way related to labor conscription. The Camerounian Africans,

contended the administration, had a taste for a wandering life, and the emigration bond was an attempt to attach them to the soil.[67] Again, defending the policy of completely forbidding women to leave or enter the territory, the administration claimed the curbs were necessary to prevent the illegal traffic in women.[68]

There is little question but that the restrictions were designed to create a stable labor market where none existed, as well as to maintain the supply of *prestation* and compulsory labor. As late as 1936, administrators in the territory were urged to forbid Africans to leave their home administrative areas if they had signed a labor contract with a European employer or were seeking employment on native plantations.[69] Several voluntary labor exchanges were set up, but the administration continued to maintain that it was "undesirable to shift labor about the territory."[70]

In all, conditions were such that much outside pressure was put on the administration to do something about them. In any event, the situation seemed not to have been as idyllic as the French government represented to the Permanent Mandates Commission: "The railway was being constructed by workers who did not complain at all of their conditions and who, in the majority of cases, returned to their villages not only in good health, but usually much better off [than before]."[71]

As a result of the pressures exerted by the Permanent Mandates Commission and public opinion in France, Great Britain, and the United States, the French administration ameliorated conditions on the works projects after 1927. Additional medical personnel and facilities were provided, recruitment practices were sharply revised, and the workers' wages, housing, and food were considerably improved. Commissioner Marchand was able to report in 1931 that working conditions on a proposed rail line to the north would be much better than those that had prevailed on earlier projects. New workers ("very active and in need of wages"—probably Bamiléké) were becoming available from the east, and they would work under excellent conditions and in plateau country. Labor requisitions would be avoided as much as possible, and the cost per kilometer would be more than double that of the 1921-1926 project. The higher cost would permit not only a raise in rations, but pay at three times the former rate. In addition, a loan of seventeen million francs from the *métropole* had been received to improve health conditions, especially to fight the widespread sleeping sickness.[72] The construction project never got started, however, because of the difficult economic situation caused by the depression.

Despite the improvements in the labor situation after 1930,[73] the memory of the former exactions continued to rankle with the rural populations. An illuminating insight into this situation was provided by Margery Perham, a visitor to the Cameroun in 1933:

The country was still full of grim stories of the extension of the railway through the unhealthy forest region to Yaoundé. The able and humane governor who just retired, Mr. Marchand, remedied these conditions, but memory dies hard. While I was in the Cameroons, at the mere rumour of further construction, a tribe much valued as "labor" was dancing the gestures of shovelling earth, with the song, "How many of us will be taken for railway work?", and the counter-question, "How many of us will come back?"[74]

The French continued to employ *corvée* labor during the 1930's but on a lesser scale. Instances were reported of the use of women for porterage, children for road work. Complaints were frequently made that administrators paid too little attention to the welfare of laborers entrusted to their care. The system of forced labor did not go completely out of existence until 1952, when the Labor Code for Overseas Territories plugged the loopholes in Act No. 46-645 of April 11, 1946, the latter statute itself in execution of the International Forced Labor Convention of 1946. In a larger sense, it was the termination of the system of the *indigénat* and the practice of differentiating between *citoyens* and *sujets* that spelled the end of forced labor in the French territories and the Cameroun. With the disappearance of artificial distinctions that maintained the majority of French Africans in a position of legal inferiority, it became indefensible to force anyone to work against his will. The old system, however, continued to color relations between the French and the indigenous elites in areas where former exactions had been heaviest.

CONCLUSIONS

The total picture of French administrative institutions during the interwar period shows them to have been admirably suited for the role for which they were designed, that is, for the *politique de protectorat* in which association rather than assimilation was the key element. The system as a whole gave a measure of participation to the African Camerounian, but also maintained the political, if not the cultural, gap between French and *assimilés* on the one hand, and the *indigènes sujet* on the other. It was based, fundamentally, on the notion that the education of the *indigène* toward the French ideal was and would be a slow process and that institutions must therefore measure and pace that growth. The published reports, especially the earlier ones during the twenties, abound with references to the need for gradual change, to the difficulties encountered in guiding the *indigène* to French civilization. Commissioner Marchand, in a statement before the Permanent Mandates Commission in 1929,[75] epitomized this view:

Important progress had been made in the Territory along various lines in the course of the last three years, but M. Marchand did not think it had been so great as to deserve special attention. *It was not,* moreover, *the wish of the local Administration that too rapid progress should be made;* it wished to prevent any disturbance of balance in the organization of the native tribes, which were still backward, and whose evolution should proceed steadily and reasonably. [Italics mine.]

The statement speaks for itself; the shortsightedness of this position can be measured by the speed with which both official and popular French attitudes changed during and after World War II. The flaw in the French position was not that change was undesirable—indeed, progress was desired and awaited—but that it was assumed that political progress could be controlled, paced to suit the rate of cultural and economic progress. France failed to understand that political wants are as insatiable as economic and social needs, and that the former cannot be regulated by simply satisfying the latter.

B. EARLY POLITICAL DEVELOPMENTS IN THE FRENCH CAMEROUN

Opposition to the French administration during the interwar period seems to have been directed mostly at the system of the *indigénat,* with the semiautocratic administrative and judicial powers it gave to local *administrateurs;* at the *prestation;* and at the suppression of the native courts and the emasculation of the powers of the traditional chiefs. These matters called forth indignation and anger among many Camerounians. The opposition manifested was usually individual, or if collective, was expressed in largely undifferentiated, unorganized ways. Thomas Hodgkin has perceptively pointed out that, as a consequence of the *indigénat* and the restrictions it imposed upon African political organization, there were few channels during this period through which a developing public opinion could express itself.[1] For the most part, therefore, political activity in the Cameroons was desultory between the wars. When it did occur on any organized scale, it centered about Douala, and usually raised issues whose ramifications involved few people beyond the Douala area.

One such situation involved the United Native Church, the successor to both the German Baptist mission and the native branch of Alfred Saker's English Baptist mission. When the German Baptist mission withdrew, it left its work with one Lotin Samé, head of the Native Baptist

Church. During World War I, Lotin Samé effected a fusion between the two Baptist organizations to form the United Native Church. After the war French missionaries reëstablished a measure of European control in the United Native Church, and in 1922 secured Samé's expulsion on the grounds of unconventional attitudes to polygamy and politics. It was charged that he baptized polygamists, meddled in politics, refused to obey European missionaries, and had engaged in trade to the detriment of his religious duties. Lotin Samé's expulsion split the church, and dissident congregations openly protested the move.

Buell reported that, in the months following Samé's expulsion, battles arose over the possession of certain church buildings. Spurred on by a visiting Garveyite sailor, Lotin Samé's followers took to the streets of Douala to demand the return of their leader. The sailor in question, according to Buell, had come to Douala in May, 1921, had spoken to many leaders of the church, and had promised that Marcus Garvey's Black Star Line would help the blacks in their fight against the whites. During 1922 and 1923, the whole town of Douala seethed with this religious "revolt," in which Samé's followers paraded up and down the street singing anti-European hymns.[2] Hodgkin provides a translation for one of the hymns quoted by Buell:

This is what our life is like here below; why bewail our lot? The Germans have left; the French have come in their place. They in their turn will go; if the English or Americans come in their place, it will be just the same, until the day we have our freedom. Meanwhile, take my corpse; throw it in the grave; liberty is on its way; in spite of all, sing Alleluia![3]

Pressure from the administration forced the elders of the church to capitulate; the church lost its independence and returned to European control in May, 1923. Lotin Samé was prohibited from preaching, but, on request from his followers, was permitted to return to his pulpit on condition that his sermons remain clear of racialist doctrine.

The agitation caused by Lotin Samé flared up briefly during the early years of the mandate period; it was virtually forgotten by 1930 (except in religious circles). Of longer duration was the situation and series of demands having to do with the desire of the Douala chiefs to recover the lands taken from them by the Germans in 1909. The Douala chiefs, their representatives, and those who pretended to speak for them, maintained a steady stream of petitions to the League of Nations and the French administration, instigated protest meetings, wrote memoranda to all who would listen, and in general continued to press their cause well into the mid-1930's. Originally, the gist of the protest was against French maintenance of the German expropriations; however, as the Douala chiefs were gradually relieved of their traditional powers under the new regime, the matter became less a demand for redress of injury and more a general attack on the French administration. The political experience gained by the Douala spokesmen during this period later enabled them to take the lead in forming political groups with broader programs and wider clienteles. In a very real sense the Douala were the first politically minded Camerounians. Their superior education and knowledge of European ways enabled them to organize for action and to focus their discontent much more effectively than their less sophisticated brethren elsewhere in the territory.

It will be recalled that in 1909 the German government decided to move the four native villages in the Douala area (Bell, Akwa, Deido, Mbassa) away from the water front to new sites several miles into the interior, and that they built a model European city upon the land thus vacated. The Germans offered to reimburse the Douala at a rate of 90 pfennigs a square meter (the estimated price of land when the protectorate was established) and to build model villages an hour and a half's walk from the river's edge. One such village, New Bell, was in fact constructed. However, the Douala refused to sell at less than three marks a square meter, a price the administration refused to accept as it contended the increased value was owing to European activity. The Douala claimed they had already given up their middleman position vis-à-vis trade in the interior, and that hence they wished to keep their villages where they were. The chiefs retained a German attorney to represent their interests in Germany, and petitioned the Reichstag for redress.

The Reichstag, fearing scandal, pressed the government to send a commission of inquiry to Douala. The investigation came to naught for two reasons: the imminence of war in Europe, and the local administration, which, claiming that Bell had plotted with Germany's enemies, had him hanged along with two of his lieutenants. With Bell out of the way, the administration forcibly expropriated the inhabitants of the Joss Plateau and moved them into New Bell. Its plans to move the other three villages were thwarted by the outbreak of the war, and in 1914 General Dobell's expeditionary forces occupied the contested Joss Plateau.

The matter did not remain long without being reopened. In 1918 the Douala chieftains drew up a memorandum on the whole subject of administration in the Cameroons, including the expropriation of the

Joss Plateau, which they attempted to have brought before the Paris Peace Conference. The memorandum never reached Paris owing to the intervention of the French authorities.[4]

The French government took the position that it was not legally liable for the debts the German Empire incurred in the Cameroun. It considered the matter settled, and maintained that inasmuch as the expropriated lands had become imperial lands by virtue of the fact of expropriation, the present administration received the lands as "the exclusive property of the Domain."[5] It offered, however, since the Germans had not indemnified the dispossessed Douala, to pay the so-called proprietors according to the rate set by the Germans. Further, it agreed that in the event it did not use all the land in question, the remainder would be sold and the proceeds used toward the construction of houses for the dispossessed.

After much fruitless negotiation, the Douala held a public meeting in 1926 and rejected the French offer. In their turn they declared their willingness to give the government what land it needed for public buildings, to forego living on the plateau, and to lease what was left to the government or to private persons. But they insisted that the land remain their property, and that they have complete control over any leasing arrangements. The administration replied with an offer for a mass indemnification, and appropriated some half-million francs for the purpose. An agreement which ostensibly resolved the issue was signed by "representative" Douala late in 1926. The signers agreed to accept the money and to relinquish their claims on the land.[6]

The "agreement" seemed not, however, to have settled anything. Very few Douala came forth to claim the indemnity, and only 40 of 330 claimants to land on the Joss Plateau applied for free plots on the Bali plateau, which the government had made available for those previously dispossessed. Some Douala at first signed for the free land, then, on counsel from the chiefs, rescinded their decisions. Still others simply waited to see what would happen.

After 1926, the Douala's campaign took on new dimensions. On the one hand, the Douala chiefs began petitioning directly to the League of Nations, and, on the other, they began urging their case directly through a representative in France proper. Between 1927 and 1933 a dozen petitions and communications were received by the Permanent Mandates Commission either directly from the chiefs or from their representatives abroad.

Most of the early petitions were confined to demanding the return of expropriated land or else adequate payment for such property.[7] A petition of a different character grew out of a "Big Public Meeting under the protection of the chiefs who in their capacity as independent sovereigns concluded the political treaty of 1884 with the German Reich." The petition was signed by Ngaka Akwa, "Chief of Akwa"; Eyum Ekwalla, "Chief of Deido"; Maipe Branga, "Chief of Bonaberi"; and Theodore Lobessell, probably Lobe Bell. All had been authors or coauthors of previous petitions. The interesting aspect of this petition is not that it represented another sally into the land question, but that it set out certain local grievances and charged the administration with keeping the African "at the lowest level" in the dispensation of justice, training, and education. Moreover, the document denounced the cupidity of all colonial powers that, enforcing identical systems, "will not tolerate the idea of national autonomy among the lower races entrusted to their care."[8] The petition claimed independent juristic status for the Douala chiefs with an implied existence of a sovereign Cameroon Kingdom. It is also significant that the petition departed from the usual demands for the return of the Douala lands to launch into a wholesale condemnation of the colonial system; views such as this had not been heard since the Lotin Samé affair. For the first time, broadly "Camerounian" sentiments were expressed, though within the context of the Douala chiefs' displeasure at the general state of things.

Early in 1931 the Douala chiefs found a spokesman in the person of one Vincent Ganty who, according to the French authorities, was an African who had formerly been in the customs service in Guinea. Ganty arrived in Douala, and apparently joined forces with the Douala chiefs. The administration claimed that Ganty "played on the credulity of negroes in one district [Douala] by means of wonders and pseudo-miracles." Ganty and the chiefs so increased the pace of their agitation that the administration jailed him and similarly penalized the most active of the chiefs. Upon his release, Ganty went to Paris, there to continue his fight.[9]

Once in Paris, Ganty began bombarding the Permanent Mandates Commission with petitions and memoranda. He styled himself "Delegate in Europe of the Cameroons Negro Citizens," and, with one of his memoranda, submitted a letter signed by fifty-four chiefs, notables, and common people, and conferring upon him the title of "Sole Agent in Europe of the Cameroons People" with plenary power to conduct any and all business on their behalf. The administration charged that Ganty styled himself "defender of the oppressed negro people," that he attempted to set up a paper Cameroun Republic, and that he charged fees in the form of subscriptions from the Douala people. The French estimated that Ganty took in about a hundred thousand francs a year from sale of his subscription cards and from similar schemes.

The administration called Ganty's assertions "scandal-mongering romance."[10] Scandal-mongering romance or no, Ganty's first petition to the League of Nations called for the withdrawal of the mandate and the creation of a Cameroun Republic.[11] In a series of petitions beginning in June, 1931, Ganty demanded the withdrawal of charges against "King Akwa" and his son, Betote Akwa, accused the authorities of violence and instances of maladministration, and demanded that the people be given the right to "give effective financial aid to their delegate in Europe."[12]

By far the most arresting of Ganty's communications was a sixty-five page memorandum that he attached to a petition to the Permanent Mandates Commission, dated August 21, 1931. The document set out a lengthy critique of the administration, and attempted to prove the illegality of the mandate and the legal existence of a kingdom of the Cameroons recognized by the treaty of 1884 with Germany. Ganty demanded the restoration of the "Kingdom" under the League of Nations. An obviously bemused Permanent Mandates Commission reported:

The petitioner's memorandum . . . is a curious document, full of contradictions, in which the author seeks to prove the inevitable racial antagonism between white and black as a justification for the constitution of an African state whose evolution is to follow native conceptions.[13]

Insofar as Ganty had abandoned his pretensions to the presidency of a "Cameroons Republic," the memorandum represented an enlarged exposition of the thesis propounded by the Douala chiefs at the "Big Public Meeting" in 1926. Their claim to hegemony over all the Cameroons was, of course, without historical foundation. It is sufficient to point out that the Douala chiefs who signed the treaty of 1884 actually ruled little more than the general area of the several villages at the estuary of the Wouri River, and that the chiefs' "kingships" were unofficial titles conferred by Europeans and without any traditional legitimization. At any rate, the entire series of events surrounding the agitation by the Douala chiefs provides what is probably the first stirrings of Camerounian nationalism. If a recognition of a community that transcends local boundaries is a factor in defining feelings of nationalism, the Douala can be said to have had early intimation of it.

In at least one other instance, Ganty did more than voice the political demands of the Douala chiefs. Under the organizational signature of the *Ligue de défense de la Race Negre*, Ganty called the

Mandates Commission's attention to the disturbance in Douala involving women's demonstrations against certain new taxes. The Commission reviewed the matter and reported that positive amends had been made by the administration to a woman injured by a policeman.

The Annual Reports to the League after 1934 continued to make oblique references to disaffection among the Douala and to the efforts of the local authorities to extend the Douala's participation in local assemblies. Once again, however, the imminence of war diverted Douala discontent and, happily for the administration, channeled some of the Douala's political energies into activities in support of the government.[14]

In 1937 a quasi-political organization calling itself *l'Union Camerounaise,* consisting (according to the administration) of "young inhabitants of the Cameroons who, in general, were more advanced than their fellow citizens," made its appearance and petitioned the League of Nations to convert the Cameroons into an "A" mandate. The president of the organization and signer of the petition was one Mandessi Bell, apparently of the Douala Bell family, already experienced in political matters. The French noted somewhat waspishly that the organization's members "would be quite glad to indulge their liking for politics if there were a change of regime in the territory."[15] By 1938, on the eve of World War II, the organization, now composed of "European and native leaders" with the aim of "[looking] after the interests of the Cameroons," sent identical letters to Franklin D. Roosevelt, Neville Chamberlain, and Prime Minister Daladier, protesting against any possible return of the territory to Germany.[16]

In 1938, what Hodgkin termed "the first legal Cameroonian political organization"—*Jeunesse Camerounaise Française*—was founded by a young Douala, Paul Soppo Priso, with the government's blessings. The new organization's program consisted of opposition to Germany, a suggestion that the Cameroun mandate be incorporated into France, and the general furtherance of patriotism.[17] After the war, *Jeunesse Camerounaise* became the seminal group from which the leadership of postwar political parties was drawn. In a very real sense, the organization was a school for Camerounian politicians. It provided a rostrum, albeit a circumscribed one, for the new young voices, all speaking in French, and beginning to demand for Camerounians the rights of Frenchmen. The war served to amplify their demands, and circumstances and events outside the Cameroun gave them the leverage they would need if some of the demands were to be realized.

FRENCH CAMEROUN: SUMMATION

From the standpoint of economic and physical development, the program of the *mise en valeur* in the French Cameroun proved a notable success between the two world wars. The total trade rose from a value of 96,000,000 francs in 1922 to 467,171,000 francs in 1938, approximately a fivefold increase, given fluctuations in the value of the franc. For a moderately rich country, almost wholly dependent on its exports of palm oil products, cocoa, and timber, the figures can almost be seen as a tribute to the success of the *mise en valeur*. Moreover, the Cameroun came through the world depression of 1928-1932 in fine style: at its lowest ebb total trade never went much below the 1924 level of 120,000,000 tons, and by 1935 it was back up to the 1930 level of 168,000,000 tons. The financial aspect of this picture is almost the same, with the small difference that here the decline began a year earlier (1929) and ended a year later (1936). This summary statement does not, of course, tell the entire story, but it is enough to show that the Cameroun's economic development was favorable in most respects, reflecting intelligent management on the local level, as the main source of funds continued to be local revenue.

From the political standpoint, of primary concern here, the record is not quite so favorable. It must be admitted that the *mise-en-valeur* owed much of its success to a heavy tax burden and the use of conscript labor, the latter mostly during the 1920's. The extensive road network, which had been almost completed by 1933, the enlargement of the port of Douala, and the proliferation of European and native plantations, usually seemed to have been accomplished at the expense of the local populations. The administration thus not only developed the economy, but left a legacy of ill-will because of its methods.

The machinery of administration, designed to slow the pace of political growth among the African Cameroonians, did more to foster political consciousness than to retard it. The *indigénat* and its indignities, the wholesale suppression of traditional authority through direct administrative methods, the *prestation,* all called forth increasingly active opposition from both traditional leaders and the newly educated elite. It was one of the paradoxes of the period—a paradox not uncommon elsewhere in colonial Africa—that the French undermined their administrative policies by the very education they took such pains to encourage. All this does not in the least minimize the important part played by the missions, especially through their schools which, although they offered the officially prescribed courses, inculcated values whose effect was to encourage challenge to the regime. The difficulties encountered by the administration in the Douala area are symptomatic of the wide gap between the aims of French policy and the actual state of political sophistication among a population already Westernized to a much greater extent than elsewhere in the territory.

It is fair to suggest that the political reforms the administration began to institute in the three or four years preceding World War II, as well as the official sanction given to new politically oriented groups, owed much less to internal pressures for reform than to the government's need to stimulate support for itself among the more politically conscious elements of the African population. The very real fear that Camerounians might balk at supporting France in her effort against Germany probably gave both local and metropolitan governments some disquieting moments, especially in the face of massive German propaganda for the return of her former colonies.

C. GERMANY AND THE CAMEROONS—1916-1940

Some of the effects of Germany's attempts to recover her former imperial colonies were felt directly within the British sphere of the bifurcated Cameroons. The return of most of the German plantation proprietors to the British Cameroons made that territory a center for pro-German agitation between the wars. Yet it was in the French Cameroun where former German plantations had been sold to non-Germans or preëmpted by the government—and Germans were excluded in the coastal trade and occasional inland farms—that the German colonial irredentist campaign had the most effect. It was suggested earlier that pro-German sentiment lingered among many Camerounian Africans, and that it tended to grow in proportion to the unpopularity of certain French institutions and practices. Some of the reforms undertaken immediately preceding World War II were undoubtedly instituted to offset any effect German propaganda might have had on the Cameroun, as well as to rally support for the French regime.

GERMANS IN THE CAMEROONS

Under Articles 297 (b) and 120 of the Treaty of Versailles, the Allied governments were empowered to retain or to liquidate all German property within their territories, including that found in the mandates. Compensation for such seized property was to be according to the laws of the country within which the property lay. After satisfying creditors and other claimants, the governments were obligated to credit any balance to Germany's reparations account.[1]

The French disposed of German property in Togo and the Cameroun according to special procedures worked out for the two mandates. Here, a tribunal established the conditions of disposal, and most properties were sold at auction. By 1925 the French administration had liquidated 116 German firms holding 362 different properties. Of this number, 219 were sold at public auction; and a total of 107 were taken by "pre-emption" by the government. Forty properties also passed to the government under provisions in the Treaty of Versailles providing for the direct acquisition by the Allied governments of properties belonging directly to the German Empire or to German states.[2] It will be recalled that, under this section of the treaty, the French government claimed the Douala river properties.

Of the properties sold at auction, 132 were acquired by Frenchmen, 40 by Englishmen, and 29 by African Cameroonians. The government, under its "pre-emptive" powers, took over any property it wished upon payment of one franc. In this manner the Nordbahn (partly owned by a private firm) was acquired for one franc. Similarly, the government acquired five former German tobacco plantations in the vicinity of Dschang and turned them over to a private company, the Compagnie des Tabacs, for a term of sixty years. Buell claimed that the administration had disposed of this property without allowing anyone else to bid on it.[3] The transaction may have irritated some of the other potential bidders, but there was nothing illegal about it.[4]

With the disposal of all former German property in the French Cameroun, the return of German citizens to the area was almost precluded. A number, of course, returned with various French, British, and German trading companies that had dealings in Douala and Kribi. Several small plantations were eventually sold to Germans, the most notable of which was a tobacco estate near Yaoundé, owned by a Herr Oellerich.[5] The situation was completely different in the British Cameroons, however. Here, the Germans not only repurchased most of their former properties, but even on the eve of World War II constituted the largest group of Europeans in the territory. (In 1938 there were about sixty Germans in the French Cameroun, where they had been allowed since 1926.)

When the old Kamerun had been split between France and Great Britain in 1916, General Dobell (governing the British sections) had sent a naval captain, Fuller, to administer the more than 264,000 acres the Germans had held by freehold grant before the war. Fuller, together with a representative of the Nigerian government, continued to work the plantations and had, by the end of the war, showed a profit of some three million pounds ($14,580,000), which was credited to the cost of the Dobell expedition. When the British Cameroons became a mandate, the Nigerian government took over management of the properties and sought to "preserve" rather than "develop" the estates. Upon representations by the Nigerian government that the upkeep on the estates was financially prohibitive, the Lloyd George government tried to sell the properties in 1922.

Initial attempts to sell the estates proved almost completely fruitless; only a small number of lots were sold. On the whole, the London merchants proved indifferent, even to favorable conditions of sale that excluded ex-enemy nationals or their agents from consideration. It appeared that most of the takers were unwilling to put up the large sums of money needed both for the initial purchase and for the necessary subsequent development. Another factor was French pressure; the French strongly objected that the Germans might come back.

The MacDonald government waited until August, 1923, and then quietly offered the properties for sale again, this time without reservations or qualifications. The London *Times* ran the following advertisement for six months before the November, 1924, dates of the sale:

An opportunity occurs on the 24th and 25th inst. to acquire going concerns either on a large or small scale when ex-enemy properties in the British sphere of the Cameroons will be offered for sale by auction at Winchester House, Old Broad Street, E.C., under the direction of the Colonial Office, whose instructions to Messrs. Hampton & Sons, the auctioneers, of 20 St. James Sq., London S.W., are that the estates are to be submitted absolutely without reserve and irrespective of the nationality of the owners.

A short campaign by some of the London dailies against the proposed sale did not deter the government, and nearly all the properties were repurchased by their former German owners.[6] Of the more than 264,000 acres once in German hands, more than 207,000 returned to them. (Table 11 shows the extent of the German holdings on the eve of World War II.) The total acreage involved is slightly larger than that of the 1924 sales, owing to the opening of new plantations in the Tombel area. The remaining acreage, about 60,000 acres, was owned by British, Dutch, and Swiss firms.

The sale brought the Germans back into the Cameroons with a vengeance. They became the most numerous national group in the British mandate. In 1925, one year after the sale, Germans already

TABLE 11

GERMAN PLANTATIONS IN THE CAMEROONS, 1938

Name of plantation	Owner	Total acreage	Acreage in use	Capitalization in reichsmarks
Westafrikanische Pflanzungsverein (WAPV), Bota	West African Plantation Co., Victoria, and Berlin	18,790	6,585	no info.
WAPV, Ngeme and Sachsenhof sections	same	no info.	no info.	no info.
WAPV, Molyoko, incl. Malende	same	5,687	3,602	3,700,000
WAPV, Prinz Alfred, Misselele	same	6,042	4,692	no info.
WAPV, Bimbia and Mabeta	same	11,083	3,018	no info.
African Fruit Co.	African Fruit Co., Hamburg	12,172	7,109	4,000,000
Likomba	Likomba Kamerun Bananen Gesellschaft, A. G., Hamburg	15,672	5,945	1,024,800
Moliwe	Moliwe Plantation Co., Berlin	34,000	7,636	1,000,000
Holforth Plant. Co.	O. Holforth	1,617	1,617	no info.
Ombe	Rein and Wesel, Oberhausen, Rhineland	603	600	no info.
Bibundi and allied plantations	Bibundi, A. G.	31,000	5,994	458,000
Debunscha	Debunscha Pflanzung, Berlin	4,329	1,025	220,000
Oechelhausen Plantage	Wilhelm Scipio, Mannheim	4,490	1,137	no info.

Table 11—*Continued*

Name of plantation	Owner	Total acreage	Acreage in use	Capitalization in reichsmarks
Isobi plantation	Bibundi, A. G., lease to K. Pröving	1,000	544	*See* Bibundi
Kamerun Eisenbahn Gesellschaft (KEG), Tombel	Kamerun Eisenbahn Gesellschaft, Berlin	17,500	2,500	1,380,000
Mukonje estate	Kamerun Kaut- schuk Co., A. G., Berlin	5,250	4,500	1,200,000
Ikassa estate	Gesellschaft Süd- Kamerun, Hamburg	17,375	1,130	1,105,200
Mbonge, Davo, Beafa, Kumbe, Mukoko, Eboka, Transport and Boa plantations	Deutsch Westafri- kanische Handels- gesellschaft, Ham- burg	20,289	5,990	710,000
Hernsheim planta- tion	Hernsheim and Co., Hamburg	2,964	2,964	540,000
Scheitlin's estate, Tombel	Mme. Scheitlin	260	112½	no info.
Totals		207,979 (322.78 sq. mi.)	28,113	

(Full citation of these works will be found in the bibliography.)

Sources: *Report on the Cameroons (1938)*, pp. 139–143; Kemner, *Kamerun . . . ,* p. 185.

outnumbered the other groups. Their numbers increased until, in 1938, there were three times as many German as British nationals in the territory (see table 12).

The extent of German agitation in the Cameroons itself is difficult to assess, as information on the subject is hard to find. What indications there are suggest that it must have been considerable. During the middle and late 1930's Germany intensified her propaganda campaign for recovery of her colonies, hoping to frighten the French and British governments into colonial concessions. German and Italian visitors became more frequent in the Cameroons, and reports were widely circulated that many African Cameroonians ardently wished

TABLE 12

NON-AFRICAN POPULATION; REPRESENTATIVE YEARS
(BRITISH CAMEROONS)

(n.d. = no data)

Nationality	Adult males	Adult females	Children	Total	Years
British	n.d.	n.d.	n.d.	*ca.* 60	1925
	45	10	—	55	1927
	61	23	1	85	1937
	66	16	4	86	1938
German	n.d.	n.d.	n.d.	125	1925
	147	25	7	179	1927
	176	52	25	253	1937
	200	56	29	285	1938
Dutch	n.d.	n.d.	n.d.	n.d.	1925
	6	—	—	6	1927
	20	6	—	26	1937
	19	8	—	27	1938
Swiss	n.d.	n.d.	n.d.	n.d.	1925
	6	6	1	13	1927
	8	9	3	20	1937
	10	7	6	23	1938
Other	n.d.	n.d.	n.d.	n.d.	1925
	6	—	—	6	1927
	16	8	—	24	1937
	23	17	1	41	1938
Totals, all nationalities	155	19	5	179	1925
	204	41	8	253	1927
	283	98	29	410	1937
	306	102	40	448	1938

(*Full citation of these works will be found in the bibliography.*)

SOURCES: Kuczynski, *Cameroons* . . . , pp. 267–268; *Report on the Cameroons* (1938), p. 107.

a return of the German administration. One German visitor to Douala in 1935 noted, at the time of his arrival, that

. . . the French administrators are quite nervous. After the Saar plebiscite it was feared that the Douala might stage a pro-German rebellion. Consequently, all of the homes of French administrators were occupied by soldiers which were not withdrawn until fourteen days later, when all was peaceful again.[7]

In March, 1938, came Nazi Germany's Austrian *Anschluss*. The event was greeted with joy by Germans living in both Cameroons, who took the occasion to prepare a celebration in Douala. The following is a French account of the affair:

On the occasion of the *Anschluss,* Germans established in the Cameroons manifested great joy and activity.

A banquet brought together German notables in Douala during the course of which the recent successes of the Reich were exalted, and the increasing power of Germany was compared with France's declining prestige. In private conversations, certain German nationals did not hesitate to announce the certain return of the territory to its first occupants.

The account went on to note the increased numbers of visitors to the territory:

Moreover, in the last few weeks the Cameroun was visited by numerous Germans on study tours, who are going about the territory for various reasons: journalistic inquiries; medical, economic, technical research. The most recent arrivals are M. Kurt Broschek, director of the *Hamburger Fremdenblatt* . . . and Dr. Gustave Siefert, on a mission of social hygiene in Africa.[8]

The *Anschluss* was also celebrated in the British Cameroons by the sizeable German contingent in the Victoria area. A German propaganda work describing the joys of German colonists in the Cameroons shows local demonstrations following announcement of the *Anschluss* and includes pictures of a banana train carrying German settlers and emblazoned with banners reading "Der Führer in Kamerun"; the hoisting of a Nazi flag at Victoria, and the visit of an official ship to Tiko. The work in question stressed the "home away from home" aspect of German life in the territory and was filled with descriptions of family life among the Cameroons' German planters.[9] A measure of the effect of the German demonstrations is the fact that within a few weeks, on April 15, the French government felt called upon to sponsor a mass meeting in Douala at which Frenchmen, Americans, and other Europeans in the area testified to the strength of their support for France and their opposition to any German plans to retake the territory.[10]

A French-language newspaper favorable to the German cause was published in Douala, at least after 1933. A French critic of the journal noted that it carried the Hitlerian motto "For Truth, Liberty, and Law" on its masthead, and that it engaged in long diatribes against the French government as well as whitewashing of the Nazi regime,[11]

Viewed in perspective, however, whatever agitation the Germans in the Cameroons managed to promote becomes insignificant in the face of the large-scale international propaganda campaign launched by the Weimar and Nazi regimes to regain the old German colonies. It was the latter campaign whose repercussions were most widely felt in the two mandates; to a large extent both the local German agitation and the French and British responses were shaped by it, not to speak of the reactions of the home governments in Europe proper.

GERMAN CLAIMS ON THE CAMEROONS: INTERNATIONAL CAMPAIGN

The campaign conducted by the Weimar and Nazi regimes for the recovery of the former German colonies is discussed elsewhere in detail;[12] we shall not be concerned with it here except in its relation to the Cameroons. A short background summary will suffice to show the general outlines and thrust of the campaign.

German reaction to the loss of her colonies was immediate; Article 119 of the Versailles Treaty produced a lengthy exposé by the German delegation to the conference, in which it was suggested that colonial questions be handed over to a commission of inquiry, and that Germany be permitted to administer her own colonies as a mandatory of a League of Nations.[13] The proposals were rejected by the Allies, as France and Britain were already in de facto control of Germany's African colonies.

There was little talk of German claims on her former colonies until 1925-1926 when Dr. Streseman, at the Locarno talks, raised the issue. Similarly, German entry into the League of Nations in 1926 focused attention on the problem. Also in 1926, three important German organizations began to wave the flag of German colonial irredentism. One was the so-called *Korag* (*Kolonial-Reichsarbeitsgemeinschaft*), consisting of thirty groups with colonial interests; another was the *Deutsche Kolonialgesellschaft,* with 250 branches and 30,000 members; and the last was the colonial committee (*Kolonialausschuss*) of the Reichstag.[14] From then on, important figures in the government took an increasingly large part in the activities of these organizations, a development which more and more identified the government with these groups' irredentist aims. Messrs. Curtius, Schacht, and von Neurath, Chancellor von Papen, and even President Hindenburg were quoted in ever bolder declarations about Germany's colonial rights and aspirations. Former Governor of German East Africa Heinrich Schnee and Ritter Franz von Epp were foremost among the leaders of the various colonial societies.[15]

After Hitler's accession to power, the German government openly made the return of the colonies an official policy aim. In his *Mein Kampf,* in speeches, notes, and other official communications, Hitler made the colonial demands of the Third Reich a key part of his *Grossdeutschland* program.[16] Ritter von Epp (who became head of the Reich Colonial League in 1936 and the principal propagandist for the colonial cause), Hermann Göring, and Hjalmar Schacht, among others, carried on a constant verbal drumfire to keep the issue alive in the German and international consciousness.[17]

With the success of German policies in Europe, Hitler began applying pressure on France and Britain for a "solution of the colonial problem." By 1937 some British and French leaders appeared willing to consider colonial concessions (rationalized as "redistribution of natural resources"), as a way to avert war. Sir Samuel Hoare suggested that the German demands deserved consideration, and Sir Arnold Wilson and Neville Chamberlain argued that Germany ought to get her colonies back if it meant avoiding war. Even Prime Minister Stanley Baldwin did not discourage some consideration of an "equitable" settlement. In 1938, Mr. Pirow, the South African Minister of Defense, on a tour that took him through Germany, gave the impression that the South African and British governments might be ready for a settlement with Hitler.[18] In France, apprehension was aroused by the publication of a number of equivocal official statements on the colonial problem. It was feared that Prime Minister Daladier and Foreign Minister Bonnet, in the spirit of the Munich conference, were preparing to offer Germany some of the mandated territories.[19]

Another dimension of the problem was the Italian role in the campaign. After securing Ethiopia in the face of weak-kneed League sanctions, serious conversations were held between representatives of Germany and Italy with a view to obtaining Italy's fuller participation in a projected Axis territorial redistribution of African territories. Since 1932 Italy had cast envious eyes at the African mandates, and toward the beginning of World War II it almost appeared as if Germany and Italy had agreed on a partition of the continent.[20]

The German argument centered about four main points: (1) the need for colonies to receive the surplus population from overpopulated Germany, (2) the need for basic resources to help Germany feed her people and supply her industries, (3) the inequity of the situation that deprived Germany of colonies she was perfectly able to govern, and (4) the assertion that Germany's prestige could no longer tolerate the indignities of the Versailles settlement which placed her at a shameful colonial disadvantage in Africa vis-à-vis France and Britain.[21] Italy's campaign followed much the same lines and seemed, at times, to clash with Germany's. The Italian line paralleled the German, except that stress was placed on the point that Italian prestige demanded colonies to suit her new position in the world.

The German campaign to regain the Cameroons included the publication, for both internal and external consumptions, of books, pamphlets, and articles stating the official colonial argument or in some way advancing the purported values of German civilization and the excellences of German ways. Much significant material appeared illuminating the brief German colonial period, and, even though it tended to idealize the accomplishments of the various German administrations, it presented valuable material for those interested in the subject.[22] For the most part, though, the material was mainly aimed at keeping the issue alive, and appeals were directed to every social, educational, and economic level of German and world opinion. Some books published for domestic consumption dealt with the heroic deeds of German colonists and soldiers; witness such titles as *Massa wann kommst Du wieder; Zwischen Tschadsee und Götterberg, Erlebnisse im Kampf in Kamerun* ("Master, When Are You Coming Back; between Lake Chad and Mount Cameroon, adventures of the Struggle in the Kamerun"); *Der Kampf um unsere Schutzgebiete* ("The Struggle for our Protectorates"), subtitled *Ein Beitrag zur Wiedergewinnung unserer Kolonien, Eine Lebensfrage für unser Deutsches Volk* ("A Contribution to the Reconquest of our Colonies, Vital Question for our German People").[23] Youth was not neglected in the propaganda barrage. A work entitled *Kampf im Urwald: Von Urwald Göttern und Schicksalen Deutscher Pflanzer und Soldaten in Kamerun* ("Struggle in the Jungle: Of Jungle Gods and the Destiny of German Planters and Soldiers in the Kamerun"), dealing with the reminiscences of a former colonist in the territory, contains the following interesting postscript:

I wrote and drew the pictures in this book for my boys. Hence it should also delight all true boys—and you as well. These stories are so true, that they might happen any day again. I don't know where you are now. Perhaps you have read these stories at a campfire on a trip, or under a rain-soaked tent. Perhaps you are also one of those who, late in the evening, read them through by the secret light of a flashlight under your bedcovers. Now close your eyes. All the characters of this book will come back to you —those fearless German men with their faithful black companions. Then you may well wish: I'd like to be like that! And when you are a grown lad you too may become a warrior and fighter in our German colonies.[24]

The colonial propagandists operated on other levels with equal skill. Following the Göring-Mussolini talks in January, 1937, ostensibly called to discuss armaments and Italian colonial aims, the official Rome radio began presenting weekly programs on "Pioneers of German Colonization," and the German government opened an exposition in Berlin of colonial postage stamps.[25] Besides postage stamps, radio broadcasts, colonial rallies, extensive pamphleteering, the propagandists sought space in foreign publications of all sorts. Dr. Schacht, Ritter von Epp, Dr. Schnee, and others wrote pieces for American, British, and French publications in which they attempted to demonstrate the reasonableness of the German position.[26]

On the diplomatic front, the Germans made it amply clear that their special colonial interests focused on the mandates in Africa. It was claimed that the wealth of the African mandates motivated the push for what both Germany and, later, France and Britain euphemistically called the "equitable allocation of the world's resources."[27]

The German government, in order to maintain pressure on the French and British governments, occasionally released stories through the Berlin press declaring that it had made some sort of "deal" with France, a maneuver invariably followed by an embarrassed silence before the French government or its spokesmen would deny that any transfer of *French* colonies was contemplated. One such story, released in March, 1937, claimed that Germany and France had reached an agreement over a joint exploitation of the Cameroun; a commercial accord had been reached, the story claimed, by virtue of which 51 per cent of the Cameroun would remain in French hands, and 49 per cent in German.[28] There was no official confirmation of the "agreement" from either side, but the French did not make the customary disavowal. One possible reason for this silence was that their government had probably been corresponding with the German government on the subject. Another probable reason was the closeness of the impending November, 1937, Anglo-French talks at Downing Street to discuss a "general settlement" of outstanding international problems. Among other matters, the talks were to take up Hitler's demands for a colonial settlement that included a return of Togo and the two Cameroons. The talks were inconclusive, it might be added, inasmuch as the principals, Messrs. Chamberlain and Eden (for England) and Chautemps and Delbos (for France) could agree only that the "colonial question cannot be discussed in isolation," as it involved other nations.[29]

We have already noted two obvious French responses to the German colonial demands over the Camerouns. One response was an increased liberalization of administrative institutions, with the aim of stressing the assimilative aspects of colonial policy—an aspect long neglected in the Camerouns. The other was the official sponsorship of mixed European-African organizations with patriotic aims. Both responses were designed primarily to secure the loyalty of the African Camerounian to the French cause, a loyalty that at times seemed to waver in the memory of some of the more stringent policies of the twenties and early thirties. Undoubtedly the presence of the German planters and merchants also served to keep alive a favorable image of the old Kamerun days.

In a broader sense, the Cameroons floundered (as did the other French and British mandates) in the sea of French and British attempts at colonial appeasement. Anxious as the local administrations were to preserve their hold on the mandates, the final decisions did not lie with them, but with their metropolitan governments. The period between 1937 and the beginning of the war in Europe in 1939 saw the development in the Cameroons of a policy vacuum within which the local French administration could eventually assert itself independently of Paris. The *métropole* was too concerned with European affairs and the immediacy of the Nazi threat to pay much attention to the fate of the mandates. (There was no question about the "colonies"—they would remain French at all costs). At times it appeared that France was willing to let the mandates go to appease Hitler's insatiable territorial demands. It was the Cameroon's good fortune that both France and Britain did not come to terms with Hitler on this question; whatever the reason for this, it enabled the vigorous French administrators and colonists to seize the initiative when the *métropole* capitulated to Germany in 1940.

The mandate period really ended in 1940, even though the formal interment of the mandate system did not take place until the League of Nations was replaced by the United Nations in 1947. For all intents and purposes, the League of Nations died with World War II; it had grown out of the peace settlement following World War I, and when the equilibrium it was designed to preserve collapsed, the League went under as well. With the disintegration of the League, the mandates reverted to the actual if not legal possession of the administering regimes. The only seemingly important question at the beginning of the war was whether the mandates could be kept out of Germany's hands. In the case of the Cameroon's, the picture became blurred because of the presence of the nominal government in Vichy after 1940. That Vichy failed to maintain the loyalty of the Cameroons is probably attributable to the vigor of the local administration, which, although it did not like Pétain and the Vichy government, liked the prospects of a return of German rule even less.

CHAPTER

V World War II and Postwar Constitutional Changes

The collapse of the *métropole* in June, 1940, left the French overseas possessions temporarily stranded and without direction. It was not long, however, until the Vichy regime moved to fill the vacuum and to secure its possession of the African territories. By the end of June, 1940, most of the territories of French West and Equatorial Africa had sworn their allegiance to Pétain.

Two centers of potential resistance remained, the Chad and the French Cameroun. In the Chad, Governor Félix Eboué and his military aide, Colonel Marchand, remained aloof from the shifts of allegiance that were taking place to the west and in the AEF. Eboué's and Marchand's determination was reinforced by the French settlers in Fort Lamy who were almost wholly hostile to Vichy and were resolved to resist incorporation into the new regime.

In the French Cameroun, the majority of the French settlers, and most of the African elite, found the prospect of joining the Vichy regime an unappealing alternative to resistance. What undoubtedly strengthened this feeling was the realization that capitulation to Vichy would also mean the eventual incorporation of the territory into Hitler's *Grossdeutschland*. After all, had not much of Hitler's colonial propaganda centered on the return of African mandates to Germany?

When the *métropole* fell, French Cameroun Commissioner Brunot sought to form an African bloc of French African possessions to repudiate the armistice and continue the war in Africa. Brunot's cables to the various French governors in Africa elicited either negative or equivocating responses.[1] Brunot met with British representatives in Douala and Yaoundé and organized public meetings at which the determination of the territory to continue the struggle was reaffirmed. He even received encouragement from AEF Governor General Boisson, shortly before the latter changed his mind and opted for Vichy. In mid-July, steps were already being taken to institute an independent Council of Government in the Cameroun under Brunot, and to form a military and economic alliance with neighboring British colonies.

131

Between July 19 and 20 the Cameroun was visited by Rear Admiral Planton, who was sent to enforce obedience to Vichy. His reception was cool, and he was soon followed by Inspector of Colonies Huet, who established a nominal Vichy regime with the aid of some local Pétainist supporters.

It was not long until the unpopular Vichyite administration in the Cameroun was upset. During the night of August 26 and the morning of August 27, De Gaulle's emissary, Colonel (later General) Leclerc, sailed from Tiko to Douala (via pirogue) with twenty-four companions. They were met in Douala by a group of partisans, and by morning had taken over the administrative buildings of the town and rallied its French population to De Gaulle. Leclerc at once dispatched two companies of *tirailleurs* to Yaoundé by the midlands railway, and the town surrendered without a struggle. Leclerc notified De Gaulle that the Cameroun had fallen to him, and De Gaulle dispatched the following cable to the Secretariat of the League of Nations in Geneva:

. . . I have the honor to inform you that on August 28, 1940, in response to the expressed desire of the population, and in my capacity as leader of the Free French, I took over the administration of the Cameroun under French Mandate, together with the powers and obligation this mandate entails. Lieutenant Colonel Leclerc will act as Commissioner to see that order is maintained, and to look after the welfare of the population and defense of the territory. . . .[2]

In the meantime, on August 26 two other Free French representatives, Colonel Jean Colonna d'Ornano and René Pleven, had reached Fort Lamy, and Governor Eboué and Colonel Marchand declared the Chad for Free France. Two days later, in a bloodless coup in Brazzaville, Gaullist Colonel de Larminat, aided by local sympathizers, took over the rule of the vast Equatorial African territories from General Huet. The Gabon, however, did not fall to the Free French until the beginning of November, when a mixed force of two thousand, led by Colonel Leclerc, took Libreville, the territory's capital. On August 30, De Gaulle announced that all AEF territories except the Gabon had rallied to Free France. On October 8, 1940, De Gaulle himself landed in Douala to symbolize Free French return to French soil.

Colonel Leclerc left Yaoundé after several months, turning his administrative functions over to Free French civilian officials, and made his headquarters at Fort Lamy. From this town, situated almost at the center of the continent on Lake Chad, some 650 miles from the Libyan frontier, Leclerc organized a series of daring raids upon Italian forces. These raids culminated in the conquest of the Fezzan and the fall of Tripoli. On one such operation, aimed at the Koufra oasis, Leclerc led a small mechanized force some 900 miles over the Sahara to strike at the rear of the Italian forces.[3]

Leclerc's campaigns from Fort Lamy extended until 1943, when Tripoli fell to combined Free French and British forces. The necessary logistical support for Leclerc came through the AEF and the Cameroun. In 1941, the British, Free French, and Belgians concluded an agreement by which the currencies of the Cameroun, the Belgian Congo, and the AEF were pegged at a fixed sterling rate, and Britain undertook to purchase a great part or most of these countries' staple output.[4] Britain also extended the offer on the same terms to all French colonies that joined with Free France.[5]

Two things of importance stand out during this period as having a direct bearing on later political events. One was that France had been forced to cultivate the educated Camerounians as a lever against the administration, a lever that could also be used to support later political demands. Another was the implied promise of the De Gaulle visit in October, 1940; significantly, De Gaulle chose the Cameroun as the first French soil to receive his footsteps after the defeat of France. The Cameroun thereby took on a new importance, a status that was reinforced by the series of talks the General held with both French *and* African leaders at the time. A new political spirit was growing, one that finally found its expression at the Brazzaville Conference of 1944. This and other events attending the birth of the Fourth Republic, as well as those leading to the creation of the United Nations Organization, provided the context within which Camerounian political life received what was practically a new start.

Three major developments set the stage for the postwar political evolution of the Cameroun. The first was the oblique shift in policy orientations manifested at the Brazzaville Conference and in the 1946 French constitution. The second was the set of institutional changes created under the new constitution. The third was France's assumption of the UN trusteeship over the Cameroun. All three developments had important implications for the shaping of political forces in the Cameroun; together, they implied a major step forward. For the first time, the Cameroun would have a significant institutionalized, legally sanctioned share in determining its own future and the shape of its political and administrative life. For the first time, domestic political forces could begin to play whatever role their impetus and strength might determine for them, and, more important, test the effectiveness of their appeals by institutional means.

A summary of these developments may help to place them in their proper perspective:

1) *Brazzaville:* The Brazzaville Conference, convoked by the Free French in January, 1944, represented the point of view of colonial administrators concerned with tropical African territories.[6] It maintained the traditional assimilationist aims of French colonial policy, recommending administrative decentralization as a *policy* and political assimilation as a *goal.* The distinction was implied in the conference's recommendation of greater administrative freedom in the individual territories, in combination with some type of federal structure uniting the *métropole* and the overseas territories. The distinction enabled it to reject any conception of autonomy for French dependencies, but to insist that these territories should have a voice in the construction of the new constitution, as well as an increased participation in the representative organs of the Republic. It was not enough, however, to increase overseas representation in metropolitan organs; the Conference felt the colonies' permanent interests in the political life of France should be recognized by the creation of some sort of colonial parliament, preferably a federal assembly. This assembly would work with local assemblies to be established in each territory. The local assemblies, suggested the Conference, would have wide powers of decision in economic and financial matters, subject only to the approval of the Colonial Ministry. They would represent both European and African interests, by election where possible, and, failing that, would represent the African elite.

The Conference also recommended the abolition of the *indigénat* and all forms of forced labor. Under the influence of Félix Eboué's 1941 Circular Letter on Native Policy, the Conference recommended the adoption of a policy that would seek to maintain traditional political institutions, not to act as tools of administrative policy, but to promote political and economic growth along lines most appropriate to each situation. Eboué had written of the creation of an African elite, legitimized by tradition and trained to responsibility: it would not be a collection of "museum curios," but an active group capable of mediating the contact between old and new. There is little question but that Eboué had viewed the development of the British policy of "indirect rule" with favor; he bade those who thought the creation of a responsible native elite an "illusion" to consider that the "illusion" had been responsible for the building up of British Nigeria.[7]

2) *The constitution and reforms (1946):* The constitution of 1946 retreated somewhat from the Brazzaville positions in that it stressed assimilationist doctrine more and converted the federalist hopes of the Conference into the reality of a centralized "French Union."[8] The political structures created by the constitution, however, rang true to many

of the recommendations voiced at Brazzaville, if not to all its aspirations.

The document provided a titular niche for all the French dependencies, according to the degree to which they had achieved political assimilation to the *métropole*. On the outer edge of the structure were to be the Associated States and Associated Territories, categories designed to identify territories that had not been formally annexed to France. The Associated States designated were the protectorates of Indo-China, Morocco, and Tunisia; the Associated Territories included only the French mandates. The constitution also established legislative and executive organs for the French Union. As far as the Associated Territories were concerned, these were limited to participating in the Assembly of the French Union, but not in its High Council. More significantly, and directly in line with the Brazzaville recommendations, the new constitution guaranteed all French dependencies voting participation in the French National Assembly and Council of the Republic. The Assembly of the French Union—and indeed its nominal executive, the High Council—was an emasculated version of the Brazzaville suggestion for a federal assembly. The Assembly of the French Union had little more than an advisory role in regard to legislation affecting the overseas territories. As if to make up for this and to dramatize the emphasis on integration, the dependencies were given full rights in the French parliament itself. Initially, of the 627 deputies in the National Assembly, 41 came from overseas, and of this number 32 represented African territories. The French Cameroun sent three deputies, elected from a dual roll (two representing the African voters: Jules Ninine and Douala Manga Bell; and one representing the Europeans: Louis Paul Aujoulat). In the Council of the Republic, 50 of the 320 senators represented overseas constituencies; of these, 34 came from African territories.[9]

Important as was the introduction of overseas participation in metropolitan institutions, by far the greatest and most important innovation of the 1946 reforms was the creation of local representative assemblies in the French dependencies.[10] Most of these legislatures were given few independent legislative powers: the Constituent Assembly had envisaged a continuation of the practice whereby the metropolitan government legislated through ministerial decrees. With the exception of the Associated Territories, the local assemblies of the African dependencies shared their powers with the interterritorial *Grand Conseils* and the metropolitan ministries. The two Representative Assemblies set up in Togo and the Cameroun combined the roles of Territorial Assemblies and *Grand Conseils* of French Equatorial and West Africa;

that is, they had powers of decision (*déliberation*) on economic and fiscal matters (subject to certain controls by the *Conseil d'Etat*, which, if not exercised in ninety days, made the proposed legislation self-executing). They had to be consulted by the administration on all regulations concerning the disposition of public lands, labor conditions, education, or the execution of development programs. On other than political questions, they were entitled to pass resolutions (*voeux*) for submission to the appropriate metropolitan ministry. They were also given deliberative powers on the local budget, which was prepared by the administration but could be supplemented by the Assembly. If any expenditure were struck out by the local Assembly, the administration might nonetheless make a provisional allocation for it in the budget, subject to ratification by the *Conseil d'Etat*.

The new Assembly's political role was somewhat circumscribed. It might elect senators to the Council of the Republic and councilors to the Assembly of the French Union. (Members of the local Assembly and deputies to the French National Assembly were to be elected from a dual roll in popular elections.)

The only subsequent modifications affecting the Cameroun Representative Assembly, prior to 1956, were enlargements in the electorate and a change in the name to Territorial Assembly, indicating that the legislature would not only be representative, but would stress greater popular participation in the actual government of the territory.

The creation of these new representative institutions had important consequences for the growth of political activity in the French territories. One effect, certainly, was that most political activists, groups, parties, and the like, were forced to realize that if their activity was to be meaningful, it would have to be channeled through the new assemblies by way of the elective process. This realization molded territorial political orientations by forcing the creation of political groups that operated most effectively on the territorial level, whatever their trans-territorial or metropolitan affiliations. Contributing to this development was the combined impact of the creation of the new assemblies plus the radical extension of suffrage and citizenship under the 1946 constitution and its executory legislation.

The 1946 constitution extended French citizenship to all inhabitants of the French dependencies, but distinguished between those who were subject to "civil law" and those who "preserved their personal status," that is, remained under customary law. All "citizens" became also "citizens of the French Union." For Togo and the Cameroun the law stipulated that those who were not "French nationals" would also not be "French citizens." They became, under the new regime, *administrés français*, a category that included almost all African Camerounians—who would, however, be covered by a "citizenship of the French Union." Furthermore, members of this category also enjoyed the same rights of citizenship as the "citizens" of the overseas territories. In effect, this put Africans of the trust territories under a different rubric, but with rights equal to "citizens of personal status."[11]

Among the civil rights guaranteed by the preamble to the 1946 constitution and by Article 82 was the right to vote. It was in the exercise of this right that the constitutional distinctions between citizens of "civil status" and those of "personal status" became operative. All members of the former category exercised the right without reservation; but only those of the second category who were specifically enumerated by law might vote. The first enumeration (1946) included practically all Africans who had at any time held posts of responsibility in private or public enterprises, or who were veterans, owners of property whose title had been legally registered, or holders of hunting or driving licenses. The basic list was supplemented in 1947 to include all persons literate in French or Arabic; in 1951 to include tax-paying heads of families, mothers of two children "living or dead for France," and civil or military pensioners; and in 1952 to include without reservation all heads of families.[12] The distinctions permitted the creation of dual electoral rolls (the so-called dual college) in most French dependencies, including the Cameroun. However, as the list of eligibles in the "second college" increased, so did the electoral lists themselves between 1946 and 1953 the second college grew from 38,000 to 592,331.[13] The rate of growth was even greater after 1953 (see Appendix B). Even though the administration had granted the vote to "citizens of personal status" and *administrés français*, it was not also prepared to grant equal weight to the exercise of that suffrage. By law, at least two-fifths of the members of the Representative Assembly in the Cameroun had to be elected from the "first college." (Similar proportions prevailed in other "double college" territories.) In 1952, the proportion was reached to one-third for elections to the new Territorial Assembly.

In sum, then, the reforms between 1946 and 1952 gave the Cameroun a constitutional and institutional framework for political action. Its limitations not only provided the boundaries within which such action might take place, but also helped define the issues from which demands for reform might be made. The configuration of events leading to the reforms of 1946 gave the Cameroun, among other French territories, the essentials of a political theater: an electorate, a representative proscenium, stage rules, and some of the lines of the play to unfold within it. The play needed a plot: in the creation of the trusteeship system the United Nations supplied one.

3) *The trusteeship:* An observer of African political patterns has suggested that the remarkable number and type of political movements that have appeared in Togoland and the French Cameroun is explained in part by the fact that they were the only areas in French tropical Africa where both the legitimacy and the ultimacy of French authority were seriously in doubt.[14] The observation, made in 1955, still rings true after nine years of headlong development. The uncertainty regarding the Cameroun's political future can objectively, without doubt, be attributed mostly to the United Nations and the ambivalent promises of the trusteeship arrangements.

If the structure of the French Union and the phraseology of its constituent documents are any indices, had the French had their way, and the mandates not been committed to trusteeship, the Cameroun would have been marked for early integration into the *métropole.* Certainly nationalist feeling would not have developed so soon after 1946. The trusteeship agreements and the French acceptance of the United Nations Charter committed the *métropole,* whether it wished it or not, to the furtherance of the aims of trusteeship. These were aims that went much further politically than those stipulated under the mandates; moreover, an enlarged world community in which colonial powers were already a minority would watch French actions with increasingly critical eyes. As far as the Cameroun and Togo were concerned, France had been pushed downhill, and the best she could do was make the descent gracefully.

The League of Nations, which had lingered in a de facto limbo since the beginning of World War II, declared itself juridically extinct at the last meeting of the League Assembly on April 18, 1946. Among other resolutions, it adopted one in which it noted the intent of those powers administering mandates to continue to administer them in the spirit of the mandate agreements until new arrangements might be made with the United Nations. It also noted the assumption of the League's mandatory functions by the United Nations under the appropriate Chapters in the Charter.[15] By 1950, all the former African mandates that had not acceded to independence, with the exception of Southwest Africa, had become trust territories under the provisions of Chapter XII of the Charter of the United Nations.

Article 76 of the Charter set forth the political objectives of the trusteeship system:

... to promote the political, economic, and social and educational advancement of the inhabitants of the trust territories, and their progressive development towards self-government or independence as may be appropriate to the particular circumstances of each territory and its peoples and the freely expressed wishes of the people concerned, and as may be provided by the terms of each trusteeship agreement. . . .

In the Trusteeship Agreement for the Cameroun, France undertook to exercise the duties of trusteeship as defined in the Charter and to promote the basic objectives of the trusteeship as laid down in Article 76. The Agreement permitted France full legislative, administrative, and jurisdictional powers in the territory "in accordance with French law as an integral part of the French territory."[16] However, by Article 5 of the Agreement, France undertook to ensure the local inhabitants a share in the administration of the territory by the development of representative democratic bodies. Further, in due course, France promised to arrange appropriate consultations to enable the inhabitants freely to express an opinion on their political regime and thus to ensure the attainment of the objectives prescribed in Article 76 (b) of the Charter.

By accepting the principles of Article 76 (b) of the Charter and the provisions of the Trusteeship Agreement, France was committing herself to the possibility of a political development for the Cameroun exceeding anything implied by the constitution of 1946. The Charter opened an alternative—independence—which was not open to the other French territories (except Associated States) under any interpretation of the 1946 statutes. Self-government was an aim France could well foresee as the result of its progressive grants of increased responsibility to its overseas dependencies; it would be self-government, however, within an integrated, *métropole*-centered political community. Independence was another matter: except in the case of the trust territories, the French constitution-makers shrank from the alternative. One suspects the eventual independence of the Cameroun came less as a surprise to France than the attainment of similar status by the several territories of French West Africa between 1958 and 1960.

CONCLUSION

Examination of the political development of the Cameroun prior to 1947 reveals an almost complete absence of organized political activity in the territory. The march of events suggests an interesting conclusion: the first genuine attempts to give the African Camerounian a share in formulating political goals came about not so much as a result of the desultory, interest-group-oriented political activity before 1940, but as a result of events occurring outside the Cameroun itself, or caused by such events. The Brazzaville Conference, which reflected a new colonial liberalism and awareness of the new forces shaping the colonial world, was an outgrowth of the war itself, a catastrophe with which the Cameroun would have liked to have had as little to do as possible. The constitutional and institutional reforms of 1946-1947 were the reflection of a change in regime in the *métropole* itself, and of the accompanying aura of progress within which the Fourth Republic was born. The trusteeship, which provided radically new political alternatives for the Cameroun, was again a *mariage d'amour* reflecting the union of Charter principles with the new postwar French colonial policies. In none of the three developments discussed in the foregoing section did local sentiment play an appreciable part; the initiative always lay outside the territory. The growth of political activity in subsequent years reflected the fact of external beginnings. The first political groups were local branches of movements begun elsewhere, and their first tasks were not always organizational, but centered about the search for goals and symbols which could find local support.

Given the new institutional and constitutional framework, the emergence of political groups and the formation of political goals during the postwar era may now be examined in perspective. The subsequent discussion will, however, touch only peripherally another important question, that of the role of the trusteeship in the political development of postwar Cameroun. Its position as a United Nations trust territory certainly had a direct influence on the political formation of the Cameroun; this will be discussed, but in the perspective of the internal political evolution of the territory. A detailed analysis of the role of the trusteeship is beyond the scope of this work; the question has been elsewhere ably examined by David Gardinier.[17]

CHAPTER

VI *The Ferment of*
Party Politics—1945-1955

INTRODUCTION

In any analysis of the postwar political development of French *Afrique noire*, it is important to distinguish between the patterns of development in the French African trust territories on the one hand, and in French West and Equatorial Africa on the other. Essentially, the context of political advancement in French West and Equatorial Africa lay in the attempts to work out an accommodation between the centripetal aims of French policy (of which the constitution of the Fourth Republic and creation of the French Union are evidence) and the persistent African demands for the maximum political and administrative autonomy possible. The problem, it must also be pointed out, involved French African leaders such as Senghor, Houphouet-Boigny, and d'Arboussier in what was often a conflict between their own deep attachments to France and the need to assert independent lines of action and policy for French Africa against the *métropole* itself.

The force of these dilemmas was largely vitiated for the Cameroun and Togo by the extraordinary position in which the trust territories stood vis-à-vis France. Even though France hoped that eventually the Cameroun would become part of a broad Franco-African political system, and even though the Cameroun sent representatives to the same metropolitan and French Union organs as did the AOF and AEF (French West and Equatorial Africa), France was nonetheless committed to permitting a political development in the Cameroun different both in objectives and content. Some of these objectives and their implications were discussed in the previous chapter. In essence, the Cameroun was a case apart, and its political development became in a large measure a function of France's obligations to the United Nations, and, in a broader sense, to world opinion.

One of the consequences of this distinction was that institutional arrangements for the Cameroun were not the subject of as much con-

141

troversy as elsewhere in French Africa, a situation clearly deriving from the fact that the political objectives of the Cameroun were more or less clearly stated and generally understood by the principal political leaders in the territory. Constitutional and institutional matters became important issues only to the extent to which they furthered the aims of trusteeship or to the degree they accorded or failed to accord with the aspirations of the Cameroun's political leaders or parties. In the succeeding two chapters the fifteen-year period from 1945 to 1960 will be covered, focusing primarily upon the growth of political movements, the activities of political leaders, and the significant political events at home and abroad that affected the territory's advance to independence. Institutional and constitutional matters will be treated within the context of this analysis, not because they are unimportant, but because the peculiarities of the Camerounian situation made them peripheral, rather than central preoccupations.

The fifteen-year period divides conveniently, because of the pattern of events within it, into two distinct part or phases. The first phase, from 1945 to 1955, is the formative era of Camerounian political party life; during these years the party system took shape and the territory's political leaders learned the essentials of political and parliamentary life. The phase ends with the abortive revolt of the radical Camerounian left, the growth of which is central to the development of the party system as a whole. The second phase, between 1955 and 1960, analyzed in Chapter VII, was highlighted by the territory's slow recovery from the shock of the events of 1955, and by its struggle within the United Nations to achieve final independence.

THE POLITICAL INVASION
OF THE CAMEROUN

The end of the war in 1945 signaled the resumption of the political wars in France. Initially, only two groups emerged untainted by Vichy collaboration: the Communists, and the new and as yet amorphous Catholic left which found political expression in the *Mouvement Républicain Populaire* (MRP). These two were soon joined by a rejuvenated SFIO (Socialist) party, and by the pseudo party which coalesced around De Gaulle, the *Rassemblement du Peuple Français* (RPF). In Africa, Felix Houphouet-Boigny and his colleagues launched the *Rassemblement Démocratique Africain* (RDA) at Bamako, in October, 1946. The RDA, dedicated to seeking greater political rights for French-speaking Africans, became the first African political party to operate on an interterritorial basis in France's sub-Saharan territories.

In the Cameroun, the *Jeunesse Camerounaise Française (Jeucafra)*,

founded in 1938, survived the war as the only quasi-political association through which African Camerounians might address themselves
to political matters. Events elsewhere, however, gave excellent reasons
to expect that the time was at hand when organized political activity
in the territory could begin in earnest. The Brazzaville Conference was
one, and certainly the reformist spirit of the leaders of the Free French
movement was another. No one doubted that once the war was over
a wave of constitutional reform would sweep both the Brazzaville
spirit and increased political participation over all parts of French
Africa. Yet, interestingly enough, it was not the metropolitan parties
that gained the first foothold in the Cameroun, but the trade union
movement, even before the war had ended in Europe.

On August 27, 1944, trade union activity was legalized in the Cameroun, and it was not long until the *Confédération Générale du Travail*
(CGT), Communist dominated and the largest trade union in France,
established a local branch in the Cameroun. In September, the CGT
founded the *Union des Syndicats Confédérés du Cameroun* (USCC).
The new organization immediately embarked on a mass propaganda
campaign designed to enlist membership and bestir political feeling.
In July, 1945, a group of trade unions met in Douala to challenge the
labor code of June 18, 1945, drafted according to the proposals of the
Brazzaville Conference. The heady atmosphere this meeting created
in Douala and the departure of one of the founders (Charles Assalé)
of the CGT from the Cameroun for Paris to attend a CGT conference
touched off a series of wildcat strikes in Douala between September
21 and 30, 1945. The strikes degenerated into riots, and the militia
was called in. By the time calm had been restored, nine persons had
been killed, and some twenty wounded.[1]

In the meantime, *Jeucafra* was undergoing rapid transformation.
The events of September, 1945, galvanized it into action. A few days
after the Douala strikes, the organization called a conference to present
a series of demands to the territorial and French governments. It proposed the suppression of the *indigénat*, the expulsion of European
traders from rural areas and from the periodic local markets, elected
regional councils, the Africanization of cadres, and the creation of a
Territorial Assembly with legislative powers. *Jeucafra* then transformed
itself into the *Union Camerounaise Française (Unicafra)* and sent a
delegation to Paris[2] to plead its case.

By the time the elections of November and December, 1946, were
held under the new constitutional arrangements, the French *Front Inter-
colonial,* and the Socialist and RPF parties had begun the formation of
branch parties in the Cameroun. Also, a local group, the *Mouvement*

Démocratique Camerounais, had made its appearance. All three parties had an ephemeral existence in the Cameroun; the first two had difficulty in obtaining support, despite what seemed like promising starts; the third lasted only a few months. In any event, the legislative elections of 1946 represented a victory for the moderates, many of whom had *Jeucafra* affiliations.

At this juncture the trade unionists, and especially their European backers, their fingers burned by the September, 1945, strikes, shifted their tactics. They now sought to overwhelm *Unicafra* and capture its leadership positions. Between March 30 and April 6, 1947, *Unicafra,* the USCC, and several other groups met to discuss their joint prospects. Extremists and moderates disagreed violently on the course to follow; the former, led by the USCC, demanded a general strike, the latter advocated using the new representative institutions as springboards to change. The trade unionists lost the argument, but in succeeding weeks had their revenge by taking over the organization that grew from the conference, the *Rassemblement Camerounais (Racam).* It was a pyrrhic victory, one observer noted, since *Racam* never succeeded in going beyond a small circle of officials in Douala,[3] and in fact, disintegrated after only several months' existence.

THE LEGISLATIVE SPRINGBOARD

While the trade unions were attempting to find political leverage by using *Unicafra* and *Racam,* the new Representative Assembly was becoming a tribune for the most able of the Camerounian politicians, many of whom had been promoters of older organizations. Endowed with little more than advisory powers on most matters, the new Assembly wasted no time in demanding greater responsibility. During the ordinary session in 1946, the Assembly unanimously passed a resolution urging that its powers be considerably extended. In his speech at the close of the session, the President of the Assembly signified his approval of this development:

You have carried out the mandate entrusted to you, Gentlemen, by drawing attention to the fact that the powers granted to this Assembly are insufficient to allow it to take a genuine part in the country's administration. You have placed on record your regret at the fact that it constitutes a "council of notables" rather than a democratic assembly endowed with real powers.[4]

Another time, the Assembly registered a vigorous protest at the government's failure to take its opinion into account. On a further occasion, members criticized the government for going to the Assembly on matters on which its opinion was not expressly required, while debarring it from amending the proposed texts. In addition, the Assembly challenged the government's interpretation of the legislative texts setting up the Assembly, and affirmed its desire to exercise greater initiative in preparing its own agenda. In all, the Assembly was showing itself capable of considerable vigor and self-direction. In the process, certain personalities began to attract attention, such as Doctor Louis Aujoulat, a physician in the service of the Catholic missions, first elected from the "European" College, later from the "African"; Paul Soppo-Priso, a wealthy and eloquent *assimilé* from Douala; Charles Okala, founder of the Cameroun branch of the SFIO, ex-seminarian, former sports star; and Betoté Akwa, a descendant of the original Akwa king who signed the 1884 treaty with Germany.

The legislators began casting about for organizational bases on which to build more solid political support. The first elections to the Assembly had been largely fought and won on the personal appeal of the candidates involved. Most voters took little account of the existence of the several political groups and voted according to what local pressure dictated or to which personalities they recognized.[5] The legislators were not slow to recognize the key role that parties and political associations would play in future elections when the electorate had become more aware. Initially, they tried two organizational approaches. One was to form local branches of metropolitan parties; in this spirit the SFIO, the RPF, and the MRP all had Cameroun sections by the year 1947.[6] Another was to use what organizations already existed in the territory, and, if they were not already politically oriented, to give them a political direction. Thus, *Jeucafra* became a key organization (though its value to the legislators was lost as its successors were engulfed by the trade unions), as did such traditional associations as *Ngondo*, which became the tool of the more ambitious of the Douala politicians. Yet, aside from the trade unions, most of the organizations that made their appearance or became politically oriented during 1946 or 1947 failed to generate much excitement among the voting public. Parties were still the playground of the political elite, and by and large their programs, created elsewhere and clumsily adapted to Camerounian conditions, struck little popular response. Except for the activities of the labor unions and the personalities in the Assembly, by the end of 1947 politics in the Cameroun had aroused little enthusiasm. The time was ripe for truly Camerounian political parties, and for issues with more general appeal. Both were not long in appearing.

NEW DIRECTIONS: THE UPC

The trade unionists, beaten in the legislative elections in 1946 and 1947, singed by the 1945 riots, had withdrawn to lick their wounds and take stock. One result of their reappraisal was their absorption of *Unicafra* via *Racam.* Another result was a shift in propaganda, both in the direction and the substance of the message. Before 1947, the trade unionists had attempted to use the doctrine of the class struggle as the main carrier of their message. The approach had been unsuccessful; they saw that in a country in which the majority of the population was rural, with a virtually nonexistent bourgeoisie, class consciousness was nonexistent as well. Much less could it be exploited for political ends. Moreover, what there was of a proletariat (if it could be called that) was based in Douala, and even it was composed mainly of unsophisticated, semiskilled laborers.[7] The 1945 strikes in Douala had been, admittedly, poor proof of the militancy and class consciousness of that proletariat.

The trade unionists produced both a new organization and a message they hoped would have more appeal. On April 10, 1948, Ruben Um Nyobé, a one-time government clerk turned labor organizer, Félix Moumié, Ernest Ouandié, Abel Kingué, and several other labor leaders formed the *Union des Populations du Cameroun* (UPC) from the ruins of *Racam.*[8] On June 17 the UPC incorporated the local RDA group and became the official Cameroun section of that party. The new organization announced what was essentially a two-point program: the unification of the two Cameroons and rapid progress toward complete independence under the terms of the United Nations Charter. The UPC quickly gained the support of the *Ngondo* and newly formed (May 10, 1948) *Kumsze,* so-called Bamiléké Traditional Association, founded by a local chief and UPC sympathizer, Mathias Djoumessi. Initially, the two "traditional" organizations proved useful allies of the UPC. By 1949, however, *Ngondo* had become disenchanted with the partnership, and by 1950 so had *Kumsze.* Both later actively opposed the UPC.

In formulating its program, the UPC had been inspired by two considerations: the terms of the trusteeship and the example of Togo. Togolese politicians had acquired and held the attention of the United Nations and of the world by a skillful manipulation of the Ewe issue.[9] (The Ewe people, through their spokesmen, demanded that, in settling the future of both British and French Togo, Ewe tribal lands, split by the border between the two trust territories, be reunited.) In Togo the Ewe problem had substantial basis in fact; in the Cameroun no such basis existed for a similar appeal. Neither the Douala nor the Bamiléké people could claim that their ethnic brethren in the British Cameroons had much interest in a unification of the two Cameroons. Over thirty years separation had effectively muted any ethnic irredentism; moreover, even though both Douala and Bamiléké had maintained contact over the frontier, no active demands for unification on ethnic grounds had ever been advanced before. The only previous manifestations of the unification issue had arisen in the context of pan-Douala demands which were directed not at Douala solidarity, but at an alleged Douala hegemony over the *whole* of the Cameroons. However, in the context of the political climate in 1948, the issue came to be an effective political horse which could be ridden far by adroit riders. Each for its own reasons, the UPC, the *Kumsze,* and the *Ngondo* joined hands on this issue.

Soon after the creation of the UPC, its leaders contacted Mr. R. J. K. Dibonge, a Douala living in the British Cameroons. With Dibonge as its head, the French Cameroons Welfare Association (later Union) was formed with the dual purpose of mobilizing the Douala in the British Cameroons and spreading the unification idea. Thereafter, the French Cameroons Welfare Association, and later other British Cameroonian political groups (including the Kamerun United National Congress, of which Dibonge was the first president), maintained active contact with the UPC's leaders. The Association had, at one time, a membership exceeding four thousand. Parenthetically, it may be noted that Dibonge's organization later also became disenchanted with the UPC, and broke with it on the question of maintaining an organization separate from the Kamerun National Congress, in whose formation Dibonge had been instrumental.[10] In any event, the unification issue remained as a permanent factor in the politics of the British Cameroons. In the early days of the British Cameroons' political formation it was, however, used more as a weapon against continued association with Nigeria than as a positive force for reunification.

On the organizational front, the UPC moved ahead just as rapidly. It began by building on the recognized RDA pattern—a pyramidical structure, based on *comités de village* in the country and *comités de quartier* in the towns.[11] In 1950, following its first congress at Dschang, the UPC reorganized itself into a tight, hierarchically structured organization. At the base of the pyramid were the local committees, found in the various quarters of urban centers and in some bush villages. Initially, almost half the local committees were in the Sanaga Maritime Region, home of the Bassa people, of which the UPC's General Secretary, Ruben Um Nyobé, was one. Besides those in Bassa country, the largest and strongest locals were in and around the urban centers in which trade union activity flourished among the laborers and plantation workers, centers such as Douala, N'kongsamba, M'balmayo, Eséka, and, later, Edéa. The second level was represented by the Central Committees, a number of intermediate bodies whose essential function was to transmit orders from the higher echelons to the local committees. The Central Committees were set up according to the number of UPC members in a given area, rather than along the lines of the official administrative divisions. Third came the Regional Committees, each designed to coördinate the activities of the combined memberships of several Central Committees. Finally, at the top of the pyramid, was the Central Executive Committee (*Comité Directeur*), elected by the Congress of the party, and comprising a political Bureau, a Secretariat, and a Treasury.[12]

In addition to this highly sophisticated organizational structure, the UPC took pains to create subsidiary and complementary organizations such as *Les Amis du Progrès*, a "cultural" society in Yaoundé; the *Comité féminin de l'UPC* (later known as *L'Union démocratique des femmes Camerounaises*, or UDFC); *Solidarité Babimbi, Association des anciens combattants*, and *La voix du peuple Bafia*. In the beginning, these groups were little more than names, although, as propaganda vehicles and petition-writing agencies they often assumed an importance far exceeding their numerical strength. Later, other organizations joined the list: the *Jeunesse Démocratique Camerounaise* (JDC, 1952), *Amis des Nations Unies, Comité du défense de la paix;* and, after 1955, such pro-UPC or UPC front groups as the *Union des associations traditionelles du Cameroun, Union nationale des mères Camerounaises, Comité de défense des droits des refugiés, Comité pour la réconciliation et l'amnistie*, and *Comité pour le regroupment des forces nationalistes*. From it all, the important fact emerged that the UPC operated on several organizational levels and in a number of social sectors, each varied according to the tactical role assigned to it. The main party carried the brunt of the political attack; the subsidiaries operated as propaganda centers and as organizational cocoons within which prospective or fledgling leaders of the party could gain valuable experience.[13] In addition, the party published a monthly newspaper, *Voix du peuple du Cameroun*, in which the leadership presented its views and laid out the party's program.[14] By 1955, three more UPC publications had appeared (*L'Etoile*, a weekly, *Lumière*, a bimonthly regional journal, and *La Vérité*, a youth bulletin).

By the time the first United Nations Visiting Mission arrived in the Cameroun in November, 1949, the UPC had crystallized along the main lines of its organizational and programmatic development. Within a year it had become by all odds the best organized political party in the Cameroun. Furthermore, it had taken on the coloration of a truly Camerounian party, and had developed the first effective body of doctrine based (at least it was advanced as such) on exclusively Camerounian themes. By the end of 1949 it had proclaimed itself the first party of Camerounian nationalism; its tactical and organizational boldness lent considerable substance to the claim. The other political parties certainly suffered by comparison; after 1949 their programs and strategies reflected attempts to preëmpt the themes and tactics of the UPC. No more dramatic testimony to the UPC's general effectiveness could have been found.

THE WAR OF PREËMPTION—1949-1955

Even though the UPC structured itself on a nationwide basis and launched a program designed to attract the widest popular support, it was not yet in any sense a "national" party. Its cadre, though dispersed throughout the country, had only a limited initial success in enlisting members, recruiting them almost exclusively in the southwest. Its program, though dealing with potentially irresistible themes, had not as yet attracted either the attention or understanding that a more experienced electorate might provide. Most Camerounians had little comprehension of the nature of the trusteeship or the implications of the trusteeship agreement, and few of them had any interest in the unification issue. It is probably fair to say that most Camerounians who thought about the matter in 1949, 1950, or 1951, showed little inclination to become excited over it.[15] Not even a meeting of nationalist groups from both Cameroons in May, 1949, or another one in August, 1951, or a United Kamerun National Congress held in Kumba, British Cameroons. December 12 to 17, 1951—to which Um led a twenty-six man UPC delegation—roused much enthusiasm for the UPC or "reunification" in the French Cameroun.

All this gave the other Camerounian parties heart; there was still certainly much room for other groups to emerge and for new ideas to develop. Even though a realistic perspective showed the UPC to be neither as powerful nor as attractive as it claimed to be, realism also dictated the wisdom of admitting the obvious—that it was better organized and led, and had a more coherent program, than any other group in the territory. These considerations drew the battle lines between 1949 and 1955. The UPC and its affiliates ranged against the other parties, using the local legislature as their lever and sounding board, with both sides putting much emphasis on appeals to tribal or ethnic loyalties.

In 1948 the first of the anti-UPC political groups was organized. In the Bamiléké region, pro-Administration chiefs created the *Union Bamiléké* to counter the pro-UPC *Kumsze*. When the latter renounced its UPC ties in 1950, the former lost its raison d'etre and faded away.

In 1949, the *Evolution Sociale Camerounaise (Esocam)* was organized. Its program (particularly after the Kumba Congress in December, 1951, which its leaders attended) also was essentially in opposition to the UPC; its founders, Bassa *notables*, tried to oppose every UPC cell in the Sanaga Maritime Region with an *Esocam* cell. An organization with aims similar to *Esocam's*, the *Renaissance Camerounaise (Renaicam)*, was created in 1949 at Abong-Mbang, in the eastern part of the country, also with an ethnic referent (Ewondo-Maka).[16]

When the next round of elections came up—in June, 1951, for the French National Assembly and in March, 1952, for the Territorial Assembly—a full panoply of parties stood ready to contest them. These included not only the UPC and the older parties, but also the *Bloc Démocratique Camerounais* (BDC), founded by Aujoulat in July, 1951. Once again the UPC lost both elections; even Um Nyobé failed to get a plurality in his own Bassa constituency.[17] Once again the moderates all but swept the field, with Aujoulat, Soppo Priso, Okala, and the future prime minister, Ahmadou Ahidjo, all reëlected to the Assembly. And once again the UPC retired to ponder the causes of its defeat.

The Assembly itself, by this time, had begun to take on the appearance of a sovereign legislature. Few of its decisions were annulled by the *Conseil d'Etat*, and its recommendations were almost always followed. Within the Assembly, the various chairmanships and *rapporteur* positions passed increasingly into African hands. Louis Aujoulat, now a deputy of the "African" College, actively campaigned for a reform of the legislature, and in the process was elected Assembly president. Soppo Priso and Charles Okala gave brilliant, polished performances on the floor of the Assembly while keeping the administration under constant verbal assault.

The legislators' activities were not confined entirely to forensic displays, however. A series of concrete proposals for legislative and administrative reform began emanating from the Assembly. Louis Aujoulat proposed the creation of a single electoral college and the enlargement of the Assembly's powers. Soppo Priso, who in 1953 finally succeeded in displacing Aujoulat as Assembly president, undertook extensive official tours of the southland, making speeches and attempting to build up a popular image. Soppo also introduced into the French Union Assembly, of which he was a deputy, legislation which would have converted the Cameroun into a semiautonomous state in which power would have been divided between a French High Commissioner and an executive council of commissioners elected from the Assembly.[18] Soppo began to look and act like a *premier commissaire*, and there were those who claimed he had ambitions to be the first Camerounian prime minister. Charles Okala advanced a program similar to Soppo's. He suggested that the Assembly be elected from a single electoral college, have extended powers (though still subject to the veto of the *Conseil d'Etat*), and that a sort of executive council be created, composed of a premiere and several assistant commissioners.[19]

Furthermore, the politicians, heartened by their electoral successes, embarked on the creation of still more political groups. Aujoulat formed his *Bloc Démocratique Camerounais,* and drew into it such diverse personalities as Ahmadou Ahidjo from Garoua, and André Mbida, imposing politician from the south. Specifically to counter the UPC-dominated CGT, in 1952 Aujoulat founded a territorial branch of the CFTC (*Confédération des Travailleurs Chrétiens*) in Yaoundé. Okala, who had nurtured the Cameroun section of the SFIO since its beginnings in 1947, only to see it gradually wither, formed the *Union Sociale Camerounaise* in 1953 from the remnants of the older group. Launching itself on a program of anticapitalism and anti-imperialism, the USC attempted to set up a number of sections in Bulu Territory and in Douala, but failed to gain much mass support among either workers or peasants. An anti-UPC group, *Coordination des Indépendents Camerounais (Indecam)* was formed in Edea in 1952 after a vigorous pamphleteering campaign. It, too, remained weak, torn by leadership rivalries.

Charles Assalé, one of the key personalities in the creation of the Camerounian trade union movement, himself organized a local political machine on a Bulu ethnic base. His *Association Traditionelle Bantoue Efoula-Meyong* proved a success, driving all other parties out of Bulu land. Riding his "traditional association," Assalé was elected to the Territorial Assembly in 1952 with what he later described as "an almost plebiscitary majority."[20] The lesson was not lost on the other politicians. Almost all of them, with varying success, tried to create their own "traditional" associations, usually basing them on existing, genuinely traditional formations. Djoumessi reinforced his *Kumsze,* Betote Akwa and "Prince" Douala Manga Bell reworked the organization and program of the *Ngondo;* other "traditional" organizations were initiated among the Bamoun, the Eton, the Ewondo and Beti, the Fulani of Ngaoundéré, the Musgum, and the Batanga.[21] Some of the latter group took on the character of ethnic "welfare" associations primarily interested in articulating a particular ethnic interest; others performed not only this function, but also advanced candidates for election to the Territorial Assembly.

Meanwhile, the UPC had shifted its tactics again. After its electoral defeats in 1951 and 1952, the organization underwent a structural and strategic reorientation. The structural changes, which were accelerated during 1952, 1953, and 1954, have already been noted. Insofar as strategy was concerned, the UPC decided to make full use of the various means of access to the Fourth Trusteeship Committee of the UN General Assembly and, it was hoped, to world opinion. Once again, the Togolese example proved fruitful. The UPC leaders observed with interest the amount of space devoted by the foreign press to the appearance of Togolese leaders before the Trusteeship Committee. In December, 1952, Um Nyobé made the first of several appearances before the Trusteeship Committee to testify in conjunction with a number of UPC-sponsored petitions.[22] Um reiterated his party's objectives: rapid advance toward independence, severance of ties with France, a UN-guaranteed unification of the two Cameroons. He also accused the French of unprovoked hostility to the UPC. The administration sent to New York Okala, Jules Ninine, and Daniel Kemajou (a Bamiléké who was at the time a member of the Assembly of the French Union) on its behalf.[23]

Um's appearance before the UN was played up as a great triumph for the UPC and, on his return from New York, Um undertook a tour of the country, allegedly to report directly to the people about the success of his mission and the work of the Trusteeship Committee.[24] In truth, Um's appearance before the Fourth Committee rebounded both to his and the UPC's prestige and influence. The UN connection, conjuring up a "Jehovah-like figure in New York," was stressed by Um, and the UPC gained thereby in the reflected glory. One commentator noted that the unificationist case was much stimulated by the UN connection, giving "those people who come within its protection the sense of being an elect."[25] Um pointed out that if the aim of the trusteeship (something entirely different from the old mandate) is self-government, then self-government cannot be realized unless the Cameroons were reunited.

Um's appearance in New York signaled not only a new phase in the personal politics of the UPC leadership, but also opened the gates to a flood of petitions from the UPC and its affiliates. The Trusteeship Council, the Security Council, the Secretary-General of the United Nations were all addressed by the Camerounian petitioners. United Nations Visiting Missions were subjected to a veritable bombardment of petitions, some of them arriving in bundles containing several hundred sheets, each written or printed with a single phrase or word, or printed uniformly with the same message.[26]

One of the UPC's founders, Dr. Félix Moumié, returned from Dakar in 1953 and brought with him an open admiration for Marxist teachings (especially that of Mao Tse-tung) and direct action. Moumié's arrival on the scene probably contributed to the change in UPC domestic tactics observable in 1954: intense propaganda campaigns coupled with a multiplication of local incidents of violence. By 1954, the UPC had begun to take on the appearance of a communist-inspired movement; at least the external trappings were there: participation in a number of "peace" conferences, world youth festivals, and WFTU congresses; the use of Marxist language in its petitions and publications; an organizational structure resembling Communist parties in eastern Europe and southeast Asia. Um denied, however, that either he or his party had Communist connections.

The party was ready for another, more direct phase of action. The events of 1955 turned the UPC from a radical nationalist party into a revolutionary one. Up to 1955 the UPC had accomplished little of real substance; its primary contribution to the Cameroun political scene was catalytic. The UPC had been the first and remained the best organized party in the country. The other politicians and parties quickly turned their energies into creating anti-UPC parties, using many of their enemy's organizational techniques. Moreover, the UPC had produced the first coherent body of party doctrine. The other politicians and parties followed suit and attempted to preëmpt the issues raised by the UPC. By 1955, almost all the parties (even the BDC) had accepted as their goals the eventual independence of the country and the unification of the two Cameroons. The UPC had led the rest in bringing the political issues of the Cameroun to the UN; it was not long until the other parties had established beachheads in New York. The war of preëmption had ended in a virtual stalemate; the UPC found its operations the object of increasingly hostile attentions by the administration.[27] By 1955 the leaders of the UPC had failed to achieve even a semblance of the RDA's successes in the AEF or elsewhere. Their mood, coming into 1955, was one of frustration, undoubtedly tinged by the bitterness of successive domestic defeats. To a radical party in this mood, violence was bound to have a certain attraction.

THE RECOURSE TO VIOLENCE—
1955 AND AFTER

If any one event could be said to have been the precipitating factor that drove an already restive UPC into a campaign of violence, it was the arrival in the Cameroun of High Commissioner Roland Pré, replacing High Commissioner Soucadaux in November, 1954. It is possible that the UPC had already been preparing for a resort to violence and that Pré's arrival made little difference, as the administration always contended. Or, it may have been Pré's policies (as the UPC claimed) that finally drove the UPC to extremes.

Whichever it was, Pré arrived determined to tolerate no foolishness from the UPC or any local political organization. He immediately took the offensive against the UPC's activities and its propaganda. Further, he insisted on a strict interpretation of the texts from which the Territorial Assembly and its elected members drew their powers. The result, a limitation of the Assembly's powers, served to alienate most of the African members of the Assembly including its president, Soppo Priso.[28]

On the other hand, the UPC appeared to have been responsible for a series of rumors, the most fantastic of which were apparently designed to play upon antiforeign sentiment and primitive superstitions. The French claimed the UPC circulated rumors alleging Europeans were abducting local inhabitants in order to decapitate them and use their heads for witchcraft.[29] In the Bamiléké Region, one former administrator claimed, the UPC circulated leaflets stating that a campaign of innoculation in the region was in fact a plot whereby the colonialists planned to depopulate the Bamiléké by killing off their children.[30] Moumié and Um were reported to have made repeated statements promising early violent abolition of the regime, and accusing the administration of various sanguinary acts of repression against UPC members.[31] In March, Pré ordered the transfer of all UPC-affiliated civil servants to Douala. The move proved to be a tactical error since Moumié was one of those affected and his new location enabled him to pursue his agitation more directly. From March 1 to 4 the *Confédération Générale Kamerunaise du Travail* (CGKT) launched a series of short strikes on the Douala waterfront. On April 22, the officers of the UPC, JDC, UDEFC, and its affiliated labor unions, the *Union des Syndicats Confédérés du Cameroun,* issued at Douala a "joint proclamation" declaring the termination of the territory's trusteeship status and the establishment of a sovereign Camerounian state. They requested, *inter alia,* the election of a constituent assembly and the formation of a United Nations commission to supervise the installation of the organs of the new state.[32] Everywhere, incidents involving the UPC multiplied; among the most notable were a series of demonstrations in the Bamiléké Region involving Um and Moumié. By the end of April, the situation was extremely tense. In the Bamiléké, Mungo, Sanaga-Maritime, and Nyong-et-Sanaga *régions* feelings ran high, and most of the larger urban centers in the south and southwest experienced increasingly serious incidents. With the coming of May, the volatile situation finally ignited.

Before detailing the events of the May uprising, however, mention must be made of the conflict that erupted between the UPC and the Catholic Church at the beginning of 1955, a conflict that served to heighten the prevailing tension and which, not improbably, may have helped inflame the already restive UPC into violent action.

From the party's inception, its leaders had taken care not to arouse religious feelings in the heavily Christianized south. Um himself claimed to be a professing Protestant, his party announced that it tolerated all religious groups, and early statements by Um and some of his followers reveal neutral or favorable references to God. At the second UPC congress in 1952, for example, Um declared that, "speaking from a Christian viewpoint, everyone recognizes that God created the Cameroun as one. . . ."[33] As the UPC became progressively more radical, it began to attack religion and the missions as "disguised colonialists." The organized opposition of Aujoulat's organization, *Ad Lucem*, the BDC, and the CFTC—all Yaoundé based and Catholic in orientation—served to exacerbate the increasing mutual hostility between the Church and the UPC.

On Easter Sunday, 1955, the Catholic bishops in the Cameroun circulated a pastoral letter that warned the faithful of Communism and the UPC:

Marxism . . . is the gravest danger that menaces our civilization . . . we are putting Christians on their guard against the present tendencies of the party known under the name of the UPC, not because it defends the cause of independence, but because of the spirit which animates and inspires its methods; because of its hostile and malevolent attitude to the Catholic mission and because of its connections with atheistic Communism, condemned by the Supreme Pontiff.[34]

The letter, read from pulpits throughout the territory, provoked an almost immediate response in Bafia and New Bell (Douala), where some violent incidents occurred. Further, three written replies appeared within several days: a UPC press communiqué addressed to Catholics in Bafia, a letter from a "Catholic of Sangmélima" entitled "When the U. P. C. teaches the Bible to the Bishops' (both on April 14), and a curious eleven-page mimeographed letter by Moumié (April 22) in which he denounced the collusive relation between religion and colonialism and argued that "God is with those who fight against colonialism and seek their country's independence."[35] The outbreak of the UPC-Church conflict was submerged in the furore of the more spectacular events that immediately followed. That it continued to persist, however, is attested to by the several Catholic missions burned or attacked, and by the numbers of priests and nuns who lost their lives through terrorist activity after 1955.

In the period between May 22 and 30, a series of disturbances took place at Douala, Yaoundé, Bafoussam, Meiganga, Nkongsamba, Mbanga, Loum, Penja, Dschang, and Ngambé. The beginning of the outbreaks coincided with the inauguration of the bridge over the Wouri, one of the major public works achievements of the Administration. The demonstrators attacked persons and property with almost wanton fury; they hurled themselves into the streets in large groups, killing or wounding Africans or Europeans who happened to be in their path. Numerous houses were burned, cars demolished or put to the torch, and considerable other property damage was incurred in most of the towns concerned in the outbreaks. In Douala itself, some three thousand rioters, armed with nail-studded clubs, machetes, axes, iron bars, and some firearms, stormed the central radio station and spread havoc throughout the New Bell section of the town. In Yaoundé, the demonstrators stormed the police station, freeing a number of UPC prisoners, invaded the Territorial Assembly, and set up a roadblock on the road to Douala. Elsewhere similar incidents were reported, and by the time the authorities had restored order (on May 30) twenty-six persons had lost their lives, and 176 had been wounded.[36]

If the UPC had expected a general uprising to follow the May riots, it was deceived in its hopes. The demonstrations had been limited to the Yaoundé area and the regions of the southwest; that it never spread any further north was due to the UPC failure to enlist the support of the Muslim populations in the northern centers. The riots accomplished little, insofar as their instigators were concerned. On July 13, 1955, a decree of the Council of Ministers dissolved the UPC and its two affiliates (the UDFC and the JDC). In an attempt to disassociate itself from the uprising, the USCC-CGT severed its connections with the French CGT, and called itself the *Confédération Générale Kamerunaise du Travail* (CGKT). This did not prevent the CGT's leaders, Jacques Ngom and Mayoa Beck, from being arrested, although they were released during 1956. Also, some 637 persons were indicted for diverse acts of violence or destruction.[37] Um Nyobé, who had been in Nigeria when the rebellion broke out, and most of the rest of the leaders, including Moumié, Kingué, and Ouandié, fled to Kumba in the British Cameroons to set up new headquarters.

Even though the revolt had miscarried, it left the political air heavy with suspicion and recrimination. The 1955 UN Visiting Mission, which visited the territory in October, noted the strained atmosphere and remarked that the riots and the aggressive propaganda of the UPC in the north had increased northern hostility to the UPC, even to the point where it encompassed the whole south. The administration, the UPC, and the local politicians all appeared divided and hesitant, and the Visiting Mission felt that if Cameroonian unity were not immediately threatened, it was at least jeopardized.[38]

It took several months until the shock of the May events had worn off sufficiently for political activity to resume with any spirit. By the autumn of 1955, however, in the wake of the increased hostility between Commissioner Roland Pré and the African legislators (who blamed him for the May riots), members of the dissolved parties as well as such personalities as Soppo Priso and André-Marie Mbida were appealing for a political amnesty and a reconciliation of all Camerooni-ans. The new spirit of reconciliation seemed to spread to the *métropole,* and an amnesty bill drafted by the administration was discussed in the French National Assembly. The effect of the new spirit could also be seen in the results of the January, 1956, Cameroun elections for deputies to the French National Assembly: Louis Aujoulat, the incumbent and representing the "hard line" of opposition to the UPC, was defeated by ex-seminarian André-Marie Mbida by 64,397 votes to 18,915.[39] (As it turned out, Mbida, who owed his political education to Aujoulat, subsequently became as violently anti-UPC as his mentor, but at the time he appears to have posed as a moderate, if not a reconciliationist, interested in furthering the growth of Camerounian autonomy.)

In the meantime, a series of constitutional reforms was being drafted in Paris, culminating in the *loi-cadre* of June 23, 1956.[40] The *loi-cadre* marked the beginning of a new era for the Cameroons, signaling the introduction of the first really large-scale reforms made in the territory since 1946. Constitutionally, *loi-cadre* gave the Cameroons its first important push to independence.

The importance of the *loi-cadre* for the Cameroons was threefold. First, it reduced one of the main difficulties that had hindered the earlier introduction of institutional reforms in the Cameroun—that is, the delays in the parliamentary process. According to Article 9, these were to be minimized by the provision that the French government, taking into account the Trusteeship Agreement, could inaugurate institutional reforms by decrees made after consultation with the Territorial Assembly and the Assembly of the French Union. Second, by making this special provision for the Cameroun, the law specifically recognized the possibility of the trust territory following a political development suited to its particular circumstances and status and, if need

be, different from that envisaged for French overseas territories proper.
Third, Article 10 provided that future elections to all assemblies in the
territories under French administration should be held on the basis
of universal adult suffrage and from a single electoral college.

In accordance with these provisions, and in consultation with
Cameroun representatives in French assemblies, the French government drafted a Statute of the Camerouns which was to give the
Cameroun a wide measure of autonomy.[41] So that a new assembly,
elected on the basis of the *loi-cadre's* provisions, might pronounce on
the proposed Statute, the old Assembly, elected in March, 1952, was
dissolved in November, 1956 (three months before its official expira-
tion date), and elections were scheduled for December 23 of that same
year. In preparation for the election, electoral rolls were specially revised, and the number of registered voters almost doubled. The total
increased from 853,932 to 1,685,059, almost 56 per cent of the total
population of the Cameroun. Also, by a special amnesty law (August 2,
1956), the administration permitted the UPC leaders to participate in
the election, providing they did so peacefully.

The institutional and constitutional reforms at hand did not, however, provoke much enthusiasm among the Camerounian politicians.
The "spirit of reconciliation" still pervaded the political atmosphere,
carrying with it unabated Soppo Priso's dislike of the administration
and a general distrust of French intentions. On June 6, seventeen days
before the *loi-cadre* went into effect, Soppo launched the so-called
Courant Mouvement d'Union Nationale, whose alleged purpose was
to unite the political parties in a common "minimum program." Its main
themes: rejection of the *loi-cadre,* unification of the Cameroons, recon-
stitution of the Assembly through universal suffrage, and proclamation
of a general amnesty throughout the territory. The movement was at
first warmly received in the south of the Cameroun and was joined
by a large number of prominent people, including some of the leaders
of the USC, BDC, *Indecam, Esocam,* and the UPC. Mbida, Ahidjo, and
leaders of the north remained aloof, suspicious of the new organization's authenticity and composition.

The movement's basic weakness soon became apparent: though most
of the component organizations agreed on general principles, they
could not do so on a common program. On November 28, extremists
and moderates clashed at the movement's congress at Ebolowa. The
latter were prepared to participate in the December elections (although
Soppo had earlier given indications he would refuse), and the former
demanded abstention and an active boycott. The split led to the disappearance of the *Union Nationale* from the local political scene, put-

ting an end to an experience that had lasted less than five months. The UPC, unable to prevail over its erstwhile confreres, went underground to prepare its campaign against the forthcoming elections.

Seen in perspective, the *Union Nationale* represents an important event in the political development of the Cameroun. It marked the real end of the war of preëmption. The movement, even though it lasted a few months, drew together the most important political personalities in the Territory on a program, however vague, that contained all the elements of the nationalist creed as the UPC had first proclaimed it. Soppo, Okala, Aujoulat, Assalé, and others who had earlier balked at the suggestion of a rapid attainment of independence were swept along to the point where they were forced to adopt the full panoply of Cameroun nationalist symbols, as well as some of the unique Camerounian nationalist demonology. There was probably not a little political opportunism in the formation of the movement; the moderates undoubtedly feared that if they did not also endorse the more radical aims of the UPC they would be overwhelmed by the nationalist sentiment that organization had succeeded in arousing. The split probably occurred partly because the moderates were not prepared to relinquish a chance to accomplish by constitutional action what the UPC had failed to do by force. Moreover, the moderates benefited by their participation in the *Union Nationale;* they had gained semirevolutionary respectability by their association with the UPC, and could henceforth present themselves to the voters as full-fledged supporters of what had now become common nationalist goals.

The election campaign was conducted along essentially regional lines, and the choice between the voters was not so much between clearly defined political movements as between prominent local personalities and the other candidates associated with them. Independence was a popular theme, as were unification and thinly masked attacks on the administration. The UPC played a more systematically organized part in the campaign than any of the legal political movements, but its part was a negative one, and limited to a small section of the territory. Late in November it had decided to carry on a campaign for voting abstention, which was in fact punctuated by acts of sabotage. In the month of the election numerous incidents of violence took place, in particular at Douala, Yaoundé, and in the Sanaga-Maritime, where two candidates, Dr. Charles Delangue (first Camerounian to be promoted to the position of Chief Physician and politically close to the UPC) and Samuel Npoumah, were assassinated.

Twice, within less than two years, the UPC had resorted to violence to gain its objectives, and each time it had been repulsed, in the process gaining the active enmity of some political groups and the distrust of others. It passed from a militantly nationalistic mass party to a clandestine, underground movement whose support was neither organized nor stable. There is little doubt that it commanded a good deal of sympathy; the *Mouvement d'Action Nationale,* which Charles Assalé and David Mvondo formed out of the *Ngondo* and the Association *Efoula-Meyong* in March, 1956, continued to press for a general amnesty and "reconciliation" throughout 1956, 1957, 1958, and 1959. The list of sympathizers did not, however, include the British Government, which, in June, 1957, expelled the so-called UPC government in exile (consisting of Moumié and ten others) from Kumba. Egypt and the Sudan offered the group asylum, and it migrated to Cairo and the protection of President Nasser. Um and his able confederate, Mayi-Matip (head of the JDC), returned to the Cameroun to resume the leadership of the embattled Bassa rebels in the Sanaga-Maritime. The UPC was down, but not out; its very presence and continued underground activity remained the key to political developments during the next three years, influencing if not shaping the configuration of parties and issues facing the first two Camerounian governments.

The focus of the violence and sabotage that gripped the south central and southwestern portions of the territory was the Sanaga-Maritime, whither Um Nyobé retired after the failure of the *Union Nationale.* Using the strong kinship obligations of the Bassa, Um had been able to incite his ethnic brethren to acts of extreme violence and sabotage. For example, during a twenty-four-hour period, between December 18 and 19, an engine was derailed just after crossing a bridge; iron ties were torn up and thrown into a river; telegraph lines were cut at intervals of about fifty feet over the distance of about one mile; roadblocks and barricades were erected at almost every crossroad leading out of the area; gullies, some as deep as ten feet, were cut across main roads; and a number of white men driving their cars on personal business were manhandled and their cars overturned.[42] The UPC burned a number of polling places, and, where they were unable to burn the polls, the voters' houses were set on fire. French and Cameroun troops were finally moved into the area and nominal order was restored. Thousands of Bassa fled to the hills, and the houses of known UPC followers were burned in retaliation.

The arrival of the troops also enabled individuals with grudges against their neighbors to settle old scores; many innocent persons were denounced by their personal enemies as members of the UPC, and were shot.

The final toll of killed or wounded in the Sanaga-Maritime during

December, 1956, and January, 1957, is still a matter of conjecture. Hundreds were wounded by beatings, shootings, and the like, and the number of dead may have reached two thousand, according to one observer.[43] It was not until February that the troops were finally withdrawn, leaving behind them an uneasy calm. They also left behind a core of UPC supporters who had gone into hiding, ready to harass the local populations.

The results of the elections (see Appendix B) reflected the limited nature of the UPC campaign and the genuine hostility toward it expressed by northern and eastern elements. Only in two regions of the nineteen, Wouri and the Sanaga-Maritime, did the UPC campaign materially affect the normal rate of abstention. In the Wouri region, consisting mainly of the city of Douala, only 22 per cent of the registered voters cast ballots. In the Sanaga-Maritime, the area of greatest UPC *maquis* activity, only 12.5 per cent of those registered voted. However, the two regions contained only about 9 per cent of the total population of the territory. Elsewhere participation was high: in the Mungo region 66 per cent of those registered voted, in the Nyong-et-Sanaga Region (the Yaoundé area) 70 per cent voted, and in the Ntem Region, 80 per cent voted. Although the UPC claimed the low voting percentages in the northern regions were owing to their efforts, the 1958 UN Visiting Mission concluded that the abstentions were owing to other circumstances, such as a lesser interest in politics and the extension of the vote to women in areas where local tradition against female suffrage was still strong. In all, the average for the entire territory was about 55 per cent of those registered who voted.[44]

CHAPTER

VII *The Politics of Consolidation—1955-1960*

THE FIRST CAMEROUN GOVERNMENT OF MBIDA

As soon as it began its session on January 28, 1957, the new Assembly spent a month studying the proposed Statute of the Cameroun, which it passed on February 22 by a vote of fifty-nine to eight. One important modification was made in the draft Statute: the territory would henceforth be called the State of the Cameroun, a change which did not alter its legal position but did appear to satisfy the desire of some legislators for recognition of the Cameroun's new status. Only the deputies of the *Action Nationale*, whose eight members finally cast the eight negative votes, argued against the draft Statute, proposing instead an alternative text of thirteen articles. This latter text would have recognized the immediate independence of the Cameroun and stipulated that all jurisdictions France reserved under the draft Statute—finances, diplomatic representation, commercial law, external commerce, penal code, and external defense—would pass at once to the new state. Furthermore, the alternative text envisaged early application for membership in the United Nations.[1] As one observer put it:[2]

The illogicality of this project, inferior to the documents usually prepared by its drafters, betrayed their [real] irritation: in effect, they were too well informed not to know the defects of their text and the quality of the Government's draft, but through their text they were aiming at the Camerounian promoter of the draft Statute: M. Mbida, who concealed neither his opposition to an early independence, nor his desire to wipe out the U. P. C. by force.

The new Statute, which went into effect on April 4, provided that, except for jurisdictions to be retained by France, residuary powers would pass to a Cameroun Legislative Assembly and a Cameroun government whose head, the Prime Minister, would be chosen by the High Commissioner, but invested (*investi*) by the Assembly.

As for the newly elected Assembly, which began thus auspiciously,

162

from the outset its members formed themselves into groups along regional lines, following the areal origins of the most important leaders:

1) the north: the *Union Camerounaise* (UC), headed by Ahidjo and Arouna N'Joya, with thirty seats,

2) the center: the *Démocrates Camerounais,* with Mbida, and twenty seats,

3) the west: the *Paysans Indépendants,* headed by Djoumessi and Njiné, with nine seats, and

4) the coast: the *Action Nationale,* headed by Soppo and Assalé, with eight seats.

All these groups, except the *Paysans Indépendants,* represented actual political organizations. The *Paysans* was a parliamentary grouping consisting mostly of Bamiléké deputies.

On May 15, 1957, the Assembly confirmed Mbida as premier, at the head of a coalition government which included members of all groups except the *Action Nationale,* which became the opposition.

The Mbida government had its troubles from the start. They stemmed from two things, Mbida's personality and Mbida's politics. His manner eventually so antagonized his political friends, to say nothing of his enemies, that by the time his policies came under fire, few regretted his departure. To a considerable degree, however, Mbida was a victim of circumstances, since he was caught almost from the beginning on the horns of a dilemma which, on the one hand, dictated strong measures to deal with a resurgence of UPC-inspired terrorism in the Sanaga-Maritime, and, on the other hand, required a good deal of finesse in dealing with demands for a peaceful solution of the same problem. His misfortune was that he lacked both that finesse and the room within which to maneuver to accomplish his purposes. Mbida started well, but soon began to show signs of developing an authoritarian (some called it dictatorial) style. His detractors claimed that his head was turned by the power he wielded and that it was not long after his investiture that he began to govern without the advice of his cabinet.[3] Moreover, he made the tactical error of maintaining the unpopular position that the Cameroun was not ripe for independence, finally proposing (in January, 1958) the drawing up of a ten-year program of economic, social, and political development at the end of which the situation could be objectively reconsidered. As if this were not enough, his group decided not to include reunification in the program.[4] Objectively seen, Mbida's views might have been extremely realistic and tenable, but they were nonetheless clearly impolitic. Moreover, since almost all political groups in the Cameroun had already espoused early independence and reunification as realizable goals, his isolation became that much more acute.

Mbida's views were well known when he took office; they provided the UPC with fresh ammunition. The Kumba group lost no time in issuing a series of declarations reaffirming its unequivocal stand on independence and reunification.[5] At home, the *Action Nationale*, which included some of the most able of the Cameroun politicians (Soppo Priso, Assalé, Behlé) flooded the Assembly with radical nationalist declarations following the defeat of their counterproposal in April. One of Soppo's important supporters, Dr. Marcel Beybey-Eyidi—known for his sympathies to the UPC—opened the pages of his newspaper, *L'Opinion au Cameroun,* to Um Nyobé and other members of the banned UPC. Some of the articles were so critical of the Mbida regime that Beybey was imprisoned for two months on charges of aiding an outlawed organization.[6]

The following example of Beybey's colorful exposition is also representative of some of the UPC writings, though the style adopted by the latter tended to be more turgid. Writing of the situation in 1958, Beybey described its main lines:[7]

a) An Assembly elected in a climate of troubles, agitation and of terror (which imposes its law on the land) whose members have agreed to remain in office as long as possible;

b) Dissipation of the nation's resources and graft have become semi-official policies: they were consecrated by the very first law voted by the Assembly, which accords exhorbitant salaries to deputies and ministers, and this in a country as poor as is the Cameroun. . . .

c) A people unhappy, starving, impoverished, fleeing a hinterland made uninhabitable in certain regions, driven to silence by a well organized system of repression and by the extreme limitation of the freedom of the press;

d) A total "political vacuum," arising from the absence of a legal opposition movement, leaving the field free to the Assembly and the Government even on the very hour when reunification and the coming accession of the Cameroun to full independence is discussed.

Even though the above excerpt was published in 1958, it reflects UPC (and Beybey's) views of 1957. In June edition of *L'Opinion,* Um Nyobé had written along similar lines, condemning the "political" vacuum and urging its "liquidation."[8]

On July 13, 1957, Um Nyobé addressed to the Prime Minister and the High Commissioner "proposals for a moral and political *détente*," reiterating the usual UPC demands for amnesty, reunification, and independence, followed by threats of violence if they were not taken into consideration. The proposals were rejected and several weeks later, on September 5, 1957, fresh outbreaks of violence and terrorism occurred in the Sanaga-Maritime *Région.* Attackers sought out planters and village chiefs, killing some, kidnapping others, or sacking or burning their houses. In the view of the High Commissioner's office, these were more frequently acts of simple banditry than of political terrorism, even when they were committed in the name of politics. Similar incursions were made in the Bamiléké and Mungo *régions,* frequently by bands who came from the British zone and returned there after their raids. Mbida sought to stem the tide by going to Um Nyobé's birthplace, Boumnyebel (Sanaga-Maritime) to plead with the Bassa and threaten that all *maquis* who had not returned to their villages in ten days would be considered as "rebels against the Camerounian Government and treated as such."[9] Mbida's pleas and threats availed as little as an earlier (February) meeting between Bishop Thomas Mongo and Um in Douala, during which the former offered himself as an intermediary between the rebels and the government in an effort to effect a *détente* between the antagonists.[10]

On December 15, a deputy from the Bamiléké, Samuel Wanko, and six others were slain in an ambush near Bafoussam.[11]

Mbida went to Paris seeking two or three companies to supplement the single battalion on duty in the Cameroun. He got his troops and the government moved military reinforcements into the Sanaga-Maritime.[12] The authorities began a systematic hunting out of the bands of terrorists, at the same time regrouping the populations along the main roads into stockades supplied with alarm signals and some weapons. Some ten to fifteen thousand persons were thus regrouped along the so-called *Zone de Pacification (Zopac).* By the end of the year between a hundred and a hundred and fifty arrests had been made, and most of the rebel bands forced to flee further into the forests.

Mbida's vigorous countermeasures to the resumption of violence and terrorism did not, however, win him new friends or discourage his enemies. On the contrary, his political opponents made it plain that they considered his measures too harsh, and they renewed their demands for a general amnesty for political acts committed after 1955. The *Action Nationale* found support in the government's camp, and the demands for such an amnesty increased by the end of the year. Other indications had signaled the imminence of Mbida's downfall: on September 27 he lost his only supporter among the Bulu, Gaston Médou; on October 8, "his" candidate for the presidency of the Assembly was beaten, and Ahmadou Ahidjo reinvested; on December 14, his own ministers gave only apathetic opposition to a bill designed to organize his fall.

On February 7, 1958, the long-awaited amnesty bill was finally passed by the French National Assembly and promulgated ten days later[13]—but it came too late to save Mbida. It is doubtful if anything could have saved him by then.

Earlier, on January 26, 1958, Mbida had virtually given himself the coup de grace (and his opponents the overt provocation they needed) by issuing the *Démocrates'* ten-year program for an undetermined political future without reunification. The *Union Camerounaise* (with five of the eight ministers in the government, including Ahidjo as vice-premier) balked at this policy and asked its ministers and one parliamentary secretary to resign. Mbida tried to replace the ministers who had resigned with members of his own party, but High Commissioner Jean Ramadier (son of French ex-Premier Paul Ramadier, and only just arrived in Yaoundé) refused confirmation of the nominations. It was clear that officially Ramadier had no choice but to confirm the nominations; by his refusal he exceeded his authority. Mbida complained to Paris and Ramadier was hastily withdrawn. It was all in vain, however. Knowing that the Assembly would never confirm his nominations, and faced with three separate motions of censure, one from each group, Mbida finally resigned on February 17.[14]

In restrospect, it is obvious that Mbida's difficulties were to a large part of his own making. As the Camerounian who had done most to engineer the new Statute of the Cameroun, he had been the near-unanimous choice of his colleagues to assume the first Camerounian premiership. Mbida was also a deeply religious man, and most of his electoral support came from the heavily Catholic Yaoundé region. His religious training, one is tempted to guess, may well have carried over into his public life; he held his opinions as if they were dogma, and possibly derived some of his ideas about political gradualism from his religion, whose methods presuppose just such an orientation. Whatever the cause of his political maladroitness, by the end of his tenure he had managed to antagonize nearly all his former supporters except the deputies from his *Démocrates Camerounais.* No one questioned his honesty or devotion; the consensus was simply that he was not in step with the times. In January, 1959, he fled to Conakry, claiming that he feared assassination at the hands of the UPC. It is ironical that almost simultaneously with his arrival in Conakry, Felix Moumié and the rest of the "external" UPC leaders themselves arrived in Conakry from Cairo. Mbida claimed that relations between himself and the UPC exiles were strained, although later, in 1959, they joined in a common declaration of policy. Mbida did not return to the Cameroun until February, 1960.[15]

THE AHIDJO GOVERNMENT

Mbida's fall eased the prevailing tension, and the official policy of the government changed from repression of the rebels to attempts at conciliation. Ahmadou Ahidjo, former president of the Assembly, ex-Minister of the Interior in the Mbida cabinet, leader of the northern Young Muslim movement, and head of the *Union Camerounaise* group (once an adjunct of the *Démocrates Camerounais*) was appointed by the new High Commissioner, M. Xavier Torre, and invested on February 19, 1958, following a vote of forty-five in favor and sixteen abstentions. The abstentions were in Mbida's group, now reduced in strength, although its chairman explained that the abstentions did not mean the *Démocrates* were declaring themselves as a formal opposition. The new government was a coalition of the *Union Camerounaise* group, led by Ahidjo (with two ministers), the *Paysans Indépendants* (with one), and the former opposition group, the *Action Nationale* (with two). A sixth minister was unaffiliated, and three others were appointed from without the Assembly. One of these was subsequently replaced by a member of the *Union Camerounaise*.

Ahidjo's ministerial selections proved happy ones. The two MANC ministers (Assalé and Behlé) had been among the most vocal critics of the former government's policies, and by including one of the cochiefs of the Bamiléké-oriented *Paysans* (Michel Njiné, who became vice-premier), Ahidjo incorporated some of the potentially fractious elements into the cabinet. In this way he also gave his cabinet a regional equilibrium which it certainly would not have had if most of the ministers had been of his own party, at that time still predominantly northern-based.

The new prime minister's program could not but please most of the legislators as it incorporated the old warhorses of independence and reunification as well as the following aims: full internal autonomy, establishment of a timetable for the independence of the Cameroun, national reconciliation, and coöperation with France in an atmosphere of reciprocal cordiality and confidence.[16] Only the Mbida faction, faithful to its embittered leader, decided to remain in opposition. To be sure it was not a "formal opposition," as the group had disclaimed such a role, but nonetheless it was an opposition, labeled by some a "rightist" bloc.

Having thus set out its objectives, the Ahidjo government lost no time in trying to implement them. The new High Commissioner gave the government official assurance that France would support a schedule for independence, and on June 12 the Assembly adopted a government motion to "modify the Statute of the Cameroun so as to recognize its option for independence upon termination of the Trusteeship."[17] As for Mbida, who had previously asked for independence in ten years, he now demanded it on January 1, 1959, claiming that Ramadier's behavior had proved France's incapacity to continue as the administering power. His *volte-face* cost him still more support in the Assembly, and by the time he left, in January, his *Démocrates* had been reduced from sixteen to eight members. Confused and leaderless, the *Démocrates* continued their ineffective opposition until 1960.

With the mandate given to him by the Assembly, Ahidjo began talks with the French government in Paris. The talks, which began in June and extended to October, terminated with formal French recognition of the Camerounian option for independence. In addition, agreement was reached on the broad outlines of the new statute (which would take effect on January 1, 1959), accompanied by nine conventions[18] providing for the transfer to the Cameroun of all powers except foreign affairs, defense, and monetary and foreign exchange policy. During the negotiations, Ahidjo did not ask for a specified date to be fixed for independence; this was to be left to the Cameroun Assembly for determination. On October 18, 1958, the draft statute and the conventions were placed before the Assembly,[19] and six days later the Assembly adopted a resolution proclaiming the desire of the Cameroun for independence and the termination of the trusteeship on January 1, 1960.

On October 28, France announced the text of the Cameroun Assembly's resolution to the Fourth Committee of the UN General Assembly and signified its assent to Cameroun independence on January 1.[20] In the ensuing debate, Félix Moumié, recently arrived in New York from the African Peoples' Conference in Accra, presented himself as a petitioner and asked that the Camerounian request be denied. He dwelt on old themes; the present government was unrepresentative, reunification had not been guaranteed by the UN, the Ahidjo regime was little more than stooge for France, the individual liberties of the Cameroun people had been severely curtailed, and so forth. For a time, the Fourth Committee was undecided, but at length it sponsored a resolution[21] to put off final consideration of the Cameroun question until a UN Visiting Mission then in the field should have had time to report. The Mission, which visited the Cameroun between November 14 and December 6, 1958, had been specifically charged with ascertaining the views held in the territory on the question of independence, and to see whether some sort of consultation should be needed to test popular opinion on the matter. An extraordinary session of the Assembly—to be convoked on February 20, 1959—would deal definitively with the future of the Cameroun and the British trust territory.

One of the most important of the Ahidjo government's objectives was in the process of realization. By the end of 1958 it seemed as if the UPC problem might also be well on its way to a final solution. That this expectation proved premature was not because of any lack of good will on the part of the government, but, rather, external support kept the movement alive up to and beyond the date set for independence. A few words about the activity of the UPC after 1957 will explain the tortuous path of the party as a clandestine, self-styled "revolutionary" organization.

It will be recalled that after the UPC was ejected from the British Cameroons and sought refuge in Egypt, there developed what were in fact two separate UPC's. One wing, led by Moumié, Ouandié, and Kingué, was ensconced in Cairo under the aegis of Colonel Nasser, who permitted them to open a so-called information bureau and broadcast over Radio Cairo. The information bureau published a bimonthly journal, *La Voix du Kamerun* (which issued from Cairo even after Moumié had shifted to Conakry), and a large number of propaganda pamphlets.[22] Some of the pamphlets were printed in such diverse places as London, Rabat, and Casablanca. As for the broadcasts, they appear to have been dismal failures. The UPC program, "La Voix Cameroun," was beamed toward the west coast of the continent in both French and Arabic. Unfortunately, the largest number of receiving sets are in the south of the Cameroun, and what transmission came through was in Arabic, which is little spoken in the south. What receivers exist in the north are mostly in the hands of the traditional chiefs and some merchants, almost all Fulani and almost wholly anti-UPC.[23] From Cairo also, Moumié traveled to the United Nations to appear before the Fourth Committee, and in Cairo Nasser gave him a post in the secretariat of the amorphous Afro-Asian solidarity movement.[24]

During 1958, Moumié and his colleagues moved the seat of their operations to the newly independent Guinean Republic and placed themselves under the protection of President Sékou Touré. Conflicting reports, possibly circulated by Moumié himself, claimed that Touré had made Moumié a private secretary, his ambassador, and the like. Official Guinean sources denied the reports, but in any event Moumié was given extensive financial and political support by Touré; as a matter of fact, until 1960 the Guinean position on the Cameroun followed point for point that of the UPC, even changing as the UPC position changed.[25]

More uncertain is the extent to which Guinea contributed financial and logistical support to the UPC groups within the Cameroun proper. Cameroun and French authorities repeatedly captured Czech pistols from UPC militants in the country, and the implication drawn is that Guinea, the only African country on the west coast at that time receiving Czech arms, had sent them in as part of its support of the UPC.[26] At any rate, most of the continued terrorism in the Cameroun during 1958 and 1959 was directed by the UPC. The *Comité Directeur* made no attempt to conceal its connection with various acts of violence or sabotage in the Cameroun, issuing bulletins and communiques allegedly emanating from the *Bureau de l'information et de l'inspection* of its so-called *Armée de liberation nationale kamerunaise* (ALNK).[27]

The other wing of the UPC, led by Um Nyobé, retreated into the forests of the Sanaga-Maritime, there to continue agitation among the Bassa and conduct sporadic forays upon the Cameroun and French troops sent into the area to maintain order. Following his installation as Premier, Ahidjo issued a series of appeals to the rebels to return to legal ways, promising to receive them with open arms, and hinting at a revision of the Amnesty law of February 17, 1958, which applied only to acts committed prior to January 2, 1956, and involved a lengthy process of judicial exoneration. By the end of August, the administration reported that since January there had been some 785 defections from the UPC, and noted that acts of personal violence and property damage had decreased everywhere, even in the Sanaga-Maritime. On September 13, 1958, an unforeseen event completely altered the situation in the troubled areas. Um Nyobé was killed by a patrol near Boumnyebel, his birthplace, and a few days later his close associate, Theodore Mayi-Matip, who had escaped the trap set for Um, surrendered to the authorities.[28]

With Um's death, the heart went out of the rebellion. The numbers of defectors rose significantly in the months following: September, 272; October, 607; November, 406. By the end of the year the authorities stated the belief that there were no more than 50 to 100 persons left in the forests.[29] The Sanaga-Maritime became relatively quiet again, and the administration expressed confidence that the revolt had all but ended. It admitted that occasional acts of violence still occurred in the Mungo and Bamiléké Regions, but termed these "effervescences" and ascribed them to "bandits" who had come across from the British Cameroons.[30] The UN Visiting Mission listed the official toll for the period from September 5, 1957, to October 31, 1958; as 75 civilians killed, 90 wounded, and 91 abducted, and approximately 200 houses set on fire; 371 rebels killed, 104 wounded, and 882 arrested.[31]

Um's death also marked the end of a legend whose force and vitality profoundly affected all who came in contact with it. Among his Bassa people, Um was thought to be superhuman, invulnerable to bullets, and fostered this belief by playing cat and mouse with the authorities and letting conclusions about his invulnerability be drawn when he repeatedly evaded capture. He was said by some to have possessed a powerful *ju-ju* (magic) which made him not only invulnerable, but invisible as well. His death was explained by his having left behind his fetish amulet immediately beforehand, hence becoming both visible and vulnerable. The force of his character, his honesty, sincerity, and loyalty was recognized by all, including his enemies. After his death, his erstwhile foes praised him in the Assembly, and Ahidjo, Soppo Priso, and Betote Akwa all joined in the general mourning. Doubtless the fact that Um was a powerful political figure and symbolized the force of Cameroun nationalism had something to do with the reactions of his former enemies. In any event, the combination of Um's personality plus the politico-magico-religious aura that surrounded him made him an extremely compelling figure.

MAKING THE TRANSITION—1959

The governments of the Cameroun and France looked to 1959 as a year of transition during which the modalities for the transfer of sovereignty would be worked out between the two countries. The final word, of course, rested with the United Nations; it would have to give its approval to the termination of the trusteeship and determine the conditions under which the change from trusteeship to independence would take place. No one, however, anticipated any difficulties at the UN.

Both France and the Cameroun understood that the transition would not be easy. If the Ahidjo government saw 1959 as the last step toward independence, the UPC saw it as the last chance to come to power under favorable conditions. The UPC realized that unless it could use the combined leverage of its international support and its popularity within the Cameroun to gain power, it could not hope to do so after independence. If it failed to seize power by January 1, 1960, Dr. Moumié knew that his friends abroad would eventually desert him, choosing instead to coöperate with the newly independent state rather than to range themselves against it. Moreover, 1959 might be the last year during which the UPC could use the extraordinary facilities of the United Nations as sounding boards for its views. So long as the Cameroun remained under trusteeship the UN would admit "petitioners" of almost any stripe to its halls; once the Cameroun was independent and a member of the UN, it would become increasingly difficult, if not impossible, for unofficial "spokesmen of the Cameroun people" to appear at UN sessions. Finally, the UPC was faced with the prospect that it might not be able to retain the loyalty of its adherents within the country if they were faced with a choice between an independent Cameroun and a UPC whose leaders could find no place within the new nation.

In short, everything pointed to the conclusion that the key to events of 1959 would be found in the bitter struggle between the governing elements of the Cameroun and a UPC grown lean and desperate in its hunger for power. As it turned out, the conflict was carried on within the Cameroun, at the United Nations in New York, and was fanned from Conakry, Cairo, and Accra. It took every form from diplomatic pressure and legal polemicism to outright physical violence, murder, and pillage. At stake was not only the directive apparatus of a country, but also the legitimacy of fourteen years of UN trusteeship and the hope it represented for an orderly transition to self-government.

Examined in the light of the government-UPC dichotomy, the events of 1959 unfolded in three distinct phases. The first phase lasted through the beginning of June and included the "Cameroons session" at the UN and the events in the Cameroun that immediately followed it. During this period, the first full confrontation of the Franco-Camerounian and the UPC points of view occurred before the UN and resulted in a vindication of the official French and Camerounian positions. The second phase lasted from June through early October and included most of the weeks during which a recrudescence of UPC-inspired violence caused new waves of fear and tension to sweep the Cameroun. The final phase opened in an atmosphere somewhat less charged but still volatile. It covered the opening of the October session of the Cameroun Legislative Assembly and lasted through the November session of the UN, at which the Cameroun question appeared for the last time, to the end of the year.

The distinguishing element in each phase was a major test of strength between the government and the opposition. It is true that each test involved a set of circumstances that, for the most part, originated in events occurring before the phase in question. Nonetheless, there are factors in each period that are unique and warrant individual treatment.

PHASE I: THE UP "CAMEROONS SESSION" AND ITS RESULTS

The year began auspiciously for the Cameroun government. When the special UN "Cameroons session" opened on

February 20, M. Ahidjo was able to bring with him to New York two major items of evidence attesting to the progress and stability of his regime. One was the 1959 Statute of the Cameroun, and the other was the highly laudatory report of the 1958 UN Visiting Mission. A brief analysis of the Statute and the report reveals the extent to which they helped give the Cameroun a favorable standing at the UN.

The 1959 Statute was promulgated by France for two main reasons: to give the Cameroun government a free hand during the year, and to forestall criticism that the Ahidjo regime was a "French tool."[32] The law gave the Cameroun full internal autonomy, reserving to France only jurisdiction over money and exchange rates, foreign policy, frontier security, and the right to intervene in the event of armed insurrection or war. Most important, the preamble to the Statute formally acknowledged that the Cameroun legislature had asked for independence on January 1, 1960, and that France had agreed thereto. In unmistakable language, the preamble affirmed that "the present Statute . . . marks the last stage in the evolution of the Cameroun institutions before the termination of the trusteeship, to occur under conditions stipulated by the Charter of the United Nations and the Trusteeship Agreements."[33]

Accompanying the Statute was a series of bilateral conventions defining the limits of France's reserved powers and outlining the terms of the technical, financial, and economic aid that France would accord during the year. In sum, the new Statute and the conventions, taken together, were designed to reinforce the government's position and leave it the widest possible room within which to maneuver at the United Nations.

The UN Visiting Mission that had been in both Cameroons during the last three months of 1958 presented its report to the Trusteeship Council on January 25, 1959, and on most matters its conclusions supported the Franco-Camerounian position.[34] During its three weeks in the French Cameroun, the Mission found that there were "no grounds for doubt that the independence which the Cameroons will enjoy on the termination of the Trusteeship will be full and complete."[35] The manner in which the Legislative Assembly and government had exercised the powers transferred to them encouraged the Mission to believe, "with the Administering Authority, that the Cameroonians have the capacity to assume the responsibilities of independence."[36] The Mission concluded that the "great majority of the population" supported the request for independence and decided that it would not be necessary to consult the population on this subject before the termination of the trusteeship.

Next, broaching a subject that was later to become controversial, the Mission found the Cameroun legislature representative, and added:[37]

There are certainly insufficient grounds . . . for the holding of new General elections under United Nations supervision before the termination of Trusteeship. Furthermore, the Mission sees no reason why fresh elections to the Legislative Assembly should be a precondition to the attainment of independence. It must be remembered that it was the present Legislative Assembly and Government which demanded and obtained from France the commitment to grant independence on January 1, 1960. It would be ironic if their representative character were to be called in question.

The report then went on to comment on the course of the rebellion in the Sanaga-Maritime, the death of Um Nyobé, and reported, with obvious approval, that the government was planning a broad amnesty to be presented sometime in January. Finally, the Mission recommended that the Trusteeship Council propose Camerounian independence to the General Assembly.

Basking in the glow of the report's approbation, the government immediately introduced, and the Cameroun Assembly passed, the amnesty bill discussed in the Mission's report. Such action could not have been taken at a more opportune time; it provided tangible proof that the government was ready and willing to honor its moral obligations.[38]

On February 21, Ahidjo and Assembly President Kemajou left the Cameroun for New York. They were followed by almost every Cameroun politician who could gather sufficient funds for the trip. By the time everyone had arrived in New York, the list of Cameroun petitioners (excluding the official government delegation) read like a *Who's Who* of Camerounian politics, somewhat overbalanced owing to the presence of a large number of UPC spokesmen. In all, some twenty-eight different Camerounian groups were represented by twenty-seven petitioners; numerically, the UPC had the best assemblage, with fifteen of the petitioners speaking for it or for its position. Three other petitioners identified themselves as "non-UPC opposition"; the remaining nine spoke for the official position, if not for the government.[39]

Three days before the special session opened, the Trusteeship Council had recommended, in the light of its examination of the Visiting Mission's report, that the General Assembly take a decision to terminate the Trusteeship Agreement when the French Cameroun attained independence on January 1, 1960.[40] The Council's report,[41] plus the Visiting Mission's report, accompanied by the administering authority's comments, went immediately to the General Assembly's Fourth (Trusteeship) Committee for detailed examination; it was also at this time that the petitioners were heard. For most of the following three weeks the committee debated the key issues raised by the Visiting Mission's report: the question of independence, the character of the Assembly elected in December, 1956, the demand for preindependence elections, the status and activities of the UPC, the legitimacy of the Ahidjo regime, and the nature of French intentions toward the Cameroun. It was the first time the "Cameroun problem" had been given a full-dress review in all its aspects, and all of the participants, both opposition and governmental, took full advantage of the opportunity.[42]

Without going into detailed examination of the long debate, we can trace the main lines of discussion. The UPC case, essentially a simple one, was put by Dr. Moumié. He disagreed with the Mission's report that the Cameroun Assembly was a representative one, and asked for new elections before independence. Dr. Moumié advanced three "compelling" reasons for his demand. First, the current Assembly had been elected for the sole purpose of discussing the draft Statute of the Cameroun with the government of France. Second, the election of December 23, 1956, did not reflect the will of the people as it had been held in an unhealthy social and political atmosphere. Third, the Assembly still had seven French representatives, and could not, therefore, be considered truly Camerounian. He questioned the wisdom of allowing Frenchmen to participate in the drafting of a constitution for a country that was not their own. The UPC leader felt that the Camerounian people wanted, above and before all else, a sincere reconciliation of all shades of political opinion. For the good of the country, he was willing to meet with Ahidjo and to explore all possible avenues for achieving a genuine easing of tension in the Cameroun. Further, he felt that only an unconditional amnesty and the withdrawal of the ban on the UPC would restore the normal political life of the country.

As expected, Guinea and Ghana supported the UPC position, as did Liberia and the Soviet Union. The Ghanaian representative, Daniel Chapman, pointed out that, in view of the conditions under which the December, 1956, elections had been conducted, it would only be "common sense" that the change in status should provide the opportunity for new elections to be held under UN auspices. Moreover, one of the largest political parties in the territory had not been permitted to contest the elections, and as a consequence a large segment of the electorate had been barred from exercising the right to express its wishes.

Guinea's supporting brief, presented by Ismael Touré, a half brother of Sékou Touré, continued the same lines of argument. The representative character of the present government was not sufficient reason, stated Touré, to deny a voice to the democratic organization that had been the first to espouse the principle of independence. Many petitioners had tried to demonstrate that the UPC retained all its influence in the Cameroun and that it could not be blamed for all the incidents said to be perpetrated by terrorists while nothing was said of the actions of the French troops. New elections would give substance to the desire for reconciliation expressed by the petitioners and the Camerounian government as well. Touré suggested five steps toward a harmonious solution of the Cameroun problem: (1) a total and unconditional amnesty as the basis for national reconciliation; (2) the repeal of all statutory provisions enacted against any of the territory's political movements; (3) reunification of the two Cameroons on the basis of a popular consultation held under United Nations supervision; (4) general elections under United Nations supervision before January 1, 1960; (5) the proclamation of independence, the termination of the trusteeship and the admission of the French Cameroun to the United Nations on January 1, 1960.

The USSR's Arkady Sobolev, joining with the representatives from Ghana, Guinea, Liberia, and four other African states in an eight-power draft resolution calling for elections in the Cameroun prior to independence,[43] gave his complete approval to the remarks of the UPC petitioners as well as to those made by representatives from countries supporting the UPC's position. Mr. Sobolev held that the statements of the petitioners disclosed that the administering authority had provoked the current crisis and was doing everything possible to suppress the national liberation movement of which the UPC was the avant-garde. Consequently, without the participation of the UPC, the vital problems of the Cameroun could not be solved. It was apparent, according to Mr. Sobolev, why the administering authority so stubbornly refused to hold new elections. By forcibly detaching the Cameroun from the trusteeship system, France sought to compel her to join the French community. Under such circumstances, he contended, independence would be only a fiction.

Essentially, the arguments of the UPC and its supporters on the Fourth Committee could be reduced to the simple proposition that, inasmuch as the UPC was one of the largest parties in the Cameroun, and yet had not been permitted to participate in the December, 1956, elections, the Assembly elected at that time could not claim to be representative. The logical thing to do would be to hold elections before independence so that a "truly representative" assembly could draft the new constitutional documents and assist in the transfer of sovereignty. This argument that the UPC, and, with it, a sizeable number of the electors, was not represented in the Assembly was undoubtedly correct. Dr. Moumié could reasonably claim considerable support in the south and southwest of the country. UPC sentiment was strong in the Sanaga-Maritime, in the Wouri, in the Mungo, in Nkam, and in parts of the Nyong-et-Sanaga, a fact which was widely accepted but relatively poorly documented abroad. Whether this made the 1956-1957 Assembly "unrepresentative" in the pejorative sense used by the advocates of new elections was, of course, something else. Granting even that the UPC might have won a few seats in the Assembly, it is doubtful that their presence could have effected the formation of the government coalition. In any event, the government's tactical need to keep the UPC *hors de combat* until after independence made the question largely academic. Cold logic dictated that the government could have no other recourse unless it was prepared to accept the UPC's conditions, terms under which it could not hope to survive as a government.

On February 27, Ahidjo presented his government's views. The Prime Minister assured the Fourth Committee that the current Cameroun Assembly was indeed a representative body elected by direct and universal suffrage, and that it included elements of an active opposition. Furthermore, since all the candidates elected to the Assembly had endorsed independence, and since his government had promised new elections immediately following independence, he could see no need for a prior consultation. If the Assembly was indeed representative, then elections before independence would only create new discord and inflame political passions; he urged instead that elections be held afterward in an "atmosphere of calm."

The Prime Minister then went on to characterize the new amnesty law as "extremely generous," and he pointed out that, of a total of 2,303 persons sentenced or prosecuted in the preceding three years for offenses directly or indirectly related to occurrences of a political origin, only 400 were still detained on January 1, 1959. The number of exiles, he said, could be counted on the fingers of one hand. The new amnesty was designed to help all these persons, including the UPC petitioners at the UN. Only 56 persons, condemned to death or hard labor for life, were unaffected by the amnesty, and these people were "mere bandits" to whom the political unrest had seemed an opportune time to commit murder and arson, to loot and steal.

Regarding the Cameroun's coming independence, M. Ahidjo assured any doubters that the 1959 Statute was evidence that it would be complete and unconditional. The new Republic would not accept integration into French community as this would involve asking the Cameroun people to "reinstate [themselves] under French Trusteeship."

France's representative on the Fourth Committee, Mr. Kuscziusko-

Morizet, summarized the Franco-Camerounian case and added a few refinements of his own. He drew attention to the fact that the Cameroun Assembly became fully competent as a legislature within the terms of the Statute which it had itself approved. Article 59 of that Statute empowered the Assembly to arrange the final stages of the period of trusteeship, and it was on the basis of that power that the Assembly had requested and been granted full internal autonomy from January 1, 1959, and had fixed the date for independence.

France therefore saw no reason why fresh elections should be held before the grant of independence, and in view of the territory's full internal autonomy it could not impose elections which the Cameroun government deemed unnecessary. The real questions at issue were whether the Camerounians were ready for independence, whether the basic freedoms prevailed, and whether the necessary conditions had been met to enable an independent Cameroun to respect the principles of the UN Charter and of the Universal Declaration of Human Rights.

By March 12, all petitioners had been heard and the draft resolution prepared for a vote. Roll-call ballots were first taken on the two amendments introduced by the "bloc of eight" (Ghana, Guinea, Liberia, Libya, Morocco, the Sudan, Tunisia, and the UAR). The first, recommending that new general elections, under United Nations supervision, be held before independence, was rejected by 46 votes to 28, with 7 abstentions. In the vote, the eight were joined by all the Arab and African members (except Ethiopia) of the United Nations, plus Afghanistan, Indonesia, Nepal, Yugoslavia, and the Soviet bloc. However, India and all the other Asian members of the so-called Afro-Asian group either voted against the proposal or abstained. Also opposing it were the United States and most of the Western European, British Commonwealth, and Latin American countries.

The extent of the UPC's failure to enlist support for its cause became even more apparent by the rejection of the second proposed amendment which provided for the revocation of the ban on the UPC and its affiliate organizations. The vote, 42 against, 28 for, and 11 abstaining, lined up the countries almost as they had been for the first amendment, the only change being a shift of four countries from opposition to abstention.

With the objectors defeated, the committee adopted the twelve-power draft resolution approving independence and endorsing the prospective admission of the Cameroun to the United Nations. The vote was 56 to 9, with 16 abstentions. Only the Soviet bloc, which had nothing to lose by remaining in opposition, voted against the resolution. Except for Liberia, which voted for the resolution, the countries of the bloc of eight, although defeated on the amendments, chose to abstain rather than take a position that would put them on record as opposing the independence of an African state. In abstaining, they were joined by nine nations that had previously abstained or voted for the first amendment. The next day, March 13, the General Assembly unanimously endorsed the draft resolution.[44] The question of the future of the Cameroons under British administration, which had also been discussed in the Fourth Committee, was the subject of another resolution passed that same day.

The first and most important round had gone to the official Franco-Cameroun position. The opposition had to be content with a paragraph in the resolution expressing the General Assembly's confidence that elections would take place in the Cameroun "at the earliest possible date" after independence.

Although France and Prime Minister Ahidjo were supported by the United Nations, the three weeks' performance before the Fourth Committee left a bad taste in many mouths, including Ahidjo's. In an interview published shortly afterward in the *Presse du Cameroun,*[45] Ahidjo vented some of his displeasure at the proceedings:

Every question before the United Nations, including the Camerounian question, was seized upon by the two major blocs as a means of futhering their doctrinal positions . . . France having been once and for all placed in the ranks of the so-called 'colonialist nations,' they [the Soviet bloc and the Afro-Asian nations unfriendly to M. Ahidjo] tried to show that it was impossible that she should accord independence and the ending of trusteeship without reservations, and it was sought to create a group of so-called 'anti-colonialist nations' that had to oppose the demands of France and by Government, whatever their tenor. Thus, one was able to witness the curious spectacle of the so-called 'anti-colonialist' nations voting against the Cameroun's independence.

Certain Asian and African nations that had been "poorly informed," M. Ahidjo observed, had allowed themselves to be influenced by "tendencious arguments." Some of them, however, later changed their position and voted for Cameroun independence. Obviously referring to the bloc of eight Ahidjo pointed out that

. . . certain African states who wish the Cameroun to be independent, hope equally that their friends or momentary guests [an allusion to Moumié, and his wing of the UPC, then resident in Conakry, Accra, and Cairo] might be the leaders of an independent Cameroun. This is unquestionably . . . interference in the internal affairs of the Cameroun. . . .

Ahidjo's displeasure could not, however, conceal his satisfaction with the way things had turned out. The United Nations had given him and his government what amounted to a clear vote of confidence. He could now turn to domestic matters, secure in his belief that most of world opinion was behind him.

PHASE II: RENEWED VIOLENCE AT HOME

Fresh from its victory at the United Nations, the government felt strong enough to redeem its pledge to fill the six empty seats in the Assembly that had been vacated by assassination, death, or resignation. On April 12 by-elections were held in the Sanaga-Maritime, Nyong-et-Sanaga, and Bamiléké *régions*. (See map 8.)

Taking advantage of the February amnesty, six *rallié upecistes* headed by Mayi-Matip presented themselves to the voters and were elected by decisive majorities in all three *régions*.[46] The government, apparently content to see the UPC split, put up only token opposition. Significantly, the six new deputies were elected with the wrath of the "external" UPC on their heads. On April 1, Dr. Moumié had issued a warning from Cairo:[47]

Let no one be deceived by the *ralliés*. . . . To participate in the elections of 12 April is to engage, at one's peril, in a colonialist enterprise fraught with the gravest danger for the Kamerun; it represents a betrayal of the UPC program and would make those involved guilty of national treason. . . .

Whatever else the "external" UPC might have felt about the elections, it could not but have been aware that they represented a considerable loss both in terms of its support within the Cameroun and its already damaged prestige abroad.

The next blow came at the beginning of May when Moumié, having been either expelled or asked to leave for reasons officially undisclosed, suddenly left Cairo for Accra.[48] Whatever the reason, the "external" UPC, once useful to Nasser's antiwestern campaign, appeared to have lost any value of this sort following its defeat at the United Nations. It was clear that maintaining Moumié and his group in Cairo would become, if it were not already, an embarrassing liability. On May 24, Moumié, on his way back to Cairo to get his family, tried to land in Lagos but was unceremoniously returned to his plane by Nigerian police and flown back to Accra.[49] Soon after, he arrived in Conakry to set up his new headquarters.

Moumié's departure from Cairo and his warm reception in Guinea and Ghana indicated that these countries were not yet willing to give up their hopes of seeing him in power in the Cameroun, and that the UPC might soon be expected to mount some sort of offensive from its new base of operations. On June 3, Ahidjo described the new threat in these terms:[50]

M. Sékou Touré has not renounced his dream of colonization. In New York he suggested that the Cameroun be placed under Guinean trusteeship. This ridiculous proposal evidently had the disposition it deserved. Now the Guinean chief of state returns to conquer the Cameroun with the aid of his straw men, Mbida and Moumié. His intentions, instead of being pure, are simple; to provoke troubles in the Cameroun so that his friends can assume power and make the Cameroun . . . a springboard for his ambitions. . . . We cannot doubt that M. Sékou Touré and his friends want a civil war in the Cameroun. . . .

As if to underline Ahidjo's words, on June 19, Dr. Moumié proclaimed a four-point program of action for immediate implementation: (1) continue the revolution until independence and unity were realized; (2) oppose the decision of the United Nations to accord the Cameroun independence without prior elections or proclamation of a constitution; (3) appeal to all states not to sign treaties with the Cameroun; and (4) urge investors not to bring capital into the Cameroun.[51]

The new strategy of the Ghana-Guinea- "external" UPC coalition was beginning to take form. Beaten at the United Nations, but unreconciled to defeat, the coalition was determined to show the world and the United Nations that all was not peaceful in the Cameroun and that the decision taken in March might have to be reconsidered.

The portents for new unrest were suddenly borne out by a resumption of violence. Quiescent since December, terrorists struck in six main Cameroun towns with a series of attacks beginning the evening of June 27.[52] In Douala that night a band of thirty terrorists killed five persons, wounded eighteen. In Yaoundé, on July 1, another band of forty men killed two Europeans and wounded five critically. A *gendarmerie* post was attacked at Mbanga and four police officers lost their lives. Three airplanes were burned at Penja, and attacks were launched in Mbalmayo, Loum, and throughout the Bamiléké and Mungo areas. It almost appeared as if the events of May, 1955, were about to repeat themselves.

The government reacted quickly. An alert was called in seven southern *régions*, special criminal tribunals were created in Yaoundé, Douala, Nkongsamba, Dschang, and Bafia, a large number of suspects were arrested, the *Bureau National de la Conférence des Peuples Africains* (a UPC front) was dissolved, and six pro-UPC newspapers were suppressed, among them Dr. Beybey-Eyidi's *L'Opinion au Cameroun*.[53] By the end of July the main outburst of terrorism had subsided, even though sporadic acts of murder, pillage, and arson continued in the Bamiléké and Mungo regions. Despite the fact that Dr. Moumié announced that he was prepared to negotiate with France "on all bases which secure our mutual interest and the effective independence of the Cameroun," it became clear during the first weeks of August that the government's swift reaction to the outbreaks had carried the day. As events during the next eighteen months were to prove, the terrorists would never again be strong enough to launch such concerted attacks.[54]

If the outbreaks marked a renewal in the internal activities of the "external" UPC, they also marked the beginning of widespread *ralliéments* (returns to legality) by many former *maquis*. Such ex-UPC *Comité Directeur* members as Jean-Paul Sendé, Elie Ngué, and Victor Nantia were among the *ralliés*, as were large numbers of Bassa and Bamiléké tribesmen who had either been in the *maquis* in the Cameroun itself or hiding in the British Cameroons.[55] The net result, of course, was to reinforce the position and strength of the *rallié* UPC wing, and to increase its pressure on the government for the legal reinstatement of the party. All proclaimed their opposition to terrorism, denouncing Moumié and those who still remained in the *maquis*. "We are not terrorists," announced one group of *ralliés*, "but revolutionaries."[56]

The *ralliés*, whether from a desire to capitalize on the continued unrest or from a wish for a genuine *détente*, also began playing on a theme which was beginning to have considerable currency, that of a *table ronde*. The idea, supported by Soppo Priso and the *Démocrates*, as well as by the *ralliés*, was essentially simple. Its supporters argued that national unity and internal peace could be achieved only if all Camerounian political elements could get together on a common national program. This would involve a series of round-table discussions in which the "external' UPC would participate. A "government of national union" would then be set up and it, presumably, would take the necessary steps to draft a constitution, proclaim new elections, and effect the transfer of sovereignty. In essence, the *table ronde* represented a plan to bring Moumié back to the Cameroun, and then, by obtaining his participation in a "national" government, effectively neutralize him so that a coalition of *ralliés* and southern politicians would be able to assume power. The proponents of this plan hoped that with Moumié back, but with his claws pulled, they might have both internal political peace and the credit for having brought it about.[57]

In Conakry, Moumié, Ouandié, and Mbida all strongly endorsed the idea of a *table ronde*. That they favored it for somewhat different reasons became apparent from a communiqué issued on August 13 in Conakry and signed by all three.[58] The communiqué stated that the UPC had three essential demands to make, the acceptance of which would mean peace in the Cameroun, cessation of all UPC revolutionary activity, and harmony thereafter. The three demands were: (1) a round-table conference to be held August 20; (2) immediately after the conference, the formation of a Camerounian *gouvernement du salut public;* and (3) preparation by this government for elections before the end of the trusteeship. The signatories agreed that they would "accept the good offices of independent African states . . . to try to find a peaceful, just, and democratic solution for the Cameroun's problem."[59] Moreover, the three proposed that France agree to "annul the present institutions," to "end the present state of war in the Cameroun," and to abrogate the decree dissolving the UPC. In short, the Conakry group accepted the *table ronde* in principle, but then insisted on circumstances and conditions for its implementation to which the government could not but have many reservations.

Parenthetically, it also appears that Mbida was not unaware that his new alliance with his former archenemies would raise some eyebrows. His reasons, recorded in *Le Monde,*[60] are sufficiently interesting to quote:

If Moumié were really a Communist, then don't you think that it would be a good thing if I, a practicing Catholic and notorious anti-Communist, were to get close to him so as to convert him or hinder him from doing evil? A Communist is surely a sinner whom you and I and all Catholics must convert. . . . Just as our Lord had labeled the Pharisees as false prophets, so was I tempted to call them [Moumié *et al.*] a generation of vipers. But out of Christian charity, I suppressed this temptation.

The *table ronde* was not convened on August 20, but the idea continued to find supporters, even within the government itself. Critics of the government began to contend that it was uninterested in a *rapprochement* and that it sought only to crush the opposition by the most severe means. Among these critics was Vice-Premier Michel Njiné, who resigned from the government when his disagreement with Ahidjo became obvious during a three-week period in which Njiné exercised power in Ahidjo's absence.[61] Seemingly unimpressed by the mounting clamor, the government instituted a new series of measures designed to mobilize the country against the continued incursions of the terrorists. Notable among these measures was the creation of a number of Bamiléké *auto-défense* (self-defense) militia units, recruited from the local population and designed to mount swift retaliation against marauding *maquis* bands.

By the beginning of October, it became obvious that the government would have to take a position on the *table ronde* and the increased pressure for an immediate *rapprochement* with the Moumié group. Accordingly, on October 12, the day before the Legislative Assembly was to reconvene, Ahidjo announced in guarded and involuted phrases that he was receptive to "discussion": [62]

. . . if, as in the past, we are prepared to engage in discussions with Camerounians, whoever they may be and whatever their political party—even if opposed to our government—to seek with them the necessary solutions to a realization of the wishes of the Cameroun people, we are not ready to bow before assassins and bandits so long as we remain a legal government, having the support of an assembly which invested us.

Although the likelihood of a *table ronde* increased as the year drew into its final months, the wave of violence that began in June served only to convince the government that elections before independence would bring further troubles.

On one hand, the terrorist attacks had disrupted the southern peasant economy on which the country depended for a sizeable percentage of its export crops. [63] On the other hand, the southern *départements* which had been placed under a state of alert were still tense because of recurrent incidents of murder, arson, and vandalism. Travel between the main southern towns was virtually at a standstill, and a strict curfew was in effect. Unemployment had increased, and with it a widespread feeling of discouragement among workers in both the public and private sectors. In all, social, economic, and political conditions had so deteriorated that even the most optimistic observers felt the government could not survive much beyond independence.

The next moves were, therefore, clearly up to the government, and the last session of the *Assemblée Législative du Cameroun*, which opened on October 13, showed government still capable of forceful and effective action.

PHASE III: OCTOBER TO DECEMBER, 1959

The mandate of the Legislative Assembly elected in December, 1956, was to have run for five years. The Cameroun's coming independence, on January 1, 1960, plus the fact that the country's new status would entail—by common understanding of all political elements in the country—a completely new set of constitutional and institutional arrangements, made it plain that the October session of ALCAM would be its last. It would also be the last time that the opposition would have the chance to advance its cause in a national forum. The session lasted eighteen days during which the Assembly held nine plenary meetings. Several of these meetings developed into the most agitated that any Cameroun legislature had experienced; not even the turbulent session during which Mbida lost his Government saw as much excitement.[64]

Essentially, the debate revolved about two bills introduced by the government. The first,[65] and by far the more important, sought to give the government the power to legislate by decree for a period not to exceed six months, during which time the new institutions of the country would be put into effect. The law would further empower the government to write a constitution with the aid of a consultative committee of forty-two members and composed exclusively of Camerounian nationals, twenty-one of which would be drawn from the Assembly (one for each *département*), with the remainder designated by the government "to represent economic, social or traditional interests, or . . . by reason of their special aptitude." Finally, the proposed law stipulated that the new constitution, once written, would immediately be submitted to a national referendum and promulgated within eight days of its adoption. In effect, the Legislative Assembly was being asked to "go on vacation," and to permit the government to assume all legislative powers until a new Assembly, elected on the basis of the new constitution, would convene. The request was for the classic French formula of *pleins pouvoirs*.

The other *project de loi* proposed a grant of full and unconditional amnesty to all persons in the Sanaga-Maritime and Nyong-et-Sanaga *départements* who had committed "political" crimes or who had been connected with the political unrest in those areas.[66]

Ahidjo himself introduced the *pleins pouvoirs* law. His brief rested on an analysis of the difficult economic, social, and political conditions in the country.[67] "We find ourselves," he said, "in an exceptional situation which requires exceptional solutions." He pointed out that, as things stood, the many important decisions that had to be taken before January 1 could not even be approached. "Only a Government with complete responsibility, endowed with *pleins pouvoirs* . . . will be able to resolve the problems of the hour."

The Prime Minister then went on to outline his program, should *pleins pouvoirs* be granted. First, he promised the immediate formation of a consultative committee to draft the new constitution. Next, the government would promulgate a new electoral law and revise the electoral lists so that elections could be held between the end of February and the beginning of March, 1960. Finally, the government would prepare a budget for the six months' period ending June 30, a measure designed to provide the necessary funds for the transition period, but one which would not impinge on the financial authority of the new Assembly.

Ahidjo also took a position on the *table ronde* and the demands for unconditional and total amnesty. There were those, he said, who saw in the *table ronde* a political springboard for personal ambitions; it should not become *une assemblée de bavards* (an assembly of idle gossips) whose members sought only to further their own private gain and hence contribute nothing to an improvement of the situation. If, however, a genuine confrontation of differing viewpoints were possible, then the government would be prepared to favor organizing and participating in it. As far as the amnesty was concerned, the Prime Minister promised to make it total and unconditional if, by December 1, "all crimes and exactions cease and if we are assured of the desire for peace of all our compatriots."

Three days after Ahidjo had spoken, the formal deposition of the *pleins pouvoirs* bill took place. The event was marked by a scene in which the opposition shouted, stamped on the floor, pounded on the tables, and hurled insults at Assembly President Mabaya who, at one point, was forced to suspend the sitting for five minutes because no one could be heard above the tumult. Leading the assault was Daniel Kemajou (whom President Mabaya had just replaced in the chair of the Assembly), who sought to prevent the bill from being sent to committee. During one particularly violent exchange on the floor, Kemajou turned on deputy Jean Akassou, a government supporter:[68]

Monsieur Akassou, you, do you know what *pleins pouvoirs* signify? They mean the suppression of liberty, they mean dictatorship! . . . How can you ask for *pleins pouvoirs* under such conditions? You who belong to the Government, don't you know what an electoral law is? If tomorrow the Prime Minister disagrees with you, he can make a law specificaly directed against you, he can talk of inconsistency, he can redraw the electoral districts as it suits him, he can suppress anything he wishes by decree. And you Monsieur Arouna [Arouna Njoya, Minister of Public Health], you who suffered for this country, will you countenance the continued suffering of Camerounians? Is it possible that you, Monsieur Arouna, participated in the ministers' meeting that adopted this criminal law, this despicable law?

Another speaker, Tsalla Mekongo of the *Démocrates*, saw the law bent to still more reprehensible ends:[69]

Now, as I speak, a state of alert with curfew is in effect in all the regions of the south Cameroun; you can't go out at night for fear of being killed; you've heard speak of executions. Do you want to give the Prime Minister special powers so as to give him the possibility of killing whoever he likes?

Over the protestations of the opposition, the law went to committee.

Six days later, when it emerged for general debate and final vote, temperatures again rose on the floor of the Assembly. This time the attack was opened by Soppo Priso with a prejudicial motion to which was attached a legal argument of some weight.[70]

Soppo contended that the Legislative Assembly was incompetent to pass on the question of the *pleins pouvoirs*. He argued that such a law constituted renunciation by the Assembly of the legislative powers granted it under the 1959 Statute of the Cameroun; Article 6 of that document specifically stated that the legislative power belonged to the Legislative Assembly. Moreover, the Statute was not an act of Camerounian sovereignty, but one decreed by France in the exercise of its authority as the tutelary power. Having thus "established that the Statute of the Cameroun did not stem from Camerounian sovereignty," Soppo went on to ask,

. . . in what measure then, before independence and the termination of trusteeship, may a Camerounian assembly, by a delegation of its powers, unilaterally impair—even temporarily—the spirit and principle established by this act of trusteeship, without the prior consent of the French Government which has the sole juridical competence to modify its own enactments?

Ahidjo replied that, even if the Statute were of French origin, this did not preclude the Assembly and the government from requesting a modification of its terms.[71] Before Soppo could offer a rebuttal, and over the vociferous protests of the opposition, his motion was put to a vote and rejected by a majority that was drawn up along strictly partisan lines.

Having failed with Soppo's play, the opposition once again turned to Kemajou, whose next speech was even more impassioned than his first:[72]

The *pleins pouvoirs* . . . will permit the Government to concentrate in one person's hands all legislative, judicial and executive powers; that is, install a dictatorship . . . a reign of personal whim, a police state of concentration camps, deportations, arbitrary arrests and imprisonments, summary executions, hangings, of arbitrary and abusive behavior of public servants, persecutions of students in the *lycées* and *collèges*, unemployment, black despair, of injustices following upon injustices, slavery, etc., etc., etc.!

Nor was this all, pursued M. Kemajou; independence under such a "dictatorship without dynamism" could lead only to popular disillusionment, a reinforcement of unrest, and possibly to an 18th Brumaire:[73]

The Cameroun people are deceived, profoundly deceived. The country is already in agony and M. Ahidjo comes today to ask for *pleins pouvoirs* to give it the *coup de grâce!* No and again no! Better to die in dignity than live in slavery and dishonor![74]

The other opposition speakers, following Kemajou (Tsalla, Yankana, Akono, Amougou, and Mbong Bayem), were pale by comparison, though no less impassioned. There was more shouting, stamping of feet, pounding of desks, and exchange of epithets, but all this availed the opposition nothing, for the bill was finally passed by a vote of fifty to twelve, with one abstention. The twelve votes against comprised the six *Démocrates* present, plus the *ralliés* (minus Mayi and Nonga Yomb, who were absent), Kemajou, and Soppo Priso. The majority included thirty-five of the thirty-eight UC deputies (three absentees), six of the eight MANC deputies (less Soppo, of course, and Dissaké, who was the sole abstaining vote), and all seven of a mixed bag of independents calling itself the *Intergroupe des Noninscrits.*[75]

On the following day the partial amnesty law was passed unanimously by the Assembly, but not before the opposition had castigated the government for not making it total and unconditional. To strong applause from the government benches, Charles Okala, the Minister of Justice, turned his most corruscating phrases on the opposition. The government, said Okala, had imposed a fair condition for the granting of amnesty: a laying down of arms and a renunciation of violence. Those who had already done so, such as the Bassa people, had the gratitude of the whole country and the present amnesty was a logical consequence of their act. The government could hardly do otherwise. But as for the others,[76]

. . . those who kill because they await the Messiah from Conakry, we shall build the Cameroun without them; and if it takes us a hundred years to do so, why then we will take a hundred years! And if there are no more French troops, we will arm the other regions against the vandals who want to impose their law on us. . . . Do you want war? We want peace. And if you want peace, tell your friends, the killers, to stop killing and we will talk with them tomorrow; but so long as their guns speak we shall refuse all conversation with them!

At a late hour on the night of October 30, after having passed a number of minor bills and selected the twenty-one deputies to sit on the Constitutional Consultative Committee, the Assembly adjourned *sine die.* Once again the net result of the session could be assessed as a solid victory for the government.

Meanwhile, the United Nations prepared for its final session of the year. Despite repeated requests from Conakry and from members of the opposition in the Cameroun, the United Nations refused to permit the Cameroun question to be the subject of a special agenda item. One last chance remained for the opposition: the Fourth Committee's examination of the Trusteeship Council's Report for 1958-1959.[77] Accordingly, six Cameroun petitioners (Nonga Yomb and Mayi Matip, of the *ralliés;* Manga Bile of the *Démocrates;* Ernest Ouandié of Conakry; Ntumazah of the Southern Cameroons' One Kamerun Party, and Isaac Tchoumba of the *Association Bamiléké,* a UPC front) asked for and received permission to be heard by the Fourth Committee.

The six petitioners repeated, almost mechanically, the formulas regarding the insidiousness of French designs, the undemocratic nature of the regime, the oppression of the people, the sincere wish for "unity and reconciliation," the need for preindependence elections and removal of the ban on the UPC. The old issues were presented for the last time, but their effectiveness had long since been dissipated.

Apart from the lackluster performance of the petitioners, several interesting developments marked the twenty-day debate in the Fourth Committee. One was the unexpected appearance of Leopold-Sédar Senghor with the French delegation to defend the record of the Ahidjo government and the work of France in the Cameroun.

Another was the Guinean resolution, introduced some forty-eight hours before the end of the committee's session, to send a Good Offices Commission to the Cameroun with the task of "facilitating national reconciliation." The resolution was introduced after Guinea, Ghana, and several other states had retreated from their demand for preindependence elections, and Ghana, surprisingly, had expressed "renewed sympathy toward M. Ahidjo." The committee rejected the resolution (forty-one to thirty-three, with seven abstentions) and then went on to endorse the Trusteeship Council's Report.

The Good Offices Commission resolution also marked the last concerted effort of the pro-UPC African bloc. Already during the debate some of these nations had taken the opportunity to register a new cordiality toward Ahidjo and his government. Ghana, Tunisia, Morocco, and Liberia denied ever having had any animus toward the Cameroun, and declared that they had only the best wishes for its future. At one point in the discussion, the Tunisian representative even declared that he saw in Ahidjo the "eminent qualities of a statesman." Although Liberia voted against the resolutions, most of those voting for it did so only halfheartedly. Certainly the game was almost over; nothing further could be gained by supporting a lost cause. Only the Soviet bloc and Guinea, consistent in their hostility to France and the "neo-colonialist regime of the puppet Ahidjo," remained intransigent in their opposition.[78]

While the Fourth Committee debated the latest form of the Cameroun question, the Cameroun government initiated moves to bring
about the long-awaited *table ronde*. A Committee for the *Table Ronde*,
consisting of leaders from five parties, including the UC, MANC, PSC,
and *Rapeca (Rassemblement du Peuple Camerounais*, an ally of the
Démocrates), was created in Yaoundé, but with the *Démocrates* and
the *ralliés* conspicuously absent. The committee issued a statement
calling for the participation of representatives from all political groups,
"abroad or in the Cameroun." It set up a single condition for this participation, that is, renunciation of violence, but did so in a manner
hardly likely to attract the "external" UPC:[79]

. . . as for leaders of political parties and representatives of opposition tendencies who have openly endorsed acts of assassination, they must first formally renounce this inglorious mode of political expression—constituting, in
fact, terrorism—and come as citizens obedient to the laws of their fatherland.

The statement gave the government away. It now neither needed
nor wanted a *table ronde* before the end of the year, but it was prepared to make the necessary gestures to show that it not only was
willing to have one but would even offer political repatriates a full
amnesty for past crimes. It was obvious that the "external" UPC could
not accept the committee's (and by implication the government's) condition without branding itself responsible for terrorism and "inglorious"
acts of assassination. And this, in turn, would contradict the entire
argument by which Moumié had justified the UPC's violence in the
Cameroun as "the struggle for national liberation." As expected, no
one appeared from Conakry, and the committee for the *table ronde*
quietly went out of existence toward the end of December.

The remaining few days of the year were taken up by preparation
for the Independence Day celebrations; the tall grass along the roads
was cut down, the streets were swept in all the main towns, and flags
appeared in profusion everywhere. The lists of eminent visitors grew
daily, and the government found it difficult to find enough cars for
them. Even the opposition got into the spirit of the time by claiming
that independence, after all, had been the result of its efforts and had
been won by "the blood of Cameroun patriots." The most optimistic
note, oddly enough, was struck not by the government, but by Mbida
in a letter to his friend Claude Akono. Hinting that he would like to
return to the Cameroun, Mbida "generously offered to forget the past,"
and added that,[80]

. . . sincerely for the love of God and for the good of our country, we pardon all
injustices, faults, errors, due to inconscience and vile passions . . . let us now

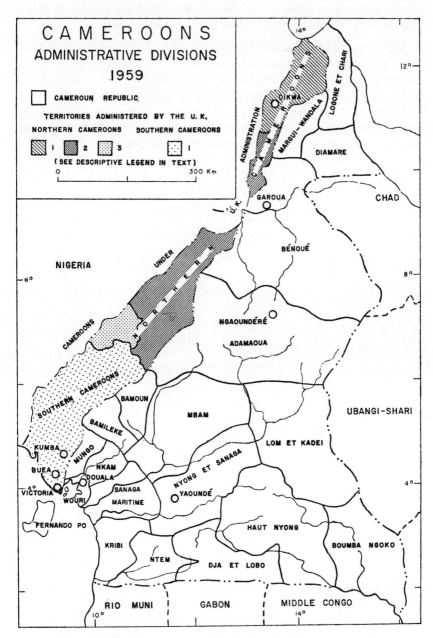

MAP 8. The Cameroons—administrative divisions, 1959

join in fraternal reconciliation in the sole interest of our country so that it may build an effective independence in peace and prosperity.

Mbida was talking about himself, but his wishes might well have been voiced by most Camerounians. Yet even the most pious hopes for an untroubled future could not conceal the fact that independence not only brought new problems, but still required resolutions of the old ones. That the old problems could not be forgotten was dramatically demonstrated on January 1, when eight citizens of the new Cameroun Republic died as a result of terrorist attacks in Douala and Yaoundé.

CHAPTER

VIII *Politics in the British Cameroons*

If, as John Kautsky[1] suggests, nationalism in many
undeveloped countries is largely a reaction against European colonial
domination, then the development of British Cameroonian nationalism
provides a deviant, if not unique, case. The "anti" positions of French
Camerounian nationalism were identifiably those centering on and
revolving about the elimination of French influence and the French
presence: independence, end of the trusteeship, reunification, and the
legal reinstatement of the first major nationalist party; the British
Cameroonian nationalists, interestingly enough, emphasized anti-British
themes only comparatively late in the game. In the hierarchy of their
nationalist demonology, the British occupied a lower rank; British
Cameroonian nationalists found that the anti-Nigerian (more specifically, anti-Ibo), anti-French, proseparatist or prounionificationist
positions paid off much more handsomely in popular support and votes
than did the anti-British or even anti-United Nations positions. This
interesting difference in emphasis is explained in part by the peculiarities of the mandate and the trusteeship which, between 1922 and 1949,
placed what was called "Cameroon Province" (loosely known as the
Southern Cameroons) under the administrative aegis of the Nigerian
Southern Provinces, then of the Eastern Provinces, and finally of the
Eastern Region.[2] From 1949 to 1954 the Southern Cameroons was
divided into two; a smaller Cameroons Province, and Bamenda Province, both administered by the Eastern Region. Under the 1954 Nigerian constitution, the "Southern Cameroons"—for the first time named
as an identifiable political unit distinct from the Northern Cameroons,
which was administratively tied to the three provinces of the Northern
Region of Nigeria until 1960—came to enjoy a limited degree of self-
government as a "quasi-federal" territory within the Federation of
Nigeria. In 1958, the designation "quasi-federal" territory was dropped,
and the Southern Cameroons attained further measures of local autonomy, including an enlarged House of Assembly, a new House of

Chiefs, and, more significantly, ministerial government. In its new status the Southern Cameroons was placed on what amounted to political parity with the Eastern and Western Provinces of the Federation, which had also attained internal self-government in 1958. This pattern of increasing devolution from Nigeria, a response to the growing separatist aspirations of an articulate group of Southern Cameroonian intellectuals, was complemented by the mounting influence of events in the French Cameroun. As the French trust territory moved toward independence, some Southern Cameroonian nationalists began to see in reunification both an alternative to Nigerian linkage and a goal for their efforts. The opposing poles of political union with the Southern Cameroons' two large neighbors, framed in terms of the goals of trusteeship, became the dominant themes of Southern Cameroonian nationalism. In the process, Britain, which had disavowed any designs of an indefinite tutelage over the territory—it is not too much to say that the Cameroons were often regarded in Whitehall as somewhat of a colonial liability—played the role of political midwife and as a consequence continued to be generally well regarded by most Southern Cameroons' political factions.

The Northern Cameroons' political evolution took an entirely different course. Only briefly, during the periods of and between the UN plebiscites of November, 1959, and February, 1961, did its people participate in the nationalist enthusiasms of the south, and then in a limited way. Administered separately since the beginning of the mandate, on the classic pattern of indirect rule, dominated by the traditional emirates of Northern Nigeria, economically and educationally much less developed than the south, the Northern Cameroons never developed a self-conscious political stratum to which themes of Southern Cameroonian nationalism had much meaning. Any discussion, therefore, of British Cameroonian development must concentrate on the Southern Cameroons, and it is primarily with that part of the territory that this chapter deals, concentrating on the events leading up to and including the termination of the trusteeship in the British Cameroons in October of 1961. The political future of the Cameroon Federal Republic which came into existence in October of 1961 is more properly a subject for later studies; possibly after enough time has elapsed to permit an evaluation of the extent to which the federation has fulfilled its basic goals.

The present chapter is divided into several sections. The first treats the period from 1922 to the termination of the mandate in 1946. The second deals with the trusteeship period and includes a turning point in British Cameroonian history, the entrance into the Cameroons of the exiled leaders of the UPC, in 1955. The third section deals with events between 1955 and January 1, 1960, when the French Cameroun became independent. The final section deals with the several United Nations plebiscites in the British Cameroons and the unification of the two Cameroons in October of 1961. Principal emphasis, of course, is placed upon the development of British Southern Cameroonian political life and upon the events that led up to and culminated in the United Nations plebiscite of February 11, 1961, in the Southern Cameroons.

THE INTERWAR PERIOD

Except for German agitation in the southern section of the territory, the political life of the British Cameroons was relatively uneventful during the interwar period. The territory, joined to Nigeria in an administrative union, was generally considered something of a backwash in the main stream of Nigerian development. The forces shaping the course of Nigerian and French Camerounian politics had few echoes in the British Cameroons; both Africans and Europeans in the territory were more concerned with economic than political problems. Moreover, the British Cameroons' relatively isolated geographic position—isolated, that is, from centers of Nigerian political and economic life as well as from forces at work in the French Cameroun—tended to reinforce an aura of quiet and calm. Isolation from the French mandate was accentuated by the administrative division between the French and British mandates; the principal contacts between the two territories fluctuated according to the tides of labor flowing between them and in relation to the scattered commercial and traditional connections. It may be added that, paradoxically, *official* contact between the mandates was greatest in the northern areas; certain common problems, particularly those involving the administration of the traditional Fulani emirates, tended to increase informal links between administrators.

Until the end of World War II, educational and economic progress was greatest in the sourthern part of the British Cameroons; first and notably in the Victoria area, later in the Kumba, Mamfe, and Bamenda areas.

By far the most important influence on the economic development of the Southern Cameroons during the interwar period was the German plantations, once again in German hands. The plantations flourished, proving the main financial and economic bulwark of the territory. Furthermore, the Germans improved much of the coastal section; they expanded port facilities at Tiko and Victoria and constructed numerous shops, warehouses, and office buildings. Not the least of their efforts

was the erection of a number of workers' camps which, although somewhat primitive in facilities and construction, nevertheless provided
plantation workers with relatively clean and comfortable surroundings.

Without going into an extensive examination of the internal economic picture in the British Cameroons during this period, the evidence
leads one to conclude that trade with Germany was the territory's
mainstay. It is important to recall that the German plantations were
returned to their proprietors in 1924, and that within two years they
were in full production. As of 1925, trade with Germany dominated
export markets in the Southern Cameroons.[3]

TABLE 13

PLANTATION WORKERS BY AREAS OF ORIGIN,
SELECTED YEARS, 1925–1955

Year	Brit. Cam.	French Cam.	Nigeria and other	Total	
1925	5,735	6,330	63	12,128	
1930	5,412	3,395	233	9,040	
1935	10,025	5,251	415	15,691	
1938	17,879	4,725	2,509	25,113	
1955[a]	15,517	1,708	6,801	24,026	
(Victoria Div.)			(Nig., 6676)		31,589
(Kumba Div.	2,107	230	2,226	4,563	(comp.
CDC only[a])			(Nig., 2225)		total)

[a] 1955 figures refer only to Cameroon Development Corporation estates, and
are therefore incomplete by over 3,000 men. The composite total includes this
3,000 figure.

(*Full citation of work mentioned briefly below will be found in the bibliography.*)

SOURCES: *Report on the Cameroons* (1925, 1930, 1935, 1938); for 1955 figures,
Ardener, Edwin and Shirley, and W. A. Warmington, *Plantation and Village in
the Cameroons* (London: Oxford University Press, 1960), pp. 400, 401.

Another important aspect of the territory's economy involved the
large number of workers the plantations drew from within the Cameroons as well as from Nigeria and the French Cameroun. The presence
of these "stranger" natives was later to have important political consequences, they were to become a political football for the main parties, ultimately wooed or caviled, depending on the shifts in political
winds. Table 13 is some indication of their numbers and origin as recorded between 1925 and 1955. It is interesting to note the large numbers from the French Cameroun, many of whom apparently entered the
British Cameroons without paying either the 500-franc bond or the
25-franc passport fee required by the French at that time.[4] Their num-

ber is also indirect testimony to the relatively good working conditions offered by the plantations between 1922 and 1927, a period in which the French administration undertook many of its major construction projects using *prestation* or *corvée* labor. Many of these laborers eventually remained as permanent settlers in the British mandate and helped to swell the steady migratory flow from Nigeria, the northern parts of the British Cameroons, and the French mandate.

Apart from encouraging economic development and supervising the German-owned enterprises in the south, the main attention of the administering authority was devoted to implementing the system of indirect rule in the territory. The system had been tailored to fit the needs of British administration in situations where explicit traditional political systems were available to cushion the impact of western institutions on traditional ones, and it was applied with great success in parts of the British Cameroons. It worked well, for example, in those areas in which the traditional Fulani institutions were still functioning (Dikwa, Bornu) and, in fact, in almost all the Cameroonian areas where explicit hierarchical authority structures existed. It had somewhat less success in areas of the Atlantika and Mandara Mountains, where the administering authority was confronted with primitive, often unpredictably hostile Kirdi tribes. Even as late as 1954 the administration was compelled to declare some areas "disturbed," and to limit travel within them. The administration was also concerned with stamping out such practices as slavery, witchcraft, and clan feuds in the more backward areas of the territory.

The problems attending British rule in the Northern Cameroons were different from those in the south. In the north, an already well established, highly developed political tradition proved readily amenable to the changes the "indirect rule" system brought with it. These changes were, on the whole, fairly easy to bring about, as the administration did not envisage a wholesale restructuring of social or political life. It may be added that the British inherited a situation whose tranquility had been assured by the Anglo-French-German reduction of Fulani power in the area during the late nineteenth and early twentieth centuries. Except for the recalcitrant Kirdi, the Muslim states in the north were easily assimilated administratively into the existing political structures of Northern Nigeria. Traditional ties, such as those with the Lamido of Adamawa and the Emir of Bornu, were handy pegs on which to hang the incorporation. Content to retain the trappings of former glory and the external semblance of power, their cherished customs and laws almost intact, northern rulers were usually entirely willing to coöperate with the British. In short, the very clarity of the traditional power relationships in the north was the greatest asset to the success of the system of indirect rule in those areas.[5]

In the Southern Cameroons, the British found a bewildering array of tribal groups, clans, chiefdoms, and other traditional political arrangements. In the extreme south, around Victoria, Tiko, and Buea, the Germans had already created a number of local chieftancies to rule the principal tribes. Further north, in the Bamenda section, the large grassland and highland areas were under the rule of traditional chiefs (fons), the natural and often autocratic rulers of a number of Tikar, Bali, and Widekum tribal groups. Throughout the territory, numerous village and clan groupings maintained their forms of political organization. Some had (and still have) explicit authority structures, complete with chiefs, "kings" (of German accolade) or fons. Others had diffused authority systems in which a tribal council, a council of elders, or an informal assembly of family heads constituted the only visible "government." Still others had intermediate forms in which leadership might be assigned to various persons depending upon position in the kinship structure and upon the occasion—such as the conduct of a war or the adjustment of a difference with a neighboring village.

In appointing "Native Authorities," the administration tried to maintain natural political structures and natural ties of family or community. Happily, the British did not repeat the mistakes they had made in Eastern Nigeria, where, unable to locate either chiefs or explicit authority structures, they had appointed a number of synthetic "warrant chiefs." The result was a period of unrest and political turmoil. Instead, this time a systematic series of "assessments," "intelligence reports," and the like were undertaken to discover the scope of the traditional groups, their political structures, and the foci of political or religious power, if such power foci existed.

By 1936, the government had recognized or created a wide variety of Native Authorities, most of them based upon a fairly accurate evaluation of the nature of the local socio-political structures. First, the fons of Bali, Nkom, Bum, and Banso in Bamenda Division, and the Fon of Bangwa (Fontem) in Mamfe Division became the Native Authorities, complete with courts and councils. Second, four chiefs in the Victoria-Buea-Mamfe districts were similarly recognized. One of this latter group, Chief John (Johannes) Manga Williams (a lineal descendant of King William of Bimbia, who sold Victoria to Alfred Saker), had also been chief under the German protectorate. Another, the district head of the Bakweri District, Chief Endeley, was the village head of Buea, and was generally recognized as a leader among the Bakweri. Chief Endeley's son, Emmanuel, later became the Southern Cameroons' first premier when the territory attained regional status in 1958. The great majority of the Native Authorities were simply village heads, by custom an elder who was considered *primus inter pares.* By 1938, almost all the territory's recognizable tribal and traditional divisions had been organized into Native Authorities. Only four, however, were considered advanced enough to administer their own treasuries and most of them (except in the Victoria, Buea, Kumba, and Bamenda areas) were still sufficiently amorphous structurally to warrant further reorganization along the lines of clan confederacies or federations.[6]

In sum then, the Southern Cameroons' principal preoccupations during the interwar period were those connected with economic conditions and local administration. There were few political stirrings in the Cameroons themselves, although toward the beginning of World War II a number of young Southern Cameroonian intellectuals had come to think in terms of organizing various sorts of common interest or mutual welfare associations among themselves. The most important of these organizations took shape outside the borders of the Southern Cameroons. The best known was the Cameroons Youth League (CYL) formed in late 1941 in Lagos by Peter M. Kale and Emmanuel Endeley, son of Chief Endeley and a medical practitioner in Nigeria. Almost inevitably the leaders of this organization, soon after its creation, became involved in Nigerian nationalist groups, particularly in the political organization Dr. Nnamdi Azikiwe was attempting to form. In 1944, Endeley and Kale, together with L. M. Namme and Namaso N. Mbile, participated in the founding of Dr. Azikiwe's National Council of Nigeria and the Cameroons (NCNC). Out of this participation grew the first Southern Cameroonian interest in developing political organizations with a peculiarly Southern Cameroonian orientation. It was not, however, until 1946 that the first major steps were taken to provide a local forum for both the new groups organized outside the territory and for those which had by then sprung into existence within it.

1946-1955

In an earlier chapter it was noted that the shift from mandate to trusteeship under the United Nations Charter in 1946 marked a milestone in the political development of the French Cameroun. The new arrangement stimulated the political aspirations of the young Camerounian elite nurtured during the war years and gave them unique opportunities to participate in the new political institutions created in France and in the Cameroun itself. Mostly significantly, per-

haps, the explicit promises of the United Nations Charter and of the
trusteeship agreements provided a goal for the political aspirations of a
number of young Camerounians who saw in the new status of their
territory the opportunity to move it to self-government and independence.

There is little question that the French had agreed with considerable
reluctance to the formation of trusteeships over their Togolese and
Camerounian mandates; they had hoped, even in the face of mounting
indications that the old ties with the *métropole* were dissolving, to
preserve the possibility of future assimilation with France. Somewhat
analogously, the British hoped that the trusteeship etsablished over
the British Cameroons would not change the direction along which
their Cameroons mandate had been moving—toward eventual integration with Nigeria. Indeed, the stipulations in the trusteeship agreement
that the British Cameroons were to be administered "as an integral
part of the Protectorate and Colony of Nigeria" permitted the British
to feel that little if anything would be changed under the new international arrangements.[7] In one declaration before the United Nations
Trusteeship Committee, the British representative declared that the
United Kingdom thought the best course for the British Cameroons
was for "all the people of the Trust Territory . . . [to] participate in
the training towards self-government which is taking place in Nigeria. . . ." Moreover, the British representative indicated that it was

. . . improbable that the Trust Territory, in view of the artificiality of its
territorial boundaries and the heterogeneity of its ethnical composition, will
ultimately become a separate political entity but . . . the people of the Territory are being fully consulted regarding their wishes and it is expected
that the forthcoming reforms to be made in local government and in the
constitution will give them both a greater measure of local autonomy and
larger representation in the Nigerian legislature.[8]

The British emphasis, then, it must be stressed, was upon continued
integration within Nigeria. Whatever else developed in the ensuing
years, it is certain that in 1946, 1947, and even in 1948 the British were
sure that the British Cameroons would eventually unite with Nigeria
when the trusteeship was lifted.

The administrative tie with Nigeria obviously had a good many advantages for the trust territory and, in particular, for the Southern
Cameroons. On the administrative level, the trust territory was able to
use the technical and economic services and expertise of Nigeria.
Further, the British Cameroons had the use of Nigerian ports, especially that of Calabar. Cameroonian farmers profited to some extent
from the operations of the Nigeria Cocoa Marketing Board, and, what

is more important, the trust territory benefited from what amounted to a subsidy of a quarter of a million pounds per annum (excess of expenditures over revenues).[9]

Insofar as its administration was concerned, the Southern Cameroons seemed, since the start of the trusteeship, to be progressing towards its eventual destiny as part of Nigeria. Under Nigeria's "Richards" Constitution of 1946, the only significant change, at least in the relationship of the British Cameroons to Nigeria, was the appearance of two Native Authority representatives in the Eastern Nigerian House of Assembly. The two were Chief Manga Williams, of Victoria, and Galega, the Fon of Bali.

In 1949, by the time the first United Nations Visiting Mission appeared on the scene, constitutional-administrative ties with Nigeria, in appearance complicated, were in reality still quite simple. The seat of government, that is to say the ultimate authority and responsibility for Southern and Northern Cameroonian affairs, remained in Lagos. There was no separate budget for the British Cameroons, nor were separate public accounts normally kept for the trust territory. Government revenues from the British Cameroons usually went into the common fund, and were redistributed to the trust territory according to need.

The trusteeship agreement had also permitted the continuation of a division between the southern and northern parts of the former mandate. Until 1948, the southern part comprised the Province of the Cameroons, a part of the Eastern Provinces of Nigeria, and the various northern sections of the trust territory were administratively tied to the Northern Provinces of Northern Nigeria. In 1948 the southern part of the trust territory was divided into the Provinces of Cameroons and Bamenda, and the new divisions put in charge of a commissioner responsible to the Chief Commissioner of the Eastern Provinces. The appointment of commissioners for both southern and northern parts of the trust territory marked an important advance. For the first time the two territories had their own administrator responsible to the Nigerian government. In 1949 the United Nations Visiting Mission summarized the administrative tie to Nigeria in the following terms:

Provinces of Cameroons and Bamenda (especially since 1948) formed part of the Eastern Provinces of Nigeria, in charge of a Commissioner who is responsible to the Chief Commissioner of the Eastern Provinces rather than to the Government; the small Tigon-Ndoro-Kentu area is administered as though it formed part of a division of Benue Province, which is a part of the Northern Provinces; and further north, there are, first, the two areas, physically divided by Nigerian territory, administered as part of the

Adamawa Division of the Adamawa Province of Nigeria, which also belongs to the Northern Provinces, and, secondly, the Dikwa Emirate which forms a division of the Bornu Province which again belongs to the Northern Provinces.[10]

The two parts of the Cameroons could, under the 1946 and 1948 Nigerian constitutions, qualify for representation in the Central Legislative Council of Nigeria, in the House of Assembly of the Eastern Provinces (for the Southern Cameroonian Provinces), and in the bicameral Northern Regional Council. The British Cameroons were in fact represented in both the Northern and Eastern legislatures but not in the central Nigerian Legislative Council. The Commissioner for the Southern Cameroons acted in a dual capacity; he was responsible to the central Nigerian government in all matters relating to the Trusteeship Agreement, but reported to the Chief Commissioner of the Eastern Provinces on administrative matters arising from the Cameroon provinces' relations to the Eastern Nigeria provinces.

If the British were convinced that the Southern Cameroons' future lay with Nigeria, it was a conviction that, after 1944—as we noted— came to have a diminishing number of sympathizers among the young Nigeria-based, Cameroonian intelligentsia.[11] At first, the sentiment took tangible form through the participation of three Lagosian Cameroons groups in the founding of the NCNC. The three groups (the CYL, the Bamenda Improvement Association, and the Bakweri Union) were apparently concerned that Southern Cameroonian identity be preserved in the Nigerian political groups that began to appear in the mid-1940's. On the basis of the available evidence, it seems probable that Dr. Endeley and his colleagues, Kale, Namme, and Mbile, might have been content to remain the Cameroons wing of the NCNC; yet in 1946, when the Cameroons trusteeships were created (the same year Endeley was dropped from the rolls of the BMA for malpractice), the already restive Cameroons groups in the NCNC began to move from the parent organization. Still in 1946, Endeley returned home to Buea and immediately plunged into local political life. In rapid succession he reactivated and politicized several semimoribund Bakweri tribal unions and associations including the Bakweri Improvement Union and the Bakweri Land Committee (concerned with reclaiming Bakweri land originally alienated to the Germans), brought together the CYL and a number of tribal unions under the organizational umbrella of Cameroons Federal Union (1947), and (also in 1947) became the first general secretary of the newly created Cameroons Development Corporation Workers' Union (CDCWU). Endeley headed the CDCWU until 1950, but his union duties did not prevent him from pursuing other political activities. In 1948, his CFU formally articulated plans that had been gaining support among the leaders of the new organizations: to take immediate steps to facilitate reunification of the two Cameroons, to teach French and English in both Cameroons, to establish a customs union permitting free trade between the two trust territories, and to create a joint constituent assembly.[12]

Apparently Endeley saw in reunification an issue that not only could embarrass the colonial administration into concessions over the Bakweri claims, but could also create support for the push toward an autonomous Southern Cameroons province within Nigeria. Moreover, Endeley was anxious for the support of a newly created organization of emigré Douala, the French Cameroons Welfare Union (FCWU; founded in 1958 by R. J. K. Dibonge), which had also, but for other reasons, made the issue part of its program. There is little question that at this point Endeley had slight genuine interest in reunification; actual reunification was something that might or might not occur in the future. His primary concern was to find political leverage with which to pry the Southern Cameroons loose within but not away from Nigeria. The first UN Visiting Mission in 1949 gives indirect confirmation of this:

In no case was complete separation from Nigeria demanded; even when requests were made . . . for unification with the Cameroons under French administration, *they were coupled with a desire to remain within the framework of the Nigerian constitution.* The demand was invariably for a greater degree of autonomy, but on a purely regional basis.[13] [Italics mine.]

One authority contends that the widespread interest in the Togo unification issue at the United Nations might also have persuaded Endeley to raise the new cry.[14]

The politicization of the Southern Cameroons proceeded apace in 1949. In May, a conference of seventeen Cameroons groups (including the CDCWU and one group from the French Cameroun) met at Kumba to discuss common problems and plan submission to the first UN mission, scheduled to visit the two territories in October of that year. One outcome of the conference was the Cameroons National Federation (CNF), which explicitly modeled itself on the NCNC, to which Endeley, Mbile, and Kale still belonged. The conference charged that the British Cameroons had been the object of "shocking neglect" and demanded, among other things, "unification in principle," removal of all frontier restrictions and regulations, teaching of English and French in all schools in both Cameroons, regional status for the Southern Cameroons, and the "constitution of an Assembly which will enable the unity of all sections of the Trust Territory . . . and as a forerunner to the provision of Article 76(b) and (c) of the United Nations Organization Charter."[15]

By the beginning of 1949, the UPC, Dibonge's French Cameroons Welfare Union, and the CNF had established informal contacts. Endeley's dalliance with the UPC seems to have been neither very serious nor extensive, for when the first of two conferences at Kumba between nationalist groups from both sides of the border took place in August, 1949 (the second was held four months later), only the groups associated with Dibonge participated in the founding of the Kamerun United National Congress.[16] (John Foncha cast his lot with Dibonge and the KUNC, as did Mbile, marking the first of the latter's several breaks with Endeley.) Two months before the second UN visit, in 1952, the KUNC and UPC met again, this time in Tiko, and once more declared that in unification lay the political salvation of the two Cameroons.[17] By the end of 1952, however, the CNF and KUNC had healed their differences and fused into the Kamerun National Congress (KNC).

At the same time, under the operation of the 1951 Nigeria constitution, Endeley, Mbile, Foncha (an old ally of Endeley, already in 1942 the secretary of the Bamenda branch of the CYL), S. A. George, Peter Motomby-Woleta, S. T. Muna, and others of the new Southern Cameroonian political elite, were cutting their legislative milk teeth in the Nigerian Eastern Regional House of Assembly. In the Assembly the thirteen (by 1953) Cameroons members sat under the NCNC banner but most of them, including Endeley and Muna, chafed at the NCNC connection; they "feared the highly sophisticated National Council of Nigeria and the Cameroons Government in the Eastern Region, and were only too conscious of the backwardness and political immaturity of their small territory."[18] Given the opportunity, Endeley was prepared to break his ties with the NCNC and actively campaign for Southern Cameroonian separatism under his own banner. The opportunity came during the January-May, 1953, crisis in the Eastern House over Azikiwe's leadership. In March, Endeley sought to enlist all thirteen Cameroons Members in a declaration of "benevolent neutrality" in Nigerian politics, but only nine went along with him. As Endeley began to reëmphasize his demands for Cameroonian autonomy, and when the nine sent a memorandum to the Colonial Secretary urging the creation of a separate Cameroons legislature, the breach became permanent. Endeley, Muna, Foncha, and George led the majority faction, retaining the designation of KNC for their group. The minority, led by Mbile, Kale, and Motomby-Woleta, formed the Kamerun Peoples' Party (KPP), urging the retention of the NCNC link and continued association with the eastern region.

In July, 1953, both KNC and KPP representatives attended the Nigerian constitutional talks in London, and Endeley pressed his demands for a separate Cameroons Region and legislature. The Colonial Secretary told Endeley that if he won an election at home on the issue of separation from Eastern Nigeria, the resumed conference to be held in Lagos in January, 1954, would abide by the decision of the voters. The KNC, now allied to the Action Group, the dominant party in Western Nigeria, captured all six of the seats allocated to the Cameroons in the new Federal House, and later won twelve of the thirteen elective seats (the KPP won the thirteenth) in the Southern Cameroons House of Assembly created under the 1954 constitution.

During 1954, and especially after the Southern Cameroons secured its distinctive quasi-federal status under the new Nigerian constitution, Endeley tended increasingly to see the Southern Cameroons of the future as a self-governing region within an independent Nigeria, and to relegate the goal of reunification to the background. Endeley's swing away from reunification and his informal alliance with the Action Group split the KNC once more, and by the end of the year John Foncha and Anthony Ngunjoh were preparing to form their own party and to occupy the programmatic ground vacated by Endeley's old CNF, advocating complete severance of political ties with Nigeria, the administration of the trust territory for the time being as a separate dependency, and ultimate reunification, on a federal basis, with the French Cameroun.

The circumstances and events leading up to the abortive UPC revolt in May, 1955, have been described elsewhere in this work. For our purposes, it is important to recall that almost from the date of its founding the UPC had maintained contacts with the nascent political groups of the Southern Cameroons, and at one time or another had supported the aims of most Southern Cameroonian political leaders. Although it is true that, by the beginning of 1955, Endeley, Mbile, Kale, Muna, Dibonge, and Motomby had moved a considerable distance from the UPC's positions, the UPC's *comité directeur*, fleeing from arrest in July, was still able to establish its headquarters in Kumba in a nominally friendly, and certainly sympathetic, atmosphere. It was, however, only the new KNC splinter, led by Foncha and named the Kamerun National Democratic Party (KNDP, formed in March), that made common cause with the exiles. The administration, it may be added, looked with some disfavor upon its new guests, but, apart from close surveillance and attempts to keep the exiles from appearing before the UN Visiting Mission that was touring the country in November and December, it refrained from overt attack upon the *upécistes*.

1955-1959

The UPC directorate not only established new headquarters for the party, but did so as well for its subsidiary youth and women's organizations, the JDC and UDFC. Once settled in Kumba, all three organizations became active again, and there were demonstrations before the UN Visiting Mission in 1955, the publication of a large amount of propaganda literature, and a vigorous campaign to recruit both members and sympathizers. The UPC even took part, albeit unsuccessfully, in the elections of March, 1957. Its nominal ally, the KNDP, very soon discovered that collaboration with the UPC meant adopting a radical activism and ideological stance rather far from its own predilections. As Ardener has perceptively pointed out, the language of anti-imperialism had always been Endeley's; the KNDP, for all its programmatic affinity to the UPC, was "in fact highly traditionalist and conservative in its image."[19] Again using Ardener's terminology, the KNDP occupied a "quasi-left" position on the Southern Cameroonian political spectrum; it based its strength on the anti-Nigerian feeling, the inarticulate mass suspicions of the "numerically powerful Bamenda rural populations [toward] the polished remoteness of Dr. Endeley and the coastal intelligentsia."[20] As such, it spoke not only for deep-seated popular sentiments, but, paradoxically, was able to attract "younger intellectuals to whom the extremism of the ideological left was repellent."[21] It became almost a foregone conclusion that the UPC-KNDP link was a *mariage de convenance* and could not last; by the time the UPC was banned in the Southern Cameroons and its leaders deported in the summer of 1957, the KNDP and the UPC had become permanently estranged. The UPC left behind two reminders of its visit; one was the One Kamerun Party, formed in 1957 by Ndeh Ntumazah, a former member of the UPC directorate, and the other was the guerilla bands that used the forests of the Southern Cameroons as bases from which to conduct raids upon their countrymen on the other side of the border.

There were other important political developments during 1957. First, despite Endeley's vacillations on the subject of unification, he was still able to muster enough strength to win the March general elections for the thirteen elective seats in the Southern Cameroons House of Assembly, but only by a slim margin. The result: KNC, six seats; KNDP, five seats; KPP, two seats. From May 23 to June 26, the principal party leaders attended the Nigerian Constitutional Conference in London, returning home with a promise of full regional status and the introduction of ministerial government. By the end of the summer, it had become obvious—particularly in light of his statements in London

—that Endeley was preparing to abandon completely the unificationist position. The retreat cost him, in September, the support of one of his staunchest followers, as well as one elective KNC seat. Solomon T. Muna, a member of the KNC executive committee and former NCNC minister in the Eastern Nigerian government, resigned from the party and "crossed the floor" to the KNDP side. Reportedly, Muna accused the KNC leadership of following a policy of "integration with Nigeria," which he claimed was contrary to the goal of unification to which he understood the KNC was still committed. Muna's defection now reduced the KNC elective seats to five; however, the party still retained the support of four of the six Native Authority members (the other two were KNDP and Independent, respectively), and in December formally sealed an alliance with the KPP, with whom it now found a good deal in common.

The new combination gave the alliance an undisputed majority in the House and permitted Endeley, early in February, 1958, to call a special session of the House to debate motions calling for the immediate introduction of the ministerial system and full regional self-government in 1959. Over the strenuous objections of the opposition, who finally walked out during the voting, the motions were adopted. The KNDP objected to the introduction of ministerial government before general elections had determined the composition of the enlarged legislature of twenty-six instead of twenty-one seats agreed upon during the 1957 talks in London. The KNDP obviously feared—and not without some justification—that, if given ministerial power, the KNC/KPP would so consolidate its position that the KNDP would be at a serious disadvantage by the time the elections were finally held. In any case, in May, 1958, Endeley became the Southern Cameroon's first premier. At the same time, for all practical purposes, he almost completely abandoned the unificationist goal: he "stated that he and his colleagues still believed in the desirability of the ultimate unification of the two Cameroons, but that the intervening events and circumstances had removed the question of unification from the realm of urgency and priority."[22] In July, the registration for the general elections was complete, but, much to the irritation of the KNDP, it was December before Endeley announced that they would not be held until January, 1959.

In January, the consequences of Endeley's vacillations and the splits in his party finally came home to him. Foncha and his KNDP won the election, garnering fourteen seats in the enlarged House of Assembly to the KNC/KPP's twelve. Foncha was named premier, and almost immediately he and Endeley set out for New York to plead their respective positions before the spring UN General Assembly session at which the future of the Cemeroons trusteeships was to be decided. As its points of reference, the Assembly had before it not only the report of the 1958 Visiting Mission—which noted that all Southern Cameroons parties had more or less agreed on a plebiscite to follow the January elections—but also an addendum to the report, filed after the January elections in the Southern Cameroons. The addendum characterized the results of the elections inconclusive insofar as the future ties of the territory were concerned, and specifically recommended a plebiscite to decide the issue.[23]

The General Assembly had little trouble in disposing of the Northern Cameroons' future; there would be a plebiscite in November, 1959, at which the voters would decide between joining Northern Nigeria when Nigeria became independent or deferring any decision until later. It proved much more difficult to find an acceptable formula for the Southern Cameroons.

Although both Foncha and Endeley agreed in principle that there should be a plebiscite in the Southern Cameroons, they differed widely as to the questions to be put to the voters. Foncha maintained that the sole issue to be decided by the voters should be that of separation from Nigeria or continued association with it. Reunification, said Foncha, could come only *after* separation, when it had been discussed with the government of the French Cameroun, and should not be a question in the plebiscite. He envisaged a short postplebiscite period during which the Southern Cameroons would work toward "complete independence," and during which the possibility of reunification, in the form of federation, would be explored by the governments concerned. Endeley, on the other hand, insisted that the choice between the voters should be clear-cut; continued association with Nigeria as a fully autonomous member of the Nigerian federation, or unification with an independent French Cameroun. Endeley pointed out that reunification had never been one of the objectives of the trusteeship; it was a matter that the Cameroonian peoples, once free, should negotiate among themselves and that should not be enforced from the outside. He even suggested that, in the light of a provision in the Nigerian constitution permitting federation with any country outside Nigeria, a federation of both Cameroons and Nigeria might someday be realized. Faced with the apparently irreconcilable positions of the two leaders, the General Assembly finally decided that a separate plebiscite should be held in each part of the British Cameroons before the date of Nigerian independence (Oct. 1, 1960), and asked the two leaders to go home and try to find some agreement on the questions to be put in the South and the qualifications for voting.[24]

In accordance with the General Assembly's wishes, an all-party conference was convened at Mamfe on August 10 and 11, 1959, under the chairmanship of Sir Sidney Phillipson. The conference deliberated for two days but failed to reach an agreement on either the alternatives to be put or the qualifications for voting. In fact, the disagreement was so sharp ("embittered," according to Sir Sidney) that only Sir Sidney's diplomacy and parliamentary skill prevented the conference from breaking up in disorder.[25]

In late September both Foncha and Endeley were back in New York, still unreconciled. Testifying before the General Assembly's Fourth (Trusteeship) Committee, Foncha explained that his party did not wish reunification as one of the plebiscite's alternatives because reunification could only be achieved through negotiation by those "who were ripe for it," and no one section of the Cameroons was as yet ready. "Independence" would first have to be achieved. According to Foncha, the KNC/KPP wanted an early plebiscite and the choice between joining Nigeria or the French Cameroun because "it hoped to use the terrorist murders in the Cameroons under French Administration in order to frighten the people . . . into voting for integration with Nigeria."[26] What his people wanted, he continued, was an opportunity to see what happened in the Southern Cameroons' two neighbors after they had attained their independence. Endeley, in rebuttal, claimed that he insisted on a clear choice, and soon, because his party could not allow the KNDP to "take the territory and its people on a joy ride to an unknown destination."[27] The continued divergence of view between the two leaders prompted another Southern Cameroonian political figure, N. N. Mbile (leader of the KPP), to suggest that the way out of the dilemma was partition of the territory, "a solution which would allow each tribe or division to make its own choice between the two alternatives."[28]

On September 30, after five days of apparently fruitless discussion, Foncha and Endeley presented the Fourth Committee with a joint statement that, in effect, admitted their inability to agree by requesting that the plebiscite be deferred until 1962. They agreed on only one thing: administrative separation from Nigeria when that country became independent.[29] There was no mention of the alternatives open to voters in 1962, nor of the "independence" to which Foncha had vaguely alluded. The statement did not please the African states that had sponsored the informal talks between Foncha and Endeley (Ghana, Guinea, Liberia, Libya, Sudan, Morocco, Tunisia, and the United Arab Republic); the Soviet delegate charged that the statement had been

written by the British, and, in fact, most of the members of the Fourth
Committee expressed serious doubts about it during the several days
following its release. The leaders were urged to reconsider their positions. On October 7 it became obvious that they had. A ten-power
draft resolution, obviously written with the concurrence of both
Foncha and Endeley, spelled out the formula that was finally decided
upon by the General Assembly: (1) a plebiscite was to be held not
later than March, 1961; (2) the questions to be put were to state clear
alternatives between joining Nigeria or the Cameroun Republic; (3) administrative separation from the Federation of Nigera was to be not
later than October 1, 1960; and (4), only persons born in the Southern
Cameroons or one of whose parents was born there were to vote in the
plebiscite.[30]

Although the record shows that Foncha and Endeley agreed on the
formula that was incorporated into the Assembly's final resolution on
the Southern Cameroons, to Foncha's colleagues back in Buea—and
one suspects to Foncha himself—the agreement was seen as a considerable political defeat. Before he had left for New York in September,
Foncha had promised to bring back a two- to three-year extension of
the trusteeship, and a guarantee for a period of independence within
which discussions of the modalities of unification with the Republic
of Cameroon could be explored at leisure. But Foncha and his colleagues, frightened by the unrest in the French Cameroun, had by
the fall of 1959 begun to retreat from their ardent unificationist positions. What they now wanted was time, time to see what would happen
over the eastern border after the French Cameroun attained independence. Consequently, the "joint statement" issued on September 30 was
received with delight in the Southern Cameroons. When the final
formula was announced, joy turned to anger: the cabinet met hastily,
wired Foncha to come home for consultation, and when he did not
reply there was even talk of replacing him as premier. Foncha's colleagues felt themselves betrayed; instead of gaining breathing space,
they had been asked to accept a decision that would force a settlement of the future of the territory before they felt it was ready to
decide calmly. An early plebiscite, even in the spring of 1961, would
they claimed, play into Endeley's hands by emphasizing the difference
between a peaceful Nigeria and a troubled French Cameroun. In any
event, Foncha's colleagues eventually accepted the final formula, however unpalatable it was to them. By way of footnote, and in all fairness
to Foncha, his colleagues' judgments of him may have been too harsh:
at the UN he was reportedly subjected to a good deal of pressure by
the African states on the Fourth Committee, and his capitulation may

have been in face of extremely insistent demands that the Cameroons quesion be decided now, not later.

In November, the plebescite held in the Northern Cameroons resulted in a surprise. Instead of voting overwhelmingly to join the Northern Region of Nigeria, the voters, 70,401 to 42,797, decided to postpone the decision until later.[31] The premier of the Northern Region, the Sardauna of Sokoto, blamed the results on "subversive activities of British officials," but Sir Andrew Cohen, at the UN, explained that the results were a reaction against certain abuses in local government. On December 12, the UN General Assembly decided on another plebiscite in the Northern Cameroons to coincide with the one to be held in the Southern Cameroons and stipulated that the same questions be asked in both parts of the territory.

THE PLEBISCITES AND REUNIFICATION— 1960-1961

During 1960, Foncha and President Ahidjo of the newly-created Cameroun Republic met several times to discuss the shape of the future arrangements under which the two Cameroons might achieve reunification if the 1961 plebiscites resulted in a vote for it. They had already talked in Buea in July, 1959; in 1960 they met in Yaoundé in January, in Nkongsamba in April, and in; Yaoundé in May, November, and December. A draft outline for a constitution embodying Foncha's concepts of a loose federation, submitted at the November meeting, was rejected, and the series of meetings managed to produce only two loosely worded, ambiguous communiqués. The communiqués, finally reprinted in a pamphlet issued by the administering authority shortly before the plebiscite, did very little to clarify a situation already muddied by Foncha's increasing reluctance to agree on anything beyond the vague outlines of a federal system. Ahidjo and Foncha did, however, agree to hold a conference *after* the plebiscite and to decide upon the details of the union then.[32] In contrast, the consequences of a vote for integration with Nigeria were spelled out clearly, as Endeley had gotten a detailed statement of policy from the Nigerian government. Symptomatic of the lack of clear communication between Foncha and Ahidjo was the fact that Foncha was completely unaware of the Ahidjo government's position on the future of the Northern Cameroons —should it opt for unification with the Cameroun Republic—until February 8, 1961, when a visiting political scientist showed him a copy of a communiqué on the subject issued by the Ahidjo government more than a month before.[33] The plebiscite itself was scheduled for February 11.

The preplebiscite campaign and the plebiscite itself have been examined in some detail elsewhere.³⁴ Suffice it for this discussion to note that the unification alterative won by more than a two-to-one margin in the Southern Cameroons, but was soundly defeated in the separate Northern Cameroonian balloting. The results were as follows:

Southern Cameroons:	For Cameroun Republic	235,571
	For Nigeria	97,741
Northern Cameroons:	For Nigeria	146,296
	For Cameroun Republic	97,659

The success of the unification alternative in the Southern Cameroons must be attributed to three main factors: (1) the skill of the KNDP leadership in translating local ethnic, economic, and political issues into votes; (2) the ineptness, compared to the KNDP, of the CPNC and its leaders in presenting the case for continued association with Nigeria; and (3), the cumulative effect of a Southern Cameroonian nationalism in which reunification was long a major programmatic goal.

The KNDP based its campaign in the Victoria and Kumba Divisions upon the exploitation of long-standing local grievances and animosities against resident southern Nigerians, an approach that paid off handsomely by denying Endeley the support of several constituencies represented in the House of Assembly by CPNC Members. This appeal attracted the votes not only of groups native to Victoria and Kumba, but also of the large number of grassfielders living in these Divisions. The fact remains, however, that even without these "friendly" votes, the unification alternative had enough support to carry Victoria Division, most of whose constituencies had been considered "safe" by the CPNC. Further, in Kumba it was only the overwhelming vote for the Nigerian alternative delivered by Mbile's district (14,738 to 555) that swung that Division for it. The only other Endeley stronghold that remained firm for Nigeria was Nkambe Division, on the northern fringe of the grassfields, long dominated by the strong personality of the CPNC's Rev. Samuel Andoh-Seh. In the grassfields (Bamenda and Mamfe Divisions, but in particular the former) it was the effective mobilization of existing party support that produced almost overwhelming support for the unification alternative. The KNDP was born in the grassfields, and its principal leaders (Foncha, Jua, Muna, Nganje, and others) could count on the strength of their personal appeal plus the strong sense of ethnic solidarity upon which the KNDP was organized. The fact that about 60 per cent of the registered voters in the Southern Cameroons lived in the grassfield areas of Bamenda, Mamfe, and Wum Divisions spurred the KNDP into concentrating its efforts there; the decision was amply rewarded by the fact that 60 per cent of the reunification votes were cast in those areas.

Where the KNDP's campaign showed tactical shrewdness, the CPNC's could only be described as lackadaisical; Endeley and his party began to show signs of energy only one month before the plebiscite, and their appeals were almost wholly devoted to unfavorable comparisons between the troubled Republic and a peaceful, well intentioned Nigeria. Moreover, the CPNC concentrated almost all its efforts in Victoria, Kumba, and Nkambe, in the belief (not altogether justified) that the grassfield divisions were already lost to the opposition. In all, the results of the plebiscite reflected the political acumen of the governing party, results all the more remarkable in the light of the indecision and difficulties found in the KNDP ranks during 1959.

The promised postplebiscite negotiations on the nature of the new federation dragged on until late July, 1961, when a Foncha-Ahidjo conference held at Foumban ostensibly resolved all outstanding differences between the two leaders and produced a draft federal constitution. One of the reasons for the delay was the anger of the Ahidjo government over the results of the Northern Cameroons plebiscite. There is considerable evidence that Ahidjo hoped that the additional potential votes for the UC to be found in the Northern Cameroons would strengthen his hand in the negotiations with Foncha, as well as offset any possible deals between Foncha and various southern-based opposition groups. The Republic officially protested the results and, during the two months following the plebiscite, vainly sought to have them annulled because of various alleged "irregularities" committed by the British authorities, aided and abetted by United Nations personnel. Even after the UN General Assembly had accepted the Plebiscite Commissioner's report, thereby confirming the results of the plebiscite, the Republic lodged a complaint on the subject before the International Court.[35] In any event, the draft constitution was approved by the legislatures in both territories, and on October 1, 1961, the Southern Cameroons trusteeship ended and the Federal Republic of Cameroun came into existence. Three months earlier, the Northern Cameroons had formally become a part of the Northern Region of Nigeria, with full provincial status. "Reunification" had been achieved, but only partly, and without full appreciation on either side of the array of problems to be faced before the new bilingual federation could be considered a success. Border tensions persisted, the economic problems attending the integration of the two territories had been only superficially considered, and even the widely heralded sense of community between the new partners had not managed to prevent the writing of a federal constitution that reflected a desire to postpone embarrassing political and economic decisions as long as possible.[36]

IX *The Cameroun and The Problems of Transition*

INTRODUCTION: THE MYTH OF INDEPENDENCE

It is a trite though valid observation that the word *independence* has a special magic that seizes alike the imaginations of the leaders of a country and those of its people. The most common manifestation of that magic is the growth of a feeling that independence is a sort of magic wand, one touch of which will resolve all conflicts, solve all problems, heal all wounds, grant all wishes, and realize all hopes. The Cameroun was not exempt from this fascination; indeed, so overpowering had its spell become that five months before independence, in July, 1959, Prime Minister Ahidjo felt constrained to address himself to it:[1]

Since the decision of the United Nations to end Trusteeship we have repeated constantly . . . that independence has fostered weighty hopes, but that these hopes cannot be realized except in the measure that we work hard to give them real content. We know, in effect, that independence will not solve all our problems, and those who profess to think so cruelly deceive their fellows. They hope to find in the inevitable disappointments the ferment which will raise thoughtless opposition and open the paths to power to them. We must unceasingly disabuse their victims; but we must also work without relaxation to save our country from the bitterness born of an independence which changes nothing, which leaves unused the enormous potential of human energy which this magic word evoked.

Ahidjo's comment gave point to both the negative and the positive aspects of the symbolism of independence: on the one hand it stimulated great expectations, which, if not realized, could only bring bitter disappointment; and, on the other hand, it created an atmosphere of hope and good will that could be productive of great things. The problem was to keep the myth within manageable bounds, a problem no less real for being intangible, and no less dangerous for being widespread.

215

In the months preceding independence a lassitude settled over much of the governmental machinery in the Cameroun, almost as if a moratorium had been called on making important decisions. The proximity of independence and the spell of its "magic" seemed to convince many Camerounians that important decisions could be put off until later, and to inhibit responsible French officials from acting in their full capacities. In the latter instance a twofold rationalization was produced: one part excused inaction by terming it resignation to the inevitable take-over by the Camerounians and the subsequent departure of the French; the other part excused it by calling it an un·willingness to take action likely to antagonize the Camerounians and to make the future of the remaining French more uncertain than it already was.[2]

The widespread misunderstanding about the nature of independence and the unrealistic expectations about it among the population is corroborated by an arresting catalogue of misconceptions appearing, surprisingly, in the January 1, 1960, issue of the *rallié* UPC newspaper, *La Voix du Peuple*. It is worth quoting in its entirety:[3]

INDEPENDENCE DOES NOT MEAN

That no one need work any longer.

That there will be neither bosses nor discipline in work.

That there will be no more laws.

That the police force will be disbanded.

That it will be possible to travel from Douala to Yaoundé without paying.

That women will be able to obtain divorces as it suits their fancy.

That the Whites will automatically go home.

That it will be possible to go into a store and take what one pleases without paying.

That Camerounization of the administrative cadres will cease.

That the Whites can be considered completely useless if it is possible to do without their services.

That racial hate should replace the hatred of colonialism.

That nothing will be done to eliminate unemployment.

That liberty will degenerate into license and everyone will be able to do as he pleases.

That civil liberties will be suspended in the name of public order.

That one may beat up [*casser la gueule*] the first citizen—preferably a European—who steps on one's toes.

That there will be freedom to install an era and a regime of corruption and favoritism.

That all the churches will be closed and all Catholics hanged.

That the clergy will have the right to use their influence with impunity to intervene in nonreligious matters.

That it will be possible to bargain away national sovereignty so as to bring the Cameroun into the Community.

The recital is as interesting for what it says as for what it implies. The fact that the opposition felt it necessary to publish the catalogue appears to be evidence of a realization that popular frustration resulting from unfulfilled hopes might rebound against the opposition rather than the government.[4]

Happily, the complex of overwrought expectations, popular euphoria, and governmental paralysis which immediately preceded and followed independence ceased to be a problem when the realities of independence began to make themselves felt. Whatever illusions had been created about the coming of independence vanished in disappointment, or dissolved in the face of old unsolved problems or in recognition of new ones that came with independence. In the Cameroun, the awakening to reality took six months, but its effect was the same as if it had taken longer: there was shock at finding that little had changed and that problems had multiplied rather than disappeared.

It would be a sterile exercise to go down the list of the particular economic, social, and political problems, old and new, that the independent Cameroun Republic faced after January 1, 1960. Such a recital would only confirm their existence without saying much more about them. A more meaningful view is to consider them in relation to the task of building a nation once a state has been created.

Independence gave the Cameroun all the classic attributes of statehood: geographical definition, a population with a common citizenship, and established central power structures in control of the country and free to regulate its relations with other states. It acquired, in short, the juridical sovereignty envisaged by the termination of the Trusteeship Agreement. Parenthetically, the 1959 Statute of the Cameroun, though it called the Cameroun a state, did not in fact make it one; the reserved powers held by France left no doubt that sovereignty ultimately reposed in Paris, not Yaoundé. Once the Cameroun became a state, however, it did not also become a nation. A *nation* is an entity much more intangible than a *state*, since the attributes which help to define a state are not adequate to define a nation. Nationhood involves building and preserving a sense of common identity that is capable of transcending local, ethnic, or partisan loyalties. This commonalty is not a juridical attribute, and international law does not require states to prove nationhood to qualify for membership in the international community. An examination of the web of internal dichotomies existing in the Cameroun on January 1, 1960, cannot but lead to the

conclusion that the Cameroun, although it had become a state, was far
from being a nation.

In the three sections that follow, three of the most important aspects
of nation-building will be discussed in relation to the Cameroun. The
first deals with the problem of finding a national commonalty within
the diversity of Cameroun society. The second considers the stability of
the Cameroun's political party system and its relation to the search for
nationhood. The third deals with the institutional and territorial framework within which the first two aspects develop. A last section will deal
with the French "presence" in the Cameroun.

FINDING A CAMEROUN COMMONALTY

Our examination of the East Cameroun's political
development reveals very few elements that might have led to the
birth of a genuine Cameroun nationalism. Broadly speaking, there are
at least two main reasons for this. One is that neither the German nor
the French colonial administration sought to encourage the growth of
a national consciousness. Within the terms of German colonial policy,
such an aim would have been both unthinkable and ridiculous. The
stated aims of French policy, at least until 1940, were assimilationist
and not particularist. France always hoped, as may be recalled, that
its colonial wards would look upon themselves eventually as Frenchmen, rather than Togolese, Senegalese, or Camerounians. The second
reason is that the demand for national identity in the Cameroun, almost
wholly devoid of ethnic reference, did not find broad political support
until the last five years of the trusteeship period. Only one major political party (the UPC) actively espoused nationalist goals before 1956.
Initially, other political groups using nationalist symbols did so more
out of tactical considerations than conviction.

Consequently, as the Cameroun moved into independence, Camerounian nationalism, though it had widespread popular support, had
yet to be translated into essentially national aims and solidarity. The
biggest obstacle to the realization of this goal lay in Cameroun diversity, which expresses itself in a variety of particularisms: regional,
urban, rural, religious, tribal, and economic. Translated into political
demands, they raise a babel of conflicting voices in which expressions
of unity, however strong, are soon lost.

The regional differences are exacerbated by their ethnic content and
perpetuated by the marked cultural differences between north and
south. The north, economically underdeveloped except for a few urban
centers, is still largely dominated by its traditional Muslim chiefs whose
hold on the northern populations, though mitigated by the presence of

the *Union Camerounaise* party, is yet strong enough to produce a monolithic bloc of deputies in the National Assembly. It is certainly no accident that most of the powerful traditional magnates of the north are also members of that bloc. Although it is true that the demographic pressure of the Kirdi population and the growth of education in the north has spurred social and political changes in the area, the chiefs and the semifeudal system they represent will weigh heavily on the political scales for a long time to come. Also, the northern chiefs have participated for ten years in Cameroun legislatures and have not challenged the institutional framework of a united Cameroun. All this, however, has not lessened the frequent north-south acrimony that arises when regional matters are discussed.

The south, in contrast, with its sharply accentuated ethnic cleavages and long history of internal discord, is by far more educated and experienced in western ways. Here Christianity has made great advances, claiming nearly a million converts. Here also are the main rail lines, most of the industrial plants, and the largest urban centers in the Cameroun. Such large cities and towns as Douala, Yaoundé, Nkongsamba, Mbalmayo, Ebolowa, Dschang, and Baffoussam, to name the more important, crystallize many of the social and ethnic tensions prevalent in the south. (These were discussed in some detail in Chapter III in relation to the problems of urbanization.) Further, there is the particularly explosive problem of the Bamiléké, at once a regional, social, political, ethnic, and economic problem of the first magnitude. It remains, unsettled, probably to bedevil the Cameroun for years to come.

Another problem of a different order centers about the uncertainty that exists on the development of the relationship institutionalized in the Cameroun Federal Republic. Cameroun nationalists never accepted the finality of the frontier between the trust territory and the Republic; to them it was an artificial and arbitrary device by which Britain and France sundered the old Kamerun. Using the image of a former "Kamerun nation" and the purported existence of an "independent Kamerun" between 1916 and 1918, Cameroun nationalists espoused the "national" objective of "unification" (or "reunification") to mobilize political sentiment.[5] It should be pointed out that such a fine disregard for the historical record is irrelevant in the face of the fact that the myth of a Kamerun nation is widely believed in both Cameroons. Having made reunification an integral part of the Cameroun nationalist creed, and having committed themselves to its achievement, the Cameroun's political leaders must now find the means wherewith to satisfy the expectations they have aroused.

In the previous chapter, we noted the circumstances under which reunification was achieved. The critical question still remains: What will be the nature of this union? Apart from drafting a constitution for the Cameroun Federal Republic, the leaders of the two Cameroons have moved very slowly in the direction of effecting the union to which the plebiscite committed them.

By the middle of 1963, only the most rudimentary common economic measures had been taken: the franc CFA had been introduced as the common currency in both states, the first federal budget had been promulgated, the flow of goods and persons between the states had been made slightly easier, and plans had been laid for a more direct overland connection between Buea and Douala, actually about twenty miles apart but hitherto mutually accessible only by way of a detour about one hundred and forty miles long. Further, the KNDP, fresh from its victory in the West Cameroon's December, 1961, general elections, was moving toward some sort of amalgamation with the East Cameroun's *Union Camerounaise* (UC) party, on the federal level. As yet unresolved were such problems as merging the two states' educational systems, separate and still based on British and French models, respectively; overcoming the yearly deficits in the recurrent budget of the West Cameroon, which in 1961 amounted to $784,000, and in 1962 to about $2,800,000; and finding substitute markets for such West Cameroonian exports as bananas and palm products after the withdrawal of Commonwealth preference on September 1, 1963.[6]

The problem of finding a commonalty for two countries separated by forty years of separate administration and by different languages, customs, and political traditions, may make the basic task of building a Cameroun nation that much more difficult.

The list of problems could be extended almost indefinitely; those mentioned above, being among the most important, serve merely to point up the dimensions of the nation-building task. To recapitulate: essentially, the task of creating a nation lies in what Karl Deutsch has called "the transformation of people, or of several ethnic elements, in the process of social mobilization."[7] In the Cameroun context, the key lies in transforming centrifugal particularisms into a self-conscious unity.

THE STABILITY OF THE CAMEROUN'S POLITICAL PARTY SYSTEM

Admittedly, a nation in the sense described above does not need a vigorous political party system in order to be a nation. The Soviet Union, Communist China, and Yugoslavia are no less nations for having single-party systems. Both the East and the West Camerouns, however, have—in the form of parliamentary and political institutions—chosen political systems predicated on democratic principles drawn primarily from French and English examples. Their commitment is to "democratic government" as John Plamenatz defines it: "Unless those who govern can be freely criticized by their subjects, and unless there is competition for popular favour between groups genuinely independent of one another, government can never be truly responsible to the people and therefore democratic."[8] The stability of the Cameroun's party system becomes, therefore, a crucial element in building a Cameroun nation as Camerounians themselves would like it to be.

Examination of the East Cameroun's postwar political history (see Chapter VI) reveals that

. . . the key element in the pattern of political grouping in the Cameroun is the absence of a national party carrying the thrust of the country's transition to and beyond independence. An all-incorporative movement on the TANU of CCP model, created to present a common political front before and immediately after the transition to independence, has no echo in the Cameroun experience. Instead, the several parties competing for power are regionally or ethnically based formations, loosely organized, more often than not coalescing around some local political personality rather than on behalf of an ideology or a program. The only true nationalist party with a dynamic organization, an ideological commitment, and a militant leadership—in short, the only party which might have grown into an all-Cameroun movement [the UPC]—dissipated its vitality in a premature attempt to seize power.[9]

The parliamentary groupings formed for the October, 1959, session of the East Cameroun Legislative Assembly (see note 108, Chapter VI) reflect this state of affairs. Only three of the five groups actually represented political parties. Similarly, the pattern of general elections in the East Cameroun from 1946 to 1960 (see Appendix B) demonstrates that candidates' party labels often had as little to do with party affiliations or programs as did electoral list titles.

No better testimony to the inherent weaknesses of the political parties can be found than the gradual collapse of multipartyism in the East Cameroun during 1960, 1961, and 1962, culminating in the arrest of the major opposition leaders and the emergence of the East Cameroun as a one-party state along lines already well defined in other African states. The story is an involved one, and has been told elsewhere at greater length; a summary will suffice here.[10]

Shortly after the election of the Cameroun Republic's National Assembly the MANC, dominated by Charles Assalé and represented

within the Assembly's *Groupe des Progressistes,* formally dissolved itself and fused with the UC. During April, 1961, the *Front Populaire
Pour l'Unité et la Paix,* a group of Bamiléké deputies that had accepted
collaboration with the Government, disintegrated following the announcement of its leader (Pierre Kamdem Ninyim, Minister of State)
that he was joining the UC. By June the whole group, which included
Victor Kanga (Minister of Justice), had been absorbed by the UC. Further, throughout 1961 and early 1962, the ranks of the PDC suffered
systematic attrition; by June, 1962, Mbida could claim only four of the
eight seats he won in 1960. In January, 1962, the UPC Congress in
Yaoundé was dissolved at bayonet point, and, during the spring of that
year, the opposition parties moved toward a merger of forces that was
announced on June 15 with the publication of an open letter signed by
Charles Okala (PSC), André-Marie Mbida (PDC), Theodore Mayi-Matip
(UPC), and Dr. Marcel Beybey-Eyidi (*Parti des Travaillistes Camerounais*). The letter declared, in effect, that Ahidjo was trying to create a
one-party state, and that if matters continued as they had the result
would be a "fascist-type dictatorship." On June 23, the Manifesto of
their *Front National Unifié* appeared. In July all four leaders were arrested on charges of "subversionary activities" and sedition, were tried,
convicted, and sentenced to both fines and imprisonment.

Behind the collapse of the opposition parties and the disintegration
of the several parliamentary groups there had been a concerted effort
by the government and the UC to move the country toward one-party
government, a trend Ahidjo observed with approval elsewhere among
both French and English-speaking African states. Ahidjo, speaking
after the fact, described his orientation on the subject:

Instead of quarreling about words, instead of disputes, we must be united
as I've already said, in one great organization, where discussion is free, where
different points of view can be confronted, and where the minority accepts
the decision of the majority. We must make use of this political organization
to mobilize all the people, to mobilize them for work, for economic and social
development. That is indispensable; all the African states that have just
become independent have understood it, they have seen that is indispensable. Some governments have even taken legal steps to realize political
unity in the interest of their countries; they have created single-party systems
[*des partis uniques*]; we haven't done this because we trust the patriotism
of Camerounians. . . .[11]

Early in 1962, Okala had characterized the *parti unifié* as the *parti
unique* in disguise; whatever the semantic difference, the East Came-
eroun had by mid-1962 become a one-party state. Accompanying the
push in this direction was a well-planned organizational expansion of

the UC; late in 1961 it could claim sections in all minor and major administrative divisions of the East Cameroun plus a steady increase in membership in southern *départements* once considered "safe" for the opposition. As the party that had won independence in 1960 and could claim the credit for reunification in 1961, the UC was able to roll out a bandwagon that many of its former opponents found irresistible. Deprived of the main planks in their programs, torn by internal rivalries, caught in a dilemma that on the one hand, dictated cautious collaboration with a government suddenly become more popular, and, on the other, the need to maintain their separate identities, the UPC, PDC, and PSC fell easy victims to the UC offense.

Part of the UC's tactical advantage came from a recognition that, during 1960 and 1961, the East Cameroun's party system still mirrored the divisive particularisms prevalent throughout the country. At root, however, much of the party system's instability lay in the parties' narrow horizons. The parties behaved much more like local interest groups than organizations conscious of broader national obligations. They displayed little concern in articulating and aggregating interests beyond those particularistic ones to which they owed their existence; they showed even less concern in politicizing the electoral masses on whom they ultimately depended for their participation in government. One is tempted to lay the blame at the door of the French administration for fostering a mentality which saw opposition as an end of political action. But even this is not wholly true. After the elections of 1956, party organization and activity had been encouraged by the French, and since then, for reasons noted previously, only the *Union Camerounaise* had expanded to any extent.

The political parties' lack of dynamism, their generally unstable character, and their limited appeal probably also lay in good measure in their inability to formulate goals with more than a heuristic value. Admittedly, they were constrained by the necessities of acting and maintaining their existence within the scope of the existing political situations. In all, however, by dissipating their energies in fruitless internecine conflicts, by failing to adapt programmatically either to independence or reunification, the opposition parties lost the initiative and with it their ability to participate effectively in the new political environment. It almost appears as if they realized their errors too late and then tried to survive by hastily banding together in the ill-fated United National Front.

There is little question but that the East Cameroun has, for all practical purposes, ceased to have a "party system"; the so-called one-party regime, with a single national organization monopolizing all aspects of political life, cannot with any accuracy be called a party system at all. The question of stability, if it is to be asked, must now be posed not in relation to the interaction of competing groups in the polity, but in relation to the *internal* workings of the regime and the nature of the forces interacting within it. If Plamenatz' proposition is taken as a point of departure, three related questions come immediately to mind: (1) Do the new circumstances permit the kind of interaction between governing and governed suggested by the definition? (2) To what extent has the new regime in fact "united" previously conflicting interests in the polity? And (3), depending on the answers to the first two questions, what are the prospects for the regime? Ahidjo has emphatically affirmed that the *parti unifié* is completely in accord with democratic principles, and at least one commentator upon the African scene has suggested that the "internal democracy" of some one-party regimes is as acceptable as the oppositional democracy of Western preference.[12] Whatever the judgments that can be passed upon "democracy" in other African one-party states, the three questions still remain largely unanswered with respect to the Cameroun, whose experience with the new form is still comparatively limited. There is at present, at least, the stability of political quiescence; whether that quiescence will last is another question.

THE INSTITUTIONS OF THE CAMEROUN REPUBLIC AND THE CAMEROUN FEDERAL REPUBLIC

On February 21, 1960, a country-wide referendum adopted the constitution drafted by the Consultative Committee created by the law of October 31, 1959. Each of the twenty-one *départements* became an electoral district, and voting took place after a vigorous campaign in which the opposition urged that the proposed constitution be rejected because it was elaborated without the participation of "an important section of political opinion." The final results were 797,498 affirmative to 531,000 negative votes. Ten of the twenty-one districts returned a negative vote, and in eight of these ten high abstention figures were registered. Significantly, all ten of the dissenting districts were in the south, and 89 per cent of the negative votes cast throughout the country were registered in those districts.[13]

The new constitution surprised even the government's staunchest supporters. The Consultative Committee had turned out a curious document that combined politics and constitutionalism, French tradition and Cameroun aspirations.

In the preamble, the document affirmed its recognition and adherence to the "fundamental liberties contained in the Universal Declaration of Human Rights and the Charter of the United Nations," and listed twenty-two "rights" and "fundamental principles" including the inviolability of the home, secrecy of the mails, prohibition of retroactive legislation and *ex post facto* laws, freedom of religion (including a statement of the separation of church and state), freedom of the press, freedom of association, right to public education and the freedom of private education, inviolability of property, the "right and the duty to work," and the obligation of the "nation to protect and encourage the family, the natural base of human society." Three other items in the preamble are also worth mentioning, as two of them are unique to the Cameroun constitution. One is a statement inviting public and private foreign development capital; the second is an expression of the pan-African ideal; and the third, apparently included to satisfy the opposition members of the Consultative Committee, is a promise to do everything possible to satisfy the aspirations of Camerounians living abroad so that they might come home to "live fraternally in a re-united Cameroun."[14]

Beyond its long preamble, the constitution bore a remarkable similarity to that of the French Fifth Republic. It created a unitary state with a national assembly elected by direct universal suffrage, but no second chamber. The resemblance is most evident, however, in the sections dealing with the presidency. As in France, the Cameroun president was designated the head of state, the "guardian of the Constitution," who in this capacity "assures the exercise of public power as well as the continuity of the state."[15] The president was to be elected indirectly by an electoral college composed of members of the National Assembly, members of "provincial" and municipal assemblies. The president was to hold office for five years, to be eligible for reëlection, to name and dismiss the prime minister, and, upon proposal by the latter, to be permitted to name and dismiss the ministers. As in France, the prime minister did not need to be invested by the National Assembly, and the government could only be brought down by the Assembly if it rejected a question of confidence posed by the government, or if it adopted a motion of censure.[16]

The Camerounian president also presided over the Council of Ministers, was the head of the armed forces, and (according to an Article nearly identical in wording to Article 16 of the French constitution) in the event of "exceptional circumstances which might endanger the integrity of the Nation [*circonstances exceptionelles pouvant porter atteinte a l'intégrité de la Nation*] the President . . . may by decree taken in the Council of Ministers, after consultation with the President of the National Assembly, proclaim a state of emergency [*état d'excep-tion*] and assume the responsibilities of Government."[17]

The National Assembly was given the power to legislate on six classes of subjects: (1) the guarantees to, and fundamental obligations of, citizens; (2) the status of persons and property; (3) the political, administrative, and judicial organization involving the functioning of the national and local assemblies, national defense, the creation or elimination of administrative jurisdictions, penal and civil procedure, the magistracy, and the civil service; (4) financial and budgetary matters; (5) social and economic programs; and (6) policies and programs of education.[18]

Finally, the constitution provided for the ratification of treaties by the Assembly; created a High Council of the Magistrature, a High Court of Justice, an Economic and Social Council with advisory powers; and defined the conditions for constitutional amendment.

Two other sections were of interest. Articles 46 to 48 designated the local units of government as provinces and communes. The larger territorial units, the provinces, were to be administered by *conseils généraux*, one in each province, which were to be composed of locally elected councilors plus the deputies to the National Assembly elected from the province. The national government was represented by a minister or a secretary of state who "assures the execution of the decisions of the *conseil général* of the province." The scheme itself would not come in for comment were it not for the fact that at independence the larger administrative divisions were the twenty-one *départements*, each of which was headed by a prefect who represented the central government. When the Cameroun Republic came to end with the creation of the new federal state, the "provinces" had not yet been created, nor had any move been made toward establishing the *conseils généraux*. The only reform of note occurred on November 4, 1960, when the Bamiléké *Département* was split into five new *départements*.

A transitional section, Article 52, called for the election of the first President of the Republic by the National Assembly. Accordingly, on May 5, 1960, M. Ahidjo was elected to the presidency by the Assembly elected April 4, 1960.

It is hardly relevant here to comment on the functioning of the institutions defined by the 1960 constitution in light of the Republic's short existence. Some critical comments can, however, be made about the document itself and the circumstances in which it was written and adopted.

First, there is some question whether the constitution was more the child of political exigency than of mature reflection. Several members of the Consultative Committee have since voiced the opinion that the government was more interested in producing almost any document and having it adopted as soon as possible than in encouraging wider discussion of its basic provisions—thus, according to these critics, accounting largely for following the French model so closely.[19]

Second, there is some question about the appropriateness of modeling the Cameroun constitution so closely on that of the Fifth Republic. The latter was written largely to accommodate the personality and political views of President de Gaulle, and was drafted in the context of the constitutional crisis that brought De Gaulle to power; the circumstances surrounding the writing of the Cameroun constitution were not in any way analogous to those existing in France in 1958. It may be further argued that even if the drafters of the Cameroun constitution had had M. Ahidjo in mind as the first president (as seems possible), neither his personality nor his political *Weltanschauung* corresponded to De Gaulle's. Indeed, if the Cameroun constitution had to be drafted to suit M. Ahidjo's personality and political views it would probably deëmphasize the role, if not the powers, of the presidency.

Early in 1960, Ahidjo characterized the governmental framework proposed in the draft constitution as a compromise between the French Third Republic and the presidential system of the United States.[20] The "compromise" turned out to be not a compromise at all, but a questionable Cameroun edition of the constitution of the Fifth Republic.

Finally, the results of the February, 1960, referendum, with its strong negative vote in the south, cast doubt on the value of the constitution as a unifying force. Although it is true that the vote might have indicated more opposition to the government of M. Ahidjo than to the basic law itself, it remains difficult to escape the conclusion that such strong opposition reflected unfavorably on the constitution proposed to the voters.

The 1960 constitution outlined a Camerounian adaptation of the Fifth French Republic; the federal constitution of 1961, however, resembled neither its predecessor nor the model it followed. The document that eventually emerged from the series of constitutional talks during the spring of 1961 defined a system combining parliamentary and presidential forms of government, a novel arrangement in which a confederal union was to develop into a federal one.[21]

First, the new constitution effected no major changes in the formal governmental structures existing in the two states prior to unification. The West Cameroun (ex-Southern Cameroons) retained its House of Assembly (renamed West Cameroun Legislative Assembly), House of Chiefs, and ministerial system, complete with prime minister and cabinet (ministers in both states are now secretaries of state). The East Cameroun (ex-Cameroun Republic) retained its own legislature unaltered save in name (from National Assembly to East Cameroun Legislative Assembly) and its ministerial system of prime minister and (now) secretaries of state. The court system in both states remained unaltered, and the courts continued to function on the pre-unification bases of the legal systems, that is, based on French principles and procedures in the eastern state, on British principles and procedures in the west. To cap the legal structure, however, the constitution created two new courts, one the Federal Court of Justice to handle appeals from the highest state courts, to adjudicate interstate or state-federal disputes, and to give advisory opinions to federal authorities in certain limited situations, and the other, a special panel court, the High Court of Justice, to try cases involving high treason, conspiracy against the state, or various crimes committed by the highest federal or state officials.

On the federal level, besides the new courts, the constitution provided for a federal president, vice-president, a set of federal ministries, and a National Federal Assembly. The federal president, in addition to the usual executive functions, powers, and prerogatives exercised by him as head of state, appoints (after "consultation") the respective prime ministers and cabinets of the states, has some vaguely defined powers to intervene in state affairs in emergency situations, may seek advisory opinions from the Federal Court of Justice on questions of the constitutionality of federal or state laws, and, in wording alomst exactly like Article 16 of the Fifth Republic's constitution, is given extraordinary powers to rule by decree in the event of national peril or crisis. "In all, the Constitution creates a hybrid President who combines the attributes of a British-style Governor-General, a Fifth Republic President, and an American chief executive."[22]

The confederal nature of the new union is clearly manifest in several ways. First and foremost is the rather extraordinary veto power given the states in the National Federal Assembly. Upon the request of the President of the Federal Republic, or of either state's prime minister, any legislation must be subject to a "second reading" and cannot be adopted unless a majority of the federal deputies of each state approve it. Usually, a simple majority of all deputies is sufficient for passage. It is, in effect, the system of the "concurrent majority." Further, the constitution provides two lists of federal jurisdictions, one in which federal organs may operate "immediately" (including defense, currency, foreign affairs, and the like), and the other, including areas now under state control (primary and secondary education, "the regime of public liberties," land law, labor regulation, for example) which will become subject to federal control after an undefined "transition period." The conclusion is difficult to avoid that the total effect of these provisions is to permit the emergence of a federal state with full powers, and at a rate that both states can regulate.

Still other provisions of the 1961 constitution tend to confirm the suspicion that what the document created was a set of mechanisms for the future creation of a federal state, rather than a federal state itself. The provisions in question, embodied in a list of "Transitional and Special Dispositions," are obviously a series of political compromises between Foncha and Ahidjo designed to maintain the political *status quo ante* in each state. (The extent to which they reflected possible mutual distrust or suspicion of the new union are tantalizing questions, but difficult to answer. A partial answer may perhaps lie in the fact that as the date for union approached, the enthusiasm of the two leaders for unification seemed to wane.) The "Dispositions" stipulate, among other things, (1) that the then-president of the Cameroun Republic (Ahidjo) would be the federal president until his term in the former office expired in May, 1965; (2) that during the term of office of the first federal president, the prime minister of the West Cameroun (Foncha) would be federal vice-president; and (3), that the respective legislatures of the Southern Cameroons and the Cameroun Republic would become, *mutatis mutandis*, the legislatures of the two states. The implication is clear that new elections would not be required in either event. Further, until April 1, 1964, the National Federal Assembly is to be composed of deputies chosen from each state legislature in the ratio of one deputy to each eighty thousand inhabitants. Accordingly, the new federal legislature is composed of ten deputies from the West Cameroon Legislative Assembly, and forty from the East Cameroun Legislative Assembly. Still further, the respective governments of the Southern Cameroons and the Cameroun Republic became the governments of the two federal states; again, by implication, without a change in personnel.

It can be argued that the 1961 constitution provides precisely that kind of room for maneuvering within which the two Cameroun states can develop the relationship best suited to the new union as it evolves, although the constitution also reflects, of course, the lack of clear thinking and concrete planning about the union that was prevalent before unification. The present Federal Republic is still clearly an experiment; the directions it will take are matters for conjecture. It may, if current trends toward political centralization persist, eventually become a unitary state. If it does, then the worst fears of many West Camerounian leaders (including members of the governing party) will

have been realized. Or, it may develop forms of accommodation between the unitary tendencies of the Eastern Cameroun and the separatist interests of the West Cameroun that will produce a viable federal state in fact as well as name. It may be trite to say, but the next
several years will indeed tell.

THE CAMEROUN, INDEPENDENCE, AND FRANCE

However devoutly many Cameroun nationalists
may have wished it, independence did not also end the "French presence" in the new republic. Considering the extent to which the Cameroun depended on French aid of all kinds, it would have been incon-
ceivable that this aid should be stopped on January 1, 1960. Continued
French aid to the Cameroun has provided ammunition to those who
claim that the Cameroun is not "truly independent," or that Ahidjo
remains the "tool of French imperialism." The extent to which France
influenced the Cameroun Republic and continues to influence the
Cameroun Federal Republic is a matter for debate, but it is a debate
that is largely academic in view of the hard facts of life which demonstrate conclusively that without French support the new state could not
survive.

Between 1946 and 1960 the total French aid to the Cameroun from
all sources totaled 173,258,813,000 old French francs (480 fr. = $1.00)
or $358,872,526. During the same period budgetary funds from Came-
roun sources totaled $175,673,372,000 old French francs, or
$360,986,190. French aid for 1960 totaled the equivalent of about
$50,000,000, and a like amount was extended for 1961 and 1962. These
sums represent over 80 per cent of the total revenues collected by the
government of the East Cameroun.[23] The figures cited for French
financial aid do not include private investment or loans, nor do they
take into account the change in the real value of the franc during the
sixteen-year period. In the form of loans, subventions, grants, advances,
and credit, public aid has come from five main sources: (1) the French
budget; (2) the French treasury; (3) the *Fonds d'Investissements et de
Développement Economique et Social* (FIDES); (4) the *Caisse Centrale
de la France d'outre-Mer;* and (5), special French economic organisms
such as the *Bureau des Recherches Petrolières.* The areas in which
French aid has played a key role are among the most important to the
Cameroun economy: (1) operating and capital expenses of national and
local administrative units; (2) balancing the Cameroun budget; (3)
support to the local treasury; (4) scientific and technical studies and
research; (5) economic development, particularly infrastructure; (6)

social services, such as health, education, urbanism, electrification, and rural housing; and (7), public aid to private enterprise.[24]

Another aspect of French aid (or, to the cynical, French influence) has been the presence of French administrators and technical experts in Camerounian ministries and government agencies. By January 1, 1960, their number had dwindled to about 70 (from a 1955 high of 160). As of November, 1961, France placed 576 civil servants at the disposition of the Cameroun. These included 50 in general administration, 26 in justice, 80 in health, 144 in technical services, 35 in telecommunications, and 241 in education.[25] Although the Cameroun government is committed to the gradual replacement of French civil servants by Camerounians, the French "technical counselors" (as they were called after independence) apparently continue to be necessary to the functioning of the government.

The most obvious evidence of the French presence is the French military personnel. French military assistance is given under the technical assistance programs, and involves considerable numbers of officers and men, plus equipment and logistic support for both French and Camerounian units. Under the terms of the provisional Franco-Camerounian accords made on January 1, 1960, France agreed to extend credit to the Cameroun amounting to 1,000,000 new francs ($4,900,000), so that by the end of the year the Cameroun could equip eight infantry companies, one mobile squadron of four platoons equipped with armored cars and jeep-mounted machine guns, and several service and administrative units. France further agreed to train Camerounian officers and noncoms, as well as to provide officers and noncoms for existing units until Camerounian replacements. The French military mission in the Cameroun, nine months after independence, still consisted of about 2,000 officers and men, of which 67 officers and men were in the training mission per se; 13 officers, 325 noncoms, and 15 non-Camerounian auxiliaries served with the Cameroun gendarmerie; and the remainder belonged to French troops stationed in the Cameroun at the request of the Cameroun government.[26]

Other forms of French assistance are less visible but just as crucial. For example, France guarantees stable prices for Camerounian cocoa, palm oil, cotton, and peanuts by supporting official Cameroun stabilization funds and by granting these products preferential treatment on the French market.

When the Cameroun became independent it rejected all suggestion that it join the *Communauté*. Ahidjo and Assalé, among others, contended that to join would only subject the Cameroun to a new form of French domination. From the point of view of political tactics, their decision was a wise one; they were assured of virtually the same sort of French aid as if the country had in fact joined the *Communauté*. The Cameroun remained in the franc zone, it continued to benefit from France's membership in the European Common Market, and France continued its financial and economic aid under the terms of the provisional accords which came into effect on January 1, 1960. On December 16, 1960, the Cameroun National Assembly authorized ratification of the Franco-Camerounian accords for economic and technical coöperation which had been signed earlier that month. The new accords were framed in somewhat different language in that they emphasized coöperation rather than aid, but the implications were clear: the Cameroun would continue to be dependent on France for some time to come. Nothing has happened during the first three years of the Cameroun's independent existence to change that pattern.

Appendixes

Appendixes

APPENDIX

A Repertory of East Cameroun Political Parties and Associations

NOTE: Official sources claimed that by 1959 there were over a hundred and fifty political groups registered or active in the Cameroun. The following list, compiled from both official and unofficial sources, is incomplete. It does, however, include all the important groups and most of the ephemeral and ethnic-based formations. Two reservations in particular must be made concerning the material presented below: (1) Political groups in the Cameroun have been somewhat unstable, in that groups were continually dissolving, forming, and reforming. The list below is, insofar as information was available, accurate up to July, 1962. (2) The definition of "political group" used as a criterion for inclusion in the list is somewhat loose but is based on the premise that a group so listed by official sources must be considered political, while yet recognizing that little distinction existed in the Cameroun between political parties and groups functioning as pressure groups, traditional formations, solidarity organizations, or social clubs. Consequently, a rather broad definition of the term "political group" has been adopted.

A. EARLY GROUPS

Name	Abbreviation	Notes
1. Comité de coordination des affaires camerounaises	Cococam	Founded *ca.* 1947, revised 1954; ephemeral; Yaoundé-based.
2. Coordination des indépendants camerounais	Indecam	Organized Nov. 8, 1952, government backed; ephemeral; vanished by 1959.
3. Evolution sociale camerounaise	Esocam	1948 to 1957; organized by administration with strong Ngondo help; later strongly anti-UPC.
4. Front intercolonial		Cameroun branch organized July 24, 1952, to represent French citizens; ephemeral.
5. Groupe des paysans indépendants		*Ca.* 1957-1958, parliamentary group composed mainly of Bamiléké deputies.

235

6. *Front national*   *FNC*   July-Sept., 1955; abortive at-
   camerounais   tempt by Soppo Priso to
                                        unite all parties.

7. *Jeunesse*   *Jeucafra*   Successor to Union Came-
   camerounaise   rounaise in 1938; early po-
   française   litical group for French
                                        and Camerounian citizens;
       had strong antifascist pro-
       gram during World War II;
       became *Unicafra* in 1945;
       leaders: Louis Aujoulat,
       Paul Soppo Priso, A. Fouda.

8. *Médiation*   *Mediacam*   *Ca.* 1951; ephemeral.
   franco-
   camerounaise

9. *Mouvement*   *MDC*   *Ca.* 1945; lasted one year;
   démocratique   ephemeral.
   camerounais

10. *Mouvement*   *MRP*   *Ca.* 1946; Cameroun branch
    républicaine   of the French party.
    populaire

11. *Rassemblement* *RDA*   Local branch of AOF-based
    démocratique   party; became UPC 1950.
    africain

12. *Rassemblement*   April 6-May 6, 1947; formed
    camerounais   of amalgam of *Unicafra* and
        RDA groups; seminal group
        for UPC.

13. *Rassemblement* *Rapeca*   Organized 1946, lasted a few
    du peuple   months; name revived Jan.
    camerounais   20, 1959, by A. Fouda,
        Yaoundé.

14. *Rassemblement* *RPF*   Cameroun branch of the
    du peuple   French Gaullist party; or-
    français   ganized in Douala, 1947,
        virtually extinct by 1954.

15. *Renaissance*   *Renaicam* Organized *ca.* Dec., 1948;
    camerounaise   with administration help;
        ephemeral.

16. *Solidarité*   Organized Sept., 1957; ephem-
    camerounaise   eral.

17. *Union*   *Unicafra*   *Ca.* 1945-Feb., 1947; founded

camerounaise française		by A. Fouda, dissolved to become *Rassemblement camerounaise.*
18. *Unité camerounaise*	*Unicam*	Organized April, 1954; ephemeral.

B. NATIONAL AND REGIONAL PARTIES AND ASSOCIATIONS

Name	*Abbreviation*	*Notes*
19. *Action paysanne*		Organized Sept. 4, 1957, to advance Dja-et-Lobo, Boulou, and Fang agricultural interests.
20. *Bloc démocratique camerounais*	*BDC*	Organized 1951 by Louis Aujoulat; had most strength among Catholics in center areas; virtually extinct by 1955.
21. *Mouvement d'action nationale*	*MANC*	Organized 1956 from merger of *Union Tribale Bantoue* and *Ngondo;* a *mariage de convenance* of Assalé, Soppo Priso; 1958-1960 in government coalition; merged with UC, 1960.
22. *Mouvement* (later *Parti*) *de l'union camerounaise*	*(M) PUC* or *UC*	Organized April, 1958, by Ahidjo, Njoya Arouna by merging local groups from Maroua, Garoua, and Ngaoundéré; government party from 1958 to present.
23. *Parti des démocrates camerounais*	*PDC*	Organized 1958 by group of deputies led by A. M. Mbida.
24. *Parti socialiste camerounaise*	*PSC*	Organized Nov., 1959, by C. Okala from USC/MSC.
Lineal precursors of PSC:		
25. (a) *Parti socialiste française*	*SFIO*	From 1947-1952, local branch of French party; became USC in 1952.

26. (b) *Union sociale camerounaise*	USC	1952-1957; became MSC in 1957. Affiliated with MSA.
27. (c) *Mouvement sociale camerounaise*	MSC	1957-1959; became PSC in 1959.
28. *Parti travailliste camerounais*	PTC	Organized Feb., 1962, by Dr. Beybey-Eyidi; became moribund with arrest and imprisonment of Dr. Beybey in July, 1962.
29. *Union des populations du Cameroun*	UPC	Organized April 10, 1948, by Um Nyobé, Kingué, Ouandié, Moumié from old RDA rump in Cameroun; banned July, 1955-Feb., 1960.

UPC affiliates and
   cover groups:

30. (a) *Comité national d'organisation*	CNO	Organized Dec., 1956; para-military branch of UPC.
31. (b) *Union démocratique des femmes camerounaises*	UDFC	Banned with UPC; led by Mmes. Moumié, Kingué.
32. (c) *Jeunesse démocratique du Cameroun*	JDC	Banned with UPC; led by T. Mayi-Matip.
33. (d) *Les amis du progrès*		*Ca.* 1948-1949; ephemeral.
34. (e) *Les amis des Nations-Unies*		*Ca.* 1952; ephemeral.
35. (f) *Les amis des patriotisme*		*Ca.* 1952; ephemeral.
36. (g) *Association voix du peuple Bafia*		*Ca.* 1948-1949.
37. (h) *Comité de défense des droits des refugiés, etc.*		*Ca.* 1951-1958; led by I. Tchoumbe Ngouancheu; ephemeral.

38. (i) *Comité du dé-fense de la paix*		*Ca.* 1952; ephemeral.
39. (j) *Jeunesse des populations du Kamerun*	*Jupokam*	*Ca.* 1952-1957.
40. (k) *Solidarité Babimbi*	*Solibabi*	*Ca.* 1948-1949; secessionist group of *Assoc. Amicale de la Sanaga-Maritime;* Um Nyobé claimed *Solibabi* had 60,000 members in 1952.
41. (l) *Union nation-ale des mères camerounaises*		*Ca.* 1949-1957; ephemeral.
42. (m) *Parti popu-laire Kamerunais*	*PPK*	Organized May, 1957; front for UPC during its period of proscription.
43. (n) *Bureau na-tional Kamerun-ais de la confér-ence des peuples africains*		UPC front; banned in 1959.
44. *Comité pour le regroupement des forces na-tionalistes*		Organized Oct., 1958, by Dr. Beybey-Eyidi at Douala; was pro-UPC; ephemeral.

C. ETHNIC, ETHNIC-BASED, PSEUDO-ETHNIC, AND LOCAL ORGANIZATIONS

NOTE: Most of the organizations grouped below—with the exception of the ethnic formations—were created to voice the political demands of various tribal elements. A number were formed as organizational handmaidens to local politicians (see text, Chapter VI).

1. ETHNIC ORGANIZATIONS

(Groups with a traditional origin, later transformed into groups having primarily a political purpose.)

Name	*Abbreviation*	*Notes*
45. *Association tra-ditionelle Anag-sama-Essolo*		Originally Eton tribal society; mobilized *ca.* 1956 to sup-port A. M. Mbida.
46. *Association tra-*		Originally a secret society;

ditionelle ban-
toue Efoula-
Meyong

47. *Assemblée tradi-*   Ngondo
    tionelle du peu-
    ple Douala, dite
    Ngondo

48. *Association tra-*   Kolo-Beti
    ditionelle Kolo-
    Beti

49. *Majong Bami-*
    léké

politicized *ca.* 1950 to aid
Charles Assale; Ebolowa
area.

De facto existence since beginning of this century; re-
constituted as political organization in 1949.

Originally Beti tribal society;
also among Ewondo; be-
came pro-UPC *ca.* 1955.

Originally adult male Bamiléké society; became politicized after 1953. (See
Kumsze.)

2. ETHNIC-BASED ORGANIZATIONS

(Groups drawing membership or support mainly from one ethnic element.)

Name	*Abbreviation*	*Notes*
50. *Association ami-* *cale "Voix du* *Beti"*	Assobeti	Organized Feb., 1948, at Mvolye-Yaoundé.
51. *Association des* *Maka dite re-* *dressement Be-* *bende*		Ephemeral.
52. *Association Mu-* *sulmane de la* *Region Bamoun*		
53. *Association des* *Notables et sous-* *chefs de la sub-* *division de Ba-* *foussam*		Bamiléké.
54. *Association* *union Bangwa*		Bamiléké, near Dschang.
55. *Conseil coutu-* *mier de Lolodorf*		Ewondo.
56. *Groupement* *anti-upéciste des* *Boulous de Dja-*		Organized *ca.* 1955 at Sang- melima.

    et-Lobo

57. *Entente des res-*
    sortissants de Ba-
    foussam à Mbal-
    mayo

58. *Jeunesse de la*   Bassa.
    Sanaga-Maritime

59. *Ligue progres-*   ***Pronord***   Organized April, 1955; Mos-
    siste des intérêts   lem Fulani; pro-UC.
    économiques et
    sociaux des
    populations du
    nord-Cameroun

60. *Union Bamiléké*   Feb., 1948, to 1952, at Ba-
                                     foussam; organized to coun-
                                     ter pro-UPC leanings of
                                     Kumsze; when *Kumsze* re-
                                     nounced UPC, Union Bami-
                                     léké vanished.

61. *Union Bamoun*   Organized Jan., 1950, at
                                     Foumbam.

62. *Union défense*
    des intérêts auto-
    chtones Manchas

63. *Union du Dia-*   Local association of *Musgum*
    maré   and neighboring groups in
                                     north Cameroun.

64. *Union des popu-*   Organized Dec., 1953, Kubi.
    lations Batanga

65. *Union (or Co-*   Organized Feb., 1960.
    mité) du salut
    public du peuple
    Bassa

66. *Union tribale*   Successor to *Union Tribale*
    Bantoue   *Ntem-Kribi;* organized 1956;
                                     President: Assalé.

67. *Union tribale*   Organized 1948, dissolved
    Ntem-Kribi   1950; at Ebolowa; founder
                                     was David Mvondo; in early
                                     days heavily infiltrated by
                                     UPC; existed as local or-
                                     ganization before 1940.

68. *Sengia Kul Meka*   Maka society claiming to be
                           "studying the Maka past";
                           ephemeral.

3. PSEUDO-ETHNIC ORGANIZATIONS

(Groups claiming traditional legitimacy but in fact little more than ethnic-based formations.)

Name	Abbreviation	Notes
69. *Association amicale des chefs traditionels du Cameroun*		Organized by Yaoundé chief Martin Abega to join anti-UPC chiefs; split from *Unatracam* in 1956.
70. *Association Bamiléké du Cameroun*		1956-1959.
71. *Association des notables du Cameroun*		1956-1959.
72. *Association des notables Bamiléké*	*Assobake*	Organized Nov., 1952, at Bafang by pro-administration chiefs; became UPC-dominated in 1958.
73. *Association traditionelle des peuples Eton-Manguissa-Batsenga*		Organized *ca.* 1956 by chiefs friendly to the PDC and A. M. Mbida.
74. *Kumsze, Association traditionelle Bamiléké*	*Kumsze*	Organized May, 1948, by M. Djoumessi, taking name of older traditional groups; originally pro-UPC, renounced UPC in 1950.
75. *Union des associations traditionelles du Cameroun*	*Unatracam*	Organized 1950 by Douala chief Betote Akwa.

4. LOCAL ORGANIZATIONS

(Local solidarity formations, many with ethnic overtones.)

Name	*Abbreviation*	*Notes*
76. *Alliance démocratique des peuples camerounaises*		Garoua; ephemeral.
77. *Association amicale de la Benoué*		Organized April, 1953, at Garoua.
78. *Association des habitants du Dja-et-Lobo*		Centered at Sangmelima.
79. *Association Amicale de Sanaga-Maritime*	*AASM*	Edea area, for Bassa.
80. *Comité de défense des interêts camerounais*		Yaoundé; ephemeral.
81. *Comité d'études et de coordination de Bafoussam*		Ephemeral.
82. *Confédération des paysans et planteurs du Ntem*		Centered at Ebolowa, represents Ntem cocoa growers.
83. *Paysans camerounais*		Organized Dec., 1958, among Bamiléké farmers by M. Njiné, D. Kemajou; dissolved 1959, incorporated into UC in 1960.
84. *Union de l'Ouest Cameroun*		Allied to *Paysans Camerounais;* formed at same time, dissolved together with *Paysans Cam.;* not as important as *Paysans.*

D. PROFESSIONAL AND SPECIAL-INTEREST ORGANIZATIONS

Name	*Abbreviation*	*Notes*
85. *Association défense des chômeurs*		Organized in Douala; claims to represent the city's 30,000 unemployed.

86. *Association des anciens élèves des colleges et lycées*

87. *Association des membres de l'enseignment au Cameroun* — Teachers' organization.

88. *Association des parents d'élèves du lycée et d'Ecole Urbaine* — Yaoundé; organized as a parents' organization for better education.

89. *Confédération des associations agricoles industrielles de l'Afrique française* — Douala.

90. *Evolution des femmes camerounaises* — **Evacam** — Organized March, 1955, by Joseph Owono; local feminist group.

91. *Groupement professionel des agents d'assurances* — Insurance agents' group.

92. *Groupement de défense des interêts des commercants du Ntem* — Ebolowa merchants' league.

93. *Union internationales des étudiants kamerunais* — **UNEK** — Cameroun students' organization; headquarters in Paris; branches in provincial universities, London, Ibadan; affiliated with *Union des étudiants noirs en France, Union internationale des étudiants.*

E. MISCELLANEOUS MARGINAL GROUPS

Name	Abbreviation	Notes
94. *Alliance démocratique du peuple camerounais*		
95. *Cercle camerounais culturel*		At first, a students' group in Paris, later (1961) also in Yaoundé with wider membership.
96. *Comité des amis de la vérité*		Organized April, 1959, by A. Fouda, Yaoundé.
97. *Communauté française*		
98. *Front national camerounais*		
99. *Médiation franco-camerounaise*		
100. *Mouvement démocratique populaire*		Organized Nov., 1959, by P. Penda.
101. *Oeuvre éducation populaire du Cameroun*		
102. *Solidarité camerounaise*		
103. *Union d'action franco-camerounaise*		
104. *Union démocratique camerounaise*		
105. *Union française au Cameroun*		
106. *Unité camerounaise*		

F. GROUPS IN THE CAMEROUN LEGISLATURE

(The rules of the 1956 and 1960 Cameroun Assemblies required that parliamentary groups have at least seven members to be eligible for membership in the functional committees. However, independents may form a group, as may deputies from two or three smaller groups or parties, although such ad hoc groups have no existence outside the Assembly. The main parties, of course, form their own groups if they have more than the requisite seven deputies.)

1. THE ASSEMBLY ELECTED DECEMBER, 1956

Name	Abbreviation	Notes
107. *Groupe d'union camerounaise*		Grew from deputies elected on UC lists; later (1958) became nucleus of UC party.
108. *Groupe des démocrates camerounais*		Established following June, 1951, election; grew from deputies elected on DC lists; later (1958) became nucleus of DC party.
109. *Groupe des paysans indépendants*		Deputies elected on *Paysans Indépendants, Paysans camerounais, Union de l'ouest* Cameroun lists.
110. *Groupe d'action nationale*		Represented MANC deputies.
111. *(Groupe) intergroupe des non-inscrits*		Ex-UPC deputies elected in by-election of April 12, 1959

2. THE ASSEMBLY ELECTED APRIL 4, 1960

Name	Abbreviation	Notes
112. *Groupe d'union camerounaise*		Deputies of UC party.
113. *Front populaire pour l'unité et la paix*		Bamiléké deputies elected on various lists; most were ex-UPC. Merged with UC in 1961.
114. *Groupe des démocrates camerounais*		Deputies of PDC.
115. *Groupe des progressistes du Cameroun*		Deputies from MANC and PSC; dissolved in 1961.

116. *Group d'union*   Deputies of UPC.
     des populations
     du Cameroun

117. *Group du Front*   Merger in 1962 of PDC, UPC,
     National Uni   PSC, and *Parti Travailliste*
                            Camerounais.

B *Domestic Legislative Elections in East Cameroun—1946-1960*[1]

(For key to abbreviations, see end of notes to this appendix.)

A. 1946-1952 (GENERAL ELECTIONS)

	Date of election		
	March 10, 1946 (with runoff)	December 22, 1946 (with runoff)	March 30, 1952
Name of assembly...	*ARCAM*	*ARCAM*	*ATCAM*
Seats contested......	{12 elective 22 appointive	34 elective 6 appointive	all elective
Seats: College I (Fr. citizens)...........	6	16	18
College II (Africans)...........	6	18 (plus 6 appointive)	32
Electoral rolls: Registered: College I......... College II........	2,500 38,000	2,611 38,976	7,788 520,605
Voted and %[2] College I......... College II........	no info. no info.	1,201 (50%) 20,490 (52%)	4,300 (60%) 330,000 (60%)
No. of candidates....	35	*ca.* 40	{Coll. I: 65 Coll. II: 238
No. of lists.........	no info.	no info.	20

Parties participating in election[3].	no info.	RPF MRP SFIO RDA MSC	RPF UPC SFIO DDC *Esocam*
Groups in assembly[4].	nonpartisan	nonpartisan	nonpartisan

B. 1956-1960 (GENERAL ELECTIONS)

	Date of election	
	December 23, 1956	April 4, 1960
Name of assembly. .	*ATCAM* (became *ALCAM* in 1957)	*ANCAM*
Seats contested (dual college abolished 1956).	70	100
Electoral rolls: Registered. . . . . . . Voted and %[2]. . . .	 1,752,902 725,000 (42%)	 1,940,438 1,349,739 (69.5%)
No. of candidates. . .	323	365
No. of lists.	86	81
Parties contesting, votes garnered, per cent of votes cast[4].	UC. . . . .249,693 (34%) GDC. . .152,000 (21%) *Paysans* *Ind*. . . 69,457 (9%) MANC. 48,666 (6.5%) SFIO. . . 18,001 (2.5%) Others. .189,000 (26%)	UC. . . . . .606,000 (45%) PDC. . . . .139,780 (10%) GPC. . . . . 60,686 (4.5%) UPC. . . . .151,379 (11%) FPUP. . .145,752 (10.5%) Indep. . . . 11,853 (0.7%) Others. . .233,789 (18.3%)
Groups in assembly, number of seats, geographic referent[5].	UC. . . . .30 (north) GDC. . .20 (So.-central) *Paysans*. 9 (west) MANC. 8 (s'west) Indep. . . 3	UC. . . . . .51 (north, east) PDC. . . . .11 (central) GPC. . . . .10 (sw, central) UPC. . . . . 8 (sw, west) FPUP. . .18 (west) Indep. . . . 2 (s'west)

C. BY-ELECTIONS

1. 1946-1952

a. April 4, 1948, one seat of College I in Ntem; no other information available.

b. September 19, 1948, one seat of College I in Adamawa, one seat of College II in N. Cameroun; no other information available.

c. June 11, 1950, one seat of College I in Ntem; no other information available.

2. APRIL 12, 1959

Six seats from two western districts were contested by forty candidates on thirteen lists; all six seats were won by candidates who later grouped into the *Intergroupe des Noninscrits* in *ALCAM*. The *Intergroupe* candidates polled 41,612 votes to their opponents' 41,087.

NOTES TO APPENDIX B

[1] The elections described herein are only those involving Cameroun legislatures. In addition to these, the territory, prior to 1957, elected representatives to various legislative bodies in France. Before 1956, three deputies (two from the second college, one from the first) were elected to the French National Assembly. Every five years the Cameroun sent three senators to the Council of the Republic (two from the second college, one from the first), five representatives to the Assembly of the French Union (four from the second college, one from the first), and two councilors to the French Economic Council. Deputies to the French National Assembly were elected at large, but representatives to the other metropolitan organs were chosen by the Cameroun legislature.

[2] The voting figures are given with the greatest reservations. In the instances of the 1952, 1956, and 1960 general elections, the figures given are my own computations from available information, official documentation being either unobtainable or unusable.

[3] Until 1956 parties seldom campaigned under their own names, but instead under the guise of list titles. Those interested knew which list represented what party. After 1956 parties began campaigning under their own banners, but quite often presented themselves to the electorate as lists with different names. To confuse matters further, candidates of the various parties often campaigned under their own names, eschewing both party or list titles. In the light of these facts, the information in this rubric is given with the following reservations:

a. The lists of parties for the 1946 and 1952 elections are extrapolations from the known affiliations of candidates. The lists for 1956 and 1960 were derived from similar extrapolations, as well as from "translations" of list titles and actual party lists.

b. The figures and percentages represent my own computations derived from the available statistics, official materials being either unobtainable or unusable.

⁴ The Cameroun legislature prior to 1956 had legislative powers per se over only a restricted number of subjects. For the most part, these legislatures could exercise only a "deliberative" (i.e., advisory) vote on matters put before them. In any event, matters of political importance were reserved to the High Commission; hence the Cameroun legislatures were "nonpolitical," and the rules forbade the formation of political groups in the body of the legislature. Being nonpolitical, presumably, the legislatures could have no interest in advancing partisan causes. As a matter of fact, political matters were quite often discussed by the legislature despite French protest.

⁵ The general area in the Cameroun from which the parties derive is given.

KEY TO ABBREVIATIONS

ARCAM   *Assemblée Représentative du Cameroun*
ATCAM   *Assemblée Territoriale du Cameroun*
ALCAM   *Assemblée Législative du Cameroun*
ANCAM   *Assemblée National du Cameroun*

For full names of parties and groups, see Appendix A.

APPENDIX

C *The* Indigénat

ARRÊTÉ determining the special infractions of the indigénat according to the application of the *décret* of 8 August 1924.

The Commissioner of the Republic of France in the Cameroun

Officer of the Legion of Honor

Noting the decree of 23 March 1921, determining the powers of the Commissioner of the Republic of France in the Cameroun;

Noting the decree of 8 August 1924, determining the exercise of the disciplinary powers in the Cameroun;

DECREES:

Article One. The special infractions restrained by disciplinary methods are the following:

1. Acts of disorder;
2. The organizing of games of chance;
2. Circulating rumors of a nature to disturb the public peace. Seditious utterances, acts showing disrespect to a duly authorized officer;
4. Giving aid to malefactors, agitators, vagabonds, natives who have fled their villages, and to all persons wanted by the Administration. Complicity in evasion of the law;
5. Refusal to render assistance in case of disaster or accident, of panic or in arrest of a criminal or delinquent;
6. Illegal wearing of official insignia, civil or military;
7. Hindering traffic on public roads, highways, paths, or waterways. Poor condition of sectors of roads whose maintenance has been charged to the villages;
8. Recruiting, on the public roads, of convoys of porters or individual porters coming to sell goods to fixed establishments in classed or unclassed urban centers;
9. Destroying or permitting the deterioration of property belonging to the Administration;
10. Vagabondage;
11. Leaving an administrative *circonscription* without authorization;
12. Leaving work without reason; applicable to porters, boatmen, convoyers, guides, workers or employees of public shops or projects. Permitting the deterioration or destroying loads or material entrusted them;
13. The practice of sorcery whose consequences do not entail appearance before a court;

14. Renewing complaints or claims to the Administration knowing them to be untrue after their settlement through regular channels, except in cases of appeal to higher authority;
15. Reluctance in paying rates, contributions, and taxes of all sorts, and to avoid *prestations*. Hindering the gathering of duties, the official census, or of any tax levy. Falsifying tax levies or any connivance therein;
16. Failure to provide articles requisitioned for essential public works;
17. Brutality by native agents toward workers who have fled public work projects;
18. Attempting to simulate or aggravate natural ills or wounds (so as to circumvent authority) in order to be dismissed from a public work project;
19. Failure to appear at official meetings [when called], without proper reasons;
20. [The possession] of contraband duly proven to have been brought in without payment of duties;
21. The knowing adulteration of products. The sale of all falsified goods;
22. The slaughter of all animals designed for human consumption without having obtained the necessary permission;
23. The slaughter and exportation, without authorization, of all large or small female cattle capable of reproduction;
24. Allowing dangerous animals or animal nuisances to stray. Allowing domestic animals to stray onto another's property;
25. Refusal to accept at their official value, all French coin or bills circulating in the territory;
26. The cutting down without authorization of fruit trees or all species of hard wood. Destruction of planted trees;
27. Refusal to work a food plantation; poor maintenance, without proper excuse, of such plantations;
28. Growing, selling, and using hemp as well as any or all other toxic materials;
29. Possessing distilled beverages or alcoholic beverages containing more than fourteen percent alcohol;
30. The making or selling of fermented beverages;
31. Permitting the straying of persons suffering from mental disorders, contagious or epidemic diseases, sleeping sickness or leprosy. Abandoning persons suffering from a contagious disease;
32. Failing to declare contagious diseases afflicting either humans or domestic animals. Failing to execute the hygienic or prophylactic measures prescribed by the Administration;
33. Burial outside consecrated burial grounds or under conditions other than those prescribed by the local authorities;
34. The practice of medicine or the use of medicines outside the control of the Administration.

Yaoundé, 4 October 1924.

MARCHAND

NOTE: The subject matter covered in this *arrêté* is interesting, particularly when considered according to topics. Seven of the sections (7, 8, 12,

16, 17, 18, 27) deal directly or indirectly with government work projects, especially the roads and the system of *prestations* connected with them. Items 22, 23, 24 are witness to the shortage of meat-animals in the south and the measures necessary to preserve their supply. Food or nutriment and matters relating to food are covered by 21, 22, 23, 26, 27, 29, and 30, a total of seven sections. It is not too far fetched to suggest that the list represents a fairly comprehensive compilation of the minor irritants the French had to face during the early days of their regime. These are infractions, it will be recalled, that did not fall under the judicial administration of the official French or native courts, nor, for that matter, of the customary courts, in areas where they still functioned.

SOURCE: Buell, *op. cit.*, pp. 384-386. (*Full citation will be found in the bibliography.* The translation is mine.)

Notes

Notes

PREFACE

[1] The most recent such study is a stimulating discussion to which K. W. Deutsch, J. R. Strayer, C. J. Friederich, H. Weilemann, R. L. Merritt, R. E. Scott, D. A. Wilson, R. Emerson, and W. Foltz contributed, incorporated in K. W. Deutsch and W. Foltz, eds., *Nation-Building* (New York: Atherton Press, 1963). Among the studies of individual African states that explicitly or implicitly develop the "nation-building" theme are James S. Coleman, *Nigeria: Background to Nationalism* (Berkeley: University of California Press, 1960); David Apter, *Ghana in Transition* (New York: Atheneum Press, 1963), a slightly revised edition of *The Gold Coast in Transition;* Raymond F. Kent, *From Madagascar to the Malagasy Republic* (New York: Frederick Praeger, 1961); and Immanuel Wallerstein, *The Road to Independence: Ghana and the Ivory Coast* (London: Cambridge University Press, 1963).

[2] Rupert Emerson, in Deutsch and Foltz, *op. cit.*, pp. 104, 105, asserts that African "nations" have been denied the opportunity to "age in the wood," one of the "prime" conditions for the building of nations.

[3] *Ibid.*, p. 105. See also two articles in the same issue of the *Cahiers d'Etudes Africaines:* A. Zolberg's study of the tribal element in the *Parti Démocratique de la Côte d'Ivoire*, "Effets de la structure d'un parti politique sur l'intégration nationale," *Cahiers d'Etudes Africaines*, no. 3 (1960), pp. 140-149; and I. Wallerstein, "Ethnicity and National Integration in West Africa," *ibid.*, pp. 129-139.

[4] Thomas Hodgkin, in an excellent essay, "A Note on the Language of African Nationalism," *St. Anthony's Papers, Number 10, African Affairs Number One* (Carbondale, Illinois: Southern Illinois University Press, 1961), argues that the ideological content of African nationalism has some highly original elements often concealed in the language in which that ideology is couched. His examples also suggest that whatever the adaptations, the ideological models of the West do serve as points of departure, if not of arrival. The point need not be belabored that the "modernization" so avidly sought throughout the continent is the modern technology of the West.

CHAPER I: *Geographic and Ethnic Context*

[1] The fullest geographical treatment of the Cameroun is found in Eugene Guernier and René Briat, eds., *Cameroun-Togo* (Paris: Editions de l'Union Française, 1951), pp. 1-28. See also summaries in the following: *Atlas du Cameroun.* Haut Commissaire de la République Française au Cameroun

(Paris: 1949 (?)); *Rapport Annuel du Gouvernement Français à l'Assemblée Générale des Nations Unies sur l'administration du Cameroun placé sous la tutelle de la France; Année 1957,* Ministère des Affaires Etrangères (Paris: 1957); Walter Fitzgerald, *Africa* (8th ed.; New York: E. P. Dutton and Co., 1955), pp. 312-319; and J. C. Froelich, *Cameroun-Togo* (Paris: Editions Berger-Levrault, 1956), pp. 1-19. See also a dated, but still interesting article by John W. Vandercook, "The French Mandate of Cameroun," *National Geographic Magazine,* Vol. LIX, no. 2 (Feb., 1931), pp. 225-260. Recent geographic summaries of the trust territory under British administration are to be found in the Colonial Office's annual report, *The Cameroons under United Kingdom Administration, Report for the Year . . . ,* especially the years 1950 and 1955; *Victoria Southern Cameroons, 1858-1958,* Victoria Centenary Committee (Victoria: Basel Mission Book Depot, 1958), pp. 1-15; Anthony H. M. Kirk-Greene, *Adamawa, Past and Present* (New York: Oxford University Press, 1958), pp. 1-14. When completed, the series of maps and commentary sheets being prepared by the Institut des Recherches Scientifiques Camerounaises (Yaoundé) should supersede all other maps and geographic descriptions hitherto published. As of 1961, their *Atlas du Cameroun* included eight plates, with descriptions.

[2] Melville Herskovits, "People and Cultures of Subsaharan Africa," *The Annals,* vol. 298 (March, 1955), pp. 11-20; *The Human Factor in Changing Africa* (New York: Alfred A. Knopf, 1962), pp. 51-112, *passim.*

[3] Joseph H. Greenberg, *Studies in African Linguistic Classification* (New Haven: 1955), pp. 1-61.

[4] George Peter Murdock, *Africa: Its People and Their Culture History* (New York: McGraw-Hill Book Co., 1959). An introductory chapter, "Language," pp. 12 ff., outlines his own and Greenberg's classifications.

[5] The position of Professor Guthrie, for example. See his *The Bantu Languages of Western Equatorial Africa* (London: Oxford University Press for the International African Institute, 1953); also C. G. Seligman, *Races of Africa* (London: 1930).

[6] *Rapport Annuel du Gouvernement Français à l'Assemblée Générale des Nations Unies sur l'administration du Cameroun placé sous la tutelle de la France; Année 1953* (Paris: 1954), pp. 14, 15. (Hereafter cited as *Rapport du Cameroun,* with the year. The designation will be used both for reports issued during the mandate years and those issued during trusteeship. The mandate reports are from 1921 to 1938. The trusteeship reports are from 1947 to 1957. No French reports on the Cameroun were issued after 1957.)

[7] *Report by His Majesty's Government . . . to the General Assembly of the United Nations on the Administration of the Cameroons under United Kingdom Trusteeship for the Year 1950* (London: HMSO, 1951), pp. 6, 7. (Hereafter cited as *Report on the Cameroons* with year. The last British *Report* was issued for 1959. The same designation will be used for reports issued during the mandate. See note 6, above, for further details.)

[8] *Bulletin de la Statistique Générale,* Supplément, Etat du Cameroun, Ministère des Affaires Economiques, Service de la Statistique Générale, Vol. 1, no. 2 (Yaoundé: Feb., 1958), p. 47. Two recent (and probably the most authoritative) works on the Bamiléké are Claude Tardits, *Les Bamiléké de l'ouest Cameroun* (Paris: Berger-Levrault, 1960); and J[ean] Hurault, *La Structure sociale des Bamiléké* (Paris: Mouton, 1962).

[9] *Report on the Cameroons* (1957), pp. 220-221; Merran McCullough, Margaret Littlewood, I. Dugast, *Peoples of the Central Cameroons,* Ethnographic Survey of Africa, ed. Darryl Forde, Part IX, Western Africa (London: International African Institute, 1954), p. 14. The estimate is based on 1953 figures cited by the above authorities, to which has been added an increment based on the rate of increase indicated by McCullough's figures.

[10] *Rapport du Cameroun* (1956), pp. 16, 17. Figures are based on the most recent (1951-52) census.

[11] *Ibid.,* p. 16.

[12] *Ibid.,* p. 16, Sec. I. I[delette] Dugast, *Inventaire ethnique du Sud-Cameroun,* Mémoires de l'Institut Français d'Afrique Noire, Centre du Cameroun (Yaoundé: IFAN, 1949), Série: Populations, no. 1, pp. 5 ff.

[13] Bertrand Lembezat, *Kirdi, les populations paiennes du Nord-Cameroun.* Mémoires de l'Institut Français d'Afrique Noire, Centre du Cameroun (Yaoundé: IFAN, 1950), Série: Populations, no. 3; Guernier and Briat, *op. cit.,* pp. 72-79; *Rapports du Cameroun* (1950-1957).

[14] *Rapport du Cameroun* (1957), p. 17. More recent but unofficial estimates give them about 750,000.

[15] *The Northern Cameroons* (Kaduna: Northern Nigeria Information Service, Aug., 1957), pp. 1-21, *passim.* "Information on the Northern Cameroons (Trust Territory Province)" (Kaduna: 1951), mimeo., p. 2.

[16] Murdock, *op. cit.,* p. 415.

[17] *Rapport du Cameroun* (1957), p. 17; *Report on the Cameroons* (1957), p. 139.

[18] *Guide Economique du Cameroun, 1959,* Chambre de Commerce et d'Industrie du Cameroun (Yaoundé: 1959), p. 24.

[19] *Report on the Cameroons* (1959), p. 120. See also note d, table 1.

CHAPTER II: *Historical Context*

[1] For two conflicting interpretations of the colonization of Africa, see Ronald Robinson and John Gallagher, *Africa and the Victorians* (London: Macmillan, 1961), and Jean Stengers' vigorous dissent, "L'Impérialisme colonial de la fin du XIX siècle: mythe ou realité," *Journal of African History,* Vol.

III, no. 3 (1962), pp. 469-491. The Robinson-Gallagher thesis is restated in more succinct form in their contribution "The Partition of Africa" in the New Cambridge Modern History: *Material Progress and World-wide Problems 1870-98* (Cambridge University Press, 1962), Vol. XI, pp. 593-640.

[2] For example, see comments by Robert Cornevin, *Histoire de l'Afrique dès origines à nos jours* (Paris: Payot, 1956), pp. 66-67. An excellent review and commentary on the various early references to the Cameroon coast is found in Joseph Bouchaud, *La Côte du Cameroun dans l'histoire, et la cartographie dès origines à l'annexion Allemande* (Yaoundé: Institut Français d'Afrique Noire, Centre Camerounais, 1952), Série: Mémoires de l'IFAN.

[3] The Cameroon coast was first more or less accurately traced on a map by the Venetian cartographer Cristoforo Soligo, *circa* 1485. On Spanish maps the name became *Camarones*, on British, *Cameroons*, on German, *Kamerun*, and on French *Cameroun*. The "prawns" which delighted the Portuguese are not actually prawns but are larger and resemble crayfish. Moreover, their occurrence at the time of the Portuguese visit seems to have been coincidental, as they appear in the Wuri estuary only every few years. Edwin Ardener, "The Kamerun Idea," *West Africa*, no. 2147 (June 7, 1958), p. 533.

[4] Edwin Ardener in Victoria Centenary Committee, *Victoria, Southern Cameroons, 1858-1958* (Victoria: Basel Mission Book Depot, 1958), p. 16.

[5] An interesting account of the suppression of slavery along the "slave coast" of Africa is found in Christopher Lloyd, *The Navy and the Slave Trade* (New York: Longmans, Green and Co., 1949). See also Basil Davidson, *Black Mother* (London: Victor Gollancz, 1961), for a general discussion of the slave trade.

[6] Among the better-known places where such trading centers grew up were Rio del Rey, about sixty miles west of Mount Cameroon, between Douala and Calabar; Bimbia and Douala, both on the Cameroon River; Malimba on the Sanaga River; Batanga on the Nyong; Kribi and Campo.

[7] For a description of the government of Victoria in the early days see Thomas Lewis, *These Seventy Years* (London: The Carey Press, 1929), pp. 46-94, *passim.*

[8] *Ibid.*, pp. 72-73.

[9] Harry Rudin, *The Germans in the Cameroons* (New Haven: Yale University Press, 1938), p. 19.

[10] *Ibid.*, p. 20, notes a letter to Victoria in 1877 from Akwa and Bell, a letter to Consul Hewett in 1881 from Bell, a joint petition to Gladstone in November, 1881, from Akwa and Bell, and "similar requests" by native kings near Bimbia and Victoria.

[11] Cited by Evans Lewin, *The Germans and Africa* (New York: Cassel and Co., Ltd., 1915), p. 138.

¹² Memorandum by Consul E. H. Hewett, December 17, 1883, cited by Rudin, *op. cit.*, pp. 22-25, and by Lewin, *op. cit.*, pp. 131, 137.

¹³ Rudin, *op. cit.*, p. 29.

¹⁴ *Ibid.*, p. 36, and Lewin, *op. cit.*, pp. 133-134.

¹⁵ There were at least three or four German newspapers that hinted at the real purpose of Nachtigal's mission. The wonder is that no one in Britain picked up the cues.

¹⁶ A historical essay by Adalbelt Owona, "Comment les Allemands mirent la main sur le Cameroun," ("How the Germans Seized the Cameroun"), *Revue Camerounaise*, 2d year, no. 10 (July-Aug., 1959), p. xiii, gives a slightly different chronology. For example, Owona notes that the *Möwe* did actually tie up in Douala until the 12th, having spent the 11th looking for the passage upriver. See also René Douala Manga Bell, "Contributions à l'histoire du Cameroun," *L'Effort Camerounais* (Yaoundé), nos. 210, 211, 212, 214-219, 222, 223 (Oct. 25, 1959, to Jan. 24, 1960, issues of this weekly newspaper); and l'Abbé Thomas Ketchoua, *Contributions à l'Histoire du Cameroun de 450 avant Jésus-Christ à nos jours* (Yaoundé: 1962).

¹⁷ Bell, *op. cit.*, gives the following list: Bimbia, July 21; Little Batanga, July 23; Plantation and Kribi, July 24; Bata, July 26. Owona, *op. cit.*, includes Malimba, July 22; Benito River, August 6.

¹⁸ Rudin, *op. cit.*, p. 43.

¹⁹ *Ibid.*, p. 123; Bell, *op. cit.*, *passim*.

²⁰ The elements of the Basler Evangelische Missionsgesellschaft which established themselves in the Kamerun represented the Stuttgart branch of the society. It was one of the several missionary bodies asked by the German government to take over the work and property of the English Baptists.

²¹ See Rudin's account, *op. cit.*, pp. 110-112. An interesting, if overdrawn, anthology of German mistreatment of natives in their colonies is found in the British Foreign Office's Historical Section's Peace Handbook Series, no. 114, "Treatment of Natives in German Colonies" (1920). Part of the material deals with incidents in the Kamerun, including the Kleist affair.

²² Norman Dwight Harris, *Intervention and Colonization in Africa* (New York: Houghton Mifflin Co., 1914), pp. 267-279. See also Rudin, *op. cit.*, pp. 97, 98; Mary Evelyn Townsend, *The Rise and Fall of Germany's Colonial Empire, 1884-1918* (New York: The Macmillan Co., 1930), pp. 322-327. A copy of the text of the 1911 Treaty is found in Great Britain, Foreign Office, Historical Section, "Peace Handbooks," no. 111, *Cameroon* (London: HMSO, 1920), p. 75. A later census in the "New Kamerun" area revealed the population to be closer to 270,000 than 1,000,000. Even this later estimate is subject to question; the leading authority on the subject, R. R. Kuczynski, *Cameroons and Togoland* (London: Oxford University Press

for the Royal Institute of International Affairs, 1939), p. 27, simply notes
that figures between 270,000 and 2,250,000 have been variously cited but
does not indicate a preference for either set.

[23] Douala Manga Bell gives a highly colored account of the affair and brings
together the relevant documents in his series of articles appearing in *L'Effort
Camerounais* beginning October 18, 1959. See note 16, above.

[24] Joseph G. Aymerich, *La Conquête du Cameroun* (Paris: Payot, 1931);
E. H. Gorges, *The Great War in West Africa* (London: Hutchinson, 1927);
Eugene Guernier and René Briat, eds., *Cameroun-Togo* (Paris: Editions de
l'Union Française, 1951), pp. 55-56; Edward Bond, "The Conquest of the
Cameroons," *Contemporary Review*, vol. 109 (1916), pp. 620-627. There
seems to be little agreement on the number of persons who actually crossed
into Spanish Guinea with the remaining German troops. Wilhelm Kemner, who
claimed to be citing the Spanish Internment Report of January 31, 1917, gives
an estimated total of 70,000, broken down as follows: 5,621 soldiers, 4,354
soldiers' wives, 980 "attached persons," and 560 children—altogether 11,515
persons—plus about 16,000 porters, bringing the number of persons in, or
connected with, the military to about 27,500. In addition, Kemner counts
3,000 grasslands chiefs and their trains, all of whom were later interned in a
special camp on Fernando Po. The rest comprised about 40,000 persons,
mostly from the Yaoundé area. All except 15,000 (Europeans and persons connected with the military) were returned to the Cameroons as soon as arrangements could be made with the Allies. The 15,000 were interned at Fernando
Po. (Wilhelm Kemner, *Kamerun* [Berlin: Freiheits-Verlag, 1937], p. 77.)

[25] Diary of (English) Major Georges, cited in Erich Student, *Kamerun's
Kampf, 1914-1916* (Berlin: Geiser Verlag, 1937). An interesting summary
account of the Kamerun campaign, as seen from the German side, is by
Dr. Alex Haenicke, "Kamerun Erlag der Übermacht," in Paul Julius Vahl,
ed., *Das Buch der Deutschen Kolonien* (Leipzig: Wilhelm Goldman Verlag,
1937), pp. 283-294.

[26] Raoul Nicolas, *Le Cameroun depuis le Traité de Versailles* (Sant-Armand/
Cherbourg: Imprimerie A. Leclerc, 1922), pp. 34-38, *passim*.

[27] Aymerich, *op. cit.*, p. 200.

[28] Nicolas, *op. cit.*, p. 36. The translation is mine.

[29] Aymerich, *op. cit.*, pp. 205-206.

[30] Anthony H. M. Kirk-Greene, *Adamawa, Past and Present* (New York:
Oxford University Press, 1958), p. 82, notes that the Arnado Kabri still has
in his possession a German rest-house book and a tax register, which he
looks on as his badge of office.

[31] Nicolas, *op. cit.*, p. 37. Nicolas was a deputy judge in Douala during the post-condominium, pre-Versailles days.

[32] Quincy Wright, *Mandates under the League of Nations* (Chicago: University of Chicago Press, 1930), p. 44.

[33] *Journal Officiel, Chambre des Députés*, September 17, 1919, p. 4395, cited in R. L. Buell, *The Native Problem in Africa* (New York: Macmillan, 1928), II, 278. Cf. also Wright, *op. cit.*, pp. 24-48.

[34] See note of December 17, 1920, *Draft Mandates for Togoland (British) and the Cameroons (British)*, Cmd. 1350 (London: HMSO, 1921), p. 2.

[35] Notably Rudin, *op. cit.*, and Townsend, *op. cit.*

[36] Buell, *op. cit.*, p. 360, and pp. 271-373, *passim*.

[37] League of Nations, Permanent Mandates Commission, *Minutes and Reports of the Twenty-Second Meeting*, 1933, VI (Geneva: 1933).

[38] See Ardener, "The Kamerun Idea," *West Africa*, June 7, 1958, p. 537; June 14, 1958, p. 559.

[39] J. P. Nicholas in Guernier and Briat, *op. cit.*, p. 49, lists some of the early pagan peoples: Massa, Muzuk, Tupuri, Wandala, Bata, Duru, Namchi, Fali, Matakam, and Kapsiki.

[40] *Ibid.*, Muzuk, Tupuri, Namchi, Fali, Matakam, and Kapsiki.

[41] *Ibid.*, Wandala, Massa, Kotoko (fusion of one part of the Wandala with the Sao), Duru, and Gisiga.

[42] J. D. Fage, *An Introduction to the History of West Africa* (Cambridge: University Press, 1956), p. 18, indicates that the Fulani are probably a mixture of some North African "whites," who settled in Ghana from the second century onward, with the Soninke, Tucolor, Woloff, and Serer peoples. By the time they reached Hausaland they had already become thoroughly African and dark-complexioned, and were speaking African languages. Their uncharacteristic height and aquiline features, as well as the similarity of the Fulani language to Serere and Wolof, betray their western and northern origins. The Fulani are also known as the Fulbe (plural; singular Peul or Pulo), Foula, Fellata, and so forth. For an extended discussion see H. Baumann and D. Westerman, *Peuples et civilisations de l'Afrique* (Paris: Payot, 1957), pp. 388-401, *passim*, and George P. Murdock, *Africa: Its People and Their Culture History* (New York: McGraw-Hill, 1959), pp. 413-420.

[42] Kirk-Greene, *op. cit.*, pp. 126-128, *passim*.

[44] Fage, *op. cit.*, p. 35.

[45] Kirk-Greene, *op. cit.*, p. 129.

[46] *Ibid.*, p. 130.

CHAPTER III: *Westernization of the Cameroons*

[1] Edwin Ardener, "The Origins of the Modern Sociological Problems Connected with the Plantation System in the Victoria Division of the Cameroons," West African Institute of Social and Economic Research, Annual Conference, Sociology Section, Ibadan, March, 1953, *Collected Papers* (Ibadan: University College, 1953), p. 92. "King" Bile (Billy) or "Williams" of Bimbia, who provided the land on which the Baptist missionary community at Victoria was founded, was given his rank by the British in 1826.

[2] Georges Hardy, in his *Histoire sociale de la colonisation française* (Paris: Larose, 1953), p. 178, notes:

Without there having been a deliberate intention to do so, almost all the principalities [sic] whose heads concluded treaties with France have either disappeared or are now little more than empty forms. The slowness and ineptitude of the local sovereigns to second the work of colonization [*l'oeuvre colonisatrice*], interpreted rightly or not as a mark of bad faith, or presented as a sign of definite inferiority, wore upon the patience of local authorities and incited them to destroy those traditional cadres which seemed to them to be more encumbering than useful, or to replace as chiefs the representatives of old families with lesser persons without prestige and often without scruples. [Translation mine.]

[3] Gabriel Almond and James S. Coleman, eds., *The Politics of the Developing Areas* (Princeton: Princeton University Press, 1960), p. 281.

[4] M. G. Smith, Senior Research Fellow, Nigerian Institute of Social and Economic Research, in a conversation with the author, in April, 1960.

[5] The modern "Traditional organization of the Douala people," *Ngondo*, a rather loose Douala-oriented association, derives its name from the old village council.

[6] Edwin Ardener, *Coastal Bantu of the Cameroons*, Ethnographic Survey of Africa, ed. Darryl Forde (London: International African Institute, 1956), pp. 51 ff.

[7] Victoria Centenary Committee, *Victoria, Southern Cameroons, 1858-1958* (Victoria: Basel Mission Book Depot, 1958), p. 47.

[8] *Ibid.*

[9] So widespread had become the practice of using money to pay the brideprice that the Germans, before they left, and later the French and British, found it necessary to impose limits on the amounts that might be spent for that purpose. The current limit is five thousand francs CFA ($20) in the East Cameroun; no limit has been imposed in the West Cameroun, although an attempt to do so was made in 1956. *Rapport Annuel du Gouvernement*

Français à l'Assemblée Générale des Nations Unies sur l'administration du Cameroun placé sous la tutelle de la France; Année 1957 (Paris: 1959), p. 219; *Report by Her Majesty's Government* . . . *to the General Assembly of the United Nations on the Administration of the Cameroons under United Kingdom Trusteeship for the Year 1957* (London: HMSO, 1959), p. 88. (The French and British annual reports for both the mandate and trusteeship periods will be hereafter cited as *Rapport du Cameroun*, with the year, and *Report on the Cameroons*, with the year.)

[10] See T. O. Elias, *The Nature of African Customary Law* (Manchester University Press: 1956), for a general discussion. Concerning the Cameroons, see Ardener, *Coastal Bantu of the Cameroons*, pp. 75-76; Merran McCullough, I. Dugast, *et al.*, *People of the Central Cameroons* (London: International African Institute, 1954), pp. 29-30, 73, 116-117, 145; R. Delarozière, *Les Institutions politiques et sociales des populations dites Bamiléké*, Memorandum III du Centre IFAN Cameroun (Yaoundé: 1950), pp. 25 ff.; and Claude Tardits, *Les Bamiléké de l'ouest Cameroun* (Paris: Berger-Levrault, 1960), pp. 69-72.

[11] Ardener, "The Origins of the Modern Sociological Problems," p. 93.

[12] Jean Claude Froelich, *Cameroun-Togo* (Paris: Editions Berger-Levrault, 1956), p. 54. Translation mine.

[13] Coleman, in Almond and Coleman, *op. cit.*, pp. 270, 272:

. . . urban centers have been the principal arenas of acculturation. . . . With few exceptions there were no cities in pre-European Africa. Thus, urban life was a new experience for most Africans. The new cities accelerated the intensification of the division of labor. As urban Africans became increasingly dependent upon their occupational specialties or salaried jobs they lost the economic security of the lineage and the self-sufficient rural community. The impersonality, heterogeneity, and competitiveness of urban life accentuated their personal insecurity as well as their individualism which became more pronounced as they sought status and prestige within the urban social structure. The cities were also centers for intensive acculturation, for it was there that Africans came into daily and intimate contact with all aspects of modernity.

[14] The role of the new achievement elite in the Westernizing process is discussed in an article by Dr. K. A. Busia, "The Impact of Industrialization on West Africa," WAISER Conference, 1953, report (see note 1, this chapter), pp. 31-37. See also Jacques Denis, *Le Phénomène urbain en Afrique centrale* (Brussels: Académie Royale des Sciences Coloniales, 1958).

[15] Harry Rudin, *Germans in the Cameroons, 1884-1914* (New Haven: Yale University Press, 1938), p. 328; Robert R. Kuczynski, *Cameroons and Togoland: A Demographic Study* (New York: Oxford University Press for the R. I. I. A., 1939), pp. 34, 53, 61, 62 ff.

[16] Kuczynski, *op. cit.*, p. 25.

[17] M'banga was segregated from Douala *circonscription* in 1926. Previous

estimates of the old Douala district, 96,740 and 94,851, are not to be trusted for reasons discussed by Kuczynski, *op. cit.*, pp. 88 ff. Figures to be cited hereafter are for the Douala *circonscription* only, without M'banga.

[18] *Résultats du Recensement de la Ville de Douala 1955-56, Population Autochtone*, Fascicule 2, Etat du Cameroun, Ministère des Affaires Economiques, Service de la Statistique Générale (Yaoundé: 1956), p. 4.

[19] Kuczynski, *op. cit.*, pp. 89, 91, 92, 93, 95.

[20] J. Guilbot, *Petite Etude sur la main d'oeuvre à Douala*, Centre IFAN Cameroun, Memorandum 1 (Yaoundé: 1948); see also his "Les Conditions de vie des indigènes à Douala." *Etudes Camerounaises*, Tome II (Sept.-Dec., 1949), nos. 27-28.

[21] Figures for 1956 are taken or extrapolated from the *Résultats du Recensement . . . de Douala, 1955-1956;* see also table 4.

[22] Almond and Coleman, *op. cit.*, pp. 273-274.

[23] Mongo Beti (pseud. Alexandre Biyidi), "Tumultueux Cameroun," *Revue Camerounaise*, 2d yr., no. 11 (Sept.-Oct., 1959), pp. 170, 171, 172. Biyidi's article criticizes current administrative practices and policies of the government. The excerpted portions are from a section of the article describing the condition of rural workers. The translation is mine.

[24] Statistical confirmation of this is found in the *Résultats du Recensement de la Subdivision de Mbalmayo (1956), Population Autochtone*, Service de la Statistique Générale, Etat du Cameroun (Yaoundé: 1956), p. 13.

[25] Cited by Georges Chaffard in "Cameroun à la veille de l'indépendance," *Europe France-Outre-Mer*, no. 355 (June, 1959), p. 65.

[26] *Ibid.*, p. 67.

[27] For a perceptive analysis of similar conditions in Brazzaville, see Georges Balandier, *Sociologie des Brazzavilles Noires* (Paris: Presses Universitaires de France, 1957). No full-scale sociological study has yet been published on Douala, but I understand that M. Gouellain, connected with the Office of Overseas Technical and Scientific Research (ORSTROM) and the Institut des Recherches Camerounais (IRCAM), is preparing a historical and sociological work on that city.

[28] Delaroziére, *op. cit.*, pp. 8 ff. See also Margaret Littlewood, "Bamum and Bamiléké," in McCullough, Dugast, *et al.*, *op. cit.* The most recent, and probably the best, works on the Bamiléké are Tardits, *op. cit.*, and Jean Hurault, *La Structure social des Bamiléké* (Paris: Mouton, 1962).

[29] Delarozière, *op. cit.*, p. 21. Tardits, *op. cit.*, pp. 110-113, lists 111.

[30] McCullough, Dugast, *et al.*, *op. cit.*, pp. 97-98; Tardits, *op. cit.*, pp. 69-76, *passim*.

[31] M. R. Diziain, "Les Facteurs de l'expansion Bamiléké au Cameroun," *Bulletin de l'Association des Géographes Français*, no. 235-236 (May-June, 1953), pp. 118, 122.

[32] *Ibid.*, p. 123. Tardits, *op. cit.*, calls them *cadets* (juniors).

[33] R. Delarozière, "Etude de la stabilité de la population Bamiléké de la Sub-division de Bafoussam," *Etudes Camerounaises* (Yaoundé), III (Sept.-Dec., 1950), 149.

[34] McCullough, Dugast, *et al.*, *op. cit.*, pp. 90-91.

[35] See table 6.

[36] Delarozière, "Etude de la stabilité . . . ," pp. 146, 147. Translation mine.

[37] Dominique Choconte, "Le grand drame Bamiléké, ses sources, ses remèdes," *La Presse du Cameroun*, Sept. 28, 1959, pp. 1, 2. Translation mine.

[38] See James S. Coleman, *Nigeria: Background to Nationalism* (Berkeley and Los Angeles: University of California Press, 1958), esp. pp. 75-77.

[39] Bertrand Lembezat, *Kirdi, les populations paiennes du nord-Cameroun* (Yaoundé: IFAN, Centre au Cameroun, 1950), pp. 51-60.

[40] I am especially grateful for the information provided by Father Desmollieres, of the Apostolic Prefecture at Garoua.

[41] *Op. cit.*, p. 16. Interestingly enough, there did not seem to be any change in the wording of this phrase in the 1954, 1955, 1956, and 1957 reports, though the situation had already begun to change by 1956.

[42] One of the few studies on this subject is an unpublished essay by an anthropologist, James Vaughn, of the University of Pittsburgh, "Culture, History, and Grass-Roots Politics in a Nigerian Chiefdom," read at the 1962 annual meeting of the American Anthropological Association. Vaughn describes the ethnic variables that explain the behavior of the Marghi tribe as observed during the 1961 UN plebiscite in the Northern Cameroons.

[43] Available information gives a list of over 150 political parties and associations in the Cameroun. Twenty-four are definitely based on tribe or ethnic group. See Appendix A for the full list.

[44] Almond and Coleman, *op. cit.*, p. 278.

[45] Father Joseph Bouchaud, C.S.E., *L'Eglise en Afrique Noire* (Paris: La Palatine, 1958), pp. 23-24, has recognized the distinction, and distinguishes

between "Christian" and "Christianized" individuals, the former having been baptized and having declared their conversion to the Church, and the latter having been "strongly touched by the missionary influence."

[46] "Education in Africa: Its Pattern and Role in Social Change," *The Annals* (March, 1955), p. 172.

[47] Rudin, *op. cit.*, pp. 354-355.

[48] Victoria Centenary Committee, *op. cit.*, p. 88. The editors are apparently citing Rudin's (*op. cit.*, p. 360) figures. Lord Hailey, *An African Survey, Revised 1956* (New York: Oxford University Press, 1957), p. 1204, cites 11,500 pupils in mission schools as against 1,194 in state institutions. J. Guidel, in Eugene Guernier and René Briat, eds., *Cameroun, Togo* (Paris: Editions de l'Union Française, 1951), p. 135, indicates that in 1913 there were 1,194 pupils in seven state schools as against 41,500 pupils in 225 mission schools. Prof. T. H. Becker, in *Das Schulwesen in Afrika* (Band XIII/2, Afrika Handbuch der praktischen Kolonialwissenschaften) (Berlin: Walter de Gruyter und Co., 1943), p. 139, cites the total number of pupils in 1912 as 43,500, and notes that in 1913 there were seven government schools and five trade or industrial schools. Becker also notes that in 1913 three new government schools were opened, bringing the total to seven, and that the 1914 appropriations envisaged the opening of six additional government schools and one trade school. Caution is probably indicated in assessing the credibility of any of these figures, especially the attendance figures. English and French sources tend to underestimate the totals, German sources to overestimate them. Rudin's attendance figures are probably fair ones.

[49] Figures are from Rudin, *op. cit.*, p. 360, and Charles P. Groves, *The Planting of Christianity in Africa*, IV (London: Lutterworth Press, 1958), 20, 21.

[50] René Costeodat, *Le Mandat français et la réorganisation des territoires du Cameroun* (Besançon: Jacques and Demontrond, 1930), pp. 118, 121.

[51] See Victor T. Le Vine and Henri M'Ballah, "[Education in] Federal Republic of Cameroon," in Helen Kitchen, ed., *The Educated African* (New York: Frederick Praeger, 1962), pp. 519-532, for a description of the systems of the two Cameroun states.

[52] See table 9 for sources of figures cited in this paragraph.

[53] *Evolution des Femmes Camerounaises*, and *Union Nationale des Mères Camerounaises*. When the UPC was banned in 1955, the latter organization was similarly proscribed as a UPC affiliate. Wives of exiled UPC leaders, such as Mmes. Martha Moumié, Margaret Ngoyi, and E. Ouandié, have been extremely active politically, even to the point of accompanying their husbands on trips to China and Russia. (New China News Agency, Peking, November 18, 1959, reports a meeting of the above ladies with Chuh Teh.)

[54] UNESCO, Camerounian Educational Planning Group, *Report Drawn upon Return of the First Mission, 10 March-20 May, 1962* (Paris: 1963), p. 12.

[55] *Rapport du Cameroun* (1938), p. 104, for the figures on the official schools' staff. The private, "recognized" schools are reported as having 120 *moniteurs indigènes* and 16 *maîtres européens.* The remaining 980 *moniteurs* and 134 *maîtres* are extrapolations from the reported attendance figures on the "unrecognized schools," estimating the ratio of *maîtres* to *moniteurs* as about 1 to 8, and pupils to teachers as about 80 to 1. The ratios are from the official figures given for 1938 and 1937.

[56] *Rapport du Cameroun* (1957), pp. 298-300, *passim.*

[57] *Ibid.,* p. 432. The estimates for the numbers of Camerounian staff are mine, derived from several conversations with Camerounian officials.

[58] UNESCO, Camerounian Educational Planning Group, *Report,* p. 14.

[59] *Ibid.,* p. 16.

[60] République du Cameroun, Ministère des Finances et du Plan, *Premier Plan Quinquennal* (Yaoundé: 1961), pp. 9, 261-265.

[61] République du Cameroun, Ministère du Plan, *Cameroun, Plan de Développement Economique et Social. Travaux Preparatoires, (Part 2) Rapport Générale* (Paris: Société Générale d'Etudes et de Planification, 1960), p. 34.

[62] According to the *Budget de l'Exercice 1959,* Ministère des Finances, Service des Etudes (Yaoundé: Imprimerie du Gouvernement, 1959), p. 184, Sec. 07.102.08 indicates the 1959 allocation to be 1,000,000 francs CFA, or about $4,100 at 1959 rate of exchange. Significant sums are also allotted to the *Maison de la France d'outre-mer à la cité universitaire* (680,000 CFA francs, or approximately $2,833), to pay transportation costs of scholarship students coming home for vacations (3,500,000 francs CFA, or approximately $14,000), and for other purposes. The 1959 exchange rate is used in these and figures following: $1.00 = 240 francs CFA.

[63] The *Union Nationale des Etudiants Kamerunais* (UNEK), the principal Cameroun students' organization in France, was affiliated with the *Fédération des Etudiants Noirs en France* and with the *Union Internationale des Etudiants* (International Students' Union). The latter organization, whose headquarters are in Prague, has been a prime organizer of the various International Youth Festivals of recent years (East Berlin, 1955, and Vienna, 1955).

In September, 1959, I visited the headquarters of the *Union Nationale des Etudiants Kamerunais* (UNEK) in Paris. UNEK utilized the facilities of the *Foyer des Etudiants Camerounais,* a student center for Cameroun students subsidized by the Cameroun government. My conversations with various members of the organization elicited a great deal of hostility toward the Cameroun government, and especially toward (then) Prime Minister Ahidjo, who was labeled a "French tool," "imperialist turncoat," and similar epithets. UNEK published a monthly magazine, *L'Etudiant Kamerunais,* and contributed most of the articles to the *Revue Camerounaise,* a bimonthly publication of the *Cercle Culturel Camerounais.* In 1960, UNEK's antigovernment activities became so irritating to the Cameroun authorities that the *Foyer* was closed, UNEK was asked to disband, and five of the organization's leaders were deprived of their government scholarships.

[64] The *Compagnie d'exploitation automobile au Cameroun* (CEAC) and the *Compagnie Française de l'Afrique occidentale* (CFAO) (the Cameroun distributor for Renault vehicles), among others, maintain such courses in the East Cameroun.

[65] It is rather difficult to ascertain with any accuracy both the extent of literacy in the Cameroun and the reliability of official figures on the subject. The confusion results from the use of such French terms as *taux de scolarisation* (level of education) and from the lack of any definite standard for assessing either literacy or educational achievement. For example, official figures indicated that in 1959 the country had a *taux de scolarisation* of 51.5 per cent. This figure was broken down into percentages for the northern areas (18 per cent) and for the southern (85 per cent). Investigation reveals that the percentages applied only to *males,* and that they referred to the percentage of males with any education at all, *not* just those who could read and write (in French). The percentages were derived from school attendance records for *all* grades. Including females in the southern percentage would reduce it by about 15 per cent; in the north the reduction would be by about 12 or 13 per cent. On a total basis, the official percentage would be reduced from about 51 per cent to about 40 per cent. The revised percentage still gives no clue to literacy (which at minimum I would define as the ability to read road and shop signs and to write out simple needs), nor do the school attendance records include students attending unofficial private and voluntary agency schools.

CHAPTER IV: *Growth of Political Life and Institutions*

SECTION A

[1] See Lord Hailey, *An African Survey, Revised 1956* (New York: Oxford University Press, 1957), pp. 206, 207, and Hans Wieschhoff, *Colonial Policy in Africa* (Philadelphia: University of Pennsylvania Press, 1944), pp. 90, 91, for succinct discussions of this theme. Two studies of French colonial policy before 1930, which expand on the problems of association, assimilation, and *identité,* are Albert Duchène, *La Politique coloniale de la France* (Paris: Payot, 1928), and Raymond F. Betts, *Assimilation and Association in French Colonial Theory 1890-1914* (New York: Columbia University Press, 1961).

[2] See Hailey, *op. cit.,* p. 332.

[3] Cited in Hailey, *op. cit.,* p. 208, from Jules Harmand's *Domination et colonisation* (Paris: Payot, 1910).

[4] Albert Sarraut, *La Mise en valeur des colonies françaises* (Paris: Payot, 1923).

[5] *Ibid.*, pp. 62-127, *passim.*

[6] Wieschhoff, *op. cit.*, p. 93.

[7] Hailey, *op. cit.*, p. 338. For the text of the *indigénat*, see Appendix C.

[8] *Ibid.*, pp. 328-344, *passim.*

[9] *Rapport Annuel du Gouvernement Français au Conseil de la Société des Nations sur l'administration du Cameroun sous Mandat* (1923), p. 142. (The annual reports for both the mandate and trusteeship periods will hereafter be cited as *Rapport du Cameroun*, with the year.)

[10] *Ibid.*, p. 81. (Translation mine.)

[11] *Ibid.*, p. 142.

[12] *Rapport du Cameroun* (1925), pp. 171-172: *Arrêté portant création de conseils des notables* (Oct. 12, 1925) and *Arrêté modifiant l'article 2 de l'arrêté du 9 Octobre 1925.*

[13] *Rapport du Cameroun* (1953), p. 43. The administrative reform of April 8, 1935, increased the number of administrative units from fifteen to seventeen, and abolished the designation *circonscription.*

[14] *Journal Officiel du Cameroun*, 1921, p. 159, cited in Raymond L. Buell, *The Native Problem in Africa*, Vol. II (New York: Macmillan, 1928), p. 310.

[15] *Ibid.*

[16] *Rapport du Cameroun* (1922), p. 59.

[17] *Ibid.*, p. 60.

[18] Buell, *op. cit.*, p. 309.

[19] *Info-Cameroun*, no. 5 (May, 1959), La Presidence du Gouvernement Camerounais, Service de l'Information (Yaoundé), pp. 10-11.

[20] The sultan invented an alphabet of 510 characters and had a history of the Bamun peoples written in it. He also maintained a museum of tribal art and antiquities at his palace in Foumban. A devout Muslim, he wrote, among other documents, one in which he synthesized Mohammedanism, Christianity, and animism. See Idrissou Mborou Njoya, *Histoire et Coutumes des Bamun* (transl. by Henri Martin) (Mémoires: IFAN Centre Cameroun, Yaoundé: 1951); I. Dugast and M. D. W. Jeffreys, *L'Ecriture des Bamun* (Mémoires: IFAN Centre Cameroun, Yaoundé: 1950); M. Göhring, "Der König von Ba-

mun und seine Schrift," *Der Evangelische Heidenbote,* LXXX, 6th year (June, 1907); Abbé Thomas Ketchoua, *Contribution à l'Histoire du Cameroun de 450 avant Jésus-Christ à nos jours* (Yaoundé: Imp. St. Paul, 1962), pp. 145-154.

[21] League of Nations, Permanent Mandates Commission, *Minutes and Reports of the Twenty-Second Meeting, 1932* (Geneva: 1932), VI, 205; *Rapport du Cameroun* (1931), p. 24.

[22] Henri Labouret, *Le Cameroun* (Paris: P. Hartmann, 1937), p. 20.

[23] This was long the traditional method of choosing chiefs in communities where the dynastic principle did not operate.

[24] See *Arrêté* of June 4, 1924, annex 3, *Rapport du Cameroun* (1925); *Rapport du Cameroun* (1938), p. 127; *Rapport du Cameroun* (1950).

[25] *Rapport du Cameroun* (1938), p. 128. Among the indigenous Moslem rulers, the rebates included not only contributions from taxes, but proceeds from annual tithes and levies on inheritance as well.

[26] *Op. cit.,* p. 310.

[27] The *allocations* are now allotted on a per capita basis amounting to about three francs per person in each chiefdom. In addition, a sum is allocated for administrative services rendered, plus the *remise* itself (*Rapport du Cameroun* [1957], p. 43). "Third degree" chiefs subsist mostly on the *remises.* The *Budget de l'Exercice 1959,* Ministère des Finances, Services des Etudes (Yaoundé: Imprimerie du Gouvernement, 1959), pp. 324, 325, provides 54,795,000 francs CFA (or approximately $223,653) for *allocations* to the chiefs.

[28] Eugene Guernier and René Briat, eds., *Cameroun, Togo* (Paris: Editions de l'Union Française, 1951), p. 107.

[29] Cited in Buell, *op. cit.,* II, 379-380. (Translation mine.)

[30] *Décret de 8 août 1924 déterminant au Cameroun l'exercise des pouvoirs disciplinaires,* cited in *ibid.,* pp. 380-384. (Translation mine.)

[31] Article 6 of the Decree gives the Commissioner for the Cameroun authority to promulgate an *Arrêté* listing the infractions to which the *indigénat* applies. The *Arrêté* of October 4, 1924, contains this list, cited in *ibid.,* pp. 384-386.

[32] French government *Décrets* of December 8, 1945, February 20, 1946.

[33] Buell, *op. cit.,* p. 314; Hailey, *op. cit.,* p. 603.

[34] Conversations with various senior Camerounian officials, September and October, 1959, in Douala and Yaoundé.

[35] *Rapport du Cameroun* (1924), pp. 62-66; *Rapport du Cameroun* (1925), pp. 37, 38.

[36] *Rapport du Cameroun* (1924), p. 64; *Rapport du Cameroun* (1925), p. 35; Buell, *op. cit.*, pp. 311-316, *passim*.

[37] *Rapport du Cameroun* (1924), p. 64.

[38] Buell, *op. cit.*, pp. 311, 312. The Permanent Mandates Commission of the League subsequently substantiated Buell's charge on both the lack of a penal code and the absence of any distinction between crimes and offenses. The Commission agreed that "this point appears to deserve attention." (League of Nations, Permanent Mandates Commission, *Minutes and Reports of the Fifteenth Session, 1929* [Geneva: 1937], VI, 247.) (For brevity's sake, references made hereafter to minutes of the Permanent Mandates Commission will list the following information in this form: (1) number of the meeting, (2) initials of the commission, (3) date, (4) page or pages. The above reference would appear as follows: XV. PMC. 1929. 247.)

[39] Buell, *op. cit.*, p. 313.

[40] I had a conversation with an elderly Cameroonian, who recalled Atangana quite well. My informant (who declined to be identified) was at one time an employee in the Yaoundé administration. He showed me some old letters purportedly written to the administration about Atangana's activities. Atangana seemed to have been involved in a wide variety of commercial activities whose costs were borne by the population, but whose benefits accrued almost solely to him. Buell mentions him in another connection, as forcing natives to work on plantations without pay. (*Op. cit.*, p. 345.) In this latter connection, the French themselves provided indirect confirmation of the charge. As Commissioner Marchand admitted, "That chiefs should employ natives for their own profit was sometimes so habitual that the Administration could only note the fact with a view to taking energetic sanctions." He further admitted that Atangana had bought an ex-German plantation from the enemy property custodian for 18,000 francs and subsequently resold it to a European company for 550,000 francs. However, the Commissioner claimed that Atangana put aside a certain amount to pay his laborers, and that there had been no "other complaints against him" from them after they had been paid. XV. PMC. 1929. 142.

[41] *Rapport du Cameroun* (1928), pp. 100-109.

[42] Buell, *op. cit.*, p. 313.

[43] Hailey, *op. cit.*, p. 672.

[44] In Lomé and Anecho the tax was graduated according to income. Cf. Buell, *op. cit.*, p. 318.

[45] Statement of the Commissioner for Togo, found in the Circular of July 4, 1922 reproduced in the *Rapport du Togo, 1922*, cited in *ibid.*, p. 320.

[46] *Arrêté* of September 16, 1923, *Rapport du Cameroun* (1925), p. 138.

[47] In Douala in 1932 a number of women demonstrated against the tax. They claimed that it was unfair, and that a local collector had embezzled some of the taxes collected from them. A French policeman lost his head and discharged a shotgun into a crowd of women, and one demonstrator was wounded. A number of other women were jailed for disturbing the peace. (XX. PMC. 1932. 221.)

[48] *Op. cit.*, p. 320.

[49] The basic rules were set down in the *Arrêté* of July 1, 1921 (*Rapport du Cameroun* [1921], p. 84), and in the *Arrêté* of September 7, 1925 (*Rapport du Cameroun* [1925], p. 141).

[50] Statement by Commissioner Marchand before the Permanent Mandates Commission. (XV. PMC. 1929. 137.)

[51] Only Ruanda-Urundi had little need for forced labor. (III. PMC. 1923. 276.) For general discussions of the problem see Hailey, *op. cit.*, pp. 1357-1376; Lucy P. Mair, *Native Policies in Africa* (London: Routledge and Sons, 1936), pp. 201-209, *passim*; Quincy Wright, *Mandates under the League of Nations* (Chicago: University of Chicago Press, 1930), pp. 250-254, 463-464; and the annex at III. PMC. 1923. 276.

[52] "La puissance Mandataire devra ... interdire tout travail forcé ou obligatoire, sauf pour les travaux et services publics essentiels et sous condition d'une équitable rénumeration." French Mandate for the Cameroons, Article 3, cited in Wright, *op. cit.*, p. 617 (English version); in Buell, *op. cit.* p. 374 (French version).

[53] VI. PMC. 1925. 16.

[54] *Arrêté* of September 7, 1925. See note 49, this chapter.

[55] IV. PMC. 1924. 18.

[56] *Ibid.*

[57] *Op. cit.*, p. 345.

[58] *Ibid.*

[59] *Ibid.*

[60] XV. PMC. 1929. 247.

[61] *Ibid.*, p. 142. Also see note 40, this chapter.

[62] Buell, *op. cit.*, p. 324.

[63] *Ibid.*

[64] IX. PMC. 1926. 70.

[65] Buell, *op. cit.*, p. 330.

[66] *Décret* of July 9, 1925, *Rapport du Cameroun* (1925), p. 88.

[67] III. PMC. 1924. 19.

[68] *Ibid.*, pp. 35-38.

[69] *Circular Concerning Native Labor and Movement of Natives, May 1, 1936* (Paris).

[70] XXX. PMC. 1936. 45.

[71] VI. PMC. 1925. 42.

[72] XXI. PMC. 1931. 135.

[73] The Forced Labor Convention, drawn up largely because of the practices in Africa, was adopted in 1930 by the International Labour Conference. By 1940 most colonial powers had ratified and executed the treaty. Only Portugal failed to put it into effect, though it had ratified it by 1956. (International Labour Office, *African Labour Survey* [Geneva: 1958], pp. 297, 695).

[74] "France in the Cameroons," *The Times* (London), May 17, 1933, p. 15.

[75] XV. PMC. 1929. 131. Italics mine.

SECTION B

[1] Thomas Hodgkin, "The French Cameroons" (third of five articles), *West Africa*, December 4, 1954, p. 1133.

[2] Raymond L. Buell, *The Native Problem in Africa* (New York: Macmillan, 1928), II, 303-304.

[3] Hodgkin, *op. cit.*, cites Buell, *op. cit.*, p. 304. The hymn is in a footnote; I have restored the punctuation as given by Buell, and translated *sepulcre* to the more colloquial "grave," rather than "sepulchre."

[4] Buell, *op. cit.*, p. 342.

[5] *Ibid.*

[6] *Rapport du Cameroun* (1926), p. 78.

[7] Petition of September 16, 1926, from Joseph Bell (XVI. PMC. 1929. 183-184); Petition of August 11, 1929, from Theodore Lobe Bell, Eyum Ekwalla, Mbape Bwanga, Ngaka Akwa (XXI. PMC. 1932. 172, 142); Petition of September 5, 1930, from Richard Manga Bell (*ibid.*).

[8] Petition dated December 19, 1929 (XIX. PMC. 1930. 195). The petition further stated a vague program for the reorganization of the territory under the League of Nations, with the coöperation of a number of countries, including the United States.

[9] XXII. PMC. 1932. 214. See also *Rapport du Cameroun* (1931), p. 26; XXI. PMC. 1932. 142, 217.

[10] See XXI. PMC. 1932. 142, 217, relating to Ganty's petition of March 18, 1931.

[11] *Ibid.*

[12] Petitions of June 19, August 14, and August 21, 1931 (XXIII. PMC. 1933. 178).

[13] *Ibid.*

[14] Another matter of interest, but on which evidence is lacking, is the extent to which the Spanish Civil War of 1936 affected the political consciousness of the more articulate Cameroonians. It is a matter of record that France gave asylum to political refugees from Fernando Po and Spanish Guinea. These refugees stayed in the Cameroons before going on to France.

[15] XXXV. PMC. 1938. 113.

[16] *The Times* (London), Oct. 29, 1938, p. 11.

[17] Hodgkin, *op. cit.*, p. 1133.

Section C

[1] See Quincy Wright, *Mandates under the League of Nations* (Chicago: University of Chicago Press, 1930), pp. 447-448.

[2] Article 120: "All movable and immovable property in such territories belonging to the German Empire or to any German State shall pass to the government exercising authority over such territories, on the terms laid down in Article 257 of part IX (Financial Clauses) of the present Treaty. The decisions of the local courts in any dispute as to the nature of such property shall be final." See Raymond L. Buell, *The Native Problem in Africa* (New York: Macmillan, 1928), II, 294-295.

[3] *Loc. cit.*

⁴ Soon after Buell's book appeared, the International Bureau for the Protection of Native Races petitioned the Permanent Mandates Commission to investigate some of the charges made in it. Among other matters, the *Compagnie des Tabacs* affair was mentioned. The Mandates Commission looked into it and agreed that there was nothing illegal in the transaction. XV. PMC. 1929. 242, 246, 247.

⁵ Wilhelm Kemner, *Kamerun* (Berlin: Freiheitsverlag, 1937), pp. 225, 258.

⁶ *New York Times,* November 23, 1924, Sec. II, p. 5. See also C. K. Meek, *Land Tenure and Land Administration in Nigeria and the British Cameroons* (London: Colonial Office, Research Studies, no. 22, 1957), p. 355; Kemner, *op. cit.,* pp. 165-170.

⁷ Kemner, *op. cit.,* pp. 243-244. The employees of the Westafrikanische Pflanzungs-Gesellschaft "Victoria" (WAPV) showed Kemner a nationalistic poem being circulated among the Germans in the territory (translation mine):

> Noch immer schweifen die Gedanken
> Zurück zum Kameruner Land,
> Um herzlich tausendfach zu danken
> Den Männern dort am Meeresstrand.
>
> Ihr zeigtet uns in frud'gem Stolze,
> Was Ihre geschafft auf heisser Erd',
> Die reife Frucht am grünen Holze,
> Die Eurer Müh' und Arbeit wert.
>
> Oft glauben wir, als ob im Traume
> Wie in ein Märchenland gestellt,
> Wenn wir in grossem, weitem Raume
> Die Wunder sahn der Tropenwelt.
>
> Mit bittrem Schmerze wir empfinden,
> Dass man geraubt uns dieses Land.
> Drum wollen laut und ernst wir künden:
> Es muss zurück zum Vaterland!
>
> Das unserem Recht Erfüllung werde,
> Dass bald die Deutsche Flagge weht
> Auf Kameruns alter deutscher Erde,
> Ist unsere Hoffnung und Gebet.

Translation:

> Ever my thoughts are turning
> Back to Kamerun-land,
> A thousand thanks returning
> To the men on that ocean strand.
>
> You showed us in joyful pride,
> What you wrought from that hot soil,

Ripe fruits from green boughs,
Redeemed by your care and toil.

Often we seem, as in a dream,
In a fairy-tale land to be,
When in that vast, expansive land,
The tropics' wonders we see.

We with bitter pain our feelings name:
This land from us was stolen.
So, earnestly do we proclaim:
It must return to the Fatherland!

Our pleas and aspirations lie
To see our rights fulfilled,
That soon the German flag may fly
On Kamerun's old German soil.

[8] *Bulletin du Comité de l'Afrique Française,* 48th year, no. 6 (June, 1938), p. 281. The text is of a telegraphic cable sent to the journal *Petit Parisien,* dated March 27, 1938.

[9] Eva MacLean, *Unser Kamerun von Heute* (München: Reichskolonialbund by Fichte Verlag, 1940), facing p. 70. The book was notable for lengthy eulogies of German women in the Kamerun, praising them as the mothers of the new Germany.

[10] *Bulletin du Comité de l'Afrique Française,* 48th year (June, 1938), p. 281.

[11] *Ibid.,* 43d year, no. 7 (July, 1933), p. 385.

[12] See Royal Institute of International Affairs, *Germany's Claim to Colonies.* Information Department Papers, no. 23 (2d ed.; London: Royal Institute of International Affairs by Oxford University Press, 1939); A. L. C. Bullock, ed., *Germany's Colonial Demands* (London: Oxford University Press, 1939); F. S. Joelson, *Germany's Claim to Colonies* (London: Hurst and Blackett, 1939); Rayford W. Logan, *The African Mandates in World Politics* (Washington, D.C.: The Public Affairs Press, 1948); Malbone W. Graham, "The Diplomatic Struggle for Africa," in the volume edited by the Committee on International Relations, University of California, Los Angeles, *Africa, the Near East, and the War* (Berkeley: University of California Press, 1943), pp. 175-212.

[13] "The German Delegation's Comments on the Condition of the Peace," *International Conciliation,* no. 143 (Oct., 1919), p. 1249.

[14] *Germany's Claim* . . . , p. 24.

[15] A statement of the German case, under the authorship of Dr. Schnee, appeared in English in 1926. See Heinrich Schnee, *German Colonization, Past, Present and Future: The Truth about the German Colonies* (New York: Alfred Knopf, 1926).

[16] See the 1930 edition, pp. 741, 742, 753, 754.

[17] Space does not permit a full listing of the relevant citations. The works cited in note 12, this chapter, contain either ample bibliographical notes or bibliographies on the subject.

[18] *Germany's Claim* . . . , pp. 65-82.

[19] *Ibid.*, pp. 82-85. See *New York Times,* Jan. 3, 1937, p. 8; March 18, 1937, p. 13.

[20] Cf. Graham, *op. cit.*, p. 175; Logan, *op. cit.*, pp. 184-204; *Bulletin du Comité de l'Afrique Française,* 42d year, no. 9 (Sept., 1932), p. 600; no. 12 (Dec., 1932), p. 741; 46th year, no. 2 (Feb., 1936), p. 484; no. 8 (Aug., 1936), p. 484; no. 9 (Sept., 1936), p. 484; 48th year, no. 2 (Feb., 1938), p. 86.

[21] Hjalmar Schacht, "Germany's Colonial Demands," *Foreign Affairs* (Jan., 1937), pp. 223-234.

[22] For example: Kemner, *op. cit.;* Heinrich Schnee, ed., *Das Deutsche Kolonialreich* (Leipzig: Deutsche Kolonial-Gesellschaft, 1930); Georg Escherich, *Kamerun* (Berlin: H. Riegler, 1938); Paul Rohrbach, *Deutsche Pflanzungen in Kamerun* (Hamburg: P. Hartung, 1937); Ewald Bergfeld, *Die Französischen Mandatsgebiete Kamerun und Togo* (Greifswald: H. Adler, 1935); Dr. Adolph Friederich, *et al., Das Buch der Deutschen Kolonien* (Leipzig: W. Goldman, 1937); Helmuth W. A. Och, *Die Wirtschaftsgeographische Entwicklung der früheren Deutschen Schutzgebieten Togo und Kamerun* (Königsberg: 1931); Reinhold Schober, *Kamerun: Neuzeitliche Verwaltungsprobleme* (Berlin: E. S. Mittler u. Sohn, 1937); Joachim H. Schreiber, *Deutsche Kolonien unter besonderer Berücksichtigung; Hierstellung als Mandate des Völkerbunds,* Volksrechtsfragen, no. 43 (Bonn: Dümmler, 1939); Karl H. Dietze, "Die Englisch-Französische Mandatsgrenze in Kamerun," *Zeitschrift, Gesellschaft für Erdkunde* (Berlin: 1937), pp. 321-348; August Full, "Kamerun," *Kolonial-Rundschau* (Sept. 12, 1932), pp. 279-447.

[23] Full citations: Fried Lange, *Massa Wann Kommst Du Wieder; Zwischen Tschadsee und Götterberg, Erlebnisse im Kampf in Kamerun* (Düsseldorf: Völkischer Verlag, 1942); P. Joseph M. Abs, *Der Kampf um unsere Schutzgebiete—Unsere Kolonien Einst und Jetzt, Ein Beitrag zur Wiedergewinnung unserer Kolonien, Eine Lebensfrage für unser Deutsches Volk* (Essen/Ruhr: Friedrich Floeder, 1926).

[24] Translation mine. Max Breul, *Kampf im Urwald* . . . (Leipzig: Julius Klinthart, 1940).

[25] *New York Times,* January 14, 1937, sec. 9, p. 2.

[26] For example: Franz (Ritter) von Epp, "Germany's Case for Colonies," *Living Age,* vol. 351 (Nov., 1936), pp. 235-241; Schacht, *op. cit.*

[27] See Logan, *op. cit.*, pp. 90-150, for a perceptive review of the diplomatic maneuvers relating to the mandates between 1936 and 1939, during which period German colonial propaganda reached a peak.

[28] *New York Times,* March 18, 1937, sec. 13, p. 2.

[29] *Ibid.,* December 1, 1937, sec. 1, p. 4.

CHAPTER V: *World War II and Postwar*
Constitutional Changes

[1] A. Sicé, *L'Afrique Equatoriale Française et la Cameroun au service de la France* (Paris: Presses Universitaires de France, 1946), pp. 110-114. Sicé quotes the reply of de Coppet, Governor of Madagascar, surely a masterpiece of ambivalence: "Madagascar has decided to remain French until the end."

[2] *Free France,* Special Issue no. 4, New York, November, 1944, p. 5.

[3] Leclerc's activities became almost legend in the annals of desert warfare. See General Ingold, *L'Epopée Leclerc au Sahara, 1940-1943* (Paris: Berger-Levrault, 1945); Paul Moynet, *Victory in the Fezzan* (London: Fighting France Publications, 1944).

[4] *The Times* (London), February 3, 1941, p. 5.

[5] *Ibid.,* January 22, 1941, p. 3.

[6] See *Free France,* Special Issue no. 2, New York, September, 1944, pp. 6-13, for a résumé of the recommendations of the conference. See also the résumé in French in "L'Evolution Recente des Institutions Politiques dans les Territoires d'Outre-Mer et Territoires Associés," Ministère de la France d'Outre-Mer, *Documentation Française, Notes et Etudes Documentaires,* no. 1847 (March 11, 1954), pp. 1-3. For commentary see Kenneth Robinson, "The Public Law of Overseas France Since the War," *The Journal of Comparative Legislation,* third series, Vol. XXXII (1950), reprinted as no. 1 of the Reprint Series of the Oxford University Institute of Colonial Studies.

[7] F. Eboué, "Politique Indigène de l'Afrique Equatoriale Française" (Brazza-ville: 1941); English translation, *Free France,* Special Issue no. 2, pp. 15-34.

[8] The constitution was approved by the referendum of October 13, 1946, and came into force on December 24, 1946. The sections dealing with the French Union are grouped in Title VIII, Articles 60-82. See also Robinson, *op. cit.*, pp. 9-27.

[9] Lord Hailey, *An African Survey, Revised 1956* (New York: Oxford University Press, 1957), p. 213.

[10] The specifics are spelled out in a series of decrees dated October 25, 1946 (*Journal Officiel,* République Française, October 27, 1946, pp. 109-129,

150). See also the summary in *Notes et Etudes Documentaires, op. cit.*, pp. 26-31; and Hailey, *op. cit.*, pp. 342-344. For the relevant statute regarding the creation and powers of the Representative Assembly in the French Cameroons, see *Décret No. 46-2376 portant création d'une Assemblée réprésentative au Cameroun* in the *Rapport du Cameroun* (1947), pp. 220-226.

[11] Articles 80, 81, 82, of the constitution of 1946. The seeming quibble over the status of various persons in the former mandates preserved the old formal distinctions of which the *indigénat* was evidence, if not actual substance. The abolition of the *indigénat*, and consequently of the distinction, forced the constitution-makers to look for a new formula which would incorporate (1) the extension of citizenship rights (i.e., suffrage), (2) "citizenship of the French Union," (3) the possibilities of change in authority foreseen by the trusteeship arrangements and (4), the difference in status between the "administering" and the "administered." The result appears undeniably awkward, but sufficiently pliable to meet most objections to it.

[12] The applicable legislation is reviewed in *Notes et Etudes Documentaires, op. cit.*, pp. 16-17.

[13] *Ibid.*, p. 17.

[14] James S. Coleman, "Current Political Movements in Africa," *The Annals of the American Academy of Political and Social Science* (March, 1955), p. 97n.

[15] League of Nations, Twenty-first Ordinary Session of the Assembly, *General Questions, Report of the First Committee to the Assembly* (Geneva, April 17, 1946), L. N. Doc. A. 33, 1946, pp. 5-6.

[16] *Trusteeship Agreement for the Territory of the Cameroons Under French Administration*, U.N. Doc. T/8, March 25, 1947, p. 39.

[17] David Gardinier, "French Policy in the Cameroons, 1947-1957." Unpublished Ph.D. Dissertation, Yale University, New Haven, 1960. See also his book, *Cameroon, United Nations Challenge to French Policy* (London: Oxford University Press, 1963).

CHAPTER VI: *Ferment of Party Politics—1945-1955*

[1] *African Transcripts* (African Section, University Museum, University of Pennsylvania), no. 7 (Jan., 1946), p. 25; *ibid.*, no. 8 (March, 1946), p. 58. For an interesting description of the general condition of the Cameroun in 1945 and 1946, see Robert Delavignette's letter in *African Affairs*, vol. 46, no. 184 (July, 1947), pp. 151-155.

[2] Marc Ducat, "Du mandat à l'indépendance," *Marchés Tropicaux* (Nov. 21, 1959), p. 2548-2550.

[3] *Ibid.*, p. 2549.

[4] *Reports of the United Nations Visiting Mission to Trust Territories in West Africa.* U.N. Doc. T/798 Supp. no. 2 (New York, 1951), pp. 49-50. This and subsequent reports of United Nations Visiting Missions will be cited hereafter as *Visiting Mission Report*, with the year. Full citations of these reports will be found in the bibliography.

[5] *Ibid.*, pp. 48-49.

[6] *Rapport Annuel du Gouvernement Français à l'Assemblée Générale des Nations Unies sur l'Administration du Cameroun placé sous la tutelle de la France, Année 1947* (Paris: 1949), p. 92.

[7] J. Guilbot, *Petite Etude sur la main d'oeuvre à Douala* (Yaoundé: IFAN, Centre au Cameroun, 1948) provides statistical confirmation of this.

[8] Descriptive or analytical literature about the UPC is not extensive. See Ducat, *op. cit.*, pp. 2549-2550; Thomas Hodgkin, "The French Cameroons, Contemporary Political Alignments," *West Africa* (Dec. 11, 1954), p. 157; "Le problème national au Cameroun," *Le Bulletin—Documents et Recherches*, no. 6 (April 1, 1956), pp. 19-27; André Retif, "A Propos de l'Union des Populations du Cameroun: Communisme et Religion au Cameroun," *l'Afrique et l'Asie*, no. 33 (Nov., 1955); J.-M. Zang-Atangana, "Les forces politiques camerounais" (mimeo. *Mémoire* submitted to the Faculté de Droit de Paris, 1961); Fritz Schatten, *Afrika Schwarz oder Rot* (Munich: A. Piper, 1961), pp. 87-105, 249-254; "Zhertvi 'Krovavoi ruki'," *Aziia i Afrika Segodnia*, no. 6 (1961), pp. 38-41, and no. 7 (1961), pp. 49-51. See also the discussions in the United Nations Visiting Missions' Reports on the Cameroons under French administration as follows: U.N. Doc. T/798, Supp. no. 2 (New York, 1951), pp. 52-55; U.N. Doc. T/1110, Supp. no. 5 (New York, 1954), pp. 13-14; U.N. Doc. T/1240, Supp. no. 4 (New York, 1956), pp. 40, 41, 43-47; U.N. Doc. T/1427 (Jan. 23, 1959; mimeo.), pp. 28-78, *passim*. There is relevant commentary in Paul-Marie Gaudemet, "L'Autonomie Camerounaise," *Revue Française de Science Politique*, Vol. VIII, no. 1 (March, 1958), pp. 58-62; and in an unpublished study by George Horner, "The Response of Selected Cameroonian Ethnic Groups to French Political Institutions" (1958), which describes the events of the 1957 uprisings in the Sanaga-Maritime and the involvement of the Bassa people. Valuable insight into the UPC role in the development of Cameroun political life is provided in Franz Ansprenger, *Politik im Schwarzen Afrika* (Köln and Opladen: Westdeutscher Verlag, 1961), pp. 192-208, 392-404, and by David Gardinier, *Cameroon, United Nations Challenge to French Policy* (London: Oxford University Press, 1963).

[9] See James S. Coleman, "Togoland," *International Conciliation*, no. 509 (Sept., 1959), pp. 30-37.

[10] Interview with Mr. R. J. K. Dibonge, October 2, 1959. Mr. Dibonge claimed that when his French Cameroons Welfare Society allied itself with the UPC he was unaware that the UPC had Communist connections. When the matter came to his attention later on, he withdrew his affiliation.

[11] Hodgkin, *op. cit.*

[12] The French administration submitted a report to the 1955 U.N. Visiting Mission in which it detailed the "organization, activities, and propaganda methods" of the UPC (*Visiting Mission Report, 1956, op. cit.,* pp. 43-47). The French report gives the impression that the UPC organizational structure was set up during 1953 and 1954, yet petitions to the 1949 Visiting Mission from UPC groups indicate the pattern described in 1955 had already been initiated by 1949, a fact confirmed by Um Nyobé in his speech before the Kamerun United Congress at Kumba, December, 1951.

[13] A former UPC official, who wished to remain anonymous, described the process whereby the UPC set up local affiliate organizations, drawing into them young Camerounians, many of them well educated, who "burned with the fires of reform." He indicated that Douala offered the best locale for the formation of such groups, because of the presence of many young labor leaders, secondary-school graduates, and *emigré notables.*

[14] No. 1, Vol. I, was issued in April, 1948. *Visiting Mission Report, 1951, op. cit.,* p. 53. In 1960 a faction of the legally reinstated UPC began publication of *La Voix du Peuple,* ed. T. Mayi-Matip and J. P. Sende. The only connection between the two journals is the name.

[15] *Visiting Mission Report, 1956, op. cit.,* p. 16; Thomas Hodgkin, "French Cameroons" series, no. 5, "One Cameroons?" *West Africa* (Dec. 18, 1954), p. 187. See also Um Nyobé's speech to the Kumba Congress (Dec., 1951) in *Réunification Immédiate,* issued by the UPC (Douala: 1952), pp. 9-18.

[16] *Esocam* virtually disappeared by 1955, *Renaicam,* by 1957.

[17] In 1951, Um obtained 3,077 out of the 16,950 votes cast in the electoral district concerned. In the elections of March, 1952, the UPC put forward three candidates in three of the nineteen regions. None were elected. According to official figures they received 2,860 (Um), 803 (Kingué), and 211 (Moumié), votes respectively. Um attributed his party's electoral defeats to the administration's hostility, asserting that the elections were irregular and that the administration had placed every obstacle in the way of UPC candidates (*Visiting Mission Report,* 1954, p. 14).

[18] *Projet du Statut du Cameroun de 24 July 1953.*

[19] *Documents Parlementaires,* 1953 C. R., no. 122. At the time, Okala was a senator in the Council of the Republic, as well as a member of the local Assembly. Such duplication was not rare; Louis Aujoulat, Paul Soppo Priso, Ahmadou Ahidjo, Alexandre Douala Manga Bell, Charles Assalé, Jules Ninine, Charles Okala, Arouna N'joya, Daniel Kemajou, André-Marie Mbida, and others all served at one time or another in the metropolitan representative organs and simultaneously as members of the local Assembly. The dual role was possible because the sessions of the Assembly were shorter or at different times than those in the *métropole.* The point is important; the Camerounian legislators were able not only to gain experience at home, but learned parliamentary lore and the ways of the French political system first hand. The urbanity and skill of Okala, Soppo Priso, and Assalé show the result.

[20] Interview with Charles Assalé, October 16, 1955, in Yaoundé.

[21] Bamoun: *Union Bamoun, Assemblée Traditionelle du Peuple Bamoun;* Eton: *Association Traditionelle des peuples Eton-Manguissa-Batsenga;* Ewondo; *Kolo;* Fulani: *Koupé;* Musgum: *Union du Diamaré.*

[22] See U.N. Doc. A/C.4/SR. 309, 310, 311, 312 (Dec. 17 and 18, 1952); A/C 4/226/Add. 1 (Dec. 17, 1952). His subsequent appearances, at some of which he was accompanied by Moumié, Kingué, or Quandié, were in December, 1953 (see U.N. Docs. A/C.4/SH. 392 [Dec., 1953], A/C.4/261 [Dec. 5, 1953]), and again in November, 1954 (see U.N. Docs. A/C.4/SR, 442, 443 [Nov. 24 and 25, 1954], A/C.4/280 [Nov. 25, 1954], A/C.4/280/Add. 1 [Nov. 29, 1954]).

[23] At subsequent appearances for the UPC, testimony was given by Dr. Marcel Beybey-Eyidi, Jacques Ngom (General Secretary, Confederation Générale Kamerunais du Travail [CGKT]) and Ndeh Ntumazah (a British Cameroonian, who after 1957, headed the UPC affiliate in the British trust territory); testimony for the administration and for themselves, was given by Soppo Priso, Jean Ekwabi, and Dika Akwa. After 1956 Moumié carried the burden of the UPC appearances at the U.N. See U.N. Docs. A/C.4/SR. 714-728 (Nov. 22 and Dec. 3, 1957).

[24] Um claimed to have held no less than eighty-five public meetings in this connection. He had the text of his remarks before the UN printed in pamphlet form, entitled *Qu'est ce que veut le peuple Camerounais,* but claimed that 10,000 copies were seized by the French authorities at Douala. (U.N. Doc. A/C.4/SR. 393 [Dec. 5, 1953], p. 526.)

[25] Hodgkin, "The French Cameroons, Contemporary Political Alignments," p. 157.

[26] The 1955 Visiting Mission to the Cameroun estimated that it received 40,000 communications, 90 per cent from UPC sources. During 1954 and 1955 the Trusteeship Council received approximately 15,000 petitions, most of them from the UPC or its affiliates. In 1956 it received 33,026, 95 per cent of which came from UPC sources. See *Visiting Missions Report, 1956,* p. 17; *ibid.,* 1959, *op. cit.,* Annex I; U.N. Doc. T/L 671 (June 4, 1956).

[27] At his various appearances before the Fourth Committee, Um claimed that he, his lieutenants, and his party had been subject to a constant barrage of harassment, culminating in several assassination attempts against himself and Moumié. See "Le probleme national au Cameroun," *op. cit.,* for a partial recital of the UPC charges and specifications against the regime. How much of this is true is hard to assess. Certainly the administration did not like the UPC and made no effort to conceal the fact; it protested Um's appearance before the Fourth Committee, the reception of petitions and petitioners of the UPC by the visiting missions, and the appearance of Félix Moumié before the United Nations after 1955. The administration took every opportunity to label the organization *sovietique* and Communist. The evidence suggests that, as it grew more apprehensive about the UPC, the

administration took more active steps to keep it within bounds. It is also certain that UPC behavior often left much to be desired: it frequently directly incited local incidents and the language used by its spokesmen and in its publications was often inflammatory in the extreme.

[28] Ducat, *op. cit.*, p. 2551.

[29] *Petitions Concerning the Cameroons Under French Administration, Observations of the French Government as Administering Authority.* U.N. Doc. T/OBS.5/71 (Dec. 6, 1955), pp. 9, 10, 11.

[30] Interview with Administrateur de France d'Outre-Mer Jean Ribo, November 2, 1959.

[31] *Petitions Concerning the Cameroons . . . Observations of the French Government . . .* , pp. 9-12.

[32] *Report of the Trusteeship Council,* U.N. Doc., A/3170 Supp. 4 (New York, 1956), p. 151, and Petitions T/PET.5/612, T/PET.5/613.

[33] *Reunification Immédiate,* p. 26.

[34] Cited by Retif, *op. cit.*, p. 53, also found in full in "Vraie ou fausse independance," *Afrique Nouvelle,* April 15, 1955. Translation is mine.

[35] Félix-Roland Moumié, "Religion ou colonialisme" (Douala, April 22, 1955). A few sentences from this remarkable document give some indication of Moumié's argument and of its tone:

When there is a God-given promise to protect "the land that God gave us," then it is easy to understand that God cannot remain neutral in a struggle for national liberation. The Bible teaches us that as the Philistine invaders sought to lay waste to the land of Israel, God armed the young shepherd, David, with a sling to strike down General Goliath, the chief of the invaders. . . . Also, the advent of Jesus Christ is itself in part founded on the principle of the national liberation struggle. When Christ was born, his homeland was not an independent country, but a Roman colony, as the Kamerun is today a French colony. . . . The Magi, simple people from the land, went to Governor Herod to find out about the birth of the "new king of the Jews," but the Soucadeaux or Roland Pré of that time could not suffer any competition. He ordered the massacre of the newborn not to get rid of a prophet; in those days there were prophets in every crowd, and they didn't bother him since prophets at that time were mostly accomplices of Roman imperialism, just as the Graffins, Bonneaus, Bouqués, etc., [the bishops who authored the pastoral letter] of today are accomplices of colonialist oppression. King Herod wanted no newborn leader who would seize power and end Roman imperialism. . . . We ask the question: On whose side is God? Whenever God is on the side of Goliath and Pharaoh, Herod and Pilate, we submit that He sanctions colonial oppression. But when, on the other hand, as Scripture shows, God is on the side of David, Moses, Jesus Christ and the oppressed Palestine, we can draw the opposite conclusion, namely, that God is with those who fight against colonialism and seek their country's independence.

My translation is from a dittoed copy kindly sent by Professor David Gardinier.

[36] These are official figures, which break down as follows: 22 dead, 114 wounded among the rebels; two Africans and one European killed by the rebels, plus one dead and 62 wounded among the police and soldiery. *Afrique Nouvelle,* June 14, 1955, p. 4. Unofficial estimates run as high as 125 killed and 300 wounded on all sides.

[37] *Report of Trusteeship Council, loc. cit.*

[38] *Visiting Mission Report,* 1956, *op. cit.,* pp. 14-16.

[39] Other results: *North:* Jules Ninine (incumbent, Socialist), 73,711, Ahmadou Ahidjo (independent, but with *Démocrates* ties), 47,260. *Coast:* Douala Manga Bell (Independent), 22,619, Daniel Kemajou (Radical Socialist), 14,532, Marcel Beybey Eyidi (Independent), 6,996. Cited in Ansprenger, *op. cit.,* p. 201.

[40] Loi No. 56-619 de 23 Juin 1956. Earlier proposals had included a *projet de loi* (no. 11543, Oct. 6, 1955) which would have given the Cameroun a Council of Government consisting of four elected and four nominated members, with investigative and "informational" powers in respect to certain branches of administration; a *projet de loi* (no. 11600, Oct. 21, 1955) which would have instituted a Council of Government under the presidency of an elected official, with eight elected and five *ex officio* members; and the *projet de loi* ("loi Deferre" of Feb. 29, 1956) out of which the *loi-cadre* eventually grew.

[41] *Décret no. 57-501 du 16 Avril 1957 portant statut du Cameroun* (Journal Officiel de la République Française du 18 Avril 1957).

[42] See Horner, *op. cit.,* pp. 12-14, and, by the same author, "Togo and the Cameroon," *Current History* (Feb., 1958), pp. 89-90.

[43] Horner, "Togo and the Cameroon," p. 90.

[44] *Visiting Mission Report,* 1959, p. 32.

CHAPTER VII: *Politics of Consolidation—1955-1960*

[1] Text of Soppo Priso's alternative *projet* may be found in *Interafrique Presse, Bulletin Hebdomadaire,* no. 101 (Feb. 22, 1957), pp. 5-7.

[2] Marc Ducat, "Du mandat à l'indépendance," *Marchés Tropicaux* (Nov. 21, 1959), p. 2552. The official text was unavailable at the time of this writing.

[3] "The French Cameroons Today," *West Africa,* no. 2143 (May 10, 1958), p. 439.

[4] *United Nations Visiting Missions to Trust Territories in West Africa, 1958; Report on the Trust Territory of the Cameroons under French Administration* (New York: Jan. 23, 1959), p. 37. Subsequent citations of this and other

reports of United Nations visiting missions will appear as *Visiting Mission Report,* with the year. Full citations of all visiting mission reports may be found in the bibliography.

[5] *Interafrique Presse, op. cit.,* p. 4; *ibid.,* no. 112 (May 16, 1957), pp. 2-5; *ibid.,* no. 114 (May 30, 1957), pp. 2-4; *ibid.,* no. 116 (June 13, 1957), pp. 3-6.

[6] Interview with Dr. Marcel Beybey-Eyidi, October 27, 1959. I am also grateful to Dr. Beybey for copies of his newspaper *L'Opinion au Cameroun,* from which the excerpt cited in the next footnote is taken. At the time of Beybey's imprisonment, copies of the paper were also seized. Beybey later broke with Soppo Priso when the *Action Nationale* joined the Ahidjo government.

[7] "Appel au Peuple Camerounais," *L'Opinion au Cameroun,* 3d year, no. 54.

[8] *L'Opinion au Cameroun,* no. 22, May 17, 1957.

[9] *Discours prononcé le 9 Novembre 1957 à Boumnyebel* (Yaoundé: Ministère d'Etat a l'Information, Postes et Telecommunications, 1957), p. 24.

[10] A long, "Open letter to Um Nyobé," published in the January 6, 1957, issue of the Catholic-sponsored *Effort Camerounais,* preceded the meeting. The letter is remarkable for its gently rebuking tone.

[11] *Visiting Mission Report,* 1959, *op. cit.,* p. 34.

[12] Interview with Mbida in *Le Monde* (Paris), December 18, 1957.

[13] Act no. 58-148 of February 17, 1958.

[14] See also the article by George Chaffard in *Le Monde* (Paris), February 18, 1958.

[15] *New York Times,* February 28, 1960, p. 14.

[16] *Discours d'investiture prononcé par M. Ahidjo Ahmadou, Premier Ministre de l'Etat du Cameroun le 18 Février 1958 devant l'Assemblée Législative du Cameroun* (Yaoundé: Service de l'Information, 1959), pp. 5-26.

[17] Text of the resolutions is reproduced in the *Visiting Mission Report,* 1959, *op. cit.,* p. 41.

[18] As promulgated, *Ordonnance no. 58-1375 du 30 Decembre 1958 portant statut du Cameroun,* and the Conventions, as follows:
  a) *Convention Franco-Camerounaise sur l'exercice des pouvoirs reservées, les transferts et la cooperation inter-gouvernementale.*
  b) *Convention . . . relative à la situation des personnels employés au Cameroun dans les services de la République Française et dans les services de l'Etat du Cameroun.*

c) *Convention . . . relative à la défense, à l'ordre public et a l'emploi de la gendarmerie.*
d) *Convention judiciaire Franco-Camerounaise.*
e) *Convention . . . relative à la monnaie et au commerce extérieur.*
f) *Convention culturelle . . .*
g) *Convention . . . relative à l'aeronautique civile.*
h) *Convention . . . relative à la méteoroloqie.*

English translation may be found in the *Visiting Mission Report*, 1959, *op. cit.*, Annex III, pp. 1-43.

[19] See *Communication de M. Ahidjo Ahmadou, Premier Ministre de l'Etat du Cameroun le 18 Octobre 1958 à l'Assemblée Législative du Cameroun* (Yaoundé: Info-Cameroun, 1959).

[20] "Independence Foreshadowed for French Cameroons," *United Nations Review* (Dec., 1958), p. 30. See also Guy Devernois, "Cameroons 1958-59 from Trusteeship to Independence," *Civilisations*, Vol. IX, no. 2 (1959), pp. 229-234, which also contains an analysis of the 1959 Statute of the Cameroun.

[21] Resol. 1282 (XII), *Records of the Twelfth General Assembly of the United Nations.*

[22] For example: Anon., *Le fascisme n'aura aucun succès au Kamerun* (Cairo: 1958); Abdul-Baghi Maw'ndi Mohammadu Raji, *Le bluff Ahidjo* (Cairo: Direction de l'UPC, 1958); *L'O.N.U. et le problème Kamerunais* (Cairo: Service de l'Information de l'UPC à l'Etranger, 1959; *La Tutelle Internationale a l'Epreuve* (Cairo: Service de l'Information . . . , 1959). Dr. Moumié was kind enough to send me copies of the journal *La Voix du Kamerun*, which had on their covers (among other things) the official UPC emblem, a crab on a field of red. The explanation below the emblem: "*Red* of the blood of the patriots who have died for the national cause, *Crab* of the Rios dos Camaroes, original name of the Kamerun." The UPC researchers appear even worse marine zoölogists than the Portuguese: *Camaroes* refers to shrimp, not crabs, and, moreover, what the Portuguese saw were crayfish, not prawns or crabs.

[23] "Le Cameroun à la veille de l'autonomie interne, la mort d'Um Nyobé," *Le Monde*, Selection Hebdomadaire (Dec. 25 through 31, 1958), p. 2.

[24] "Doctor of Revolt," *Drum* (Oct., 1959), pp. 27-28.

[25] For example, in May, 1959, during a series of conferences between Ahidjo and Southern Cameroonian Premier Foncha on the reunification question, Ghana and Guinea issued a joint communiqué in which they stated that ". . . they were willing to take their full part in the national reconciliation of the populations of the Cameroons, and the establishment of a truly representative and democratic government before the accession of the country to independence." The communiqué went on to ask for unconditional

amnesty for condemned politicians, abrogation of the decrees dissolving the UPC, and the holding of "free" general elections before the end of 1959. The communiqué was, in essence, a restatement of the UPC position at that time.

[26] My conversations with French, Cameroun, and British officials left me with the impression that there was no doubt who was supplying rebel UPC forces in the field. All pointed to Guinea, and all felt that as soon as Guinea withdrew its support the UPC would fold up.

[27] The *Armée de libération nationale kamerunaise* (ALNK) appears to have been the successor to the *Comité Nationale d'Organisation* (formed in 1956) as the directive apparatus of the UPC militants in the Cameroun itself. It is probable that the organizational form and the name were borrowed from the Algerian *Front de Libération Nationale* (FLN), with those aims the UPC has repeatedly declared its sympathies and whose methods had been viewed with approval by Moumié.

[28] See Philipe Decraene, "La Mort d'Um Nyobe a porté un coup decisif au mouvement insurrectionel de la Sanaga-Maritime," *Le Monde*, December 19, 1958, p. 4.

[29] *Visiting Mission Report,* 1959, p. 50.

[30] *Loc. cit.*

[31] *Ibid.*, p. 51. See also "Le Cameroun à la veille de l'autonomie interne . . . ," *op. cit.*, and "End of a Rebellion," *West Africa*, no. 2174 (Dec. 13, 1958).

[32] *Ordonnance No. 58-1375 du 30 décembre 1958 portant statut du Cameroun,* Journal Officiel de la République Française du 31 decembre 1958.

[33] *Ibid., préambule.*

[34] U.N. *Visiting Mission Report,* 1959, *op. cit.* For a summary of the reports on both Cameroons, see "Mission's Reports on Two Territories," *United Nations Review*, March, 1959, pp. 31-37.

[35] *Visiting Mission Report,* 1959, par. 134.

[36] *Ibid.*

[37] *Ibid.*, par. 141.

[38] The bill itself—granting amnesty to a wide spectrum of persons involved in UPC uprisings and holding out the possibility of commutation of sentence to others convicted of capital offenses—passed the Legislative Assembly on February 14 by a vote of thirty-seven to seven. Only Mbida's *Démocrates*, leaderless and confused, voted against the measure. They claimed the bill

was not inclusive enough. See Etat du Cameroun, *Journal Officiel des Débats de l'Assemblée Législative du Cameroun, Session 1958-1959,* plenary meeting of February 14, 1959 (afternoon), pp. 253-268.

[39] Moumié arrived, accompanied by Mme. Marthe Ouandié (for the UDFC). Mbida came from Conakry. Pro-UPC spokesmen from the Cameroun included Dr. Marcel Beybey Eyidi, Martin Tchapchet, and Dr. Phillipe Mbarga Manga. The *rallié* UPC was represented by Mayi-Matip. Among the non-UPC petitioners were Moussa Yaya (UC), Benoit Bindzi (MRPC), Paul Monthé (Paysans Independants), and Gaston Kingue-Jong (AN). It should also be observed that the word "group" seems to have been loosely interpreted by the petitioners. Of the "groups" represented, only fourteen had any noteworthy membership. Most of the others had only an ephemeral existence. See Appendix A.

[40] Resolution 1925 (XXIII), of February 17, 1959.

[41] See *Official Records of the General Assembly, Thirteenth Session, Annexes* (agenda item 13), U.N. Doc. A/4094.

[42] The debates in the Fourth Committee are reported in full in *Official Records of the General Assembly, Thirteenth Session,* Fourth Committee, 845th through 871st meetings (U.N. Docs. A/C.4/SR.845-871). The debates are summarized in "Assembly Charts Course for the Cameroons," *United Nations Review,* April, 1959, pp. 45-53. See also *The New York Times,* February 22, 1959, p. 3; March 3, p. 6; March 5, p. 3; March 7, p. 2; March 11, p. 9; March 12, p. 5; March 13, p. 2; March 14, p. 23; and March 18, p. 34; and *The Economist* (London), March 21, 1959, pp. 1081-1082.

[43] See U.N. Doc. A/C.4/SR.847 (1959).

[44] Resolution 1349 (XIII). "The future of the Trust Territory of the Cameroons under French Administration." (Adopted March 13, 1959.) The operative portions of the resolution read as follows:

The General Assembly . . .

1. *Resolves,* in agreement with the Administering Authority, that, on 1 January 1960, when the Cameroons under French Administration becomes independent, the Trusteeship Agreement approved by the General Assembly on 13 December 1946 shall cease to be in force in accordance with Article 76b of the Charter of the United Nations;

2. *Expresses its confidence* that, at the earliest possible date after the attainment of independence on 1 January 1960, elections will be held for the formation of a new Assembly which should take decisions regarding the establishment, in their final form, of the institutions of the free and independent Cameroons;

3. *Recommends* that, upon the attainment of independence on 1 January 1960, the Cameroons under French administration should be admitted to membership in the United Nations according to Article 4 of the Charter.

[45] *Presse du Cameroun* (Yaoundé), April 12, 1959, p. 1. Translation mine.

[46] The seats in the Sanaga-Maritime were won by Mayi-Matip and the members of his list: Silas Mbong Bayem, Martin Inack Njoke, Jean Nonga Yomb.

Mayi's list received 35,020 votes, the next list 6,191, and a third 4,251. The winning list in the Bamiléké by-election, the *Liste Kumsze,* included Daniel Lontsi (secretary-general of the *Kumsze*) and Grégoire Ndékou Python, and received 6,592 votes. See *Presse du Cameroun,* April 14, 1959, p. 1. The French Conseil d'Etat had, incidentally, annulled the elections of the two slain deputies from the Sanaga-Maritime.

⁴⁷ *Déclaration du Bureau du Comité Directeur de l'U.P.C.,* Cairo, April 1, 1959 (mimeo.). Translation mine.

⁴⁸ An Egyptian official (who must remain unidentified) told me that Moumié's relations with Communists in Cairo and abroad had become "dangerous" to the state during 1959. He (Moumié) was unofficially told that he would get help to "fight colonialism," but not to fight "other Camerounians." Told to "make up his mind," Moumié chose to leave Cairo, but left a representative in Cairo until the beginning of 1960, when Cairo sent an official representative to the Cameroun's independence day celebration. This, according to my informant, so enraged Moumié (who felt that it amounted to recognition of the Ahidjo regime) that he began to attack the UAR publicly. My informant wished it stressed that Moumié was welcome in Cairo only so long as he was "fighting against *French* colonialism," and that during his stay he was under more or less constant surveillance. Cairo, my informant pointed out, "never accepted all his activities," and gave Moumié no more than "the usual aid to refugees."

⁴⁹ *Presse du Cameroun,* May 26, 1959, p. 1.

⁵⁰ *Ibid.,* June 4, 1959, p. 1. Translation mine.

⁵¹ *Ibid.,* July 7, 1959, p. 1. The "program" was preceded by a circular letter from Cairo, which, among other things, stated the following:

We nevertheless take as our point of departure the criterion that those who are not with us are against us, and that as such deserve the treatment reserved for traitors. We have decided to continue the revolution until the end. There is no longer any other solution. We have clearly and precisely stated that the time for words is past. We maintain that position now. Unity will be accomplished by revolutionary action inside as well as outside the party. We must nevertheless remain unyielding toward the traitors. The breathing space we granted them is over. We must, therefore, begin to act. [Translation mine.]

(*Circulaire à tous les organismes de l'U.P.C.,* no. 194/BCD/UPC/QD, Cairo, June 4, 1954.)

⁵² *Presse du Cameroun,* July 4, 5, 6, 7, 8, 9, 10, 15, 16, 17, 18, 19, 27, 28, 1959.

⁵³ The others were: *Kamerun mon Pays, Ma Patrie le Cameroun, La Nation Kamerunaise, Le Travailleur Kamerunais,* and *Le Paysan.*

⁵⁴ The pattern of terrorist depredations from the fall of 1959 onward has been one of decreasing frequency and severity. There was a marked drop in incidents after the UPC was legally reinstated in February, 1960, and by

April, 1961, most of the troubled areas had become peaceful again. Only occasional raids by terrorist gangs served to remind the public that a threat existed. During February and March, 1961, I was able to undertake an extensive motor tour of several areas in the Bamiléké, Mbam, and Mungo *départements* which had previously been considered too dangerous to be traveled without military escort.

⁵⁵ *Presse du Cameroun,* notably July 10, 28; August 20 and September 28, 1959. On the last-mentioned date, a group of 257 Bassa tribesmen *ralliés* returned from the British Cameroons. There are no exact figures on the number of repatriated and *ralliés,* but official sources have estimated that between three and five thousand persons were involved in *ralliéments* between June, 1959, and February, 1961. These represent persons of whom official cognizance was taken; no one knows how many more returned but were never officially counted. In the latter category are the inhabitants of a number of villages who were known to have been "in the *maquis,*" but are no longer so.

⁵⁶ Statement issued by a group of twenty-six *ralliés; Presse du Cameroun,* July 28, 1959, p. 1.

⁵⁷ This was brought out in a series of interviews I conducted between October 9 and 30, 1959, in Yaoundé and Douala. My sources, who refused to be quoted or identified, were authoritative, in that they spoke (or purported to speak) for specific groups or sectors of opinion.

⁵⁸ *Presse du Cameroun,* August 20, 1959, p. 1.

⁵⁹ Reference is made to the offer of Emperor Haile Selassie, as well as to the one of the foreign ministers attending the Conference of Independent African States at Monrovia in August, 1959.

⁶⁰ September 9, 1959, cited in Franz Ansprenger, *Politik im Schwarzen Afrika* (Köln and Opladen: Westdeutscher Verlag, 1961), p. 394. Translation is mine.

⁶¹ Njiné resigned on September 11; a government communiqué claimed that he had not maintained "a sufficiently energetic policy" with regard to the "present," that is, terrorist, situation. Three days later Njiné issued his own communiqué explaining that his break with the government was due to a "divergence of views on the measures needed in the current crisis." Among his recommendations, Njiné urged that the government pursue a "policy of rapprochement of all Camerounians, be they within or outside the Cameroun."

⁶² *Presse du Cameroun,* October 13, 1959, p. 1. Translation is mine.

⁶³ See Chambre de Commerce et d'Industrie du Cameroun, *Exposé sur la Situation Economique du Cameroun au 1ᵉʳ Janvier 1960* (Douala: Feb., 1960).

⁶⁴ Etat du Cameroun, *Journal Officiel des Débats de l'Assemblée Législative*

du Cameroun, Session de 1957-1958, plenary session of February 18, 1958, pp. 266-309.

[65] *Loi No. 59-56 du 31 Octobre 1959 accordant au gouvernement le pouvoir de légiférer et de préparer la Constitution Camerounaise.*

[66] *Loi No. 59-57 du 31 Octobre 1959 portant amnistie pleine et entière des faits à caractere politique ou en rapport direct avec des incidents d'origine politique commis avant la publication de cette loi dans les départements de Sanaga-Maritime et Nyong-et-Sanaga.*

[67] *Journal Officiel des Débats, Année Legislative 1959-1960.* First annual ordinary session, plenary meeting of October 20, 1959 (afternoon), pp. 15-19, *passim.* (See also radio talk by Ahidjo explaining *pleins pouvoirs* reprinted in *Presse du Cameroun,* Nov. 8 and 9, 1959, p. 1.)

[68] *Ibid.,* plenary meeting of October 23, 1959, p. 29. Translation is mine.

[69] *Ibid.* Translation mine.

[70] *Ibid.,* plenary meeting of October 29, 1959, p. 35. Translation mine.

[71] As is often true in debates of this kind, both Soppo and Ahidjo told only part of the story. Although it was true that the Assembly and the government could ask for a modification of the Statute, such modification was subject to challenge by the High Commissioner and/or subsequent annulment on the advice of the Conseil d'Etat. According to Article 26 of the Statute of the Cameroun, annulment could occur only if a law or decree were patently in derogation of the French constitution, international treaties concluded by France, or the Statute of the Cameroun. Soppo's protest, while correct in principle, was in fact beside the point. The Assembly could pass any law it wished, even one abolishing the Statute. The mere fact that such a law was patently unconstitutional and would surely be annuled could not prevent the Assembly from passing it.

[72] *Débats,* plenary meeting of October 29, 1959, p. 38. A UPC pamphlet, *The UPC Denounces the Planned Systematic Tortures in the Kamerun* (Cairo: July, 1958), listed nine alleged "concentration camps or penitentiaries" in the Cameroun: Mokolo, Marena, and Yoko, in the north Cameroun; Doume, Yokadouma, Baham, Bafoussam, Bamoungoum, Bansoa, and Dschange, in the south, with the latter five located in the Bamiléké region.

[73] *Débats,* plenary meeting of Oct. 29, 1959, p. 39. Translation mine.

[74] *Ibid.,* p. 40.

[75] The composition of the ALCAM at the beginning of the session was as follows:

Groupe d'Union Camerounaise	38 seats
Intergroupe des Noninscrits	7 seats
Groupe des Démocrates	8 seats
Groupe d'Action Parlementaire pour le Salut National (UPC ralliés)	8 seats
Groupe d'Action Nationale	7 seats
Unaffiliated	2 seats

[76] *Débats*, p. 78. I was present at this session and can confirm the frenzy with which the government benches applauded M. Okala. It was quite natural, because before Okala spoke the opposition had all the best lines. Translation mine.

[77] See U.N. Docs. A/C. 4/933–960 (Oct. 30 to Nov. 19, 1959).

[78] It is interesting to note that they did not oppose the Cameroun's entrance into the United Nations in 1960. Moreover, most of the former friends of Dr. Moumié soon granted the Cameroun official recognition. Liberia and the UAR were among the first African nations to set up legations in Yaoundé.

[79] *Presse du Cameroun*, November 17, 1959, p. 1. Translation mine.

[80] *Ibid.*, December 25, 1959, p. 1. Translation mine.

CHAPTER VIII: *Politics in the British Cameroons*

[1] John H. Kautsky, *Political Change in Underdeveloped Countries: Nationalism and Communism* (New York: John Wiley and Sons, 1963).

[2] The Covenant of the League of Nations stipulated that "C" mandates "can be administered under the laws of the Mandatory as integral portions of its territory" (Art. 22, sec. 6). Under a broad interpretation of this article, the mandates for both Togo and the Cameroons (Art. 9) permitted the mandatory power to administer them as an "integral part" of its *adjoining* territory— not of the metropolitan country itself. In the French Cameroun, early responsibility was channeled through Brazzaville. Under Article 9, Nigeria provided administrative services for the British Cameroons. By Ordinance no. 1 of 1924, the bulk of Nigerian law was made applicable to the British Cameroons. See Quincy Wright, *Mandates Under the League of Nations* (Chicago: University of Chicago Press, 1930), pp. 414-415.

[3] See *Reports on the Cameroons* for 1925, 1928, 1930, 1935, and 1938 in particular.

[4] *Décret* of August 15, 1925 (*Journal Officiel, no. 27*, Aug. 15, 1925), p. 323.

[5] The authoritative exposition of the policy is set out in Lord Frederick Lugard's *The Dual Mandate in British Tropical Africa* (2d ed.; London: William Blackwood and Sons, 1923). The British annual *Reports* for

both 1924 and 1925 provided short but concise descriptions of the aims of the mandate in "indirect rule" terms. Among the better commentaries and descriptions of the system are the following: Lord Hailey, *An African Survey, Revised 1956* (New York: Oxford University Press, 1957), pp. 186-206; Lucy P. Mair, *Native Policies in Africa* (London: Routledge and Sons, 1936), pp. 118-137; Hans Wieschhoff, *Colonial Policy in Africa* (Phila.: University of Pennsylvania Press, 1944), pp. 62-90; Donald Cameron, *Principles of Native Administration and their Application* (Lagos: Government Printer, 1934). An evaluation of the Nigerian experience under the system of indirect rule is found in James Coleman, *Nigeria: Background to Nationalism* (Berkeley and Los Angeles: University of California Press, 1958). Lugard's biographer, Margery Perham, in her excellent *Lugard, the Years of Authority* (London: Collins, 1960), contributes a lucid exposition of the system, pp. 377-641, *passim*.

⁶ *Report on the Cameroons* (1938), p. 15.

⁷ For an exhaustive discussion of the whole question of administrative unions under the trusteeship system, see Nicolas Veicopolous, *Traité des Territoires Dépendants, Tome I, Le Système de Tutelle d'Apres la Charte de San Francisco* (Athens: Institut Français d'Athenes, 1960), pp. 158-168, *vide* particularly note 300, pp. 159-166.

⁸ U.N. Doc. T/AC.14/24 (1948).

⁹ *Reports of the United Nations Visiting Mission to Trust Territories in West Africa: Report on the Cameroons Under British Administration.* U.N. Doc. Supp. no. 2 (T/798) (New York: 1951), p. 15.

¹⁰ *Ibid.*, p. 13.

¹¹ In the preparation of the several pages dealing with the development of political groups in the Southern Cameroons, I have drawn heavily upon Edwin Ardener's "The Political History of Cameroon," *The World Today*, vol. 18, no. 8 (Aug., 1962); Ardener's several articles in *West Africa* (appearing between 1958 and 1961); David Gardinier's "The Movement to Reunify the Cameroons," a paper presented at the 1960 meeting of the African Studies Association; and my own researches in the Southern Cameroons in 1959 and 1961. A detailed study of the rise of Southern Cameroons nationalism has yet to appear; therefore, my summary does not claim the completeness or the precision that Ardener—who probably knows more about the subject than anyone else—could provide. My discussion of the 1961 plebiscites is based entirely upon my own field research in both parts of the British Cameroons immediately before, during, and after the plebiscites.

¹² *Reports of the . . . Visiting Mission . . .* (1951), p. 15.

¹³ *Ibid.*

¹⁴ Gardinier, *op. cit.*, p. 3.

[15] *Petition from the Cameroons National Federation Concerning the Cameroons Under British and French Administration.* UN Doc. T/PET.4/16 (Dec., 1949), p. 10.

[16] "Intervention de UM NYOBE au Congres de Kumba (14-17 décembre 1961)," [Comité Directeur de l'UPC] *Unification Immédiate du Cameroun* (1952), pp. 9-18, *passim.*

[17] "Déclaration commune des réprésentants du mouvement national camerounais (Tiko, 22 août 1952)," *ibid.,* pp. 19-20.

[18] Ardener, *op. cit.,* p. 345.

[19] *Ibid.,* p. 346.

[20] *Ibid.*

[21] *Ibid.,* p. 348.

[22] *United Nations Visiting Mission to Trust Territories in West Africa, 1958; Report on the Trust Territory of the Cameroons Under British Administration.* U.N. Doc. T/1426 (Jan. 20, 1959, mimeo.), p. 43.

[23] *Addendum to the Report on the Trust Territory of the Cameroons Under British Administration (T/1426).* U.N. Doc. T/1426/Add. 1 (Feb. 6, 1959, mimeo.).

[24] A full summary of the discussions at the spring General Assembly session is found in "Assembly Charts Course for Cameroons," *United Nations Review,* April, 1959, pp. 16-18, 45-53.

[25] *Report of the Mamfe Conference on the Plebiscite Questions & Register, August 10 and 11, 1959* (Sept., 1959, mimeo.).

[26] U.N. Doc. A/C.4/SR 885 (Sept. 24, 1959), p. 15. The discussions during the fall Assembly session are fully summarized in "Assembly Recommends New Date for Plebiscite in Southern Cameroons," *United Nations Review,* November, 1959, pp. 10-13, 27-28.

[27] Quoted in *Daily Times* (Lagos, Nigeria), September 26, 1959, p. 8.

[28] U.N. Doc. A/C.4/SR 885, p. 17.

[29] U.N. Doc. A/C.4/414 (Sept. 30, 1959).

[30] *Report of the Fourth Committee.* U.N. Doc. A/4240 (Oct. 14, 1959).

[31] *Report of the United Nations Commissioner for the Supervision of the Plebiscite in the Cameroons Under United Kingdom Administration.* (Djalal Abdoh.) U.N. Docs. T/1491 (Nov. 25, 1959), T/1491/Corr. 1, T/1491/Add. 1.

[32] *Southern Cameroons Plebiscite, 1961, The Two Alternatives* (n.d.). (Printed By Authority [of the Commissioner for the Southern Cameroons under United Kingdom Trusteeship].)

[33] République du Cameroun. Ministère des Affaires Etrangeres. *Communiqué* (Dec. 31, 1960). The question arose during an interview with Foncha, when I asked him what he thought of the Republic's position on the future of the Northern Cameroons. Fortunately, I had a copy of the communiqué with me, but I never did get an answer to my question.

[34] *Report of the United Nations Plebiscite Commissioner for the Cameroons under United Kingdom Administration; Plebiscites in the southern and northern parts of the Territory, on 11 and 12 February 1961.* U.N. Doc. T/1556 (April 3, 1961). Reuben Frodin, "Flies in the Trusteeship Ointment," American Universities Field Staff *Reports*, RF-1-'61 (Feb. 25, 1961); Victor T. Le Vine, "The 'Other Cameroons,'" *Africa Report* (Feb., 1961), p. 5; "'P' Day in the Cameroons," *West Africa*, no. 2283 (Mar. 4, 1961), p. 236; no. 2284 (Mar. 11, 1961), p. 265.

[35] On December 2, 1963, the International Court of Justice decided that, inasmuch as the General Assembly had terminated trusteeship (Resolution 1608 [XV]), the Court could not accept jurisdiction, even for a declaratory judgment.

[36] For further discussion of the problems encountered in trying to create the new federal republic, see Victor T. Le Vine, "Unifying the Cameroons," *West Africa* (Sept. 15, 1961), pp. 774-775; and "The New Cameroon Federation," *Africa Report* (Dec., 1961), pp. 7-8, 10; "Prospects for the Cameroun Federation," *West Africa* (Sept. 30, 1961), p. 1073. The Cameroun's charges relating to the conduct of the Northern Cameroons plebiscite are found in a pamphlet edited by the Cameroun Ministry of Foreign Affairs and Secretariat of State of Information, *La position de la République du Cameroun à la suite du plébiscite des 11 et 12 février 1961 dans la partie septentrionale du Territoire du Cameroun sous administration du Royaume-Uni de Grande-Bretagne et d'Irlandie du Nord* (Yaoundé: 1961).

CHAPTER IX: *Problems of Transition*

[1] Remarks made to a group of visiting European parliamentarians, *Presse du Cameroun,* July 18 and 19, 1959, p. 1. Translation mine.

[2] Between September 26 and October 30, 1959, I conducted a series of informal interviews with various French and Camerounian officials in Yaoundé and Douala. The French attitude was expressed by a typical remark made by one administrator: "Why rock the boat while we're still in it?" A young Camerounian in the Ministry of Finances put it thus, "Nothing matters now except getting independence; when we are free, then we can worry about what to do with our freedom."

[3] *La Voix du Peuple* (Douala), January 1, 1960, p. 3. Translation mine.

[4] This was confirmed during a conversation with M. Mayi-Matip on December 17, 1959.

[5] See also Edwin Ardener, "The Kamerun Idea," *West Africa*, no. 2147 (June 7, 1958), p. 533, and no. 2148 (June 14, 1958), p. 559; J. R. Prescott, "Nigeria's International Boundaries: I, The Eastern and the Cameroons," *West Africa* (June 4, 1960), p. 628; P. C. Mafiamba, "Nigeria Kamerun Border," *West Africa* (Oct. 22, 1960), p. 1190.

[6] These themes are developed at length in Victor T. Le Vine, "The Cameroun Federal Republic," in Gwendolen Carter, ed., *Five African States* (Ithaca: Cornell University Press, 1963).

[7] Karl W. Deutsch, *Nationalism and Social Communication* (New York: John Wiley and Sons, 1953), p. 31.

[8] John Plamenatz, *On Alien Rule and Self-Government* (New York: Longmans, Green and Co., 1960), p. 66.

[9] Victor T. Le Vine, "Political Parties in the Cameroun," unpublished MS, December, 1960.

[10] "The Cameroun Federal Republic," in Carter, *op. cit.*, pp. 321-334.

[11] "La conférence de presse donnée a Yaounde le 2 Juillet par le President de la République Fédérale du Cameroun; S. E. Excellence Ahmadou Ahidjo repond aux questions des Journalistes," supplement to *Presse du Cameroun* (Yaoundé), July 22, 1963.

[12] Ruth Schachter (Morgenthau), "Single-Party Systems in West Africa," *American Political Science Review*, Vol. LV, no. 2 (June, 1961), pp. 294-307.

[13] Communiqué published by the Cameroun Ministry of the Interior, February 28, 1960. The ten dissenting *départements* were: Dja-et-Lobo, Haut Nyong, Kribi, Mbam, Mungo, Knam, Nyong-et-Kelle, Nyong-et-Sanga, Sanaga-Maritime, and Wouri. The Bamiléké *Département*, which was expected to reject the constitution, voted to accept it, 67,272 to 13,952.

[14] The full text of the three paragraphs is given below (translation mine):

The State of the Cameroun, conscious of the need to develop its economy in liberty, and of the necessity of a participation of capital from all sources in this development, is anxious to include in its institutions such codes, conventions, and contracts as will most usefully bring this about. It expects henceforth, in agreement with interested countries and international organisms, to seek all means of creating the best conditions possible for capital desiring to invest in enterprises of profit to both parties.

The Camerounian people affirms its desire for the realization of close coöperation with all African states to the end of bringing about, in independence, the formation of a free and united Africa.

It [the Camerounian people] proclaims its wish to do everything to satisfy the aspirations of Camerounians living in territories outside the fatherland, to the end of permitting them to reënter the national community and live fraternally in a reunited Cameroun. [Perhaps the closest parallel to the second paragraph is the provision in the Ghanaian constitution which promises a surrender of Ghana's sovereignty to a future pan-African political union.]

[15] Article 11 (Title III). The key phrase is "il assure par son arbitrage le fonctionnement des pouvoirs publics ... " "Arbitrage" in this context can be most meaningfully translated as "impartial intercession," a phrase corresponding to the sense in which the president is considered to be above partisan considerations and representative of the nation as a whole.

[16] Article 14 (Title III), Article 36 (Title V, Section III). Although the constitution permitted interpellations, the government could not fall because of one. Further, Articles 35 and 36 provided that the fall of a government gives the President of the Republic the option of dissolving the Assembly and calling new elections.

[17] Article 20 (Title III).

[18] Article 23 (Title V, Section I).

[19] Interviews with four members of the Consultative Committee, October and November, 1960. The four interviewees, of whom three were members of the government party, refused either to be quoted or to permit their names to be recorded.

[20] Helen Kitchen, "Cameroun Faces Troubled Future," *Africa Special Report* (Jan., 1960), vol. 3, no. 1, p. 14.

[21] P. F. Gonidec subjects the new federal constitution to an exhaustive analysis in "Les Institutions Politiques de la Republique Federale du Cameroun," *Civilisations,* Vol. XI, no. 4 (1961), pp. 370-395, and *ibid.,* Vol. XII, no. 1 (1962), pp. 13-22. His discussions of political trends and events is less noteworthy.

[22] "The Cameroun Federal Republic," in Carter, *op. cit.*

[23] Etat du Cameroun, Ministère des Finances, *Budget de l'Exercice 1959;* Haut Commission de la République francaise au Cameroun, "Aide financière apportée par la France au Cameroun dépuis la seconde guerre mondiale" (mimeo.), 1959; République du Cameroun, Ministère des Finances, *Budget de l'Exercice 1960-1961, Budget de l'Exercice 1961-1962;* US Department of Commerce, *Economic Developments in the Federal Republic of Cameroon, 1961* (W. Courtney), pp. 6-7. The reported aid for 1961 came to 3,165,000,000 francs CFA (about $13,187,500), but this figure does not include hidden charges such as market subsidies, military aid, and so on. (Gilbert Comte, "La coopération avec la France," in "Le Cameroun dix-huit mois après l'indépendance," *Europe France-Outre-Mer.*)

²⁴ See note 23, "Aide financière apportée par la France. . . ."

²⁵ *La Semaine Camerounaise*, April 1, 1963, cited by David Gardinier, *Cameroon, United Nations Challenge to French Policy* (London: Oxford University Press, 1963), p. 98.

²⁶ *Bulletin Quotidien de l'Agence Camerounaise de Presse* (Yaoundé), November 30, 1960.

Bibliography

Bibliography

BOOKS

Abs, P[aul] J[oseph] M[aria]. *Der Kampf um Unsere Schutzgebiete.* Essen/ Rhur: F. Floeder, 1926.

Almond, Gabriel, and James S. Coleman. *The Politics of the Developing Areas.* Princeton: Princeton University Press, 1960.

Ansprenger, Franz, *Politik im Schwarzen Afrika; Die Modernen politischen Bewegungen im Afrika französischer Prägung.* Köln and Opladen: Westdeutchen Verlag, 1961.

Ardener, Edwin. *Coastal Bantu of the Cameroons.* London: International African Institute, 1956. (Ethnographic Survey of Africa, no. 9.)

Ardener, Edwin and Shirley, and A. Warmington. *Plantation and Village in the Cameroons.* London: Oxford University Press, 1960.

Aujoulat, L[ouis] P[aul]. *Aujourd'hui l'Afrique.* Paris: Casterman, 1960.

Aymerich, Joseph G. (General). *La Conquête du Cameroun.* Paris: Payot, 1931.

Balandier, Georges. *Sociologie des Brazzavilles Noires.* Paris: Presses Universitaires de France, 1957.

Baumann, H., and D. Westerman. *Peuples et civilisations de l'Afrique.* Paris: Presses Universitaires de France, 1948.

Becker, T. H. *Das Schulwesen in Afrika.* (Band XII 1/2, Afrika Handbuch der praktischen Kolonialwissenschaften). Berlin: Walter de Gruyter, 1943.

Beer, George Louis. *African Questions at the Paris Peace Conference.* New York: Macmillan, 1923.

de Belleau, de Lyée. *Du Cameroun au Hoggar.* Paris: Alsatia, 1945.

Bentwich, N. C. *Le système des mandats.* Hague: Hague Academy, 1929.

Bergfeld, Ewald. *Die Französischen Mandatsgebiete Kamerun und Togo.* Greifswald: H. Adler, 1935.

Betts, Raymond F. *Assimilation and Association in French Colonial Theory, 1890-1914.* New York: Columbia University Press, 1961.

Binet, Jacques. *Budgets Familiaux des planteurs de cacao au Cameroun.* Paris: Office de la recherche scientifique et technique de la France d'Outre-Mer, 1956.

Bouchaud, Joseph, C.S.E. *La côte du Cameroun dans l'histoire, et la cartographie dès origines à l'annexion Allemande.* Yaoundé: IFAN, Centre au Cameroun, 1952. (Memoires de l'IFAN.)

————. *L'Eglise en Afrique Noire.* Paris: La Palatine, 1958.

————. *Histoire et géographie du Cameroun.* Douala: 1944.

Bruel, G. *La France équatoriale africaine.* Paris: Laroze, 1935.

Bruel, Max. *Kampf im Urwald, von Urwald Göttern und Schicksalen Deutscher Pflanzer und Soldaten in Kamerun.* Leipzig: Julius Klinkhardt, 1940.

Brunschwig, Henri. *L'Expansion allemande outre-mer du VX siècle à nos jours.* Paris: Presses Universitaires de France, 1957.

Buell, Raymond Leslie. *The Native Problem in Africa,* Vol. II. New York: Macmillan, 1928.

Carter, Gwendolen, ed. *Five African States.* Ithaca: Cornell University Press, 1963.

Chauleur, Pierre. *L'Oeuvre de la France au Cameroun.* Yaoundé: Imprimerie du Gouvernment, 1936.

Chazelas, Victor. *Territoires sous mandat de la France, Cameroun et Togo.* Paris: Societé d'editions géographiques, maritimes et coloniales, 1931.

Chot, Robert, ed. *Le Cameroun, aspect géographique, historique, touristique, adminisitratif du territoire.* Paris: Editions Alepie, 1954.

Cohen, Sir Andrew. *British Policy in a Changing Africa.* London: Routledge and Kegan Paul, 1959. (No. 2, Northwestern University series "African Studies.")

Coleman, James S. *Nigeria: Background to Nationalism.* Berkeley and Los Angeles: University of California Press, 1958.

Cornevin, Robert. *Histoire de l'Afrique dès origines à nos jours.* Paris: Payot, 1956.

Costeodat, René. *Le Mandat français et la réorganization des territoires du Cameroun.* Besançon: Jacques et Demontrond, 1930.

Davidson, Basil. *Black Mother.* London: Victor Gollancz, 1961.

Delarozière, R. *Les Institutions politiques et sociales des populations dites Bamiléké.* Yaoundé: IFAN, Centre au Cameroun, 1950. (Memorandum III Centre IFAN Cameroun.)

Delavignette, Robert. *Freedom and Authority in French West Africa.* Oxford: Oxford University Press, 1957.

Denis, Jacques, S.J. *Le Phénomène urbain en Afrique centrale.* Brussels: Académie Royale des Sciences Coloniales, 1958. (Classe des Sciences Morales et Politiques, Mémoires en 8vo, Nouvelle Série. Tome XIX, fasc. 1, 1958.)

Deutsch, Karl W. *Nationalism and Social Communication.* New York: John Wiley and Sons, 1953.

Diel, Louise. *Die Kolonien Warten! Afrika im Umbruch.* Leipzig: P. List, 1939.

Diziain, R., and A. Cambon. *Etude sur la population du quartier New-Bell à Douala.* Yaoundé: Institut des Recherches Camerounaises, 1956.

Drews, Max. *Frankreich versagt in Kamerun.* Berlin: Junker und Dunhaupt, 1940. (Schriften des Deutsches Instituts für Aussenpolitische Forschung, Heft 79.)

Duchène, Albert. *La Politique coloniale de la France.* Paris: Payot, 1928.

Dugast, I. *Inventaire ethnique du Sud-Cameroun.* Yaoundé: IFAN Cameroun, 1949. (Mémoires de l'IFAN Cameroun: Populations, No. 1.)

Escherich, Georg. *Kamerun.* Berlin: H. Riegler, 1938.

Ferrandi, Jean. *La conquête du Cameroun-nord, 1914-15.* Paris: Charles Lavanzelle, 1928.

Fitzgerald, Walter. *Africa.* 8th ed. London: Methuen, 1955.

Franceschi, Roger. *Le Mandat Français au Cameroun.* Paris: Sirey, 1929.

Froelich, J. C. *Cameroun-Togo.* Paris: Editions Berger-Levrault, 1956.

du Gard, Martin. *L'Appel du Cameroun.* Paris: Flammarion, 1939.

Gardinier, David. *Cameroon, United Nations Challenge to French Policy.* London: Oxford University Press, 1963.

Gaston, Joseph. *Ce qu'il faut savoir du Cameroun.* Brazzaville: Agence economique de l'A.E.F., 1920.

German Colonial Society, D.K.V. *Das Buch der Deutschen Kolonien.* Leipzig: Wilhelm Goldmann, 1937.

Gorges, E. H. *The Great War in West Africa.* London: Hutchinson, 1927.

Grosclaude, Pierre. *Menaces allemandes sur l'Afrique.* Paris: F. Sorlot, 1938.

Groves, Charles P. *The Planting of Christianity in Africa.* Vol. IV. London: Lutterworth Press, 1958.

Guernier, Eugene, and René Briat, eds. *Cameroun, Togo.* Paris: Editions de l'Union Française, 1951. (Encyclopèdie de l' Afrique Française.)

Guilbot, J. *Petite Etude sur la main d'oeuvre à Douala.* Yaoundé: IFAN, Centre au Cameroun, 1948.

Hailey, [William Malcolm] Lord. *An African Survey, Revised 1956.* New York: Oxford University Press, 1957.

Hall, Hessel Duncan. *Mandates, Dependencies and Trusteeship.* Washington: Carnegie Endowment, 1948.

Hardy, Georges. *Histoire de la colonisation française.* Paris: Larose, 1928.

——. *Histoire sociale de la colonisation française.* Paris: Larose, 1953.

——. *La politique coloniale et le partage de la terre aux XIXe et XXe siècles.* Paris: Editions Albion Michel, 1937.

Harmand, Jules. *Domination et colonisation.* Paris: Payot, 1910.

Harris, Norman D. *Intervention and Colonization in Africa.* New York: Houghton Mifflin, 1914.

Herskovits, Melville J. *The Human Factor in Changing Africa.* New York: Alfred A. Knopf, 1962.

Hertslet, Sir Edward. *The Map of Africa by Treaty.* Vol. I. London: HMSO, 1894.

Hurault, Jean. *Mission d'études au Cameroun, 1955.* Paris Institut Géographique National, 1956.

——. *Notes sur la structure sociale des Bamiléké.* Paris: Institut Géographique National, 1951.

——. *La Structure sociale des Bamiléké.* Paris: Mouton, 1962.

Ingold, J. (General). *L'Epopée LeClerc au Sahara 1940-1943.* Paris: Berger-Levrault, 1945.

Joelson, F. S. *Germany's Claim to Colonies.* London: Hurst and Blackett, 1939.

Johannssen, G. Kurt, and H. H. Kraft. *Germany's Colonial Problem.* London: T. Butterworth, 1937.

Kaberry, Phyllis M. *Women of the Grassfields.* London: HMSO, 1952.

Kanga, Victor Jean-Claude. *Le droit coutumier Bamiléké en contact avec des droits Europeens.* Yaoundé: Imprimerie du Gouv't., 1959.

Kautsky, John H. *Political Change in Under-developed Countries: Nationalism and Communism.* New York: John Wiley and Sons, 1963.

Kemner, Wilhelm. *Kamerun dargestellt in kolonialpolitischer, historischer, verkehrstechnischer, rassenkundlicher, und rohstoffwirtschaftlicher Hinsicht.* Berlin: Freiheitsverlag, 1937.

Ketchoua, Thomas (Abbé). *Contributions à l'Histoire du Cameroun de 450 avant Jésus-Christ à nos jours.* Yaoundé: Imp. St. Paul, 1962.

Kirk-Greene, Anthony H. M. *Adamawa Past & Present.* Oxford: Oxford University Press, 1958.

Kittler, Glen D. *The White Fathers.* New York: William Allen, 1958.

Kuczynski, R. R. *Cameroons and Togoland: A Demographic Study.* London: Oxford University Press, 1939.

Labouret, Henri. *Le Cameroun*. Paris: P. Hartmann, 1937.

———. *Colonisation, colonialisme, décolonisation*. Paris: Payot, 1952.

Lange, Fried. *Massa, wann kommst du wieder; zwischen Tschadsee und Götterberg, Erlebnisse in Kampf in Kamerun*. Düsseldorf: Völkischer Verlag, 1942.

Lecoq, R. *Les Bamiléké*. Paris: Presence Africaine, 1953.

Lembezat, Bertrand. *Le Cameroun*. 3rd ed. Paris: Editions Maritimes et Coloniales, 1954.

———. *Kirdi, les populations paiennes du nord-Cameroun*. Yaoundé: IFAN, Centre au Cameroun, 1950. (Memoires de l'IFAN, Centre au Cameroun, Série, Populations, no. 3.)

Lewin, Evans. *The Germans in Africa*. New York: Cassel, 1915.

Lewis, Thomas. *These Seventy Years*. London: Carey Press, 1929.

Lieb, A. *Deutsche Kolonialarbeit: zehn Jahre Mandatscherrschaft in Kamerun*. Berlin: Freiheitsverlag, 1932.

Lloyd, Christopher. *The Navy and the Slave Trade*. New York: Longmans, Green, 1949.

Logan, Rayford W. *The African Mandates in World Politics*. Washington: Public Affairs Press, 1948.

———. *The Operation of the Mandate System in Africa, 1919-1927*. Washington, D.C.: The Foundation Publishers, 1942.

Lugard, Sir. F. D. *The Dual Mandate in British Trophical Africa*. London: William Blackwood, 1923.

MacLean, Eva. *Unser Kamerun von Heute*. München: Fichte Verlag, 1940.

Mair, Lucy P. *Native Policies in Africa*. London: Routledge and Sons, 1936.

Manue, Georges R. *Cameroun, création française*. Paris: F. Sorlot, 1938.

Marabail, Henri J. J. *Etude sur les territoires du Cameroun*. Paris: E. Larose, 1919.

Masson, Georges. *La mise en valeur des territoires du Cameroun placés sous mandat Français*. Paris: Librairie Coloniale et Orientale Larose, 1928.

Mathiot, André. *Les territoires non-autonomes et la Chartre des Nations-Unis*. Paris: Librairie Générale de Droit et Jurisprudence, 1949.

McCullough, Merran, Margaret Littlewood, I. Dugast. *Peoples of the Central Cameroons*. London: International African Institute, 1954. (Ethnographic Survey of Africa, no. 9.)

Meek, C. K. *Land Tenure and Land Administration in Nigeria and the Cameroons*. London: HMSO, 1957.

Merat, L. *L'Existence au Cameroun*. Paris: Larose, 1928.

Moynet, Paul. *Victory in the Fezzan*. London: Fighting France Publications, 1944.

Murdock, George Peter. *Africa: Its People and Their Culture History*. New York: McGraw-Hill, 1959.

Murray, James N. *The United Nations Trusteeship System*. Urbana, Ill.: University of Illinois Press, 1958.

Nicolas, Raoul. *Le Cameroun depuis le Traité de Versailles*. St. Armand/Cher.: Imprimerie A. Leclerc, 1922.

Njoya, Idrissou Mborou. *Histoire et Coutumes des Bamun*. (Henri Martin, trans.) Yaoundé: IFAN, Cameroun, 1951. (Mémoires, IFAN, Centre Cameroun.)

Och, Helmut W. Albertus. *Die Wirtschaftsgeographische Entwicklung der früheren Deutschen Schutzgebieten Togo und Kamerun.* Königsberg: 1931.

Oxford University British Commonwealth Group, Bullock, A., ed. *Germany's Colonial Demands.* London: Oxford University Press, 1939.

Passarge, Siegfried. *Kamerun* (Vol. II of Meyer, Hans. *Das Deutsche Kolonialreich*). Leipzig: 1909.

Paulin, Honoré. *Cameroun-Togo.* Paris: L. Eyroller, 1923.

Perham, Margery. *Lugard, the Years of Authority.* London: Collins, 1960.

Plamenatz, John. *On Alien Rule and Self-Government.* New York: Longmans, Green, 1960.

Pouquet, Jean. *L'Afrique Equatoriale Française et le Cameroun.* Paris: Presses Universitaires de France, 1954.

Powell, E. Alexander. *The Last Frontier; the White Man's War for Civilization in Africa.* New York: Scribners, 1919.

Reyher, Rebecca H. *The Fon and His Hundred Wives.* Garden City, N.Y.: Doubleday, 1952.

Ritter, Paul. *Afrika Spricht zu Dir.* Mülhausen/Thur.: Bergwald Verlag, 1938.

Ritter, Karl. *Neu-Kamerun.* Jena: Reichskolonialamt, 1912. (Veröffentlichen, no. 4.)

Ritzenthaler, Robert and Pat. *Cameroons Village, an Ethnography of the Bafut.* Milwaukee: Milwaukee Public Museum, 1962. (Publications in Anthropology, no. 8.)

Robinson, Ronald, and John Gallagher. *Africa and the Victorians.* New York: Macmillan, 1961.

Rohrbach, Paul. *Deutsche Pflanzungen in Kamerun.* Hamburg: P. Hartung, 1937.

Rouard le Card, Edgar. *Les Mandats français sur Togoland et le Cameroun, étude juridique.* Paris: A. Pedone, 1924.

Routil, Robert. *Kamerun, Land und Leute.* Wien: Gottlieb Diestel, 1914.

Rowling, Cecil W. *A Study of Land Tenure in Cameroons Province.* London: Colonial Office Land Tenure Panel, HMSO, 1948.

Royal Empire Society, Information Bureau. *Notes on Conditions in the British Cameroons.* London: Royal Empire Society, 1956.

Royal Institute of International Affairs, Information Department. *Germany's Claim to Colonies.* 2d ed. London: Oxford University Press, 1939.

Rudin, Harry. *Germans in the Cameroons, 1884-1914.* New Haven: Yale University Press, 1938.

Sady, Emil J. *The United Nations and Dependent Peoples.* Washington, D.C.: Brookings Institution, 1956.

Saurrat, Albert. *La Mise en valeur des colonies français.* Paris: Payot, 1923.

Schnee, Heinrich, ed. *Das Deutsche Kolonialreich.* Leipzig: Deutsche Kolonialverein, 1930.

———. *German Colonization, Past, Present and Future.* New York: Knopf, 1926.

Schober, Reinhold. *Kamerun: Neuzeitliche Verwaltungsprobleme.* Berlin: E. S. Mittler und Sohn, 1937.

Schreiber, Joachim Hans. *Deutschen Kolonien unter besonderer Berücksichtigung; Hierstellung als Mandate der Völkerbundes.* Bonn: Dümmler, 1939. (Völkerrechtsfragen, no. 43.)

Seitz, Theodor. *Die Gouverneursjahre in Kamerun* (vol. 2 of *Vom Aufsteig und Niederbruch Deutscher Kolonialmacht*). Karlsruhe: C. P. Mueller, 1927.

Sicé, A. *L'Afrique Equatoriale Française et la Cameroun au service de la France*. Paris: Presses Universitaires de France, 1946.

Steer, George L. *Judgment on German Africa*. London: Hodder and Stoughton, 1939.

Susset, Raymond. *La vérité sur le Cameroun et l'A.E.F.* Paris: Editions de la Nouvelle Revue Critique, 1934.

Tardits, Claude. *Les Bamiléké de l'ouest Cameroun*. Paris: Berger-Levrault, 1960.

Thompson, Virginia, and R. Adloff. *French West Africa*. London: Allen and Unwin, 1958.

Townsend, Mary Evelyn. *Origins of Modern German Colonialism, 1871-1885*. New York: Columbia University Press, 1921.

———. *The Rise and Fall of Germany's Colonial Empire*. New York: Columbia University Press, 1930.

Veicopolous, Nicolas. *Traité des Territoires Dépendants, Tome I, Le Système de Tutelle d'Après la Charte de San Francisco*. Athens: Institut Français d'Athenes, 1960.

Victoria Centenary Committee. *Victoria, Southern Cameroons, 1858-1958*. Victoria: Basel Mission Book Depot, 1958.

Wieschhoff, Hans. *Colonial Policy in Africa*. Philadelphia: University of Pennsylvania Press, 1944.

Wilbois, Joseph. *Le Cameroun*. Paris: Payot, 1934.

Wright, Quincy. *Mandates under the League of Nations*. Chicago: University of Chicago Press, 1930.

Zimmerman, E. *Neu-Kamerun: Reiseerlebnisse und Wirtschaftspolitische Untersuchungen*. Berlin: Mittler und Sohn, 1913.

ARTICLES AND PAMPHLETS

ANONYMOUS

"Assembly Charts Course for Cameroons," *United Nations Review* (April, 1959), p. 15.

"Assembly Recommends New Date for Plebiscite in Southern Cameroons," *United Nations Review* (Nov., 1959), p. 10.

"Conference de Mlle. Homburger; la colonie allemande du Cameroun," *Géographie*, vol. 40, no. 8 (June, 1923), pp. 355-386.

"Doctor of Revolt," *Drum* (Oct., 1959), pp. 27-28.

"The French Cameroons Today," *West Africa*, no. 2143 (May 19, 1958), p. 439.

"The German Delegation's Comments on the Condition of the Peace," *International Conciliation*, no. 143 (Oct., 1919), p. 1249.

"Independence Foreshadowed for French Cameroons," *United Nations Review* (Dec., 1958), p. 30.

"Kamerun boyetsya za svobodu," *Sovremenii Vostok* (April, 1958), p. 12.

"Mission's report on the Two Territories, End of Trusteeship Proposed for the French Cameroons," *United Nations Review* (March, 1959), p. 31.

"Moskaus Taktik im Schwarzen Erdteil," *Ost-Problème*, 12th yr., no. 4 (Feb. 19, 1960), pp. 112-115.

"Le problème national au Cameroun,' *Le Bulletin-Documents et Recherches,* no. 6 (April 1, 1956), pp. 19-27.
"Prospects for the Cameroun Federation," *West Africa,* no. 2313 (Sept. 30, 1961), p. 1073.

By Author

Adrianov, B. V. "Etnicheskii sostav covremenogo Kameruna," *Sovetskaya Etnografiia,* 1959, no. 5, p. 56.
Amphoux, Marcel. "Le Mandat de la France au Cameroun," *Revue de Science Politique,* vol. 56 (1933), pp. 276-298.
Ardener, Edwin. "The Kamerun Idea," *West Africa,* no. 2147 (June 7, 1958), p. 533; no. 2148 (June 14, 1958), p. 559.
————. "The Origins of the Modern Sociological Problems Connected with the Plantation System in the Victoria Division of the Cameroons." (Minutes of) West African Institute of Social and Economic Research, Sociological Section (March, 1953), pp. 88-105.
————. "The Political History of Cameroon," *The World Today,* vol. 18, no. 8 (Aug., 1962), p. 341.
Beti, Mongo (pseud. Alexandre Biyidi). "Tumultueux Cameroun," *Revue Camerounaise,* 2nd yr., no. 11 (Sept.-Oct., 1959), p. 155.
Binet, J. "Conditions des femmes dans la région cacaoyére du Cameroun," *Cahiers Internationale de Sociologie,* vol. 16 (Jan.-June, 1956), pp. 109-123.
Bond, Edward. "The Conquest of the Cameroons," *Contemporary Review,* vol. 109 (1916), pp. 620-627.
Calvert, Albert Frederick. *The Cameroons.* London: T. W. Laurie, 1917. (Pam.)
Chaffard, George. "Cameroun à la veille de l'indépendance," *Europe France-Outre-Mer,* no. 355 (June, 1959), p. 65.
Chilver, E. M., and P. Kaberry. "From Tribute to Tax in a Tikar Chiefdom," *Africa,* Vol. XXX, no. 1 (Jan., 1960), pp. 1-19.
Chudeau, R. "La nouvelle situation des colonies francaises africaines Togo-Cameroun," *Géographie,* vol. 33, no. 2 (1920), pp. 193-218.
Coleman, James S. "Current Political Movements in Africa," *The Annals* of the American Academy of Political and Social Sciences (March, 1955), pp. 97-112.
————. "Togoland," *International Conciliation,* no. 509 (Sept., 1959).
Delaroziére, R. "Cameroun, inventaire ethnique et linguistique du Cameroun sous mandat français," *Journal de la Société des Africanistes,* vol. 4, no. 2 (1934), pp. 203-208.
————. "Étude de la stabilité de la population Bamiléké de la Subdivision de Bafoussam pendant les années 1946 et 1947," *Etudes Camerounaises,* no. 31-32 (Sept.-Dec., 1950), pp. 137-185.
Devernois, Guy. "Cameroons 1958-59, From Trusteeship to Independence," *Civilisations,* Vol. IX, no. 2 (1959), pp. 229-234.
Dietze, Karl H. "Die Englisch-Französische Mandatsgrenze in Kamerun," *Gesellschaft für Erdkunde, Zeitschrift,* 1937, pp. 321-348.
Diziain, M. R. "Les Facteurs de l'expansion Bamiléké au Cameroun," *Bulletin de l'Association des Géographes Français,* no. 235-236 (May-June, 1953), pp. 117-126.

Douala Manga Bell, René. "Contribution à l'histoire du Cameroun," *L'Effort Camerounais*, nos. 210, 211, 212, 214-219, 222, 223 (Oct. 25, 1959, to Jan. 24, 1960).

Ducat, Marc. "Du Mandat à l'Independance," *Marchés Tropicaux du Monde* (Nov. 21, 1959), pp. 2547-2554.

Ekang, J. N. *An Introduction to Eastern Kamerun.* Ibadan: No publisher given, 1956. (Pam.)

Frodin, Reuben. "Flies in the Trusteeship Ointment," American Universities Field Staff *Reports*, no. RF-1-'61 (Feb. 25, 1961). (Pam.)

Froelich, J. C. "Ngaoundéré, la vie économique d'une cité peul," *Etudes Camerounaises*, no. 43 (June-July, 1954), pp. 3-66.

Full, August. "Kamerun," *Kolonialische Rundschau*, vol. 9, no. 12 (1932), pp. 279-447.

Gardinier, David. "The Movement to Reunify the Cameroons," paper presented at 1960 meeting of the African Studies Association. Mimeo.

Gaudemet, Paul-Marie. "L'Autonomie Camerounaise," *Revue Française de Science Politique*, Vol. VIII, no. 1 (March, 1958), pp. 42-72.

George, S[ampson] A. *Kamerun (Unification).* London: 1956. (Pam.)

Geze, Bernard. "Notes de géographie physique et agronomique sur le Cameroun," *Annales, Institut Nationale Agronomique de Paris.* Alençon: 1941, tome 32, pp. 7-164.

Gironcourt, G. de. "Les conquêtes franco-anglaises en Afrique du Togo et le Cameroun," *Bulletin, Société de Géographie et d'Etudes Coloniales de Marseilles*, tome 40, (1917), pp. 72-89.

Göhring, M. "Der König von Bamum und seine Schrift," *Der Evangelische Heidenbote*, Année 6, no. 80 (June, 1907).

Gonidec, P. F. "Les Institutions Politiques de la République Fédérale du Cameroun," *Civilisations*, Vol. XI, no. 4 (1961), p. 370; *ibid.*, Vol. XII, no. 1 (1962), p. 13.

Gourou, P. "Problèmes de géographie humaine au Cameroun septentrional," *Cah. d'outre-mer*, vol. 44 (Oct.-Dec., 1958), pp. 426-430.

Graham, Malbone W. "The Diplomatic Struggle for Africa," in University of California at Los Angeles Committee on International Relations, *Africa, the Near East, and the War.* Berkeley: University of California Press, 1943, pp. 175-212.

[Gua-Nulla, and M. Ndumu.] Kamerun Society, "The Kamerun Society and the Nigerian Constitutional Conference, and the Unification Question" (Victoria, 1957), mimeo., 9 pp.

Guilbot, J. "Les conditions de vie des indigènes à Douala," *Etudes Camerounaises*, no. 28 (1949), pp. 179-239.

Hodgkin, Thomas. "The French Cameroons," series in *West Africa*, no. 28 (Dec. 18, 1954).

Horner, George R. "Response of Selected Cameroonian Ethnic Groups to French Political Institutions," unpub. MS (typed), 1957.

———. "Togo and the Cameroon," *Current History*, vol. 34, no. 198 (Feb., 1958), pp. 84-90.

Jeffreys, M. D. W. "An Extinct Jewish Colony (Victoria, Cameroons)," *Jewish Affairs* (Johannesburg) (Nov., 1954), p. 43.

Johnston, Sir Harry. "The Africa of the Immediate Future," *Journal of the African Society*, Vol. XVIII, No. LXXI (April, 1919), p. 161.

Kaberry, Phyllis M., "Traditional Politics in Nsaw," *Africa,* Vol. XXIX, no. 4 (Oct., 1959), pp. 366-383.

Kamerun Society. "Economic and Financial Problems of the Cameroons" (Victoria, 1957), mimeo., 33 pp.

Kirk-Greene, Anthony H. M. (for the Government of Northern Nigeria). *This is Northern Nigeria.* Kaduna: Government Printer, 1956. (Pam.)

Kitchen, Helen. "Cameroun Faces Troubled Future," *Africa Special Report* (Jan., 1960), vol. 3, no. 1, p. 14.

Knittel, Ingeborg. "Untersuchung über die Kapitalinvestierung der Vereinigten Staaten von Amerika in Afrika," *Beiträge zür Kolonialforschung.* Berlin: Riemer and Andrew Steiner, 1943. (Band. IV.) Pp. 171-185.

Lancaster, D. Gordon. "Cameroons, Ethnology," *Man,* vol. 33, no. 93 (1933), p. 91.

Leeming, A. J. "A Historical Sketch of Victoria, British Cameroons," *Nigerian Field,* vol. 13, no. 4 (Oct., 1950), pp. 184-189; *ibid.,* vol. 16, no. 1 (Jan., 1951), pp. 37-45.

Lelong, R. M. "Yaoundé, capitale du Cameroun," *A.O.F. Magazine* (Paris, 1955), no. 3, pp. 5-7.

Le Vine, Victor T., "The New Cameroon Federation," *Africa Report,* vol. 6, no. 11 (Dec., 1961), p. 7.

———. "The 'Other Cameroons,'" *Africa Report,* vol. 6, no. 2 (Feb., 1961), p. 5.

———. "'P' Day in the Cameroons," *West Africa,* no. 2283 (March 4, 1961), p. 236; no. 2284 (March 11, 1961), p. 265.

———. "Unifying the Cameroons," *West Africa,* no. 2301 (July 15, 1961), p. 774.

Logan, Rayford W. "Operation of the Mandate System in Africa," *Journal of Negro History,* vol. 13 (Oct., 1928), pp. 423-477.

McKay, Vernon. "French Aid to Africa," *Current History,* vol. 33, no. 195 (Aug., 1957), pp. 91-98.

———. "Too Slow or Too Fast? Political Changes in African Trust Territories," *Foreign Affairs,* vol. 35 (Jan., 1957), pp. 295-310.

Migeod, Frederich W. H. "The British Cameroons, its Tribes and Natural Features," *Journal of the African Society,* vol. 23, no. 91 (April, 1924), pp. 176-187.

Moncharville, M. "L'Execution du Mandat au Togo et au Cameroun," *Revue Générale de Droit International Public,* serie 2, tome 7 (1925), pp. 58-78.

Moran, William. "U.S. Technical and Economic Assistance to Africa," in Haines, C. G., ed., *Africa Today.* Baltimore: Johns Hopkins Press, 1955.

Nicod, A. *La femme au Cameroun.* Paris: Societé des Missions Evangeliques, 1927. (Pam.)

Nicolas, J. P. "Deux ports d'estuaire, St. Louis du Senegal et Douala," *Bulletin d'I.F.A.N.* (Jan.-April, 1957), pp. 259-274.

Owona, Adalbert. "Comment les Allemands mirent la main sur le Cameroun," *Revue Camerounaise,* 2d year, no. 10 (July-Aug., 1959), p. xiii.

Potekhin, I. I. "Borba za Vossoyedinenye Kameruna," *Sovetskaya Etnografiia* (1959), no. 5, p. 62.

Rathery, M. *Les produits d'exportation du Cameroun dans la conjoncture mondiale.* Yaoundé: Chambre de Commerce et d'Industrie du Cameroun (1959). (Pam.)

Retif, André. "A propos de l'Union des Populations du Cameroun; Communisme et religion au Cameroun," *L'Afrique et l'Asie, no.* 33 (Nov., 1955).

Richet, Etienne. "Voyage au Cameroun et dans le Nigeria," *Bulletin Société Royal Géographique,* vol. 47 (1927), pp. 1-46, 205-305; *ibid.,* vol. 48 (1928), pp. 1-48, 109-176, 267-333.

Robinson, Kenneth. "The Public Law of Overseas France Since the War," *The Journal of Comparative Legislation,* 3rd series, Vol. XXXII, 1950 (reprinted as no. 1 of Reprint Series of the Oxford University Institute of Colonial Studies).

Royal Empire Society, Information Bureau. *Notes on Conditions in the British Cameroons.* London: Royal Empire Society, 1956. (Pam.)

Schacht, Hjalmar. "Germany's Colonial Demands," *Foreign Affairs,* vol. 15 (Jan., 1937), pp. 223-234.

Schachter, Ruth. "Single Party Systems in West Africa," *American Political Science Review,* Vol. LV, no. 2 (June, 1961), p. 294.

Soppo-Priso, Paul. *L'Armée camerounaise et le service obligatoire de solidarité nationale "So-Kono."* Yaoundé: 1959. (Pensées et Actions, no. 2.) (Pam.)

Stengers, Jean. "L'Imperialisme colonial de la fin du XIX siècle: mythe ou realité," *Journal of African History,* vol. 11, no. 3 (1962), p. 469.

Union des Populations du Cameroun. Abdul Baghi Maw'ndi Mahamadu Rajn. *Le bluff Ahidjo.* Cairo: Service d'Information de l'UPC a l'étranger, 1958. (Pam.)

————. Comité Directeur. *Le Patriote Kamerunais, Journal d'avant garde de la lutte de libération nationale et sociale du peuple Kamerunais, numero de Novembre-Decembre 1959, saisi par la police française le 21 Janvier 1960.* Conakry: Jan. or Feb., 1960. (Pam.)

————. ————. *Unification Immédiate du Cameroun.* 1952. No place of publication given. (Pam.)

————. ————. *The UPC Denounces Planned Systematic Tortures in the Kamerun.* Cairo: 1958. (Pam.)

————. *Circulaire à tous les organismes de l'U.P.C. No. 194/BCD/UPC/ QD.* Cairo: June 4, 1959. (Pam.)

————. *Déclaration du Bureau du Comité Directeur de l'U.P.C.* Cairo: April 1, 1959. (Pam.)

————. *La revolution kamerunaise, ses objectifs, sa signification et ses repercussions dans le continent africain.* Cairo: Feb., 1960. (Pam.)

————. Moumié, Félix-Roland. *Intervention de M. Félix Roland Moumié, chef de la délégation kamerunaise.* (Second Conference, Afro-Asian Peoples, Conakry, April 11-15, 1960.) Conakry: Comité Directeur de l'U.P.C., April 1960 (mimeo.).

————. *Le fascisme n'aura aucun succes au Cameroun.* Cairo: Service de l'Information, 1958. (Pam.)

————. Moumié, Felix R., and N. Njiawue, *La révolution kamerunaise et la lutte des peuples africains.* Conakry: Sept., 1959. (Pam.)

————. ————. Ouandié, E., and A. Kingué. *Position de l'U.P.C. vis-a-vis de l'indépendance du Kamerun.* Conakry: Dec., 1959. (Pam.)

————. *L'O.N.U. et le problème Kamerunais.* Cairo: Service de l'information, December or January, 1958-1959. (Pam.)

————. Moumié, Felix R. *Rape of the Cameroons.* London: Committee of African Organizations, Nov. or Dec., 1959. (Pam.)

------. *La Tutelle Internationale à l'Epreuve*. Cairo: Service de l'Information, January or February, 1959. (Includes Memorandum of the Kamerun Society to the UN Visiting Mission to the British Cameroons, Dec., 1958.) (Pam.)

------. Um Nyobé, Ruben. *Qu'est ce que veut le peuple Kamerunais*. 1957. (Pam.)

Vaast, Pierre. *Petite Géographie du Cameroun*. Bourges: Fernand Nathan, 1954. (Pam.)

Vandercook, John W. "The French Mandate of Cameroun," *National Geographic Magazine*. Vol. LIX, no. 2 (Feb., 1931), pp. 225-260.

Vaughn, James. "Culture, History, and Grassroots Politics in a Nigerian Chiefdom," paper presented at 1962 meeting of the American Anthropological Association. (Mimeo.)

Warmington, Alan. "The Cameroons and the Fiscal Commission," *West Africa*, no. 2143 (May 10, 1958), p. 443.

------. "Saving and Indebtedness Among Cameroons Plantation Workers," *Africa*, Vol. XXVIII, no. 4 (Oct., 1958), pp. 329-343.

------. "Some Aspects of Industrial Relations in the Cameroons Plantations," *Proceedings* of the Third Annual Conference of the West African Institute of Social and Economic Research, Ibadan: University College of Nigeria, 1956, pp. 16-22.

Wrigley, G. M. "The Military Campaign Against Germany's African Colonies," *Geographical Review*, vol. 5 (Jan., 1918), pp. 44-65.

Zang-Atangana, J. M. "Les forces politiques camerounais," memoire submitted to the Faculté de Droit de Paris, 1961. (Mimeo.)

PUBLIC DOCUMENTS

Cameroun Under French Mandate (Cameroun sous Mandat Français). *Journal Officiel des Territores du Cameroun*, from 1923.

Cameroun Under French Trusteeship. Etat du Cameroun.
   a. *Journal Officiel de l'Assemblée Représentative du Cameroun*, (1947-1952).
   b. *Journal Officiel des Débats de l'Assemblée Territoriale du Cameroun* (1952-1956).
   c. *Journal Officiel des Débats de l'Assemblée Législative du Cameroun* (1957-1959).

------. Direction des Affaires Politiques et Administratives; 5eme Bureau. *Note sur les Partis Politiques au Cameroun sous Tutelle Francaise*. Yaoundé: Nov. 19, 1949. (Mimeo.)

------. ------. Ministére des Affaires Economiques. Service de la Statistique Générale. *Annuaire Démographique du Cameroun Edition Provisoire, 1946-1956*. Yaoundé: Imprimerie du Gouv't., 1956.

------. ------. ------. ------. *Bulletin de la Statistique Générale*. Yaoundé: Imprimerie du Gouv't., 1958: nos. 1-12; 1959: nos. 1-12.

------. ------. ------. ------. *Résultats du Recensement de la Subdivision de Mbalmayo, 1956, Population Autochtone*. Yaoundé: Imprimerie du Gouv't., 1957.

------. ------. ------. ------. *Résultats du Recensement de la Ville de Douala, 1955-56. Population Autochtone*. Fascicule 2. Resultats d'ensemble. Yaoundé: Imprimerie du Gouv't., 1957.

------. ------. ------. ------. *Résultats du Recensement de la Ville d'Ebo-*

lowa, 1958, *Population Autochtone*. Fascicule 1. Yaoundé: Imprimerie du Gouv't., 1959.

———. ———. ———. *Résultats du Recensement de la Ville de Yaoundé, 1957, Population Autochtone*. Yaoundé: Imprimerie du Gouv't., 1958.

———. ———. ———. ———. *Supplément au Bulletin de la Statistique Générale*. Yaoundé: Imprimerie du Gouv't., 1958: nos. 1-3; 1959: nos. 1-2.

———. ———. Ministère des Finances. Service des Etudes. *Budget d'Exercice, 1959*. Yaoundé: Imprimerie du Gouv't., 1959.

———. ———. Presidence du Gouvernement Camerounais. Service de l'information. *Info-Cameroun*, Bulletin Mensuel Information du Gouvernement Camerounais (monthly). Yaoundé: Imprimerie du Gouv't., nos. 1-7 (Jan.-July, 1959).

———. ———. Service des Douanes. *Le Commerce Extérieur du Cameroun, Année 1958*. Yaoundé: Chambre de Commerce et d'Industrie, 1958.

———. ———. Service d'Information du Gouvernement Camerounais.
  a. *Discours d'Investiture Prononcé par M. Ahidjo Ahmadou, Premier Ministre de l'Etat du Cameroun le 18 Fevrier 1958 devant l'Assemblée Législative du Cameroun.*
  b. *Communication de M. Ahidjo Ahmadou, Premier Ministre de l'Etat du Cameroun le 18 Octobre 1958 à l'Assemblée Législative du Cameroun.*
  c. *Communication de M. Ahidjo Ahmadou, Premier Ministre de l'Etat du Cameroun le 6 Mai 1959 à l'Assemblée Législative du Cameroun.* Yaoundé: Imprimerie du Gouv't., 1959.

———. High Commission of the French Republic in the Cameroons. *Atlas du Cameroun*. Paris: Editions S.E.L.F.A., 1949.

———. ———. Direction of Foreign Relations. *Cameroun, 1946 from Trusteeship to Independence 1960*. Paris: 1959. (Pam.)

———. ———. Information Service. *Cameroons 10 Years of Investments and Progress Under the Leadership of France*. Paris: Diloutremer, 1958.

———. Chambre de Commerce et d'Industrie. *Bulletin Mensuel*. Douala: beg. Jan., 1959.

———. ———. *Guide Economique du Cameroun*, 1959. Yaoundé: 1959.

Cameroun, Republic of. Chambre de Commerce et d'Industrie du Cameroun. *Exposé sur la Situation Economique du Cameroun au 1ᵉʳ Janvier 1960*. Douala: February, 1960.

———. *Journal Officiel des Débats de l'Assemblée Nationale du Cameroun*. 1960.

———. Ministère des Finances. *Budget de l'Exercice* (1959-1962).

———. Ministère des Affaires Etrangères and Secretariat d'Etat à l'Information. *La position de la République du Cameroun à la suite du plébiscite des 11 et 12 février 1961 dans la partie septentrionale du Territoire du Cameroun sous administration du Royaume-Uni de Grande-Bretagne et d'Irlandie du Nord*. Yaoundé: 1961.

France. Agence Economique des colonies autonomes. *Cameroun*, magazine trimestriel. 1926–January, 1937. (Colonial Ministry.)

———. Caisse Centrale de la France d'outre-mer (Paris). *Graphiques de l'Evolution économique du Cameroun: population, prix, budget ordinaire, investissements*. Paris. 1953.

———. Centre d'Information Documentaire (Paris). *The Work of France in the Cameroons.* 1939.

———. Comité Monétaire de la Zone Franc. Secrétariat Général. *La Zone Franc en 1957, Cinquième Rapport Annuel du Comité Monétaire de la Zone Franc.* Paris: 1958.

———. Institut d'Emission de l'Afrique Equatoriale Française et du Cameroun. *Rapport d'Activité, Exercise 1958.* Paris: 1959.

———. Ministry of the Colonies (Ministère des Colonies). Commissariat au Cameroun. *Guide de la Colonisation au Cameroun.* Paris: E. Larue, 1923.

———. ———. *Rapport Annuel du Gouvernement Français sur l'administration du Cameroun sous Mandat* (1921-1938). (Some years issued by the Foreign Ministry.)

———. Ministry of Overseas France (Ministère de la France d'Outre-Mer). *Documentation Francaise. Notes et Etudes Documentaires.* "L'Evolution Récente des Institutions Politiques dans les Territoires d'Outre-Mer," no. 1847 (March 11, 1954).

———. ———. (or Foreign Ministry) *Rapport Annuel du Gouvernement Français à l'Assemblée Générale des Nations Unies sur l'administration du Cameroun placé sous la tutelle de la France* (1947-1959).

Great Britain. Colonial Office. *Annual Report of H. M. Government to the Assembly of the United Nations on the Cameroons under United Kingdom Administration* (1946-1959).

———. [Commissioner for the Southern Cameroons under United Kingdom Trusteeship.] *Southern Cameroons Plebiscite, 1961, the Two Alternatives.* [Buea: 1960.]

———. ———. *Report by the Conference on the Nigerian Constitution,* London, July-August, 1953. Cmd. 8934. London: HMSO, 1953.

———. ———. *Report by the Resumed Conference on the Nigerian Constitution,* Lagos, January-February, 1953. Cmd. 9059. London: HMSO, 1954.

———. ———. *Reports on Mandate of the Cameroons to the League of Nations.*
1921-1922 issued as Cmd. 1647 with series title.
1923-1929 issued by Colonial Office as Colonial numbers,
1930-1938 issued by Colonial Office as Cmd. with series title.

———. ———. *Nigeria, Report of the Fiscal Commissioner (A. L. Chick) on the Financial Effects of the Proposed New Constitutional Arrangement.* Cmd. 9026. London: HMSO, 1953.

———. Foreign Office. Historical Section. *Cameroon.* Peace Handbooks, no. 111. London: HMSO, 1920.

———. ———. ———. *Partition of Africa: British Possessions.* Peace Handbooks, nos. 89-95. London: HMSO, 1920.

———. Secretary of State for Colonies. *Report by the Nigeria Constitutional Conference,* 1957. Cmd. 207. London: HMSO, 1957.

International Labor Organization. International Labor Office. *African Labour Survey.* Geneva: ILO, 1958.

League of Nations. Twenty-first Ordinary Session of the Assembly. *General Questions, Report of the First Committee to the Assembly.* L.N. Doc. A. 33, 1946. Geneva: April 17, 1947.

———. Council. *Mandat Brittanique sur le Cameroun.* L. N. Publ. 1922 ser. 6, A., no. 13, 15.

———. Permanent Mandates Commission. *Minutes and Reports.* 1921-1937.

———. Secretariat, Mandates Section. *British Mandates for the Cameroons.* Cmd. 794. London: HMSO, 1923.

Nigeria, Federation of. Federal Information Service, Lagos, for Southern Cameroons Information Service. *A Statement of Policy by Dr. E. M. L. Endeley.* Lagos: 1958.

———. Ministry of Research and Information. Information Division. *Financial Assistance to the Cameroons.* Lagos: 1959.

———. *Population Census of the Eastern Region of Nigeria, 1953.* Bulletin no. 2 (Bamenda Province), no. 5 (Cameroons Province). Lagos: The Government Statistician, 1954.

———. *Population Census of the Northern Region of Nigeria, 1952.* Lagos: The Government Statistician, 1952.

———. *Report of the Native Courts (Cameroons, Bamenda Province) Commission of Inquiry.* Lagos: Fed. Gov't. Printer, 1953.

———. *First Progress Report of the Economic Programme.* Sessional Paper no. 2 of 1957. Lagos: Fed. Gov't. Printer, 1957.

———. *Second Progress Report on the Economic Programme, 1955-60.* Lagos: Fed. Gov't. Printer, 1958.

———. Northern Region. *Statement by the Government of the Northern Region of Nigeria on the Reorganization of the Legal and Judicial Systems of the Northern Region.* Kaduna: Gov't. Printer, 1958.

———. ———. *Information on the Northern Cameroons (Trust Territory Province).* Kaduna: 1961. Mimeo.

———. Southern Cameroons. Cameroons Development Corporation. *Annual Report.* Bota/Victoria, So. Cam.: from 1950.

———. ———. *Debates in the Southern Cameroons House of Assembly.* Vol. I: First Session, October 26-November 9, 1954. Buea: So. Ca. Gov't. Press, 1955 (only to Nov. 2). Vol. II: First Session, October 26-November 9, 1954. Calabar: St. Therese's Press, 1955 (only Nov. 3 to 9), Vol. III. First Session, Fourth Meeting, December 12 to 14, 1954. Calabar: St. Therese's Press, 1955.

———. ———. Information Service. *Press Releases.* No. 1 (in 1959) to nos. in 1962.

———. ———. Southern Cameroons Production Development Board. *First Annual Report, 1956-57; Final Report, April-Sept., 1957.* Buea: So. Cam. Gov't. Printer, 1958.

———. ———. Southern Cameroons Development Agency (successor to Southern Cameroons Production Development Board) *Reports.* First Report: October, 1957, to March, 1958. Second Report: March, 1958, to March, 1959. Buea: So. Cam. Gov't. Printer. 1959, 1960.

———. ———. *Introducing the Southern Cameroons.* Lagos: Federal Information Service, 1958. (Pam.)

———. ———. *Report on the Mamfe Conference on the Plebiscite Question, Aug., 10 and 11, 1959.* Buea: So. Cam. Gov't. Printer, undated.

———. ———. *Report of the Accountant-General* (Buea, Aug. 29, 1959), Buea: So. Cam. Gov't Printer, 1959.

———. ———. *Southern Cameroons Gazette.* 1957, 1958, 1959.

United Nations. Dept. of Economic and Social Affairs. *Economic Developments in Africa, 1956-57.* Supplement to the World Economic Survey, 1957. U. N. Doc. E/3117, ST/ECA/56.

——. ——. *Review of Economic Activity in Africa*. Supplement to the World Economic Report, 1953-54. (New York, 1955.) U. N. Doc. E/2738, ST/ECA/33.

——. ——. *Scope and Structure of Money Economies in Tropical Africa*. (New York, 1955.) U. N. Doc. E/2739, ST/ECA/34.

United Nations. General Assembly. *Official Records of the General Assembly, Thirteenth Session, Annexes*. U. N. Doc. A/4094.

——. ——. Fourth (Trusteeship) Committee. *Report* (The Future of the Trust Territories of the Cameroons Under French Administration and the Cameroons under United Kingdom Administration). (March 13, 1959.) U. N. Doc. A/4095.

——. ——. ——. *Official Records*. 845-871 meetings. U. N. Docs. A/C.4/SR. 845-871 (New York, 1959).

——. ——. ——. *Petitions Concerning the Cameroons Under French Administration, Observations of the French Government as Administering Authority*. U. N. Doc. T/OBS. 5/71 (Dec. 6, 1955).

——. Trusteeship Council. *Report of the United Nations Commissioner for the supervision of the Plebiscite in the Cameroons Under United Kingdom Administration*. U. N. Docs. T/1491 (Nov. 25, 1959), T/1491 Corr. 1, T/1491 Add. 1 (Dec. 1, 1959).

United Nations. Trusteeship Council. *Report of the United Nations Plebiscite Commissioner for the Cameroons under United Kingdom Administration; Plebiscites in the southern and northern parts of the Territory, on 11 and 12 February 1961*. U. N. Doc. T/1556 (April 3, 1961).

——. ——. *Report of the Trusteeship Council*. U. N. Doc. Supp. 4 A/3822 (New York, 1958); Supp. 4 A/4100 (New York, 1959).

——. ——. *Special Report on Administrative Unions Affecting Trust Territories and on the Status of the Cameroons and Togoland under French Administration Arising out of Their Membership in the French Union*. U. N. Doc. A/2151 (New York, 1952).

——. ——. *Special Report of the Trusteeship Council, The Future of the Trust Territories of the Cameroons under French Administration and the Cameroons under United Kingdom Administration*. U. N. Doc. A/4094 (New York: Feb. 18, 1959).

——. ——. *Reports of United Nations Visiting Mission to Trust Territories in West Africa*. U. N. Doc. Supp. 2 T/798 (New York, 1951).

——. ——. *United Nations Visiting Mission to the Trust Territories of the Cameroons under British Administration and the Cameroons under French Administration, 1955. Report on the Cameroons under French Administration*, U. N. Doc. T/1240 (April, 1956).

Report of the Cameroons under British Administration, U. N. Doc. T/1239 (April, 1956).

——. ——. *United Nations Visiting Missions to Trust Territories in West Africa, 1958. Report on the Trust Territory of the Cameroons under French Administration*. U. N. Doc. T/1427 (Jan. 23, 1959).

Report on the Trust Territory of the Cameroons under British Administration. U. N. Doc. T/1426 (Jan. 20, 1959) and Add. 1 (Feb. 6, 1959).

——. ——. *Addendum to the Report on the Trust Territory of the Cameroons Under British Administration* (T/1426). U. N. Doc. T/1426 Add. 1 (Feb. 6, 1959).

United Nations Educational, Social and Cultural Organization. *World Survey*

of Education, Vol. III, Secondary Education. New York: International Documents Service, 1961.
————. Camerounian Educational Planning Group. *Report Drawn Upon Return of the First Mission, 10 March-20 May, 1962.* Paris: 1962. Mimeo.
U. S. Department of Commerce. Bureau of Foreign Commerce. World Trade Information Service. *Economic Reports,* Part I, nos. 57-63. "Basic Data on the Economy of the French Cameroons" (1957).
————. *World Trade Information Service Economic Reports,* part 1, nos. 61-68, "Basic Data on the Economy of the Federal Republic of Cameroon" (1961), *ibid.,* part 1, nos. 62-49, "Economic Developments in the Federal Republic of Cameroon, 1961" (1962).

PERIODICALS

NEWSPAPERS

Afrique Nouvelle (weekly, Dakar), 1950-1963
Le Bamiléké (weekly, Dschang, Cameroun), 1959
Cameroons Champion (Victoria, West Cameroon), 1960-1961
Cameroons Times (Victoria, West Cameroon), 1960-1963
The Daily Times (Lagos, Nigeria), 1958-1962
Le Démocrate (sporadic, Yaoundé), 1959-1960
Depêche du Cameroun (UPC weekly, Yaoundé, Cameroun), 1959
L'Effort Camerounais (Catholic weekly, Yaoundé), 1958-1962
The New York Times, 1921-1963.
The Nigerian Citizen (daily, Kaduna, Northern Nigeria), 1958-1960
L'Opinion au Cameroun (sporadic weekly, Douala, Cameroun), 1958-1959
La Presse du Cameroun (daily, Yaoundé), 1959-1963.
Le Temps (Paris), to 1945, thereafter *Le Monde,* 1945-1963
The Times (London), 1921-1963
La Voix du Kamerun (sporadic, UPC, Cairo), since September, 1958.
La Voix du Peuple (weekly, Douala, Cameroun), since September, 1959.

MAGAZINES AND JOURNALS

Africa (London, International African Institute)
Africa Report, formerly *Africa Special Report*
African Transcripts (University of Pennsylvania)
Africana Newsletter (Hoover Institution)
L'Afrique et l'Asie (Paris)
The Annals of the American Academy of Political and Social Sciences
Bulletin de l'Association des Géographes Français
Bulletin du Comité de l'Afrique Française
Civilisations
Drum (Lagos)
The Economist (London)
Etudes Camerounaises, formerly *Bulletin de la Société d'Etudes Camerounaises* (Yaoundé)
L'Etudiant du Kamerun (*Union Nationale des Etudiants Kamerunais,* Paris)
Foreign Affairs
Interafrique Presse (Paris)

Marchés Tropicaux du Monde
Neues Afrika, formerly *Afrika Zeitschrift* (Hamburg)
Revue Camerounaise (Paris)
Revue Française de Science Politique
United Nations Review
West Africa (London)

MISCELLANEOUS

Administration et Diplomatie d'Afrique Noire et de Madagascar, 1963. Paris: Ediafric, 1963.

Annuaire des Etats d'Afrique Noire, 2ᵉ Edition; Gouvernements et Cabinets Ministeriels, Partis Politiques. Paris: Ediafric, 1963.

"The Brazzaville Conference," *Free France,* Special Issue no. 2. New York: September, 1944.

Deboudaud, J., and P. H. Chombard de Lauwe, *Carte Schematique des Populations du Cameroun* (Journal Société des Africanistes, vol. 9, no. 2, 1939. pp. 197-203.)

Downs, Alice May. "Togoland, and the Cameroun, German Colonies and French Mandates." Unpublished Master's thesis, University of California, 1926.

"The French Cameroons," *Free France,* Special Issue no. 4. New York: November, 1944.

Gardinier, David. "French Policy in the Cameroons, 1945-1957." Unpublished Ph.D. dissertation, Yale University, 1960.

Institut des Recherches Camerounaises. *Atlas du Cameroun* (Plates 1-8). 1961.

Le Vine, Victor T. "Political Parties in the Cameroons." Unpublished MS., December, 1960.

Tompkins, Dorothy C. *Cameroun: A German Colony and a French Mandate.* Unpublished Master's thesis, University of California, 1937.

Union Nationale des Etudiants Kamerunais (UNEK) *Statuts.* 1958. (Mimeo.)

Union des Populations du Cameroun. Bureau du Comité Directeur (Conakry) mimeographed items:

  a. Armée de Liberation Nationale Kamerunaise, Etat-Major, Bureau de l'Information et de l'Inspection. "Communiqué," April 4, 1960, by Pengoye Leconstant.

  b. "Communiqué sur les élections du 10 Avril 1960," signed by Moumié and Kingué, April 19, 1960.

  c. "Conference de Presse," April 23, 1960, by Moumié.

  d. "Coup d'oeil sur la république neo-colonialiste d'Ahidjo," signed by Moumié, Kingué, and Ouandié, April 9, 1960.

———. Personal letter from Félix-Roland Moumié to Victor T. Le Vine, dated April 28, 1960.

Index